The TOUGHEST HALF

Women Who Underpinned Britain's Greatest Industry

ELIZABETH STEWART

RYAN PUBLISHING

First published 2021 by Ryan Publishing
PO Box 7680,
Melbourne, 3004 Victoria,
Australia
Ph: 61 3 9505 6820
Email: books@ryanpub.com
Website: www.ryanpub.com

RYAN PUBLISHING

 A catalogue record for this book is available from the National Library of Australia

Title: The Toughest Half : Women Who Underpinned Britain's Greatest Industry
ISBN: 9781876498610 : Paperback
ISBN: 9781876498672 : Hardback
ISBN: 9781876498733 : eBook

Copyright © Elizabeth Stewart

Apart from any fair dealing for the purposes of private study, research, criticism or review, as permitted under the Copyright Act, no part may be reproduced by any process without written permission. Inquiries should be addressed to the publisher.

Internal design by Luke Harris, Working Type Studio, Victoria, Australia.
www.workingtype.com.au
Other Creators/Contributors: Graeme Ryan, editor.
Cover: Designed by Luke Harris & Graeme Ryan.

Contents

Acknowledgments ix

Prologue xi

Introduction: Memories of a Grandmother xxiii

Chapter 1: A Poor Collier Lass: Rebecca's memories 1

Rebecca's young life is one of poverty and deprivation. As a small child she is employed to work down a coal mine, alone and in the dark. The only semblance of affection she receives is from her older sister with whom she shares her penurious existence in a tiny hovel. Rebecca sees the appalling conditions in which women and girls, sometimes little older than herself, are forced to work until an act of Parliament brings an end to these conditions. Only then can Rebecca finally begin to hope for a better future.

Chapter 2: Let's Talk about Women 13

In the Victorian era, the home is regarded as the rightful place for women. Women who work outside the home are seen to be contravening the prevailing patriarchal, middle class ideal of femininity. Women who endure the harshest working conditions are held in particularly low esteem; even their working apparel is considered an affront to the complacent emerging bourgeoisie. Although the 1842 Mines and Collieries Act eventually prohibits women and girls from working underground, it is prudery rather than altruism which brings about its passage.

Chapter 3: Coming of Age **39**

Nan, whose life story is woven into this history of women and coal mining, is introduced. World War I and its effect on mining and the role of women are discussed. Social conditions, including childbirth, are chronicled against the background of Nan's early life and career choice, a choice which is relevant to this book.

Chapter 4: Jenny and Tommy **69**

The story of Jenny and Tommy epitomises the story of a young miner and his wife. It tells of their backgrounds and how Tommy comes to be a miner and Jenny a miner's wife. Jenny describes the life and routine of a young miner's wife in a growing mining community from the beginning of the 20th century.

Chapter 5: Where there's muck: Birth of a Coal Community **85**

1900–1914: Describes the environment in which Jenny and Tommy grew up. The chapter documents the origins of Creswell, the village central to the book. It narrates the history of the sinking of the mine, building the village and the beginning of its social life, emphasising the role of, and effect on, the women who became miners' wives.

Chapter 6: Cleanliness: Women's Work **117**

The beginning of Nan's career coincides with the post WWI era of freedom for women. However, the optimism of this new found emancipation is not shared by all women. Through the medium of a small Welsh mining village in 1920, the chapter describes the harsh conditions endured by working miner's wives

Chapter 7: Every heart deserves a mate: Carys's Dilemma **129**
The chapter introduces Meg and Gwyn Thomas. It tells of their meeting and marriage but, more importantly, the story of Gwyn's sister-in-law. Carys is a typical miner's wife at that time – young, numerous children, influenced by nonconformist preaching and the victim of paternalism. She is also largely ignorant in matters of contraception.

Chapter 8: Godliness and Childbirth: Matters of Fertility **157**
A discussion on birth control, the work of Marie Stopes and its relevance to women in such mining communities.

Chapter 9: Not a penny off the pay… **177**
1918–1927: The background and events leading to the 1926 General Strike and subsequent lockout of miners are narrated. The strike has significant unfortunate consequences for miners and their wives.

Chapter 10: Isn't it marvellous? **205**
1926–1927: Conditions experienced in mining communities are contrasted with the attitude of the upper classes towards the strike and the harsh effect of the miners' lockout on the wives and families of miners. Many notable women emerge from this turbulent time but the adverse effects of the lockout are long-lasting. An epilogue to the chapter summarises the lives of three remarkable women and their work during the time of industrial unrest.

Chapter 11: Solo Once More **239**
During the years 1930–1947 Nan's career advances. She meets Jack and marries but unexpected circumstances eventually bring her to Creswell and to her future life. Two important government initiatives affect her life and her career.

Chapter 12: Taking off the 'L' plates **265**
1948–1950: Nan moves to Creswell and eventually to the colliery. The village has prospered after experiencing the effects of WWII.

Chapter 13: Dirt and Dust: Miner's Safety, at last **287**
Mid-19th century–1948: The chapter describes the dangers to health faced by coal miners and outlines early safety interventions which led to the development of occupational health nursing and its application to coal mining.

Chapter 14: Pit boots, Sutures and Foreign Bodies **305**
1950–1967: Nan begins work at Creswell colliery. This chapter describes the contemporary social life of a village community, Nan's work as a pit nurse and anecdotes associated with her work culminating in her retirement.

Chapter 15: Fire! *327*
Tragedy strikes and Nan is in the midst of the disaster. The chapter describes events and the technical factors leading up to the colliery disaster, the rescue attempts and the aftermath.

Chapter 16: Sweetheart and Wife: Freda's Story **351**
Freda was born into and lived in the Creswell mining community all her life. Her husband is killed in the 1950 disaster. We are re-introduced to Meg, now an elderly widow.

**Chapter 17: 1984, Beginning of The End: Losing the Battle
The strike to end all strikes** **373**
Events leading to the 1984–85 miners' strike: The strike – including the main protagonists, police behaviour and its conclusion.

Chapter 18: The Aftermath **401**
Nan views from afar the chaos tearing 'her community' apart

Chapter 19: Annette's Memoirs, 1984 .... **405**
Annette, the wife of a striking miner, narrates events which occur during the year of the strike and how, in particular, the strike affects her and her family.

Chapter 20: We are women, we are strong **429**
The work of miners' wives and the role they play in supporting the strike.

Chapter 21: Extinguishing the Spark: The end of coal? **449**
1987 onwards: The end of the coal mining industry in Britain and its effect on coal communities.

Chapter 22: Last Look **459**
Present day: Dr Davey Thomas, Meg's grandson, visits Creswell after 30 years working overseas. He describes his impressions and memories of the village, acknowledging the lives of his mother and grandmother, typical miners' wives.

Post Scriptum **479**
Appendix: Igniting the Spark: How this mineral changed so many lives **481**
Bibliography **495**
Index **497**

Acknowledgements

Writing this book was a relatively isolated process. I confided my intent to write to very few people. Who, I thought writes their first a book in their seventies, and then expects that it will be published? However, those in whom I did confide rewarded my confidence with an abundance of support, moral and practical, which encouraged me to see the project to its conclusion.

Foremost among my confidants and supporters is my husband, Con O'Brien. With the utmost patience he guided me through the (to me) intricacies of the computer, was a constructive and sympathetic sounding board for my ideas, a painstaking editor of early drafts and never complained when he returned home to find the dining room table occupied by a computer and littered with numerous files and papers instead of any evidence of dinner. Thank you Con!

My daughter, Jacquie O'Brien, an ardent feminist and professional communicator cheered me on when at times I thought my efforts were futile. Her succinctness and eye for detail were invaluable.

When I considered the book was complete, further encouragement came from Graeme Ryan at Ryan Publishing who pronounced the book "publishable". This was when the real work began! Thank you Graeme for your professional help, advice and patience, and for introducing Luke Harris from Working Type who compiled the book, designed its cover and organised the illustrations which transformed the manuscript into an actual book.

Although I cannot acknowledge any practical assistance from my mother, Nan Stewart, the story of her life was predominantly the inspiration for this book. She spent much of her life living and working among mining women in a coal mining community.

Because of this close relationship many of the children of mining women became my childhood friends. Indeed, many of them may well have eventually become miners' wives. Being invited into their homes gave me an insight into their lives and into the uniqueness of their community. This book also acknowledges their hard work, sacrifice and contribution to coalmining, once Britain's greatest industry.

Prologue

The evening of Monday 25 September 1950 was the 268th evening of the year. After a sunny but cool summer, autumn had brought cloudy weather and showers. The meteorological forecast for the following day was for unsettled weather accompanied by frequent thunderstorms. A total eclipse of the sun would also occur on that day, although it would only be visible in certain parts of Asia. UN troops would capture the South Korean capital of Seoul during the vicious war being fought on the Korean Peninsula. Harry S. Truman was the Democrat President of America where, on the same day, credit cards were introduced. George VI was the reigning monarch of Great Britain and Clement Atlee, despite a swing to the Conservatives at the February election, had been re-elected Prime Minister of a second post-World War II Labour government.

There was nothing to foretell that the following day would be different from any other weekday in Creswell, a mining village in the north east midlands of Britain. The fact that George was King and Atlee was Prime Minister — even more importantly a Labour Prime Minister, true to its mining heritage this was Labour heartland — were probably the only events about which the villagers knew or cared, apart from the weather forecast.

I was five years old on that day and, already in my third week of infants' school, was beginning to feel rather grown up as I walked to and from school on my own. Most of my new school friends were still being accompanied by their mothers. My mother had accompanied me only once, as was mandatory, on my first day.

As they returned from school on that Monday afternoon, my friends' mothers probably turned on the wireless to listen to Mrs.

Dale, wife of country GP Dr. Jim, recounting yet another day in her diary. Later in the evening after the children had eaten their tea and been sent off to bed (after all, tomorrow was another school day) their parents probably relaxed, laughing at the gags of Dick Bentley in *Take it from Here*.

In 1950, the lives of the women in colliery villages had not changed markedly since the beginning of the century when this particular mining community had originated. Early marriage, large families and a routine of housework, dictated by the times of their husbands' shifts at the pit, were the norms for most of them. In our village, our friends' mothers were stay-at-home mums who made beds, washed dishes and clothes — particularly clothes discoloured by ingrained coal dust from underground work — accompanied by the sound of Teresa Brewer's *Music, Music, Music*, courtesy of the BBC Light Program *Housewives Choice*. Housework was a perpetual struggle to keep at bay the interminable black grit and smut which covered their furniture and windows.

Like our mother they cooked Sunday 'dinner' to Billy Cottons raucous "Wikey! Wikey!" prelude to his *Band Show* broadcast on the radio each Sunday lunchtime. Television sets in Creswell at that time were few and far between, but those lucky enough to own one would probably sit their children in front of BBC, the only TV channel, to be distracted by the antics of *Muffin the Mule*, *Andy Pandy* or *The Flowerpot Men* and their friend, Little Weed thereby allowing their mums the opportunity to prepare tea free from hindrance. Later, after the kids were put to bed, their mothers could relax in front of another edition of *Come Dancing*. Sometimes there would be a special treat such as going out to see *Annie Get Your Gun* or, possibly they swooned over Cary Grant dreaming of a different life in the upstairs seats of the Regors Cinema.

The routine in *our* house was anything but comfortably

predictable. In those days my mother, having separated from our father in 1945, was a working mum. I doubt if she ever tuned into — nor even cared about — the minutiae of Mrs Dale's day.

Each day after school as I retraced my route home from school I would be hopeful of catching up with my brother Alistair who, two years older than me, had graduated to the junior school. Alistair and I were ahead of our time. We were, although the phrase hadn't then been coined, 'latch-key kids'. We would let ourselves into the empty house where mum would have left a flask of tea and we would make toast in front of the fire. Part of mum's morning routine had been to 'lay' the fire in the grate so that, when the weather was cool, all we had to do was apply a lighted match and *hey presto!* a welcoming fire just like all the other kids came home to. Laying a fire was an art at which she excelled: newspaper at the bottom, followed by a layer of sticks and, finally, strategically placed lumps of coal. The secret of success, she maintained, was not to screw up the newspaper too tightly, make sure there was plenty of air.

It would be another three years before we became the proud owners of a new twelve inch screen, black and white television set, just in time for us to watch the live broadcast of the Coronation of the new Queen. In the meantime, my brother and I watched what programs we could in the homes of neighboring children whose parents were lucky enough to have a TV. *Housewives' Choice* never provided background music for our mother's chores and, instead of sitting down to listen to comedy on the radio each evening she adhered to a routine of housework. Tuesday evenings were dedicated to cleaning upstairs bedrooms, Wednesdays to cleaning bathroom and toilets and Friday nights to washing. I'm sure the intervening evenings were equally well occupied, yet our mum still found time to oversee homework, listen to our reading, correct spelling and, more often than not, read us bedtime stories before we were old enough read them ourselves.

After two hard years as district midwife in the village and its environs, a position which involved a 24 hours a day, seven days a week on-call roster, she had, a few months earlier, commenced working for the recently created National Coal Board as an industrial nurse managing the medical centre at the local coal mine. She had hoped that this position with its 9 to 5, Monday to Friday plus half day on Saturdays working hours would be a much more family-oriented option.

Being the only midwife in the village, her previous inflexible on-call roster had meant leaving us in the care of a paid housekeeper, which used up most of her salary, while she drove around streets of coal blackened rows of houses clustered round the pit, or along country lanes to outlying adjacent villages to deliver babies single handedly.

One of the benefits of her work as a midwife was a subsidised council house. Her resignation to take up employment with the National Coal Board meant that she had to find alternative accommodation for the three of us. With her meager savings and her small salary, she bought a three-bedroom, detached, 1920s-style house in what was then, arguably one of the 'better' streets in the village. In the summer of 1950, we had moved in to our own house.

Her new position worked well. Although her working hours didn't quite correspond with school hours, it was manageable for all of us, although she had little spare off-duty time. On school holidays, Alistair and I were packed off to stay with an aunt, my mother's sister, who had no children of her own. She and her elderly husband kept a farm on the edge of the Pennines in Yorkshire where, with no neighbours to worry about, we were allowed lots of freedom to run wild.

We seemed to be a happy, self-sufficient little family. Although lack of money was a constant theme, for a five-year-old, the routine felt safe and secure.

Coming downstairs on Tuesday morning 26 September 1950, I was, therefore surprised to find, instead of my mother busy in the kitchen preparing breakfast, a family friend sitting in the corner of our dining room. He told me that my mother wasn't there as she'd had to go to work. "T ' pit's on fire. They came for your mam early this morning."

Since we had no telephone, a messenger had been sent to collect her. She had no option but to leave us alone in the house, asleep, until help arrived. When it did arrive, it came in the form of Fred Clarke who was sitting in a small chair by the fire which he had thoughtfully lit for us. Fred was a pit top worker and he, his wife May, and two children lived in the Model Village in a house owned by the National Coal Board, close to the pit.

After experiencing the unpredictable working hours of her midwifery routine, we weren't particularly perturbed by the fact that she had been called away. Even though she had only worked at the pit for a short time, it was still not unusual for her to be called out each time one of the miners had been injured. Yet this was the first time she had been called out during the night. We ate our breakfast and went to school as usual. We had learned to be adaptable.

Shortly before this we had spent a Saturday with Fred and May while mum had attended, coincidentally, a disaster planning meeting, along with other colliery officials (mine manager, underground manager and other relevant officials). As part of her personal plan, it was decided that, in the event of a crisis, the Clarkes would be informed and either Fred or May would come to take care of us while the other would stay with their own children.

Arriving at school, on what I recall was a dark, damp morning (the weather forecast had been accurate for once) the school hall seemed to be full of children. There was an air of excitement and tension. Many of the children had fathers working underground on the night shift that night. Like a mantra there was a constant murmur. "Pits on fire", they whispered to no one in particular.

That day, I suppose, was an ordinary school day except that rather than enjoying tea and toast in front of our own fire, we went home from school to the Clarke's. In retrospect, I wonder what awaited many of the other children when they arrived home that afternoon.

That night, and for the next few nights, we stayed at Fred and May's house, sharing their children's beds. On the first evening of that long day, just as we were about to go to bed, there was a muffled knock on the door and my mother tumbled in. She had come to say good night to us. She collapsed into a chair, exhausted and distraught. Seeing her in tears was, for me, probably the most frightening part of the whole experience. Not only did she know all the missing and dead men, having delivered many of their children, she also knew their wives.

Distressing as it was to see her so distraught, we were relieved to see her. She had not even taken off her overcoat when there was another knock on the door. "Sorry, Sister, can you come back?"

After she had left home in the early hours of that Tuesday morning, she went immediately to an emergency meeting to plan what action should be taken in the face of the catastrophe. By that time mine rescue teams had arrived from other pits in the area and were already underground. From the meeting she went straight to her medical centre to make the necessary preparations and gather what equipment she thought might be necessary. The area nursing and medical officers were informed. Extra resources were called in. She was then taken to the pit top to assess what emergency medical equipment needed to be sent underground. Cloistered in a small building, surrounded by miners, rescuers and officials, she waited anxiously for events to unfold.

By the time she left the pit top daylight was already beginning to fade and it took a while for her eyes to adjust to the gloom. As she was escorted through the pit yard she turned and was astonished to see that it was crowded with people, all silently waiting for news of the men trapped below. What she found so poignant was the complete silence in which these people waited. No one uttered a sound.

There was little hope of finding survivors and the task now was to prepare to receive the bodies. The local Drill Hall was commandeered as a makeshift mortuary. This hall was the venue of so much communal entertainment — vegetable shows, amateur dramatic and operatic society productions, each Thursday evening's 'sixpenny hop', old-time dances. Most of the dead miners, with their wives, children and girlfriends, had found amusement in this place. They would be brought here to be cleaned and prepared for identification. Nurses from surrounding collieries, many of them close colleagues of my mother, came to assist in this harrowing task. Afterwards she said she was struck by the irony of her situation. Having arrived in the village to deliver babies, she was now occupied with the grim task of providing the final duty of care for their dead fathers, fathers these babies would never know.

I can't recall precisely how long we were separated from our mother, but it must have been at least several days. When the three of us were reunited we returned thankfully to our own home.

Later that week, there followed two days of funerals. As we lived close to the cemetery where many of the men were to be buried, the area nursing manager and colleagues who had assisted my mother, descended on our home. I remember the long convoy of hearses and funeral cars as they passed our house. It seemed to last the whole of those two damp, dreary days. My mother and her colleagues were present at as many of the funerals it was possible to attend.

Because of the presence of poisonous gases down the pit, it was considered too hazardous to attempt to retrieve all the bodies. The area containing the bodies was sealed off and there they remained, sepulchered for a further six months until it was considered safe to take down lead lined coffins and bring them home. Even then, two bodies remained underground for a further six months until they were retrieved almost a year after the fire which had killed them.

Despite the disaster and the entombed miners, the pit re-opened almost immediately. Like the men, my mother returned to work without a break. Many of the miners had friends and even relatives whose bodies were close to the sites where they were working. One man recalled how he helped to seal off the section of the pit which enclosed the body of his father. There was no debriefing or trauma counselling. Post-Traumatic Stress Disorder was neither named, nor would be recognised, for another three decades.

The magnitude of the disaster was profound, leaving hardly a family in the village untouched. A national disaster relief fund was established immediately, and millions of pounds were rapidly donated to assist the wives and families of those killed. Of the 80 men killed on that day in September 1950, the youngest was 25, the oldest 63. All these men left families — wives, daughters, sisters and mothers. Many of the fatherless children were our school friends.

The tireless efforts of various rescue teams were justifiably applauded. An official government inquiry followed. Sadly, there appears to be no acknowledgment, nor even mention of the efforts, dedication and sacrifice of the nursing services in general or of my mother in particular. In the report of the enquiry, not one woman is mentioned, by name or otherwise.

Doubtless our mum never expected this. She was, after all, just doing her job.

In all subsequent accounts the omission is ubiquitous. This is not surprising. The term *miner* has become synonymous with men. Coalmining has relied on the heavy work done by men. History is replete with accounts of coalmining disasters which claimed the lives of hundreds of *men*. *Men* strike for better wages. However, the aphorism 'Behind every great man is a great woman' could well be applied to women of British coal communities. In fact most people are surprised to learn that women once laboured underground alongside men in conditions just as appalling.

Although not a natural product of a coal mining community, most of my pre-adult life was spent in a Derbyshire mining village and was, therefore, vicariously affected by the nature of coal mining.

I saw and heard the miners going to and from work and, despite the installation of pit head baths, saw the whites of their eyes illuminated in their blackened faces as they emerged from underground. I watched them working in their allotments, glad to be in the open air. I heard them singing as they wove their way home on Saturday nights after closing time from any of the four pubs in the village. School holidays coincided with the annual fortnight's holiday when many families decamped to National Union of Mineworkers' holiday camps in Rhyl or Skegness.

Like other villages, we marked the time of day by the siren which announced the end of one shift and the beginning of the next. Most of my friends were the children of miners and I spent time in their houses where a coal fire perpetually burned in the grate and there was always a hot meal ready to put on the table regardless of the time the men came home from working underground.

I heard the sound of the brass band practicing in the impressive Edwardian Miners' Institute and the clinking of glasses on long summer evenings when wives joined in for a game of bowls on the adjacent, immaculately curated green.

I've walked through lines of washing flapping in communal yards, past groups of colliers' wives, clad in pinafores, heads turbaned as they gathered in groups to gossip on street corners. I've seen them on their hands and knees scrubbing their door steps or leaning on their brooms after sweeping their yards. I've been inside their houses during spring cleaning when carpets were draped over washing lines waiting to be beaten with old tennis rackets as women scraped off the previous year's grimy wallpaper before hanging a new coat. There were few practical skills to which these women could not turn their hands. I've also seen them trying to quell their nervous shivering while being whisked off in a neighbour's old car to the local casualty department, always prepared for the bad news which followed an accident at work. Life has seldom been easy for miners' wives, but few of them expected that it would be.

This book is an attempt to acknowledge the lives of mining women — wives, mothers and daughters, a rare breed of women whose underground and above-ground toil, hard work and bravery, have been largely overlooked by history. I have attempted to describe their lives in an historical context to show how they survived adversity, ignoring their own needs while simultaneously nourishing their families and supporting their men. I have endeavoured to bring some of their experiences to life by inventing certain characters and allowing them to tell their own stories. Although I have put the words in their mouths, they are words I imagined they would use. By doing this I hope their communal voices can now be heard; one voice speaks for many.

Woven through this book is the true story of my mother who, although not a miner's wife, was once a miner's daughter. Her life too was hard and closely entwined with coal mining to which she made, over many years, a considerable contribution not only to the men in the industry but also to their wives. She died in 1990, coincidentally, the time of many pit closures.

Wife and mother — mutual support.

Introduction

Memories of a Grandmother

The lump in my throat was growing. It hurt to swallow, but swallow was all I could do to hold back the tears. This was my first funeral. I didn't know what was expected of me. I had spent all the previous day trying to select what I hoped would be the most suitable outfit. While there was not much suitable attire that can be chosen from a 14-year-old's wardrobe, I had to make sure that what I was wearing was just right. In my head I wanted to hear my Grandma's words, "don't you look smart".

I was entering my teenage, rebellious years, so I didn't want to look 'too smart'. Nor did I want to show too much emotion at my Grandma's funeral, and that meant crying. What if someone should see me? This was Perth, after all. It's the sort of place where you run into people you know all the time — mainly when you don't want to.

I finally settled on a paisley top (just like Morrissey's, or so I thought), a black skirt, short but not too short, and a black jacket, tights and shoes (black of course).

The funeral was small, intimate, family members only. It was a dignified, understated affair for what was a dignified, understated life. My Grandma was laid to rest, cremated at Karrakatta Cemetery in Perth in August 1990. She died three days after complications associated with a fractured femur. My mother, Grandma's last surviving child, followed the dignified, understated air of the occasion. She was upset, yet calm and in control.

My earliest memories of Grandma are bitter sweet. She was a

generous, almost too generous, woman. A constant 'feeder'. You would never leave her house hungry. In fact, you would leave virtually on the edge of sickness from too many sweets, chocolates, biscuits, whatever your tiny grand-childish heart desired. And you would always leave with a pocket full of coins and dollar notes that she would thrust at you from her oversized purse. "Don't tell your mother", she would say in a matronly, yet hushed manner.

But Grandma also had a dark, tortured side. A devoted Jehovah's Witness, every visit would end with her quietly taking you aside and reading passages from garishly illustrated bibles that promised paradise for those who worshiped the deity. Ruin and constant torment awaited those who did not. Grandma wanted us, me and my two older brothers to join her in paradise. My parents, she would say with her head shaking, were too selfish to join us.

My Grandma's relationship with my parents, particularly my mother, was challenging. Mum was a loving and devoted daughter. She had taken on responsibility for Grandma's welfare in early adulthood, after her brother, my Uncle Alistair, died in a car accident in Zambia in June 1968, aged just 26. My mother's father was not around so both my mother, Elizabeth and Uncle Alistair, were raised solely by Grandma in the 1950's and 1960's, a time that was not generally kind to single mothers, particularly working single mothers in coal mining villages like the one in which my mother was raised.

On the many occasions that I would sleep over at Grandma's, she would tell me stories about Creswell, their mining village, the home of my mother and uncle. I loved the way her slight Northern accident would pronounce the words, "Creswell". It reminded me of roast beef and Yorkshire pudding. It sounded comforting like slippers and a hot water bottle.

She would reminisce about her garden in Creswell, how she converted an old air-raid shelter to a garden bed and how she constructed a pond complete with fish, stone pathways, and a small orchard. Rows of perennials brightened up each dull, smut-covered spring.

She was the beneficiary of expert tips on how to get the best out of her garden. On long summer evenings she would put the children to bed and escape to a couple of hour's gardening. "Evenin' Sister", was usually the prelude to conversations and gardening advice over the back fence which separated her garden from a 10 acre plot of miners' allotments.

Her garden was not just her joy, it was her paradise. It was also her refuge, probably not unlike the one about which that she would sermonise during her Jehovah moments. The only impression I have of it is from the black and white photos of my mother growing up. As old and grainy as they are, there is no doubting the beauty of that garden, the result of painstaking hours and effort making it a floral hideaway from the gritty and sometimes gory reality of the mining village where she spent her working days looking after the miners.

My Grandma was a colliery nurse.

1

Poor Collier Lass

*

My name's Polly Parker, I come o'er from Worsley
My mother and father work down the coal mine
Our family is large, we have got seven children
So I am obliged to work down that same mine
And as this is my fortune I know you'll feel sorry
That in such employment my days I must pass
But I keep up my spirits, I sing and look cheerful
Although I am but a poor collier lass

By the greatest of dangers each day I'm surrounded
I hang in the air by a rope or a chain
The mine may give in; I may be killed or wounded
Or perish by damp or the fire of a flame
But what would you do if it weren't for our labours
In greatest privation your days you would pass
For we would provide you with life's greatest blessing
So do not despise a poor collier lass

All the day long you may say we are buried
Deprived of the light and the warmth of the sun
And often at night from our beds we are hurried
The water is in and barefoot we run
And though we go ragged and black are our faces
As kind and as free as the best we'll be found
And our hearts are more white than your lords' in high places
Although we're poor colliers that work underground

I'm now growing up fast, somehow or another
There's a young collier laddie runs strange in my mind
And in spite of the talking of father and mother
I think I should marry if he is inclined
But should he prove surly and will not befriend me
Another and better chance may come to pass
And my friends here I know to him will recommend me
And I'll be no longer a poor collier lass

1 Poor Collier Lass

My name is Rebecca Booth. I am about 60 years old and live in a village called Monk Bretton in Yorkshire. I have been asked to tell the story of my life and how it is connected to coal mining. It might sound funny, but I can't ever remember a time before I was married when the pit wasn't part of my life.

I remember very little about my family before I came to work in the mine when I was a little child. That must have been when I was about five or six. I only know what I've been told about my family, my Mam and Dad, that is, by my sister. Thirza and me are the only people left of my family. Certainly, I never went to school and to this day can neither read nor write and have to make my mark with **X**.

It seems as though my parents and two younger brothers (I don't remember their names) all died of a disease called Typhus. People told me that my father was a shepherd and that we had very little money for clothes and food. Then my father got a job working at Oaks Pit not far from where I live now. In those days all five of us lived in a little cottage with only one room. Although I can remember hardly anything of my family, I have a dim memory of us all going to sleep together at night on the floor, mainly to keep warm, and I remember being afraid of the rats that used to run all over us. Or perhaps I imagined that. Much more of that I can't tell you, because I don't know myself.

After my family all died, I went to live with my older sister, Thirza, and her husband, Enoch Holmes. Although Enoch agreed to take me in, he wasn't a very kind man either to me or Thirza. I don't think I knew what kindness was in those days. Like my dad, Enoch was also a coal miner at Oaks Pit. Enoch and Thirza had been married just before my family all died and Thirza too went to work down the pit for her husband. Because there was no one to look after me when I went to live with them, they used to take me down the pit with them.

In the winter we used to have to get up while it was still dark and walk all the way to the pit which seemed to be a very long way for my little legs. In winter it was still dark when we got to the pit. We came home in the dark too after Enoch and Thirza had worked their shift. In fact, when I look back, it always seemed to be dark in those days.

Once we got to where we used to work, we were lowered into the pit where we stayed all day and didn't come up again until it was once again dark. We didn't see much daylight. Going down into the pit was like going down a well except that we sat in baskets rather than buckets. We went down two at a time sitting cross-legged. The baskets were wound up and down with a big wheel operated by an old woman. The first time I went down I was terrified, but Thirza was with me and held me tight.

Enoch worked at hewing — digging the coal out of the rock with a pickaxe. He was a very strong man. The mine was very deep, and it was very hot. Because it was so hot, and wet too, Enoch like all the other men and boys mostly used to work without any clothes on. Most of the time the men used to have to dig out the coal while they were lying down as the roof was too low for them to stand up. The only way they could see was by the light of a little candle.

When the coal had been dug out it was shovelled into big tubs or corves. Then the corves had to be taken from where they were filled to the bottom of the pit so they could be pulled up to the ground above. The corves were very heavy and had no wheels, only runners like sleds have on the bottom of them. They had to be dragged over what was very rough ground through very low tunnels which seemed to go on for miles. The work was done by the women and older girls who were called hurriers.

My sister Thirza worked as a hurrier and used to have to pull the heavy corves full of coal. As you may imagine it was hard, backbreaking work. Sometimes children called thrusters used to help by pushing the wagons from behind while the women dragged them at the front. I was too little at the time to be much help.

I remember that Thirza, like all the women, had a belt buckled round her waist which was fastened to a chain that went between her legs. This chain was attached to a big hook at the front of the corf. She would have to go down on her hands and knees to drag it along, just like a harnessed animal. So she could see where she was going, she too had a candle which was fastened to her head with a strap.

Where the roads were steep, she had to hold onto a rope to help her to pull the heavy load. If there was no rope, she would try to catch hold of a rock, anything to help and steady her especially as in many places the ground was very steep. Sometimes there was no tunnel where the coal was dug, and it had to be carried in big baskets and sacks over rough ground and sometimes up ladders so it could be tipped into the corves to be taken to the pit bottom. The women carried the heavy baskets and sacks on their backs. The baskets had straps which passed round their foreheads to stop them from slipping. This meant that the women carriers were able to use their hands to help them to climb the ladders, or sometimes staircases which went round and round. You could always tell these women because the straps from the baskets used to wear away their hair, so they were quite bald at the front.

The pit was very wet and when it rained it would come in through the roof so that many times the water would be halfway up our legs. We used to get soaked through.

The women used to wear their men's old trousers to work in, but often the trousers were full of holes which had been made by the rubbing of the chains. Thirza also used to get really bad sores because of all the rubbing. The sores never got a chance to heal because she was always working with the chain on. Because it was so hot a lot of the women used to work naked from the waist up just like the men, although Thirza always wore an old shirt to try and protect her modesty. Mind you, most of the time it was that wet through with sweat and the damp from the pit that you could see right through it anyway. There used to be lot of goings on between some of the miners and these women which we children could see as well as hear. I used to be very frightened by some of the noises they made and there were lots of stories of some of the women giving birth to bastards. Thirza had seen this happen and told me she always used to be careful to keep close to the other women because she was very frightened of what some of the men might do to her.

My sister hated the work and told me that she was very afraid of being down the pit. She also hated the way a lot of the women used to curse and swear at the men and at each other. I didn't understand a lot of what they said, but what I did understand frightened me. There was also a lot of fighting among the women about whose turn it was to take a load of coal. Those that carried most coal got paid more. Sometimes Thirza worked so hard she never even got time to eat her dinner which she used to take down the pit. Sometimes the rats used to eat her food before she got the chance.

When I'd been going down the mine for a little while, Enoch told me he'd got me a job working underground as a trapper. Like lots of other children who worked as trappers my job was to open the trapdoors along the roadways to let the corves pass through. I had to be sure to close them properly again afterwards. This was important as it helped to keep the mines properly ventilated. I worked very long hours, mostly in the dark and often in water which sometimes came most of the way up my legs. I always worked alone. They preferred girls to boys to do this work as we were smaller and could fit through smaller spots.

I used to work from five in the morning until five in the evening. Enoch got my pay which was about ten pence a day. Although the work wasn't all that hard, I didn't like being on my own and used to be very frightened most of the time. I was always in the dark as there was no light for us. The only light I used to see was the glimmer of the candles as the corves passed through. Sometimes I couldn't even see to eat my dinner — usually a crust of bread with perhaps a bit of dripping which Thirza gave me before we left for work. There was never anything to drink. I could hear the rats running around and feel them running over my feet in the dark. Also, because it was dark and I was on my own, I never knew what time of day it was so sometimes I used to eat my dinner too early and then have nothing left for the rest of the shift. A lot of the time I used to sing and talk to myself to try to stop me from feeling so scared, but it didn't really work. I didn't dare to leave my post for more than a minute for fear of being in trouble for neglecting my work.

Enoch used to keep all the money the three of us earned, Thirza's as well as mine. A lot of the coal miners used to beat their wives and children. Enoch didn't beat us, but he used to shout at Thirza and me, especially if we weren't ready in time to leave in the morning. Poor Thirza; like me she was always tired. The sores she got from the chains rubbing her used to turn into painful boils. Even when she was young, she used to walk like an old woman. She found it very hard to walk properly as she was always bent over or crawling along at work pulling those heavy tubs. She was always wet through and she always seemed to be coughing a lot.

I reckon we all worked about fourteen hours a day and Enoch never shared the money we all earned I think it was only a few shillings and mostly it was paid every month. He said all the money went to pay for our little house, which was just a hovel and there was never much food, let alone proper clothes.

We all used to come home together at night and, as I said, it always seemed to be dark. Where we lived was like the place I lived when my family was alive, but it had a little room upstairs, reached by a ladder, where Enoch and Thirza used to sleep. I slept on the floor in the corner of the room downstairs. There was no bed, just a little table and two rickety chairs. There used to be a little fire sometimes, but it never gave off much warmth.

After we had eaten our meal at night — usually a few potatoes which Thirza boiled in an old kettle — we just used to go to bed. Many times we were too tired to wash ourselves so that we went to work again the next morning still wearing the same grime and coaldust from the day before. Often Thirza after she got home from work would just fall asleep on one of the chairs, too tired to climb up the ladder to bed. I know she tried to be kind to me and look after me but, like me, she was tired out all the time. Life was miserable for all of us.

The only day we didn't work was Sunday. Some families, at least the children, used to go to Sunday school but I never did. I used to like to try and run about a bit outside which was nice after being in the old dark pit for the rest of the week. I didn't know or understand anything about God and Jesus in those days.

One day when I'd finished work there was only Enoch waiting for me. He told me that my sister was already at home as she had been taken ill. Later she told me what had happened that day.

She hadn't felt well when we all got up that morning and it was hard for her to keep up with Enoch and even me when we were hurrying to work. Enoch got very angry again and kept shouting at her that we would all be late. Although she tried to do her work pulling the corf, she had such bad pains in her stomach. After a while she took off the belt and chains and crawled into a little cold, damp passage off the roadway. Here, all alone, she gave birth to a child. She wrapped it in her dirty, wet shirt — the only thing she could find — and crawled with the child under her arm to the bottom of the pit where she managed to climb into the basket and was wound up to the pit top. In the daylight she unwrapped the child, but she could see that it was dead. She struggled back to our little hovel where she buried the baby. The next morning, she was back at work with us. She never had any more children; or perhaps she did and they too, like this one, were born dead.

Then one day, Thirza and I were told that we were no longer allowed to work down the pit. It seems there had been a bad accident at a pit near us and a lot of children had perished in a flood. It was thought to be too dangerous and work that should not be done by women and children. So a law was passed forbidding all the women and the younger children — boys under ten and girls — from working underground.

The women who had pulled the corves were to be replaced by ponies. We were pleased that we would not have to go into the dark and work hard all day but many of the women were also very angry. What would they do for money? Enoch didn't have any sons so his would be the only wage in our family. By this time Thirza was old beyond her years, worn out with hard work, the many injuries suffered through her work and having babies that did not survive. I realised that it was up to me to try to keep on working and earn enough money to help out.

Even though I was still little for my age I was able to get a job working at the pit top. Lots of the older girls and some of the women who had been hurriers worked there. We were called pit brow women. The work was still hard but at least we worked in the daylight and we were no longer on our own. There were also some men working with us, usually men who'd been injured and could no longer dig the coal. Although we all did the same sort of work, the men used to get paid more than the women and girls did. A few of the men didn't like us working there as they said it took the work away from men who had families depending on them.

Our work was to check through the coal after it had been brought out of the pit and pick out lumps of rock and stone. As the tubs of coal arrived at the top of the mine some of the men and the stronger girls and women used to drag them out and, with a hard shove, sent the tubs along a rail where we met them. By pushing and pulling the tubs, we managed somehow to get the coal onto the tables, or screens, to be sorted. The screens were long moving belts which carried the coal and we stood on either side of them. The belts were about three feet wide and a few feet from the ground. As I was one of the smallest of all of them, I found it hard to reach the tables so someone gave me two bricks to stand on. There we picked out the rubbish with our fingers as the coal moved slowly past. If the stones stuck to the coal, we had to use a hammer to loosen them.

Although it was much safer than working down the pit we were sometimes hurt, especially us younger ones when large lumps of coal fell off the belt.

However, working with the coal we still used to get very dirty. So when we worked we used to wear trousers which covered our knees with an old dress or an apron over them. We used to cover our heads with a tightly wound handkerchief to stop the coal dust from getting into our hair so that only our faces were left uncovered. On cold days we used to wear an old jacket as we worked out of doors. On our feet we wore wooden clogs.

While I was working as a pit brow lass, I became friendly with Joseph, one of the men I worked with. He had worked down the pit until his leg had been crushed by a rock fall. He was no longer able to hew coal as he wasn't able to crawl along the low narrow passages at the coal face, so he was given work at the pit top instead.

Joseph was a kind man, and apart from Thirza's tired attempts, not many people had been kind to me in my short life.

One Sunday, Joseph invited me to his house to meet his family. Although it wasn't much bigger than the house we lived in, it seemed much brighter and cleaner and everyone seemed much happier than we were. Joseph had a daughter who was away working as a maid somewhere as well as three sons. Eventually I began 'walking out' with Samuel, the middle son. Joseph had vowed that none of his sons would ever go to work down the pit. One became a charcoal maker, and another worked as a knife grinder. Samuel was a farm labourer. As a small child he had spent some time in school and was able to read and write a little. With Enoch and Thirza's blessing we were married. I was just eighteen years old.

Pit brow women at Rose Bridge Pit 1884

Thirza died shortly after my marriage. I had never known much love in my life until I met Samuel, yet I realised that Thirza had tried to love and care for me as best she could. But her life had been one of drudgery, brutality and poverty, completely lacking in any comfort. She too had never known much love in her lifetime. Enoch continued to work in the mine. I don't suppose he very much missed the meagre pay that Thirza and I earned now he was on his own. On 12 December 1866 he was one of 361 miners killed when an explosion caused by firedamp tore through the mine. Fire was the thing we most dreaded in the mine. I know it was sad for Enoch, but at least Thirza had already gone and didn't have to go to the poor house.

I suppose you could say that the mine had claimed both Thirza and Enoch's lives but, with my marriage to Samuel, I could say that, for the first time in my life, I at least was now forever free of the mine and all its dangers.

The Women in Pants Who shocked Victorian Britain
AtlasObscura
https://www.atlasobscura.com/articles/
pit-brow-lasses-women-miners-victorian-britain-pants
*https://thoroglove.wordpress.com/2015/03/12/
trappers-hurriers-and-hewers-working-in-a-coal-mine/

2

Let's Talk about Women

It is pertinent to the content of this book to examine the ambivalent Victorian attitude to femininity, motherhood and, indeed, womanhood in general. The Victorian era was largely populated by, and under the influence of the emergent middle-class hegemony and its inherent ideal of femininity. The home was considered to be the *locus* of a woman's authority. A woman's place, it was considered, was in the home. Domesticity and motherhood were regarded as the pinnacle of female fulfilment. Any labour undertaken by women outside the home demeaned them to the extent that they were unsuitable for motherhood, insidiously implying that children raised by working women were somehow disadvantaged and, therefore, probably inferior. The comfortable middle class believed that women who transgressed their doctrine of femininity were beneath contempt.

There were, however, certain iconoclasts who rebelled against this doctrine. Florence Nightingale (1820–1910) and Gertrude Bell (1868–1926) both fought hard to defy social and family constraints in order to pursue their ambitions. Flying in the face of contemporary social mores, both women overcame parental opposition to achieve independence and luminary status. Both women, however, had the advantage of coming from wealthy, enlightened backgrounds and neither married nor became mothers.

Paradoxically the patriarchal perception of the Victorian era was that, although women were *physically* weaker than men, they

The Bourgeois notion of femininity was idealised in fashion. Silks, laces and shawls emphasised the vulnerability of women who were regarded as paragons and guardians of morality whereas working women were considered almost a subspecies.

https://www.pinterest.com.au/bonnieturko/softer-generation/

were considered to be *morally* superior, and a counterbalance to inherent male iniquity. As guardians of morality, it was women's responsibility to prepare the following generation and perpetuate these ideals.

Contemporary Victorian industrialism and its associated urbanisation wrought social upheaval with the emergence of the working class, undermining pre-existing values. In the interest of production and profit a 'contract of convenience' was expediently negotiated between the forces of patriarchy and capitalism which permitted the prevailing ideal of womanhood to be compromised. Since *working* women were less of a drain on expenditure, being paid about one third to a half of the wage paid to men, the traditional idealisation of femininity was pragmatically modified. However, women who worked outside the home for wages continued to be regarded as somehow outside, or irrelevant to society, and perhaps even regarded as a subspecies. Women who performed the demeaning work associated with new industrialism were treated even more dismissively. How could women accustomed to such work be expected to know much of household duties, or how to make *a man's home?*

Laissez-faire, literally translated from French 'let do', or to leave things to take their own course, free from government interference, was the economic philosophy of Victorian England. It also became a euphemism for greed or, as Karl Marx put it, 'the basis of *laissez-faire* was profit'. A. N. Wilson, in his eponymously titled book, described the Victorians, hypocritically believing that their God had created the working class in his own image and had no qualms about treating them every bit as appallingly as the sugar plantation proprietors in the West Indies treated their slaves.

> 'The Victorians .... were uncharitable people .... not intent on creating a more equitable society ... providing aid for orphans [or] the exploited women of the northern mills and mines.'
> (Wilson, A. N. (2003) *The Victorians* p 120).

The aristocratic and developing industrial bourgeoisie were extensively involved in, and profited from, many commercial industrial ventures and, with a readily available cheap, productive and expendable workforce, they were completely lacking in incentive to invest more heavily in machinery.

Nowhere is this philosophy better exemplified than in the coal mining industry where hewing coal was done by hand. At this time there was no mechanical substitute for the pick and shovel. The unskilled labour of men *and* women was still needed to dig the coal and deliver it to the surface.

* * * *

From 1840, the birth rate in Britain began to fall, not unrelated one could assume, to the long, harsh working days of women. Industry had turned to women, mostly unmarried or childless, to fill the gaps in the workforce. Although there is abundant literature describing the appalling conditions suffered at this time by women and children working in factories, particularly the textile manufacturing industry, there is a deficit of information about the arguably more atrocious conditions in coal mines. As complacent Victorian families warmed themselves in comfortable drawing rooms in front of fires most would not have known, nor cared, that the coal which burned in their grates had been dragged to the surface by women, and children as young as six, through long underground tunnels too narrow for a man to negotiate.

An act of 1842 to redress this undesirable situation was greeted with fierce opposition from the colliery owners and it was a further three years before the Liberal government of Lord John Russell even gave consideration to limiting the working hours of women (and children), believing it would interfere with the *freedom* of workers!

> 'Mining is an industry which has always been male-dominated, regardless of geographical location. There have been positive steps which have helped to integrate women into the industry, but females continue to be under-represented and mining is still largely a man's domain.'

The above paragraph was published in 2014 as part of an

article entitled 'Let's talk about: women in the mining industry'. (*Mining [DOT] Com* April 15 2014 at https://www.mining.com/lets-talk-about-women-in-the-mining-industry-31775/)   How times have changed! One does not have to search the archives very thoroughly to discover that women and young children worked alongside men in British coal mines long before the Act of 1842 prohibited this. In 1841 about 216,000 people were employed in the mines including women and children as young as four, five and six. Working in appalling conditions they received a fraction of the modest wages paid to men.

Children were left alone, usually in dark, damp passages, frequently having no work to do at all. By contrast, transporting the coal was very hard work and was usually done by older girls and women called 'hurriers'. They carried sacks and baskets of coal weighing over 100 kilograms (over 200 lbs) from the coalface along tunnels often over a kilometre in length (up to a mile long). During the journey these sacks and baskets had to be hauled up several ladders to reach their destination, along passageways just wide enough to allow women and children to pass, before being emptied into large tubs. The tubs had no wheels and were pushed and pulled over the uneven floor of the mine by women and girls harnessed to the tubs by chains threaded between their legs, attached to a second chain around their waists and then to the wagon. The chains, through constant chafing, caused skin sores. In places, the passageways were so steep they had to hold on to ropes to find their way. Where there were no ropes, they clutched on to anything at hand to steady themselves. Uneven floors and water leaking from above meant they were often ankle deep in water and in some places it reached their thighs. They worked constantly in saturated and scant clothing. In some places it was so hot and the work so hard that many women worked bare breasted together with naked men and

Harnessed to the corf by means of a chain between the legs and attached to one around the waist, young women pulled tubs or corves loaded with coal. Each corf weighed over 600 kg (over half a ton) and had to be pulled and thrust along tunnels often only 60 cm (2 feet) high.

'The "Pit Brow Lasses" of the nineteenth century: History Extra; BBC World Histories Magazine
https://www.historyextra.com/period/victorian/women-nineteenth-century-mining-lancashire-pit-brow-lasses-mines-collieries-act/

children, their only clothing being old trousers. These women often came to work leaving small children in the care of other women who did not work and were not always family members.

Working hours could be up to 14 hours a day and the women were frequently required to work double time, meaning that they could be underground for 24, or even 36 hours. They were paid a rate of seven shillings a week. Wages were usually paid monthly and, to ensure working numbers were maintained, they were frequently paid a month in arrears.

Swearing and fighting among the women was common. There are also recorded cases of rape and other sexual abuses perpetrated by male miners on these vulnerable women. These offences were frequently committed in the presence of children. Accidents were frequent with recorded instances of bones being crushed by derailed wagons. There was no sick pay or compensation.

COAL BEARING AND ITS DANGERS.

> Where there were no underground roadways, the coal was carried in baskets, weighing about 150 kg (200 lb) each. Often there were no ropes to steady the women and they clutched at anything close to hand, even jagged rocks, to steady themselves.
>
> *The Mining Folk of Fife: Scottish Mining Website: http://www.scottishmining.co.uk/502.html*

Women married young. They were usually illiterate since starting work as young children had deprived them of the opportunity to attend school. If they became pregnant, they frequently miscarried because of the brutal nature of work and conditions. Those whose pregnancies lasted a full term would frequently work until imminent delivery, some going into labour as soon as they reached their homes. There are many reported incidents of women simply undoing their chains and crawling into the nearest cranny to give birth, not even having the opportunity to go above ground. All this, however, was about to change.

Like two children emerging from underground, this memorial honours the 26 children who were killed at Huskar Pit, Yorkshire in 1838. The disaster was the impetus for the Ashley Royal Commission which, in 1842 resulted in an act, which prohibited children from working underground.

https://www.flickr.com/photos/andy_milner/33575720875

On 4 July 1838, there was a serious accident at Huskar Colliery in Silkstone, near Barnsley in Yorkshire. It had been an unusually hot day and, like many hot English summer days, it ended in a thunderstorm with about four inches of torrential rain, accompanied by hailstones. The machinery used to pull the coal and miners to the pit top was powered by steam, but the rain had put out the fire, disabling the engine and stranding the miners underground. Among the miners were many young boys and girls. A message was sent underground telling them to make their way to the base of the pit shaft where they were to wait until the engine was repaired and they could be evacuated. After about nine hours, when this failed to occur, many of them decided not to wait any longer. They were tired, hungry and, no doubt, frightened. Some of them decided to use an alternate exit. From an adjoining wood was a drift, a horizontal passageway used for ventilating the mine. At the end of the drift was a door which allowed the entrance of air into the mine. The children went through this door and they made their way up the drift. Suddenly, they were overpowered by a gushing torrent of water that washed them off their feet and carried them back to the ventilation door. The water rose against the door where they were trapped. Twenty-six children were drowned. When their bodies were eventually recovered, their faces were washed and they were delivered to their homes and waiting parents on a cart. Among the twenty-six children were two sets of brothers. Several other children shared the same surnames and were most likely related. The loss to the small mining community would have been enormous. A monument was built in Silkstone to honor the dead children.

(In 1988, a hundred and fifty years after the disaster, Silkstone Parish Council made funds available for the upkeep of an old memorial to the children and a new memorial was built at the site of the drownings.)

An inquest into the disaster was held at the Red Lion Inn in Silkstone, near Barnsley. Robert Coldwell Clarke, the mine owner, had inherited the land which accommodated the coal mine from his father, a Barnsley solicitor with a substantial property portfolio in the district including Noblethorpe, a hamlet near Barnsley. Clarke worked the coal seams on the estate on a large scale and, after increasing his considerable wealth, built Noblethorpe Hall as his residence. After his early death at 46 in 1846, his wife Sarah became heir carrying on with the business and adding considerably to the estate. (Ironically, not all coal owners were male. Lucy Thomas, also known as the mother of the Welsh steam coal trade, took over the running of her husband's coal mine after his death in 1833. There is no available information on the way she treated her employees.)

Three years after the Silkstone disaster, miners from the pit reported that Robert Clarke had installed and maintained good ventilation and lighting in his pits. A local surgeon when interviewed about working conditions of children down mines commented that he considered it a healthier lifestyle than that of weaving, or even farm labouring. (There is no accompanying information as to whether he had children and, if so, whether he was willing to let them work down the mine.) However, Robert Clarke, who employed 91 boys and 53 girls, did reluctantly admit that he regarded underground work unsuitable for girls, although it was sometimes the only means of support available to their families. He went on to tell the enquiry, "If I had a girl of my own I would rather send her to the pit than to the [workhouse], but if I had a choice I would rather send her to some other work". (Clarke had a son who was not employed in the mine.) Both Clarke and the surgeon, however, agreed that "the employment of girls was injurious to their morals!"

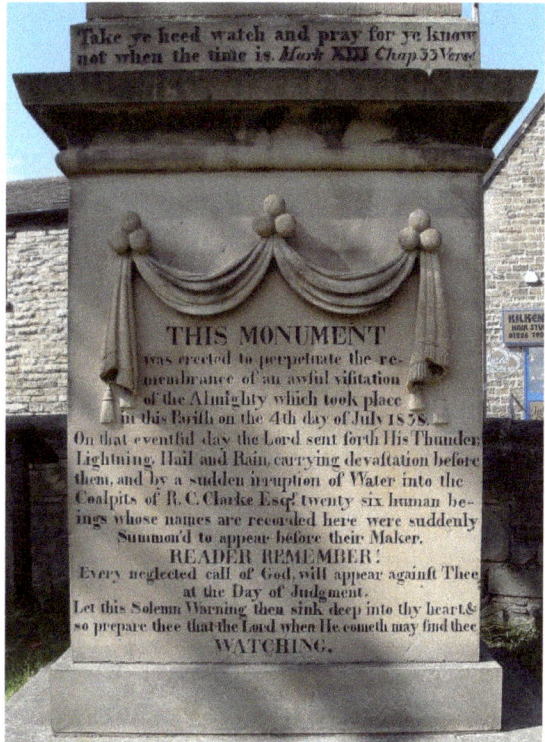

THIS MONUMENT was erected to perpetuate the remembrance of an awful vision of the Almighty which took place in the Parish on the 4th day of July 1838. On that eventful day the Lord set forth his Thunder, Lightning, Hail and Rain carrying devastation before them, and by a sudden irruption [sic] of water into the Coalpits of R. C. Clarke Esq., twenty six human beings whose names are recorded here were suddenly Summon'd to appear before their Maker. READER REMEMBER! Every neglected call of God will appear before Thee at the Day of Judgment. Let this Solemn Warning then sink deep into thy heart and so prepare thee that the Lord when He cometh find thee WATCHING.

https://www.flickr.com/photos/30120216@N07/6561351611

Reports of the accident appeared in London newspapers and came to the attention of Queen Victoria who subsequently exerted pressure on then Prime Minister, Lord Melbourne, to hold an inquiry into the working conditions in both factories and mines. In 1840, Lord Melbourne appointed his nephew-in-law, Anthony Ashley-Cooper 7th Earl of Shaftesbury, arch Tory politician and 'champion of the poor', to lead a royal commission of inquiry into the working conditions (mainly of children) in coal mines. Ashley, like his contemporary social reforming fellows, was a devout Christian who believed in the literal truth of the Bible. His underlying belief behind rescuing women and children from the mines was based on the premise that God had chosen to come to earth in the form of a poor person and that every child was made in His image, having both dignity and rights. Ashley also regarded *laissez-faire* as 'state tyranny'. He also believed that the state should take responsibility for the welfare of its citizens. This idea was anathema to *laissez-faire* economists.

For over two years Lord Ashley and the other commissioners undertook a fact-finding mission, visiting collieries and coal mining communities throughout the country — much to the outrage of the mine owners. Four commissioners were appointed to collect and compile evidence and, for the purposes of the royal commission, the country was divided into districts. A sub-commissioner was assigned to each district. They had a hard task ahead of them to inspect every coal mine, often going underground, to collect information about working conditions. They heard and saw, at first hand, the human degradation and exploitation of these workers, and interviewed a wide range of people from mine owners, who displayed a disparaging lack of concern and responsibility for the welfare of their employees, to children who carried out the work.

They investigated the number of women and child workers

and the age at which they were employed, how they were hired, their working conditions and the way they were treated. The commissioners were also charged with investigating and publishing a report on any accidents and long-term effects on the well-being of the employees. Evidence was given to the commissioners under oath and a written record was made of every interview. The report also included explicit engravings of conditions underground adding authenticity to the findings.

Samuel Scriven, one of the commissioners, had been previously appointed by the House of Commons to investigate working conditions in the in the textile industry and potteries. What he saw and heard about the conditions in the coal mines shocked him most of all. Children as young as six were employed to work in dangerous conditions, side by side with men and women both stripped to the waist, in the extreme heat of the pits. Although he was horrified at the women's nakedness, he was equally scandalised that many of them were wearing trousers! "Some of them would pass without much trouble as brawny, well-proportioned members of the stern sex", he was said to have remarked. In fact, by putting on trousers and, sometimes discarded jackets of their fathers or brothers, they were attempting to protect their modesty. In the intolerable heat, more flimsy clothing, even if available to them, would have revealed even more their contours as it clung to their perspiration-soaked bodies.

Some workers made light of their evidence, fearing reprisals if they gave damning reports as to the real nature of their working conditions, while many more took the first opportunity presented to them to tell, in graphic detail, of the wretchedness of their plights.

Women described how they had first gone to work down the mine when they were small children, often working there for the next 10 or 15 years. Many women described how they had given birth while still at work. Those women who managed to come above ground to give birth told the commissioners of how, within a day or two, they returned to work, leaving the newborn infant, if it survived, in the care of relatives or friends. Women were forced to take their older children to work with them. Because of the harsh workload, many suffered complications associated with childbirth, including miscarriages and still births. Work-related accidents were common often meaning they were unable to work. Permanent deformities caused by work were common.

The women used to get up about four in the morning, starting work as soon as they had descended the mine and working the whole time apart from an hour for 'dinner' which usually comprised bread only. This was usually mid-morning, if they had time. Sweat poured down their bodies and, by the time they eventually finished their shifts and returned home, they were often too exhausted to wash and often fell asleep sitting in chairs. The commissioners formed the opinion that:

> 'The collier's home [cannot possibly] be comfortable. He makes his wife and children toil with him in the mine: he married a woman from the mine; and neither she nor her daughters know anything of housekeeping. How can disorder be prevented from creeping into the collier's dwelling, when no one is there in the daytime to attend to it? Then all the money which they can save from the Tommy-shop, (of which I shall speak presently) goes for whiskey. Husband and wife, sons and daughters all look after the whiskey. The habits of the colliers are hereditarily depraved: they are perpetuated from father to son, from mother to daughter; none is better nor worse than his parents were before him. Rags and filth--squalor and dissipation--crushing toil and hideous want--ignorance

and immorality; these are the features of the collier's home, and the characteristics of the collier's life.'
(MacArthur-Reynolds, G.W. (1845) *The Mysteries of London*; Library Of Alexandria: USA)

The brief of the commission had been to collect information about the conditions of the mines, publish the findings and advise on any ensuing laws and/or recommendations. The information revealed to them, together with the visual images of the horrendous working environment and conditions that supplemented the narrative record of the information they had gathered was outrageous and appalling. When the report was published, it made harrowing reading and caused a public outcry.

Although the commissioners were shocked into public displays of disapproval it was ironically, *not* primarily the brutalisation of these women nor the abhorrent conditions in which they were forced to work that elicited their disapproval. According to one of the commissioners, one of the most 'disgusting' sights he had ever witnessed was "young females dressed in trousers like boys, crawling on all fours with belts round their waists and passing through their legs as they loaded wagons." One girl gave evidence, sparing no detail, of how "the chain….had worn large holes in [her] trousers", causing one of the commissioners to respond, "Any sight more disgustingly indecent, or revolting can scarcely be imagined than these girls at work. No brothel can beat it." In his view, these women violated Victorian virtues of feminine purity and moral superiority. Recorded incidents of sexual abuse could, therefore, be blamed on the women who, by the conventions of the day, were regarded as guardians of male morality. Tellingly, it was the garb — or lack thereof — that disgusted and revolted the upright commissioner rather the sight of them in chains loading and hauling.

In an era when lace, silks, cashmere shawls and crinolines were emblematic of middle class notions of femininity, bourgeois ideals led Victorian society to consider that women who performed physical labour were 'masculinised', seen as culturally aberrant and the antithesis of being female. The spectacle of naked or semi-naked women down mines horrified their collective sensibilities. By Victorian standards even a woman, albeit respectably dressed, who exposed her legs was obviously associated with prostitution. At the very least, appearing to breach the feminine construct was enough to make such women unsuitable to become wives and mothers.

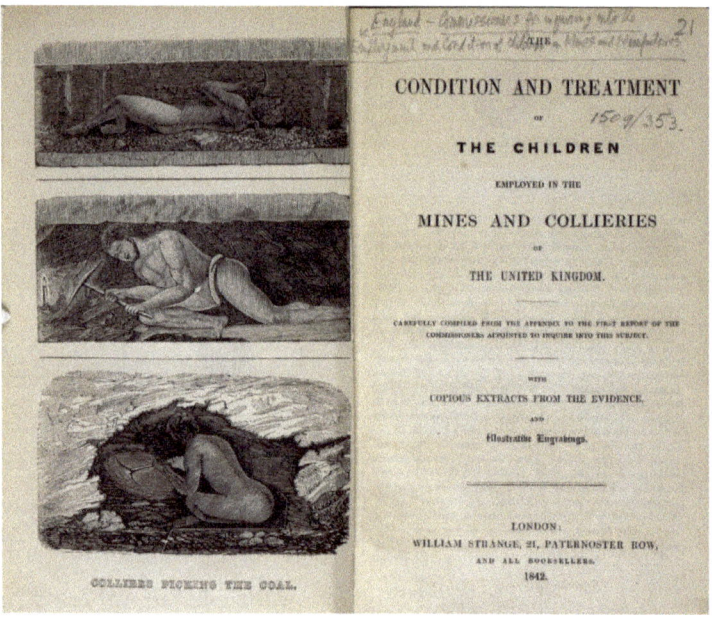

The Report on Child Labour, 1842
The Women in Pants who shocked Victorian Britain; *AtlasObscura*

https://www.bl.uk/collection-items/report-on-child-labour-1842#

The harshness of the commissioners' report, it seems, appeared to offend the Victorian ideal of virtue rather than decency. The description by Wilson (*ibid*) of the Victorians as:

'Ruthless, grabbing, competitive male dominated society stamping on its victims and discarding its weaker members' appears to be, on this occasion, suitable.

In order to ensure the passage of the Act pursuant to the Royal Commission, Lord Ashley appealed, not to the pity or revulsion at the inhumane conditions in which these women were forced to toil, he appealed to Victorian prudery.

Within a week of the report being published, Ashley gave notice that he intended to take the Mines and Colliery Bill through Parliament. After a long, eloquent preamble, he introduced his bill:

> [Women's] labour… is wasteful and ruinous to themselves and their families… They know nothing that they ought to know, they are rendered unfit for the duties of women by overwork and become utterly demoralized. In the male the moral effects of the system are very sad, but in the female they are infinitely worse, not alone upon themselves, but upon their families, upon society, and, I may add, upon the country itself. It is bad enough if you corrupt the women, you poison the waters of life at the very fountain.

In essence, the fault lay with the women. Did the commissioners consider they were responsible for bringing about their own hopeless situation?

The subsequent Mines and Collieries Act of 1842 stipulated:
- All underground employment of women and girls would be prohibited
- No boy under 10 could be employed underground

- Parish apprentices between the ages of 10 to 18 could be allowed to continue working underground.

Children as young as six made up a large component of the workforce in Victorian coal mines. They worked for as long as 12 to 18 hours a day in mines which were dark and dangerous and the air thick with coal dust. Because of the nature of the work many developed permanent deformities. Many more did not survive.

The 1842 Mines Act prohibited all girls and boys (under ten years old) from working underground in coal mines.

Judge, B. (2015) August 10 1842: Mines Act bans women and children from working underground
https://moneyweek.com/403857/1842-mines-act-bans-women-and-children-from-working-underground/

Two days after Ashley introduced the Bill into Parliament, it was reported that his speech detailing the Commission's findings, heard largely in silence, was punctuated by cheers from fellow members who afterwards, many with tears in their eyes, rose to congratulate him. The Bill was passed by the House of Lords on 7 July 1842, ironically almost four years to the day of the Huskar accident which had prompted the enquiry.

Although it suffered several amendments and was greeted with disapprobation by mine owners, the Act prohibited *all* women from working underground. There was to be no compensation for loss of earnings even though many families had relied on the wages of both man and wife. One woman remarked that, although she had hated her previous work, it was better than starvation. To emphasise the regard for the work these women performed, they were replaced by pit ponies which increased the costs to the mine owners. The ponies needed to be fed and roofs had to be raised to allow them to pass through.

* * * *

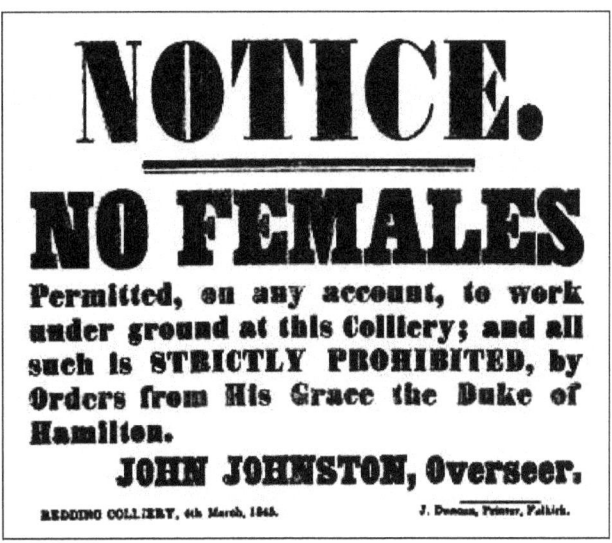

Notice at Redding Colliery, Falkirk, Scotland, 4 March 1845
Spartacus educational: Mines and Collieries Act

Only a single inspector, however, was appointed to oversee the introduction of the legislation throughout the whole of the country. Unsurprisingly, the mine owners continued to contravene the Act and in 1850 it was reported that there were still 200 women and girls, some as young as 11, employed in collieries in South Wales.

Although this revelation prompted an increase in the number of inspectors, numerous violations of the Act continued.

There followed a series of Acts addressing working conditions in mines. An Act in 1850 investigated the frequency of accidents in mines and in 1860 an Act was introduced to improve safety in mines and revise the minimum age of boys working in mines to 12 years. In 1872, there was still an enormous loss of life through mining accidents and a second Mines Regulation Act was passed requiring all managers to possess a State Certificate of Training. Miners were also given the right to appoint one of their peers as safety inspectors. In 1881, a Mines Regulation Act empowered the Home Secretary to hold enquiries into the cause of mining accidents. There still remained, however, a need for further intervention and regulation in the mining industry.

Families who had previously worked together underground relied on the wages of women and were now suffering even more financial hardship. Women again became confined to the home, losing what independence they had previously. Many women, however, insisted on continuing to work. Dressed in men's clothing, they entered the mines clandestinely through side entrances. A ten-pound fine in the event of discovery was hardly a deterrent to the mine owners who turned a blind eye to this practice and the Home Office appeared reluctant to pursue errant owners.

Many of the women who were no longer permitted to work underground found work at the pit top (or brow) sorting coal. They became known as Pit Brow Women.

Pinterest: https://www.pinterest.com.au/ pin/50595195794908878/?lp=true

Why 'pit brow lasses' were coal mining's unsung heroines: The Guardian *https://www.theguardian.com/culture/2018/oct/14/pit-brow-lasses-coal-mining-unsung-heroines-bishop-auckland-museum*

Women gradually moved into occupations at the pit top. This pleased the mine owners as they were still willing to work for lower wages than the men, and owners were reluctant to lose the cheaper form of labour. The most common form of pit top work performed by women was coal picking — inspecting the coal brought from underground and picking out lumps of dirt and rock. For these women, known as 'Pit Brow Women', work was still hard but a definite improvement on their former working conditions.

Ninety-nine per cent of pit brow women were married and formed tightly knit groups. They continued to work 12 hours a day, six days a week which left little time for leisure activities such as would have been available in those days, and time spent away from the picking tables was spent doing housework.

Coal picking work had previously been reserved for men who had been disabled in mining accidents. Unlike their male counterparts, the women had no trade union and were under constant pressure from male workers to leave their jobs so they could be done by these men. Men also believed that removing the women from the workforce would make it easier for them to demand higher wages as men were still considered the chief breadwinners with families to support. In 1887, women took part in organised protests over harsh working conditions. The result was that they were merely banned from pushing loaded wagons.

Once again, it was their unconventional working attire which appeared to cause offence to Victorian prudery. Working outside in the cold and dirt, pit brow women developed a unique 'dress code' described by one onlooker: "She wears a pair of trousers …. covered with a skirt reaching just below the knees. Her head is cunningly bandaged with a red handkerchief, which entirely protects the hair from coal dust. Across this is a piece of cloth which comes under the chin, with the result that only the face is exposed. A flannel jacket completes the costume." On their feet they wore clogs.

Images of Pit Brow women in their unique work attire were captured for posterity by Arthur J. Munby (1820–1910). A Cambridge graduate who was called to the bar, Munby failed to make a career as a barrister and worked as a civil servant in the Ecclesiastical Commissioner's Office. He had a fascination with working women whom he photographed almost obsessively. Many of his photographs became picture postcards and were bought as novelties by members of Victorian society, particularly middle class ladies and gentlemen who continued to regard the working lifestyles of these women with disdain. Neither the 'ladies' nor their husbands,

There are galleries of photographs of these women whose distinctive wardrobe appeared to fascinate the public. The photographs of these women, produced commercially and sold as novelties, were the work of Arthur J. Munby, a graduate of Trinity College, Cambridge and failed barrister with an obsession for working-class women.

https://en.wikipedia.org/wiki/Pit_brow_women

nor the purchasers of the novelty postcards, gave much thought to why the women wore these clothes or the hard work that made it necessary for them to do so. Given the opportunity, the pit brow women would arguably, with circumstances and money permitting, willingly exchange wardrobes with their more fortunate sisters.

Regrettably there is no evidence that their more favoured sisters took any part to improve the despicable working conditions of women employed by mines. However, there are copious recorded examples of the roles they played from the very inception of the campaign for abolition of slavery in Jamaican sugar plantations and cotton fields in the southern states of North America. These campaigners ranged from the aristocratic Georgina, Duchess of Devonshire (a mine owning dynasty) to middle class women such as journalist Harriet Martineau. Mary Wollstonecraft, author of *Vindication of the Rights of Women* compared men's domination of women to slavery thus,

> Half the human species, like the poor African slaves, [are] subject to the prejudices that brutalise them …. only to sweeten the cup of men'.

Substituting the words 'women down the mine' for African slaves, 'warm' for sweeten and 'British population' for men would have provided an effective slogan for a campaign to abolish the abominable working conditions of women in mines.

Nevertheless, between 1887 and 1911, there were continuous, concerted efforts to ban women completely from any work in coal mines. By the early part of the 20th century, advanced technology superseded women's labour. Washing and cleaning machines began to do the work of the coal pickers. As late as 1941, there were 600 women employed in this occupation and by 1950, there were less than 100. The last two women to be 'manually' employed in the British coal industry retired in 1972.

Women who worked in the coal mining industry, whether underground in horrendously unpleasant and dangerous conditions or later as they 'graduated' to work above ground — where conditions were an improvement but not ideal — were significant contributors to the success of British industry, not to mention the wealth of mine owners. Their working conditions, hard labour through blood, sweat and tears should never be overlooked. Never again did women in Britain work underground nor on the surface of coal mines fulfilling the backbreaking labour necessary for the industry to prosper. Despite this, they have remained an influential part of the coal mining culture providing support and security for the men who remained indentured to the industry.

> *I am an Aspull collier, I like a bit of fun*
> *To have a go at football or in the sports to run*
> *So goodbye old companions, adieu to jollity,*
> *For I have found a sweetheart, and she's all the world to me.*
> *Could you but see my Nancy, among the tubs of coal,*
> *In tucked up skirt and breeches, she looks exceedingly droll,*
> *Her face besmear'd with coal dust, as black as black can be,*
> *She is a pit brow lassie but she's all the world to me.*
> **(Anon)**

3
Coming of age

My mother was born in 1907, the oldest of seven children. Named Annie Elizabeth, she always hated the name Annie, preferring the diminutive Nan, which she used in various forms for the rest of her life. Nan's biography is not unconnected with the events of the preceding and following chapters of this book. Her story winds its way through the narrative and is a significant constituent of the warp and weft of the story's fabric.

At the time of Nan's birth, her father Harry, was employed as a miner in one of the collieries of South Yorkshire. The synchronism doesn't end there. Harry worked at Silkstone Colliery, scene of the disaster which had killed so many children sixty years earlier.

Born in 1887, Harry started work underground in the early 1900s but, unlike many of his co-workers, he and his wife Emily rented a small cottage in High Green, at that time a village, now the most northern suburb of Sheffield. Unlike many miners' houses, his was not owned by any of the local mining companies Harry, however, did not hail from a mining heritage. He came from a family of small holding farmers.

High Green was not a mining community, but a country village and it was there that Nan's birth took place on 11 June 1907. When Nan was still a baby, Emily and Harry moved to the neighbouring village of Charlton Brook where they lived for the next few years. Emily had been a long-term resident of the village where her father owned the local Bridge Inn. She had ten siblings and a large extended, close knit, supportive family. Prior to her marriage she had helped around the inn, unlike many of her female cohort, most of whom would have left the village to work in domestic service.

The Bridge Inn at High Green, owned by Nan's paternal grandfather and home to her mother's family, is still operating.

Publican Partnerships
https://www.eipublicanpartnerships.com/run-a-pub/pubs/PBO%20Reports/030320.pdf

At the time of Nan's birth Harry was working as a deputy at Silkstone, a supervisory position responsible for an area underground. As with all mining jobs, it was hard work, but Harry was young and fit and, like the rest of his mining colleagues he would walk the few miles to work. During his shift down the pit he would walk, sometimes crawl, through underground tunnels along the coal face where the miners worked, frequently stopping to talk to the men in his area or district. Part of the responsibility of his position was to supervise aspects of health and safety. In accordance with the 1911 Mining Act, a deputy was required to be on duty for every shift and at each change of shift he would report any significant events that had taken place during his time at work to the deputy designated to replace him.

Even at this time, production methods in the coal industry were antiquated. Working down the pit was still dangerous and mine safety conditions deplorably slack. Loss of life, individual and wholesale, was common. Although until the early 19th century mines had been largely unregulated, by the beginning of the 20th century there was considerable government control by legislation supported by a government inspectorate. Legislation had often followed recommendations from government inquiries, but reform was tardy and erratic as mine owners were reluctant to embrace guidelines which protected their employees claiming it would adversely affect their profits.

When Harry first went into the mine, the industry was about to undergo the transition from being largely unregulated to one which, having Parliamentary representation by miners, had progressed in line with the growing strength and influence of the emergent Labour Party.

At this time, some of the thinner, more superficial coal seams were being worked out. Thriving new mining communities were emerging throughout the Northern coalfields where shafts had been sunk to gain access to the rich, thick seams of coal which comprised the highly productive region of the Yorkshire/Nottinghamshire/Derbyshire Coal Field known as the Barnsley Bed coal seam. From the late 1800s the production and demand for coal soared without interruption until, in 1913 it reached its peak. During those years, miners constituted the largest group of industrial workers in Britain.

The first national strike by British miners in 1912 formed part of the wave of labour unrest that swept through Britain prior to World War I. Involving almost a million miners, the industrial action was an attempt by the Miners' Federation of Great Britain (MFGB) to secure a minimum wage for its members. The existing complicated wage structure, a sliding scale based on the selling price of coal, made it difficult for certain miners to earn a fair day's wage. Miners in less productive coalfields such as the Forrest of Dean coalfield in Gloucestershire earned less than their peers in the more profitable northern pits of Durham or Yorkshire. After 37 days of strike action and 38 million working hours lost to the strike, the Government intervened by passing the Coal Mines Act securing, for the first time, a minimum wage for all miners. On 28 July 1914, 'The war to end all wars' was declared and, for the duration, trade union activity ceased.

In the early stages of the war, even with many men away at the Front, the production of coal per man increased, probably due to the fact that, as is usual in times of national adversity, there was a national commitment among workers to improve productivity. Less time was lost to absenteeism, holidays and industrial action. However, despite government intervention, the initial rise in the coal production was relatively short lived. In 1916 production was 60 percent of its 1913–1914 peak. During the next four years of hostilities, both the demand and production of coal declined as it was replaced by the use of oil. 1914–1918 were watershed years in the coal mining industry. From then it declined to the point where, towards the end of the century, it ceased to exist.

The wartime decrease in the amount of coal extracted per man, together with the reduction in the number of shifts worked per year can be attributed to a general decline in the physical ability of the male workers in the industry. In the early stages of the war the youngest, fittest miners had enlisted in large numbers to fight, leaving work to older, less fit men. The industry had lost its most productive workers. Following a huge national campaign to attract volunteers to take part in the fighting, newspapers published articles and propaganda directed at young men to convince them to come forward and show their patriotism by joining the fight against Germany. In the following weeks there was a scramble for recruiting offices as thousands of young men answered the call. As many as 10,000 of Britain's youth enlisted in one day. In one week alone in September 1914, 175,000 volunteered. By the end of that month the number had risen to 750,000. Even reports of enormous loss of lives on the battlefields of Northern France and the Middle East did nothing to deter eager young men from volunteering to replace their fallen compatriots. By Christmas 1914, hundreds of thousands more had voluntarily enlisted and the stampede continued into 1915. The call for volunteers had been so successful that the government was unable to arm or equip all of those who had enlisted. Those who did not enlist faced public insults and humiliation so that it took more courage *not* to volunteer.

British coal miners came out on strike for the first time for parity of pay in 1912. The strike lasted for six weeks. Nationally miners had voted 445,801 to 115,921 in favour of the strike during which they would chant
"Eight hours work, eight hours play
Eight hours sleep and eight bob a day"

http://www.healeyhero.co.uk/rescue/individual/Bob_Bradley/Bk-2/Bk2-1912.html

"Lord Kitchener wants you!"

Undoubtedly the most famous image of WWI shows Field Marshall Herbert Kitchener, then Secretary for War, appealing for men to join the British Army. First produced in 1914, it has assumed iconic status even though it was not widely circulated outside London.

https://en.wikipedia.org/wiki/Main_Page

In March 1916, when enlistment failed to staunch the flow of the colossal numbers of dead and wounded, the Government introduced conscription. Under the terms of the Military Service Act all medically fit, single men between the ages of 19 and 41 enlisted in the armed forces on 2 March of that year. A second Act in May 1916 extended conscription for married men and the age limit was lowered to 18. Conscripted men had no choice about which service, regiment or unit they joined.   There were, however, exemptions to the Act. Certain industrial workers whose occupations were described as 'Scheduled' or 'Reserved' were not required to enlist. Among those exemptions was coal mining.

The Military Services Bill was introduced in January 1916 approving conscription of single men aged between 18 and 41. In May 1916, the bill was extended to include married men and in April 1918 the upper age was lifted to 50.

National Army Museum
https://www.army.mod.uk/firstworldwarresources/archives/1101/step-into-your-place-1916-c

After hours spent in dark, narrow tunnels in heat and water and the omnipresent threat of injury and/or death there was usually little relief when the working day was over. Many miners lived in primitive conditions where even washing away the accumulated grime and coaldust was a problem. It is hardly surprising that many miners eagerly volunteered to leave home to fight. Could life in the trenches of Flanders be any worse than these? By 1915, almost 20% of men engaged in the mining industry joined the armed forces.

Although men who were officially exempt from the fighting

were issued with papers and badges to prove they were already undertaking war work, many felt the guilt of staying behind with their wives and families while the sons of neighbours were risking their lives on the other side of the English Channel. There was also, for many, the call of adventure. This may have been true for Nan's father, who enlisted in 1916 or, perhaps, it was also a means of escape from his ever-increasing family!

In 1908, a year after Nan's birth, came a brother, and in 1911 and 1913 respectively, two sisters. In 1914 a fifth child, a girl, was born but did not survive. In 1916, Emily gave birth to another baby boy. It would be a further two years before Marie Stopes published *Married Love*, one of the most influential books of the century and there was scant readily available information on birth control.

As was common in small communities at that time, Emily's children were all born at home. For generations, women had experienced home births attended by midwives, neighbours, relatives or friends. Few pregnant women received adequate, if any, antenatal care. Pregnancy and childbirth were natural facts of life, although economic and social circumstances all influenced the related risks. Wealthier women were able to choose to have a doctor, or at least a trained midwife, present at the delivery whereas poorer women were attended mostly by experienced but completely untrained *accoucheurs*.

With the passing of the first Midwives Act in 1902 midwifery in Britain became legalised for the first time. Hitherto few, if any, of the women attending the deliveries of poorer women, had received any training and neonatal and maternal death rates reflected the standard of care. The Act established midwifery as a profession but since there were at this time relatively few trained midwives some of these 'lay' midwives were allowed to continue practicing *pro tem*. However, these women were required to register as *bona fide* and were not allowed to call themselves midwives. Under the Act unregulated and untrained 'handywomen' were no longer allowed to attend women giving birth. Such women were regarded as illiterate with dangerously unsanitary methods, although for decades they had been attending working class women during childbirth, often in primitive conditions where, to many, childbirth may have more often been an unwelcome rather than a joyful event.

Elizabeth Sanderson, widow of a Lanarkshire (Scotland) coal miner described herself as 'midwife' in the 1901 census when an estimated 95% of working-class births took place in the home. Like many women in her position, she became a midwife to earn an income, and her skill was based on her own experience of giving birth to six children.

National Records of Scotland
https://www.nrscotland.gov.uk/research/learning/features/safe-delivery-a-history-of-scottish-midwives

Nevertheless a network of these midwives survived in places such as mining communities. Legislation did not entirely change entrenched ideas and traditions which allowed many of these women to continue to practice. Nan's birth certificate gives no information about who attended Emily when she gave birth. Presumably, in 1907, it would have been a trained midwife.

Although abortion was illegal, it was during that time, the most widespread form of birth control. Used predominantly by working-class women, it was used as a means of limiting the number of children per family to help check poverty and unemployment.

Annual death rates per 1000 total births from puerperal fever in England and Wales (1911–1945)

(*Registrar General Reports*)

Leaving his family behind, Harry left for the Front sometime in 1916. There is no record of how Emily felt about his departure, leaving her with five children under ten. The following two years would have been anything but easy for either of them, but at least there would be no more pregnancies, for a while. Nan was particularly close to her father and would have missed him. However, to her, his absence would have proved somewhat of a mixed blessing. She remembered her dismay on the occasions when, coming home from school, she would be greeted by the cries of yet another new born-baby and her heart would sink. At least her father's absence would mean a respite from the added chores associated with the arrival of another sibling.

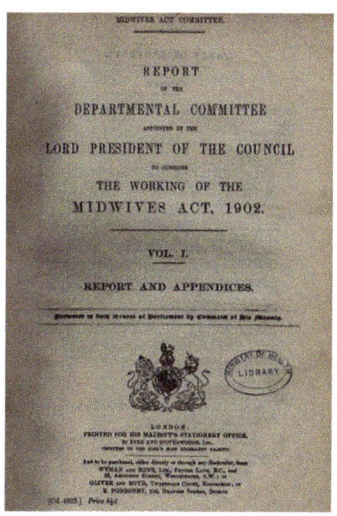

The Midwives Act of 1902 regulated the practice of midwifery and provided a penalty for women without qualifications to practise. This ensured that only qualified midwives could attend women giving birth.

https://www.cosmobooks.co.uk/pages/books/234033/midwives-act-report-of-the-departmental-committee-to-consider-the-working-of-the-midwives-act-1902

Since Harry enrolled as a Private, his wage of seven shillings a week would hardly have been enough to support his family. Fortunately, Emily remained close to her parents from whom she received both practical and emotional support. As with most large families, several of her brothers and brothers-in-law were also in uniform. This, of course, meant that support was limited as it had to be shared. Conditions at home for the next few years would be hard.

Like men, women at that time had divided opinions about the war. Many were enthusiastic supporters. Some were so avid in their support that it led them to humiliate and shame men into enlistment, often handing out white feathers as a sign of cowardice. Others were troubled at the thought of war, while still more vehemently opposed it. Neither Emily's political nor ethical stance is known, but family reports tell of her circumspection at Harry's intent to enlist. For the period of his absence, there would be little communication between them. Censorship made correspondence difficult and many families were unaware of where their men were serving.

Harry was drafted into the Durham Light Infantry. After initial training on Salisbury Plain, as part of the British Expeditionary Force, he saw action on the Western Front at Ypres, Messines, the Somme, and Passchendaele. Like most, his regiment suffered heavy losses. Six Victoria Crosses were awarded to the regiment at a cost of 12,530 deaths, including officers. By early October 1914, more than 80% of its original complement had either been killed or wounded.

By all accounts, Harry's war was bearable. As an infantryman he was assigned batman to one of the officers. Why he was chosen for this service is unknown. He never had any experience in any form of a servant's role. Among his duties were maintaining the officer's uniform, acting as a 'bodyguard' in combat, communicating orders between the officer and various subordinates and performing various tasks which his officer felt disinclined to perform. Although it could possibly be regarded as submissive, the position of batman was quite a desirable one. Such soldiers got better rations and were sometimes the recipients of favours from their officers. Because of his role, Harry was exempt from the more back breaking work assigned to his fellow soldiers. Also, the position, not infrequently came with promotion to lance-corporal, sometimes to corporal and eventually, sergeant. However, it would be gilding the lily to describe any role which involved the trench warfare of 1914–1918 as opportune. At some stage, Harry's kit was lost as he was moved up the line. The cost of replacement was deducted from his meagre pay, meaning more hardship for Emily and the family.

The Battle of Passchendaele, Belgium, took place in September 1917. Total casualties were estimated at 500,000 of whom 274,000 were British and Commonwealth soldiers. More than 200,000 German were believed to be killed and many thousands more reported missing in action.

Battle of Passchendaele: Encyclopaedia Britannica
https://www.britannica.com/event/Battle-of-Passchendaele

The absence of so many men meant a huge drain on the labour pool at home creating a need for new workers. Suddenly women were able to take on work from which they had previously been excluded — work in heavy industry, in transport and even in the police force. An estimated two million women replaced men in the labour force.

The wartime demand for an increasing workforce on the home front had a noticeable effect on the position of women of both the middle and working classes. Many middle-class women replaced men in clerical positions while the number of women in banks increased as did female representation in commerce, education and local government occupations. Undertaking clerical work was seen as an entrée to obtaining work in the Civil Service. Middle-class women, by and large, were the ones who went into nursing or joined the newly formed service organisations. Freedom and independence associated with working outside the home made chaperoning obsolete. Although paid employment was hardly a novelty for working class women, it offered a wider range of roles and hastened the demise of traditional female occupations such as domestic service. Employers of sweated labour found difficulty retaining workers who left in droves to seek better paid occupations which were now available. Almost half the first round of applicants for work at the London General Omnibus Company had previously been employed in domestic service.

However, the wages women received remained less than those paid to men who had done the same work. Anxiety about the fighting menfolk, pressure of employment and the ubiquitous demand to perform household chores took a toll on all women like Emily. Although the pressure and hard work of taking care of five young children precluded her from taking on paid employment outside her home, like other women in her situation, she remained anxious for her husband's welfare. This anxiety was not new for her. Like all women married to miners she had worried daily about the possibility of his not returning home at the end of his working day. Rather than a knock on the door if disaster struck, during wartime it could be weeks before she received any bad news, invariably delivered by telegram.

3   Coming of age

World War I female tram driver from Preston Lancashire. Over the course of two days there were more than 200 applications for the job. Most of the women were displaced from their work by returning soldiers.

From the archive, 21 May 1915: Women tram guards in wartime: The Guardian
https://www.theguardian.com/world/the-northerner/2015/may/21/women-tram-guards-wartime-1915

Although working in a munitions factory was monotonous and sometimes dangerous, it presented new employment opportunities for women during WW I.

"Munitions and Morales: How the First World War transformed women's role in the UK." Sky News: https://news.sky.com/feature/munitions-and-morals-how-the-first-world-war-changed-womens-role-in-uk-11541862

The war made its impact felt across the whole of the class structure. Even sons of the monarchy joined the war effort. Propagandists exploited the fact that women had willingly sacrificed sons, brothers, husbands and lovers, supposedly uniting all women in the fight for justice. The war called on women to maintain their family obligations while simultaneously undertaking a variety of work that made them a relevant, essential part of the war effort. Even typically 'feminine' domestic crafts such as knitting and sewing took on military significance as they produced mountains of handmade socks, scarves, gloves and balaclavas for soldiers.

Nor were children exempt from humanitarian and patriotic duties. Nan remembered her early schooldays during the war when each day began by singing the British, French and Russian National

Anthems as a mark of respect to The *Triple Entente*. Girl Guides and Boy Scouts undertook the manufacture of basic medical supplies — bandages, swabs and slings. Boys delivered messages as well as collecting eggs for wounded soldiers. Girls helped with knitting and both boys and girls wrote morale boosting letters to send to the Fronts. Everyone was urged to accept, without question, the rationing of basic food items.

Neither was the Home Front free from the exigencies of war. Under the 1914 Defence of the Realm Act, there was a sudden increase in the number of government regulations applying to all classes. Black outs were enforced as, for the first time in history, Britain came under attack from the sky. Bombing raids were carried out by colossal German airships called Zeppelins. One such attack on London on 8 October 1915 killed thirty-eight people and injured eighty-seven. Coastal towns were particularly vulnerable to attack. In December 1914, a raid on the northern towns of Scarborough, Hartlepool and Whitby killed one hundred and thirty-seven people and injured almost six hundred. Further raids on densely populated London left many women and children dead. In total there were fifty-one raids by Zeppelins and fifty-seven raids by aeroplanes killing and injuring 4,820. The attacks caused vehement public outrage as many of the victims were women and children. Emily and the children, living close to the industrial city of Sheffield would have been exposed to the same threat of danger as the city also bore its share of the bombing.

A German Zeppelin flies menacingly over London in 1915
"Giants of the Sky — The Zeppelins of WW I" War History online
https://www.warhistoryonline.com/instant-articles/giants-sky-zeppelins-ww1.html

At the outbreak of WW I, German armed forces used Zeppelin airships in strategic raids against British towns and cities. The first was on King's Lynn in Norfolk. The airships could travel at 100 km/h and carry up to 200 kg of bombs. Attacks caused widespread alarm and WW I became a 'total war' involving civilians as well as the military.

Zeppelin airships carried out 51 bombing raids in Britain killing 557 and injuring a further 1,357 people. More than 500 bombs were dropped causing £1.5 million damage. Of the 84 airships used, 30 were shot down and a further 27 were lost in accidents.

Aeroplanes carried out 27 raids dropping 111,935 kg of bombs killing 835 and injuring 1,972 people at a cost of £1,418,272 damage.

3 *Coming of age*

Damage inflicted by Zeppelin a bombing air raid on Sheffield
BBC Sounds: *https://www.bbc.co.uk/sounds/play/p01x4046*

Although proscribed from joining the forces, many women without children took on military or quasi military roles. The Voluntary Aid Detachment was made up of female civilian volunteers who went to the war fronts, initially to work as cooks and canteen workers. When caught under fire they were thrust into emergency hospital work. Although not trained nurses, as were the women of the Army Nursing Corps, they discharged their duties admirably and, with the growing shortage of nurses, went on to serve in military hospitals at various fronts. (Vera Britain gives an excellent account of her VAD experiences in her autobiographical *Testament of Youth*.) Over 57,000 women served with the Women's Auxiliary Corps on the battlefields of France where still more women volunteered to drive ambulances under the auspices of the

Red Cross. The Territorial Force Nursing Service was established in 1908 to support the Territorial and Reserve Forces. Candidates had to be over 23 years of age and have completed three years training and, from 1913, they could volunteer for overseas service. During WWI there were about 7,000 nurses and about 2,300 went overseas, including Nan's aunt Mary, Emily's sister. At home, the Women's Land Army was created to enable women to replace male agricultural workers who had been drafted into military service. As infected with war fever as men, many women willingly offered sacrifice and service to King and country.

Although their contribution to the war effort was largely applauded, unlike that of their male equivalents, it was not compulsory. Regrettably, wartime media often patronisingly conveyed the impression that the actions of women were, somehow, less remarkable. Since women were not conscripted into work their war time employment was regarded as temporary. Once the men returned, any support that had been available to them was withdrawn and facilities such as day nurseries closed.

What is significant is that, at this time, women were still denied the vote. (In 1918 about 58% of the adult male population were still unfranchised. For the duration of the war, the Women's Social and Political Union (WSPU) chose to suspend its suffrage campaign to help the government recruit women into war work. Their contribution to the war effort was perhaps sufficient proof to convince the government that women deserved the right to vote.

At the eleventh hour of the eleventh day of the eleventh month of 1918 an Armistice was signed in a forest just fifty kilometres from the battlefields of Northern France. After four years of fighting, where little had been achieved militarily, the cessation of hostilities came with a whimper rather than a bang. The news was received without fuss or pomp on the Western Front where both armies were left exhausted, depleted and demoralised. The war had claimed the lives of three quarters of a million British fighting men, most under the age of forty-five. Over one million had been wounded. Most of these men were from the working class where the war had its greatest impact. The casualty rate among middle class, junior officers had been extremely high, eradicating a generation of potential scientists, legal experts, philosophers and educators. Repatriating survivors was difficult, and it was 1919 before most of the troops, including Nan's father, returned home.

Although overjoyed at returning to their families, delight turned soon turned to resentment. During their time away, the men had formed close relationships with comrades, providing a network of mutual protection and support. Once they became separated from their mates this quickly began to evaporate. Many young men had spent their formative years in trench warfare surrounded by fear, filth and death. They now began to wonder if it had all been worthwhile. They were fearful of what lay ahead and there was resentment towards the leaders who had sent men off to certain death and afterwards seemed happy to forget them. How, they wondered, could the families who had welcomed them home so warmly begin to comprehend the horrors they had experienced?

Life was hard for able bodied, battle hardened young men as they sought to re-adapt to civilian life. For the physically maimed and disfigured, life would be even harder. A new post-war psychological phenomenon evolved during the Great War: 'shell shock or Combat Stress Reaction'. Decades before the phenomenon of Post-Traumatic Stress Disorder was acknowledged, many soldiers suffered this debilitating condition which proved to some men as disabling as physical damage.

Septimus Smith, a returned soldier in Virginia Woolf's novel

Mrs Dalloway suffers from hallucinations caused by wartime trauma. After being involuntarily admitted to a psychiatric institution as a result of his condition, he eventually commits suicide. Although a fictitious character, his was a real-life experience common to many returned servicemen.

To add a further barb to the demoralised nation came the Spanish Flu pandemic of 1918 as one of the major medical calamities of the 20th century. Hitting Britain in a series of waves, it accompanied the returning soldiers and a young Nan, then eleven years old, also succumbed to the virus — the only member of her family to do so. Deterioration was rapid and, typically as in Nan's case, the illness developed into pneumonia for which, with no antibiotics, there was little effective treatment. Fortunately, Nan did survive although she sustained permanent damage to one lung.

Like thousands of other men, Harry returned home to Emily and the children. Inevitably, like thousands of other couples after a three year absence, their relationship, had changed. Unemployment rose steeply and, for returning servicemen, there was a paucity of jobs. There were recriminations against working women who were considered to be taking men's jobs and they were the first to be sacked in order for their jobs to be given to men. After all, it was understood, their work had only been for the duration of the war.

Working and fighting alongside Australian soldiers, Harry had become enamoured with their accounts of the antipodean country with its wide-open spaces, blue skies and endless sunshine. He was also attracted by the notion of egalitarianism exemplified by the apparent lack of deference to authority exhibited by the 'Aussie digger'. Australia was a new county which seemed to offer the opportunity and space for Harry, Emily and their large family. The thought of farming also appealed to Harry. The stifling class system of Britain, and the even more stifling thought of returning to his work underground, became anathema to him. The Australians had talked about the Soldier Settlement Scheme which placed ex-servicemen on the land as one of many Australian repatriation policies for returned servicemen. It was a way of showing the nation's gratitude for the sacrifices these men had made in giving four years of their lives (not to mention the disruption caused to their families) of a war which was, to them, on the other side of the world. (Although such a scheme was undertaken by Britain on land acquired for the purpose in Kenya, it did not succeed.) In Australia, land was made available to the returned soldiers at affordable terms with monetary advancements. This was meant to enable the purchase of machinery and stock and make improvements to the land.

Harry was enthusiastic to take part in this scheme and discussed the idea of emigration with Emily. Much to his dismay, she did not share his enthusiasm. She was afraid of water and was unwilling to make the long voyage. She was also reluctant to leave the security of her village and extended family ties. Grudgingly, Harry had no option but to return to his job as a pit deputy — for the time being. However, he did not abandon the idea of farming. Ironically, although thousands of soldiers took up the challenge of the Australian settlement scheme, most did not succeed. The scheme ultimately proved to be a failure, with profound social and ecologically adverse effects.

For the duration of the war, the British coal industry had been under government control. Wages, hours and safety conditions had improved for the miners who had stayed behind. While the mines were profitable, the government was reluctant to hand them back to their owners. The miners knew that a return to private ownership would mean a return to harsh conditions and poor pay in order to maximise profits for the wealthy owners. The claustrophobia of the mine, and impending strike action, provided the stimulus Harry needed to move out of the industry. With what little savings he had and a loan from Emily's father, he returned to his roots and leased a small holding, Pottersgate Farm in Cumberworth, coincidentally also only a few miles from Silkstone. This property included a farmhouse which, although not large, was more adequate for Harry, Emily and the children than the High Green Cottage had been. A sixth child was born in 1919.

Harry specialised, with considerable success, in breeding pedigree large white pigs. Although she had initially been reluctant to pull up her roots and transplant herself to the isolated farm, Emily adapted well from the wife of a miner to be a farmer's wife. She was a hard worker who worked in the fields picking up suitable stones to help her husband build traditional Yorkshire dry stone walls. She fed piglets that were abandoned by the sow. She was frugal and, although she made sure her family was well fed, existed on a very meagre diet herself. She managed the money well but was not, by all accounts, a demonstrative mother. It was Harry who gave the children affection.

Whether or not he saw academic potential in Nan, presciently, Harry offered to pay for her to attend nearby Barnsley Girls High School. This would have entailed considerable financial hardship since Harry was in the process of establishing his farm and still had five more children to rear. It was a sacrifice he was prepared to make. Nan refused the offer, yet did agree to music lessons. Instead of school fees, a piano was purchased.

At this time Nan, who would have been about 15, decided to leave school and, much against the wishes of her parents, made the decision to find work in domestic service. Somehow, she secured work with the family of a businessman in Leicester. It had been a case — a recurring theme in Nan's life — of 'act in haste, repent at leisure'. No sooner had she arrived at the Leicester house than she realised her mistake and hated it. The work was hard and the hours long. The wage was pitiful, but worse was the condescension with which the family treated her. She was also shocked to realise that she missed her noisy, boisterous family who had been the main motivation for leaving home. Nevertheless, she gritted her teeth and persisted for a couple of years. By then she considered she could return home with dignity having acquitted herself of the responsibility for her decision.

Although the initial return home was comforting, it took only a short time for her to recognise that this wasn't where she wanted to stay. Although fond of her mother, who apparently did not overtly return her affection, she did not intend to emulate her mother's life. Nan remembered only one occasion when she was allowed to kiss her mother, and none of the children remembered Emily ever telling them that she loved them. Surely there must be something more.

Her two-year absence enabled her to appraise her family situation objectively. Her parents were now working hard to make a success of the farm, and if she stayed, she would become another unpaid pair of hands. Since her return, she was even more irritated by her rowdy siblings. She knew that, having gone against her father's wishes two years earlier she could now expect little, if any, encouragement to find an alternate life. She wrote to her aunt, Mary Harriet, fondly known in the family as 'Aunt M.H' to explain her dilemma. Being a trained nurse who had served in field hospitals in France, she was well qualified to offer advice. Aunt M. H. responded by suggesting that Nan might consider a career in nursing. Not only would it prove to be interesting and rewarding, it could provide an escape from the dreary prospect of continuing to live at home. She promised to do all she could to help her niece.

Aunt Mary had trained at Manchester Royal Infirmary towards

the end of the 19th century but thought that Nan would be more suited to a smaller, less hidebound institution. During the time of Aunt Mary's training, the preference for accepting trainee nurses was for those who had completed secondary school education or had, like Nan, at least completed elementary school. They considered that girls who had finished their schooling at thirteen or were less capable of 'taking advantage of' lectures and tuition. They also favoured girls trained in 'social arts' as it would be necessary for them to sit at meals and mix sociably with other probationers (trainee nurses). There was also concern that less well-educated girls would, once their training was complete, have difficulty fitting into any position that may be required of them. In Nan's case, they needed no such concern. She was bright and, although the product of a boisterous family, possessed the requisite social graces. Ironically, the hospital administration appeared to make a rod for its own back. In 1923, owing to difficulty attracting prospective probationary nurses with certain 'qualities', a staff shortage forced the hospital to temporarily reduce the number of beds available to the sick.

True to her word, Aunt M.H. wrote to an ex-colleague who was now a tutor at Ashton-Under-Lyne District Infirmary near Manchester. Nan was interviewed by the Matron and was accepted as a probationary nurse.

In 1919, the Nurses' Registration Act was passed by the British Parliament. It was followed by the creation of the General Nursing Council which established a register of nurses. To be enrolled as a nurse on the register it was necessary to have completed three years of training in the care of the sick, thereby ensuring that all future nurses were properly trained. For Nan, this legislation was very timely. Ashton-Under-Lyne was twenty miles from Nan's home but, under the conditions of employment, all nurses were required to live in the Nurses' Home. She would never return to live with her large family.

3 Coming of age

Ashton-Under-Lyne, now part of Greater Manchester, emerged as an important Lancashire mill town after the introduction of the textile industry in the 19th century. Less important economically there was also, coincidentally, a coal mine, Ashton Moss Colliery, which boasted the world's deepest shaft, 870 metres deep. In the early 1920s, shortly before Nan became a probationary nurse, the collapse of the overseas market sent cotton towns such as Ashton into decline. By 1930, most of the mills had closed, adding to the county's high unemployment. The Infirmary had been established in 1860 by Samuel Oldham, a local mill owner after one of his employees was badly injured in a boiler accident. It became, primarily an 'accident' hospital with the addition of a children's ward in 1908. An 'acute' hospital, with a specialty pediatrics service, it served a large area with high unemployment. Aunt M.H. and Nan had chosen wisely.

Nan enjoyed the training despite the hard work, long hours and rigid, but fair, discipline. She was paid about twelve pounds a year, requiring extreme thrift to survive independently. She never asked for financial help from her struggling parents. Although, returning to the hospital after rare visits home, she would often find an extra five shillings in her purse. Nan fitted in well with her colleagues making a handful of close friends. One in particular, René Lawton, was daughter of the youngest son of a mill owning Manchester family. Rene adopted the name Nancy for her friend and the two of them remained friends, visiting each other regularly until they were both well into old age.

After she qualified, Nan continued to work at the Infirmary for a further year as a staff nurse. At the end of that year, together with a group of training school friends including René, she was admitted to Birch Hill Infirmary in Rochdale, also a mill town in Lancashire, to train as a State Certified Midwife.

She described the conditions at Birch Hill, a former workhouse as 'pretty gruesome'. The work entailed many adverse and abnormal deliveries. Nevertheless, it was excellent training for what would come later in her life. Most of the women who gave birth there were from very impoverished backgrounds. Many of them were employed in harsh conditions at the local mills and worked until their babies were delivered. There was a high incidence of rickets amongst infants who were left in prams all day waiting for their mothers to finish long shifts at the mills. In addition to hospital deliveries, the trainee midwives had to attend a requisite number of home births. If deliveries in the infirmary were often gruesome, one can only guess what they were like on the outside.

After a year at Birch Hill, Nan graduated as a well-trained, proficient nurse. As a State Registered Nurse and State Certified Midwife, she said goodbye to her friends. She was alone in the world and had embarked on her chosen, well-earned career. Her life was about to begin, a life which would not be easy but never mundane.

In the 1920s, twenty years prior to the introduction of the National Health Service in Britain, hospital treatment was not covered by National Insurance. This was made possible largely by worker contribution schemes where member paid about three pence a week to secure free treatment. Hospitals were also supported by local communities such as the one above which delivered about 500,000 eggs in one year to county hospitals.

The main beneficiaries of hospital treatment were children and women with maternity service the fastest growing of all medical specialties.

"What was health care like before the NHS?" The Conversation
https://theconversation.com/what-was-healthcare-like-before-the-nhs-99055

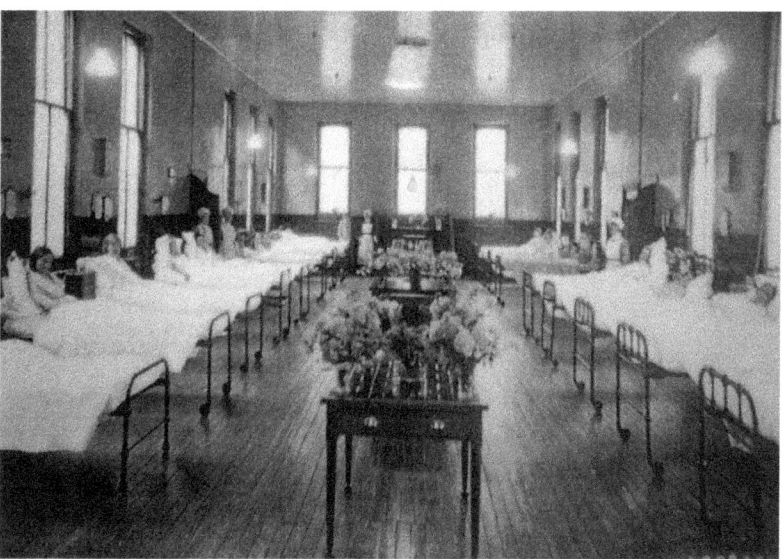

Hospital based nursing training was hard work with long hours, low wages and strict discipline as reflected in the precise neatness of this hospital ward.

http://www.alangeorge.co.uk/Images_D-H/GeneralHospital_AnneLewisWard(Ladies).jpg

Nan returning to hospital after a visit home: although these visits were sometimes a relief from hard work and study for Nan, unfortunately, because her home was isolated, they also involved walking considerable distances.

4

Jenny and Tommy

Children of Welbeck Abbey staff, Jenny's friends.

Jenny and Tommy, who appear in the following story, were both born a few years before Nan. Their story is fairly typical of couples born and reared in small, close-knit mining communities such as Creswell, which plays a significant part in this narrative. The story of their early lives does not differ greatly from that of Nan who was brought up within twenty miles of Jenny and Tommy. Eventually, their paths will cross.

At the time of this story, Creswell's emergence as a thriving coal producing community had just begun. Jenny's parents both originated in the tiny hamlet of Carburton, which bordered the nearby Welbeck Estate, country seat of the Dukes of Portland.

The Welbeck Estate, in north Nottinghamshire, is part of the district known as the Dukeries, so named because it contains four ducal seats: Norfolk, Newcastle, Kingston and Portland. The village of Carburton was in fact, owned by the Portland Estate. Tommy and Jenny's parents were both born there in the 1800s when Carburton's population was less than 200. Many of the men were agricultural workers, mostly being employed by the Duke of Portland. Few of the women at that time worked and those who did were also mainly employed on the Welbeck Estate in some form of domestic work. When she was in her eighties, Jenny was still fond of relating the story of her younger life to her grandchildren.

* * *

I was born on 24 June 1900 — mid summer's day — on the Welbeck Estate. My parents lived in one of the small lodges on the estate owned by the 6th Duke of Portland. The small ornate lodges, built of local Steetley stone, were provided by the estate for gardeners and gamekeepers. My father was then the assistant to the head gardener on the estate.

My mother had, before her marriage, worked as a maid in Welbeck Abbey, part of a huge army of hundreds of men and women employed to look after the house and estate. My parents had known each other since they were children as they were both from the same village. My father left home at the age of 12 to start work on the estate and my mother followed him a couple of years later to work as a maid in the Abbey. Although my father lived at home in Carburton and left for work every day, my mother had to live in because of her long hours and imposed discipline, and only went home on her days off. Although they were both kept very busy and worked long hours, they still managed to see one another quite often, especially when my father used to go up to the Abbey to deliver produce to the kitchens where my mother worked when she first arrived there. At the time when both my parents were working at the Abbey, they were part of a staff of over a thousand mostly unskilled people. Compared to the wages and conditions of servants in those days, the Welbeck servants were well paid and many of the employees knew they had jobs for life.

When he first inherited the estate in 1854, the 5th Duke spent huge sums of money extending and renovating the estate and the Abbey. He built a whole network of underground tunnels and rooms including an underground riding school and a ballroom equipped with a lift to convey the guests up and down. He even had a roller-skating rink built for the use of the staff when skating was a popular pastime. But the 5th Duke was an odd man. Because of his unusual building enterprises, he was known as 'The Burrowing Duke.' He was also a hermit and hated to be seen by people. Workers were instructed that, if they came across him on the estate, they were never to look at him and by no means address him. They called him 'The Workman's Friend' because he treated his workers well. Nevertheless, one of them who politely doffed his cap to him was dismissed for doing so.

When my parents were married at the small 12th century church of St Giles in Carburton, my mother had to leave her position as married women were not allowed to work, and her position was soon taken by another girl. I had a very happy childhood. The gardeners were always busy, caring for the many trees, lawns and planting miles of flower beds throughout every season of the year. When I was just a small child, my father was put in charge of the kitchen gardens. These gardens covered over 20 acres next to the Abbey and the vegetables and herbs were elaborately planted in various sections. There were strawberry beds, raspberries growing on canes and various currant bushes, red, black and gooseberry. There was an orchard and even braziers at certain places which helped to ripen the fruit. There were long greenhouses and the garden beds were bordered with elaborate arrangements of asters, geraniums and petunias.

When I was three, my sister Winifred (named after the Duchess) was born. There were lots of other children to play with around the estate and on trips to nearby Clumber Park. Of course, we were quite lucky as we lived in a nice cottage, but not all the children did. It was certainly a beautiful place to live but when the pit opened at Creswell, two miles away, we could see and smell the smoke coming from the chimney. They said the Duchess used to telephone the pit manager when the wind blew the smoke over the abbey and tell him to stop the pit from working.

When I was five, with other children from the estate, I started school in nearby Creswell. Sometimes we were taken in a horse drawn trap but mostly we walked the two miles there and back. The village was a dirty place and the smell of smoke and smut from the pit was even worse than at Welbeck. Our hands and faces were always grubby when we got home. Many of the village children seemed to be much poorer than we were. They weren't dressed as nicely, and I don't think as clean as we were. Many of the children lived in nearby Duke and Duchess Streets, rows of dark little houses, some of them only getting bread and jam for midday dinners for which most of them would walk home. As we lived too far away to go home, Welbeck children used to sit together and eat sandwiches of freshly baked bread with cold meat, cheese, fresh fruit and salad. I think a lot of the Creswell children envied our delicious fare.

There were sixty children in our class and the teachers were very strict, sitting at high desks so they could see what each child was doing, including the naughty boys at the back of the room. We were taught the usual subjects, reading, writing and sums and physical education which, was quite new at that time. The girls learned sewing and needlework while the boys learned woodwork. I suppose these skills would be useful as I expected to go to work at the Abbey, perhaps even as a lady's maid, when I had finished my schooling. Many of the village children were loud and rough and not very much given to schoolwork. Most of the boys expected to follow their fathers into the mines anyway, so didn't consider schoolwork very important. By then a lot of the girls didn't consider working in service. Many expected to go into shops or some of the local factories which were opening in Worksop and Mansfield.

During the long summer school holidays, we used to play outside all day with the other children from the estate, only coming inside when there still seemed to be hours of daylight left and mother called us for supper and then to bed. We used to walk in the nearby woods and in Markland Grips, fishing in the stream, gathering tadpoles and bringing them home in jam jars, but we were warned to watch for grass snakes. Once I remember being taken in a charabanc to Sherwood Forest in nearby Edwinstowe, home of Robin Hood, and climbing inside the huge, hollow Major Oak with several other children. People said this was the tree used as a shelter by Robin Hood. We used to spend whole days having adventures without causing any worry to our mothers. The woods were rich with hazelnuts and horse chestnut trees. In the autumn we used to collect the horse chestnuts to play conkers, providing hours of fun and always a popular autumn game in and out of the school yard. We used to drill holes through the middle and thread them with a piece of string. The boys used to take conkers very seriously and only occasionally would condescend to let the girls join in. Easter time was the time for playing with whips and tops and Christmas brought groups of door-to-door carol singers, both round the estate and in Creswell village. In winter our dad made us a little toboggan and we would sled down nearby Crag Hill after the first snow of the Christmas holidays. We used to play snowballs until our gloves were saturated with melted snow and then go inside to get woollen socks to wear instead. Our hands got so cold it was painful, but that didn't stop us from having fun. We used to make slides in the snow, until someone's mother fell on one and got hurt.

Although Tommy Green had always been in my class, I didn't really take much notice of him until I was about 13, the year before I was due to leave school. His father worked down the pit. Tommy was a quiet, very studious boy, tall with reddish hair. He used to read a lot. In fact, I rarely remember seeing him without a book and he was always asking questions of the teachers — some of which they weren't always able to answer. He had become a keen cricketer and spent many hours on the cricket pitch built at the pit top. Although he used to play football there in winter, cricket was his real love. Everybody thought Tommy would go far, destined for better things than working down the pit. His older brother, Archie went to the local grammar school on a scholarship which had been arranged by the Duchess of Portland and it was hoped that Tommy would follow in his footsteps. Unlike many of the other boys in the class, Tommy was quiet and polite. He had two younger brothers, and the family didn't have much money.

Tommy's family lived in the Model Village which was then only a few years old. Although not as picturesque as the stone lodges on the Estate, the Model cottages were modern and, unlike our homes, had indoor bathrooms. The Model was built specially for the miners and their families and had a lovely park in the middle with swings and a slide and on Sunday afternoons the band used to play in the bandstand. The children used to form rival gangs, Top and Bottom Model, and in the weeks leading up to bonfire night on 5 November they would scour the local woods for dead trees and branches to see who could make the biggest bonfire on which they would burn a made up Guy Fawkes. They used to boast about it at school and tell stories of nightly raiding parties on each other's wood piles.

https://property.mitula.co.uk/property/flats-village-worksop

Tommy and I became good friends and used to meet in the playground and talk. Tommy didn't care if the other boys teased him. Unlike them, Tommy didn't mind being seen talking to a girl. By coincidence, Tommy was very interested in gardening so was particularly interested to hear than my father was such an important gardener. He used to help his dad in his allotment which was quite close to their house in the Top Model. Although he grew mostly vegetables to feed the family, Tommy's pride and joy were large onions, almost the size of footballs which he had cultivated himself. Tommy also grew roses in the little front garden of his house. Roses grew well in the local clay soil and thrived on the pit pony manure which Tommy used to gather in little hessian sacks. When I told my father about Tommy, he was particularly impressed, and my mother told me I could invite him over for tea one Sunday and father would show him the Abbey kitchen garden. On his first visit to our house, he presented my mother with a beautiful bouquet of roses that he had grown himself, thereby ensuring further invitations. Tommy visited our house quite regularly and my father, being the father of two girls, enjoyed having a boy with whom he could discuss his work. We were allowed to go for walks around the estate and I took great pleasure in showing him the extensive buildings, but my sister always had to come with us. My mother, however, was always a little reserved with Tommy. After all, his father worked down the pit, and his mother was just a collier's wife.

Tommy's parents were also local. His mother came from Belph, an even smaller hamlet than Carburton, and quite close to Welbeck. Her father, Tommy's grandad, was a farm labourer. Tommy's father came from Whitwell, a couple of miles from Creswell. Most of the land around the area had been bought by the Duke of Portland. Whitwell was also a coal mining village and the two pits opened at about the same time. Unlike Creswell, Whitwell pit stood on the outskirts of the village which was, in any case, a much prettier village than Creswell. Tommy's grandfather had been a blacksmith in the village.

Unlike my mother, Tommy's mother had not left home to go to work but used to help her father in his work, particularly at haymaking time. Tommy's father had worked in open cut mining, travelling around the district to get work, and when the mines opened in Whitwell and Creswell, he chose to work at Creswell. The prospect of new housing was very appealing to him, especially as he and his wife already had one child and were expecting a second. It would be no exaggeration to say that my mother tended to look down on Tommy's family. I think she believed that her, and my father's, background connected them, however tenuously, to the aristocracy! Nevertheless, she was very impressed by the fact that Archie was at the grammar school, courtesy of the Duchess, and Tommy's future also looked very promising.

Then one Monday morning when I arrived at school, Tommy wasn't there. The teacher told us that his father, along with two other men, had been killed in a rock fall down the pit two nights earlier. I thought Tommy would come back to school after the funeral. When I got home that day and told my parents my father told me that he would visit Tommy's family after work that night and see if there was anything he could do to help. Dad had grown very fond of Tommy. With two daughters, he liked to be able to talk to a boy, especially one who took a keen interest in his work. I waited up for Dad to come home, but he didn't bring good news. Because Archie was older, and already doing well at the grammar school, his mother had decided that he should stay there and then go on to university to continue his studies. At least one of the boys would get away from the village and make a good life for himself. Tommy would now become the breadwinner of the family. He would become a miner himself. That was the end of Tommy's school life and any hope of a future. Tommy was 14.

In July of the same year, at the end of the school year I also left school. I was a girl, so my education wasn't that important. Anyway, I was going into service at the Abbey. My parents secured me a job as a maid. Secretly I think my mother was rather proud that I was following in her footsteps. Although she had been fond of Tommy, when he became a miner, I think she hoped it was the end of my friendship with him. Becoming a miner's wife was not something she had planned for me.

Even though we lived on the estate, it was a condition of my employment that I lived with the rest of the domestic staff at the Abbey, most likely in the same backstairs room in which my mother had slept when she started work there. In fact, I performed the same tasks as she had done — getting up each morning to open the shutters, lay the fires and tidy the family's mess from the night before. Everything had to be immaculate before the family came down at 9 o'clock. The days were long and often it was midnight before we got to bed. Each day was filled with the same chores as the day before. The maids were under the strict care of the housekeeper. No one was allowed to have a boyfriend. I found the young men I worked with mostly priggish and boring and missed the long, interesting talks with Tommy whom I no longer saw.

This was the beginning of the Great War and many of the older boys on the estate were going off to join the army. Nevertheless, a staff of 60 people continued working in the Abbey. The Duke and Duchess still did much entertaining of other rich and famous people. I remember the summer before I started working there when the Archduke of Austria, Franz Ferdinand and his wife came to stay at Welbeck, and the Archduke narrowly missed being accidently shot while on a shooting party!

During the war, some of the girls had left to work in munitions factories and hadn't come back to the Abbey so there wasn't, by then, much competition for jobs. A lot of the young men who worked on the estate had enlisted in the army and gone off to fight never came home again and of those who did, some were unfit to take up their former work. At least Tommy had been safe as mining was a reserved occupation. Mother, my sister and I did our bit for the war effort knitting socks and scarves and my sister and I did some first aid training at the hospital in Worksop. Three years passed and I had been promoted to parlour maid.

I used to go back to our little lodge on my days off and, one day when we were having tea, Dad told me he'd met Tommy again. Dad had been asked to help with organising the annual gardening show in the Drill Hall at Creswell. The show was always judged by the Duke and Duchess. Tommy was still a keen gardener and proudly carried off a first prize for his, by now, famous large brown onions. He had kept his father's allotment and spent most of his free time working there. I suppose it was a welcome relief after spending hours working underground in the dark.

At the end of the war, everyone celebrated. There was a party in the grounds at Welbeck and we were all given time off to go and enjoy ourselves. Among the crowd of people enjoying the fun and the fireworks I found Tommy. He had grown tall and strong and once he started talking, I lost all the shyness I had felt after not seeing him for so many years. He was the same Tommy, kind and at ease. He walked me home and I invited him to come in and talk to my parents. They were pleased to see him again. He told us of his work in the pit. It wasn't so bad now he'd got used to it, and at least his wage was able to support his mother and two younger brothers. Archie was now at the university in Nottingham, unsure about what he would do afterwards.

After this, we began walking out together — alone. Since the war things had changed. Life seemed freer, discipline wasn't so strict and not many girls were that interested anymore in going into domestic service. Tommy took me home to meet his mother. 'Mam' he called her. My mother had always been rather critical of miners' wives believing that they were all rather loud and, like their husbands, enjoyed a night out at the pub on Friday nights. Although she might have sat outside on a summer evening and sipped a lime and lemon with father, she would never have dreamed of going into the bar. 'Common', she had called it. Tommy's mother was very different from what my mother had described. Like Tommy, she was quiet and dignified, although it was obvious that she had, and still, worked hard. In the small front garden Tommy continued to grow roses in the rich, clay soil.

At the back of the house, in the communal yard, lines of brightly coloured washing flapped in the breeze. Although all the houses were overlooked by the huge chimney and spoil heap, Mrs Green's house was always welcoming and clean as a whistle. Along one wall was a shelf full of books — Tommy still found time for reading.

We both knew that if we wanted to marry, we would have to wait for a while. The family, even Archie, despite continuing support from the Duchess, still depended on Tommy's wages.

In 1921, Archie finished at university and got a teaching post near Leicester. His salary was enough for him to make a small allowance to his mother. Tommy's younger brothers had both left school and taken up apprenticeships. Tommy knew now that he would never work anywhere else but the mine. Both my parents were very fond of Tommy, my father in particular and, although neither raised any objections when we announced that we were wanted to be married, I knew that my mother was a little disappointed at the thought of her daughter becoming a miner's wife. Mostly, I think, it was because she knew that it would be a life of hard work and worry about Tommy's safety, just like the life Tommy's mother and all the women like her, married to miners, had led. Now that her family was almost off her hands, Tommy's Mam returned to Belph to help her mother look after her father who had suffered a stroke the previous year and, after we were married, Tommy and I took over the house in the Model Village.

Life took some adjustment. The proximity of the tall smoking chimney and the putrid fumes of the slag heap left a sooty film of dirt over everything. Hearing the pit siren going off each mid-morning, and the continuous shunting of the railway wagons at the pit sidings, was disturbing after the quiet of the estate. Strangely I used to look forward to the clump of pit boots at all hours of the day and night as the men, including Tommy, trudged to, and especially, home from work.

My days were still long and filled with work which began at the crack of dawn. I was used to hard work and long days, but now I had to get used to the routine and variation of Tommy's shifts, regularly getting up at 4 o'clock in the morning, packing his 'snap' and making sure he had a hot dinner to come home to afterwards whatever time of day, it was. The coal fire was always alight, both for cooking and heating the water. Unlike our little villa on the estate, where we used to have our bath in front of the kitchen fire, our little house had a bath in the small bedroom, complete with plumbing. Built into one of the cupboards, it was pulled down each Saturday evening for our weekly baths. During the week when he was working, Tommy would use the pit top baths bringing his dirty pit clothes for me to wash.

Each Monday, regardless of Tommy's shift, I would be up early to fill the copper and light the fire in the washhouse across the yard. Washing took up most of the morning by 'ponching' the washing in the aluminum dolly tub and rubbing out stubborn dirt on the corrugated iron rubbing board with water all over the floor and the skin of my fingers white and crinkly, then chatting to the neighbours as we pegged out the sheets and shirts. If it rained, the washing had to be dried inside in front of the fire. The women were very close to each other as most of them had grown up together. They used to stand in little groups and gossip; they all enjoyed a good laugh together, leaning on their brooms with 'pinnies' flapping. But I always felt like an outsider and always remained a little aloof. I didn't like to gossip. I think some of them thought I was a bit snooty, especially because I had worked at the Abbey. I was shy and, to be honest, a little afraid of these women whose idea of a good night out was to be invited by their husbands to the pub or club on a Friday or Saturday night. It didn't take me long to find out that most of them had hearts of gold and would never see anyone, especially a neighbour in trouble. Mrs Fletcher, at the end of our yard used to brag that she'd once had a visit from the Duchess as she was being shown round the Model Village. Hanging on Mrs Fletcher's wall, in full flight, were three plaster ducks. The Duchess told her, in no uncertain terms that, even though the ducks were plaster, she strongly disapproved of birds inside houses — they should be free to fly outside. When the Duchess left, the ducks were taken down and since then Mrs Fletcher had refused to buy even a Christmas card if it bore the image of a robin!

Tommy and I preferred long walks along the surrounding lanes to drinking in the pub or the miners' welfare, especially in the long summer evenings. We would walk down the bridle path to the estate to visit my parents or over to Belph to see Tommy's Mam. Now that he was teaching, and Archie sent her part of his wages, life became a bit easier for Tommy and me. Tommy still spent hours happily working in his allotment, no matter what the weather was like or whatever the time of year and he remained a keen exhibitor at local vegetable shows. He remained an avid reader and I often wondered what his life could have been like if things had turned out differently.

In the autumn we would pick blackberries in the hedgerows on our walks. I would make jams and pickles from what Tommy had grown. I'd picked up lots of tips from the cook at the Abbey and I always made my own bread. Neighbours' children always knew when it was baking day and would hang around waiting for a hot crust covered with homemade strawberry jam. There was always a vase of freshly cut flowers in the house, no matter what season of the year it was. On Saturday nights we sometimes joined other miners and their wives for old time dancing at the Drill Hall — the

Valeta waltz, Gay Gordons and always a progressive barn dance. On Sundays we use to enjoy joining in the singing at Evensong and at Harvest Festival we donated home grown vegetables and preserves.

Keeping on top of the dirt in the house was a constant round of hard work with coal dust everywhere, on the furniture, curtains and on window sills. Each year after Easter came the ritual spring cleaning when the carpets were taken up, placed on the washing lines in the yard and we would all be exhausted with beating out the accumulated dust. The chimney sweep would arrive, and the women would help each other to hang fresh wallpaper replacing the old layer, discoloured by the permanently burning fire. For a few days at least, the smell of pit fumes was banished from the house.

Looking back, I think we had a happy life. Only two things worried me. Like all colliers' wives, I never overcame my fear for Tommy's safety. His dad had been killed at work and so had some of the husbands of women of my age. No matter what time he left for work, I never let him go without saying goodbye. The second worry was overcome when, three years after our marriage, I discovered I was pregnant.

On the morning the baby came I wasn't feeling at all well when Tommy left for work. For the first time since we'd been married, I stayed in bed while he made his own breakfast before leaving for his early shift. Just before he left the house, he came upstairs to say goodbye and, although he was worried, he had no option but to go to work. The pains started shortly after he had gone and gradually got worse. I got up and banged on the wall for my neighbour Mrs Jenkins who, being the mother of three children, would know exactly what to do. She sent her oldest boy with a message asking the midwife to call. By the time Nurse Metham arrived, labour was well advanced. Good old Mrs Jenkins stayed with us most of the day, only leaving to get her children off to school. By the time they came home in the afternoon, there was still no sign of the baby. It just seemed to go on and on and when Tommy arrived home from work it was to find the house in chaos. Mrs Jenkins sent him next door to her house to share the dinner which she had made for her husband, both men having worked the same shift. Finally, towards evening when it was obvious there was a problem, Nurse Metham sent an almost frantic Tommy off to get Dr Manson. Poor Tommy, beside himself with worry, was made to stay at the Jenkins house.

At last, the baby arrived just before eight o'clock the next morning, after Tommy and Mr Jenkins had once more left for work. The baby was a little girl and, by then, we were all well and truly worn out — Nurse Metham, Dr Manson, me and, especially Mrs Jenkins, who had not only been there most of the night, had also had to see to her own family, and to Tommy! Although I slept most of the day, she kept a good eye on me until Tommy came home later that afternoon. We were so happy with our little girl whom we called Muriel Winifred. Although I know that secretly, Tommy had wanted a son, I was happy because no matter what happened, our child would never have to follow her father down the mine.

5

Where there's muck: Birth of a Coal Community

There was a whispering in my hearth,
A sigh of the coal,
Grown wistful of a former earth
It might recall.

I listened for a tale of leaves
And smothered ferns,
Frond-forests, and the low sly lives
Before the fauns.

My fire might show steam-phantoms simmer
From Time's old cauldron,
Before the birds made nests in summer,
Or men had children.

But the coals were murmuring of their mine,
And moans down there
Of boys that slept wry sleep, and men
Writhing for air.

And I saw white bones in the cinder-shard,
Bones without number.
Many the muscled bodies charred,
And few remember.

I thought of all that worked dark pits
Of war, and died
Digging the rock where Death reputes
Peace lies indeed.

Comforted years will sit soft-chaired,
In rooms of amber;
The years will stretch their hands, well-cheered
By our life's ember;

The centuries will burn rich loads
With which we groaned,
Whose warmth shall lull their dreaming lids,
While songs are crooned;
But they will not dream of us poor lads,
Left in the ground.
Miners, Wilfred Owen January 12, 1918

While the Industrial Revolution was taking place in Britain, the village of Creswell, at the very north east tip of the Derbyshire landscape, was also on the verge of a transformation. Once rich seams of coal were discovered beneath this landscape the charming rural hamlet, lying above the Barnsley Coal Bed, ceased to be both charming and rural. Never again would it be described as attractive. The hunger for coal transformed the rolling green hills and forests surrounding the village into a blackened industrial vista.

5 Where there's muck: Birth of a Coal Community

*https://www.google.com/search?q=map+of+derbyshire&tbm=isch&source
=iu&ictx=1&fir=N8CQlA10OJCTsM%253A%252C-OJHxX_8RyGG-
M%252C_&vet=1&usg=AI4_-kR-hVtG*

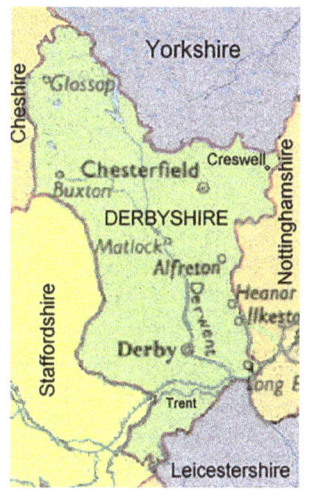

Creswell is located in the county of Derbyshire, East Midlands, four miles north-east of the town of Bolsover, 8 miles north of the major town of Mansfield, and 129 miles north of London. Creswell lies just north-west of the Nottinghamshire border.

*Travel Encyclopedia
https://www.encyclopedia.com/sports-and-everyday-life/food-and-drink/food-and-cooking/travel*

Millions of years earlier, this countryside had been a vast swamp land covered with giant ferns. Simultaneously, the subterranean chemical transformation of rotting vegetation to coal, the solid, black combustible matter was taking place. Once it became indispensable to new industry, coal became the cause of widespread environmental defilement that would climax towards the end of century and Queen Victoria's reign. Numerous unprepossessing villages which became blots on the local landscape were built over rich coal seams. Creswell was one such emerging mining community.

One of the few remaining attractive features of which the area can still boast is Creswell Crags. Here there is evidence, in the form of primitive paintings on the rock walls, of the existence of human habitation 12,000 years ago. Etchings on cave walls inform us that the area was one of the most northerly places in the world to be inhabited by humans during the last ice age. There is archaeological evidence of settlement from the Neolithic, Bronze and Iron Ages and throughout the Roman occupation.

5 Where there's muck: Birth of a Coal Community

Creswell Crags, an enclosed limestone gorge, comprises several caves that were occupied during the last Ice Age between 43,000 and 10,000 years ago. Excavations have revealed numerous flint tools and remains of prehistoric animals. The site has been declared a Site of Special Scientific Interest and, even after the eventual demise of the coal industry, is still a tourist attraction.

https://www.creswell-crags.org.uk/explore/our-caves/

Creswell's early significance derived from its relationship to Elmton with which it still shares a parish — the Parish of Elmton-with-Creswell. Long before Creswell existed, Elmton or Helmtune as it was called, was recorded in the Domesday Book, the great survey commissioned by William the Conqueror in the 11th century. There is no mention of mining in the area.

About two miles to the west of Creswell and now much smaller than its neighbour, Elmton was originally the principal medieval village of the parish. Creswell existed then only as a primitive settlement being a small outlying hamlet populated by yeomen farmers. The open countryside was green above the fertile clay soil. Creswell probably remained a sleepy farming community until the mid-18th century when, in response to the construction of a nearby turnpike road linking the two market towns of Mansfield and Chesterfield, it was about to undergo a transformation.

Most of the local population at this time consisted of small tenant farmers who paid rent to the local landowner to work the land to support their families. Cottage industries, such as spinning cloth in the home for local merchants, co-existed with farming and were a means for women to supplement the family income. However, at the end of the 17th century, landowners began to fence off their estates to maximise profits and the poorer farmers were pushed off the land. Their only chance of employment was to become hired agricultural labourers for the estate owners. Rather than trading what they produced, families became dependent on wages.

The lives of the women of this era were pre-destined by accident of birth. Those of lowly birth were unable to choose their own futures. Single women, irrespective of age, were traditionally regarded as dependent and could never hope to become self-sufficient since their wages, if any, were only half those paid to men. Marriage was the only escape from a life of reliance. The stage of a woman's life cycle determined her role within the family and two-thirds of her life revolved around reproduction. If a woman did earn a wage, once she married it was seen as a new form of dowry increasing the income of the family into which she married. At that time the average age of marriage for women was twenty-three and for men, twenty-seven. Together with reproduction, married women were responsible for running the household, feeding the family and keeping both them and the home clean.

In the late 19th century, with the advent of the industrialisation, Creswell began to expand. In the early the part of that century, when mining began in earnest, coal seams had been relatively superficial and less sophisticated engineering necessary for mining. Coal had been dug from these superficial outcrops of coal for centuries. (The first ever recorded mining death associated with this area was in 1298 in, ironically, what later became known as Silkstone.) These superficial seams were thin, in some cases less than forty-five centimetres high (eighteen inches) and although the mines were shallow, they were still uncomfortable places to work. Although they were cooler, they were still damp, and miners were unable to stand while digging the coal. The work was done mainly while they were lying down or bent over.

The Industrial Revolution greatly increased demand for coal and necessitated sinking shafts deep underground to gain access to rich, thicker seams. Previously it was dug from shallower seams in narrow tunnels too low for men to stand while digging. Although wooden props were used to support the tunnel, the danger from collapsing was a constant threat.

A Brief History of Mining: The Guardian
https://www.theguardian.com/environment/gallery/2015/dec/18/coal-mining-britain-brief-history-in-pictures

The coming of the railways increased the demand for coal to fuel steam driven engines which, in turn, could transport it to other areas of the county and to seaports for export abroad. Superficial coal deposits were no longer adequate to fulfil the new demand. Once access was available to the thicker coal seams, supply was increased significantly. Beneath Creswell, part of the Yorkshire/Nottinghamshire/Derbyshire Coal Field, ran the Barnsley or Top Hard coal seam which, in some places, was over three metres high and provided a remarkable amount of good quality coal.

Changes in lifestyles were a consequence of the expanding coal industry. Pit top communities provided a habitat for miners and became a modern demographic feature of industrialisation. When coal mines were smaller operations, miners lived in houses similar to those of farm labourers, which often had an attached smallholding. Coal owning landowners generally leased their estates to smaller freeholders who invested capital in equipment and hired miners to work for specific periods of time. Coal supply was usually local and when rivers, and later canals opened, it could be transported to more distant markets. In order to compensate for altered working conditions, deeper access to thicker coal seams meant unpleasant working conditions. Wages paid to coal miners subsequently increased to more than the amount paid to labourers and artisans.

Thicker seams made it possible for miners to work upright but because the mines were deeper, they were hotter, darker and the atmosphere foetid with the pungent smell of sweating miners and the stink of excrement from pit ponies. Deeper underground there was now the ever-present danger of explosions from coal gases. Miners dug out the coal which was then removed by children and sorted at the pit top, usually by older miners and women. Unwanted waste from the sinking of deeper mines, plus the waste sorted from coal brought up from underground, was deposited on the pit tip.

This constituted a new, ubiquitous Victorian industrial feature, or eyesore, on the landscape: the slag heap, which grew to dominate future mining villages.

The writings of D.H. Lawrence, himself the son of a miner from the nearby Nottinghamshire mining village of Eastwood, reflect the debauching effect of the new industrialisation on pastoral life, transforming once rustic scenery of a village like Creswell into a landscape of smokestacks. In his 1913 novel, *The Rainbow*, Lawrence's words paint a picture of the effect of new industrialism on the once halcyon countryside:

> 'Whenever one of the Brangwens in the fields lifts his head from his work, he sees the church-tower of Ilkeston in the empty sky .... Heaven and earth as teeming around them .... they felt the rush of sap in spring .... [the] young corn waved and was silken.
>
> In autumn the partridges whirred up, birds in flock blew like spray across the fallow, rooks appeared on the grey, watery heavens, and flew cawing into the winter.
>
> [On the women] was the drowse of blood intimacy, calves sucking and hens running together in droves, and young geese palpitating in the hand while the food was pushed down their throttle.'

This idyll was not to last.

'About 1840 a canal was constructed across the meadows .... Connecting the newly opened collieries of the [Derbyshire, Nottinghamshire border] valley. A high embankment travelled along the fields to carry the canal .... Then, a short time afterwards, a colliery was sunk on the other side of the canal, and in a while the Midland Railway came down the valley …. Looking from the garden gate down the road to the right, there, through the dark archway of the canal's square aqueduct, was a colliery spinning away in the near distance, and further, red, crude houses plastered on the valley in masses, and beyond all, the dim smoking hill of the town.

…. As they worked in their fields …. came the rhythmic run of winding engines …. the farmers of the lands met the blackened colliers trooping from the pit-mouth. As they gathered the harvest, the west wind brought a faint, sulphurous smell of pit refuse burning.'

Emerson Muschamp Bainbridge (1845–1911) was an English mining engineer and consultant. He was also a philanthropist and, as a Liberal Party member of Parliament, represented the constituency of Gainsborough, Lincolnshire from 1895–1900. In 1889, after obtaining a lease from the Duke of Portland, he founded the Bolsover Colliery Company which sank the shaft for Creswell Colliery.

https://artuk.org/discover/artworks/emerson-muschamp-bainbridge-18171892-36387

At a slightly later date than the transformation of, and only a few miles away from, Lawrence's fictional Nottinghamshire village of Cosethay, Emerson Muschamp Bainbridge, Liberal Member of Parliament, was working as a mining engineer. Bainbridge had a reputation as a philanthropist and had previously managed coal mines on behalf of the Duke of Norfolk who had invested in canal building which facilitated the transport of coal from Yorkshire. In 1890, together with Tylden Wright, a geologist and mining engineer who was a leading authority on coal mining in the country, Bainbridge formed the Bolsover Colliery Company.

Bainbridge subsequently obtained a lease from William Cavendish-Bentink, 6th Duke of Portland, to mine the 'Top Hard' or 'Barnsley Bed' coal seam beneath his 8,000 acres of land at Welbeck, a few miles from Creswell. The seam produced excellent quality coal, much of which was used for fires to heat the homes of London and the South East of the country. Bainbridge appointed John Plowright Houfton as general manager of the company in February 1890, and in June of that year Houfton, with a crew of twelve men, sank a shaft at Bolsover, about four miles from Creswell. This shaft reached the 'Top Hard' seam in September 1891. It was Houfton who also oversaw the sinking of the shaft at nearby Creswell in 1894.

At Creswell pit, in rapid succession, two adjacent shafts were sunk to a depth of 450 feet. Two huge winding wheels were erected, visible for miles around the area. One of the wheels was to operate the mechanism to transport men from the pit surface underground where they hewed the coal and haul them up again at the end of their shift. The other was to carry the coal to the surface. Coal production began in 1897 and by 1901 the colliery was producing 2700 to 3000 tons of coal daily. Creswell was, and remained for the rest of its eight-decade history, a highly productive colliery.

Early view of Creswell Colliery with twin winding wheels for shafts which were sunk in 1894. Miners enjoying a game of cricket while others trudge to and from work.

http://www.healeyhero.co.uk/rescue/individual/Bob_Bradley/Bk-6/B6-1991-P2.html

This prosperity was to continue until 1913 when the coal industry reached its zenith. The war of 1914–1918 proved to be a watershed for the coal industry after which it began a gradual decline resulting in oblivion eighty years later. The Bolsover Coal Company and its Creswell development could be regarded, therefore, as relative late-comers to coal mining.

By the 1890s, as the production of coal at Creswell increased, so did the population to service the mine. Even by 1870, some of the thinner seams of coal in the Durham and South Wales coal fields were beginning to be worked out and leaving many miners unemployed. Many of them made their way to the more profitable pits in the Midlands. Because of the hard work involved in mining it has always been the largest single employer of manual labour. Cutting coal was 'pick and shovel' work with machinery being used mainly for ventilation, lighting and powering winding equipment. The new development taking place at Creswell would have appeared an attractive mecca for unemployed migrating workers seeking to continue their livelihoods.

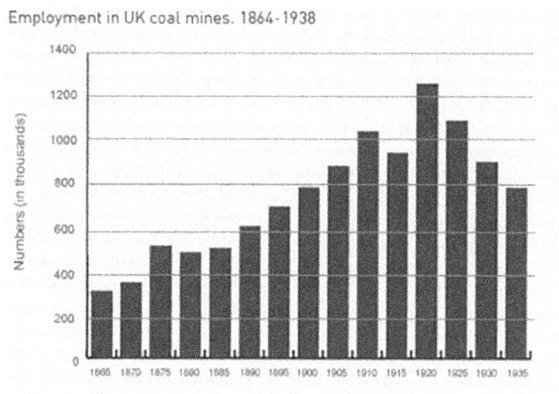

Employment on British coal mining industry 1864–1938

https://www.economicshelp.org/blog/6498/uncategorized/the-decline-of-the-uk-coal-industry/

Mining skills were readily transferable, and miners became the most mobile workforce in the country. News of the opening of a new pit spread rapidly among the mining fraternity and men came from far afield to find work there. From the ancient tin mines of Cornwall, miners and their families were encouraged to move north, bringing their mining skills with them in return for a more reliable and lucrative income. Miners arrived from the troubled coal fields of South Wales. Once settled, they rarely left the locality as the names in the village even now testify: Davies, Jones, Williams, Evans, and

Price. Most of these itinerant miners were single men who formed communes in tiny rows of houses close to the pit tops where a strong sense of camaraderie developed.

Rows of houses sprang up quickly around the pits to house the growing number of miners who moved to work in newly opened mines.

http://ppparchive.durham.gov.uk/photos/picviewer.asp?next=1607

Type of Employment	Number of women employed
Domestic Servants	1,740,800
Teachers	124,100
Nurses	68,000
Doctors	212
Architects	2

Where British women were employed in 1900.

Statistics for Creswell at this time show that typically, 40% of women in and around the village were employed in domestic service.

However, this figure may be exaggerated as women who worked on farms were not listed as being employed. Although many of the women were listed as 'maids' they were not employed in domestic service but were actually agricultural workers. In Clowne, one of the villages close to Creswell was a mill which made candlewick and sailcloth and probably provided work for the local women. Many of these women would have become miners' wives.

Undoubtedly, the new wave of single, immigrant miners changed the social equilibrium of local communities. As the workforces expanded so did the need for housing and hamlets evolved into thriving mining communities.

Every colliery owner, when he sank a pit, built houses for his workers to provide local accommodation. The accommodation was, by and large, a reflection of responsibility and the regard in which he held his employees. Typically those, who by their hard labour, had borne the brunt of fuelling the Industrial Revolution were housed in accommodation characterised by overcrowding, poor sanitation, spread of diseases and pollution. The miners were paid low wages barely affording them the means for decent housing, not to mention clothing and food. It was common for large families to live in relatively small rooms. Construction of inexpensive and poorly built rows of housing, intended for working-class people was the norm. Lack of sanitation led to the spread of diseases and, since most homes did not have running water or sanitation, people resorted to dumping their filth and waste in the street. Epidemics such as scarlet fever, typhoid and dysentery were not uncommon. The people themselves had little ability to solve these problems as they were so poorly paid that they struggled to afford even their basic lifestyles. Creswell miners, it seemed, fared better under private ownership than most mining communities.

In keeping with Bainbridge's philanthropic attitude his company, Bolsover Colliery Company, bought a further ten acres of land from the Duke of Portland's Welbeck Estate to provide housing for its employees. It was to be quality, state of the art accommodation for the Creswell miners. John Houfton, who later became Chairman of Bolsover District Council, was known to take a keen interest in the welfare of the miners and their families. He proposed to Bainbridge the ideal of building housing in addition to a social structure for the miners and commissioned his cousin, Percy Bond Houfton, to build a 'model village'.

In addition to having a certificate in mine management, Percy Houfton was also an architect whose specialty, *Arts and Craft* architecture stood for traditional craftsmanship utilising themes of medieval, romantic or folk styles of decoration. This style is apparent in the houses contained within the Model Village. The design was to incorporate two hundred houses, a miners' institute, school, co-operative store and an orphanage for children whose fathers had been killed in accidents at the mine. A Methodist Chapel, an Anglican Church, a bandstand and allotments for the miners to grow produce were also included. The village, a few hundred metres north of the colliery, was completed in 1895.

Two concentric octagons were designed to contain a total of two hundred and eighty-two cottages of various architectural designs for the miners and slightly grander 'villas' for deputies and overmen. The octagons enclosed a village green or park, bisected into 'top' and 'bottom' model parks, which included a children's play area and a bandstand where, no doubt, villagers were entertained on Sunday afternoons by their famous colliery band. Between the two parks was a tramway which delivered coal to the houses and was stored in coal cellars.

The above is typical of the Arts and Craft architecture popular in the late 19th century. It attempted to re-establish traditional skills and craftsmanship which were being threatened by mass production. Its main exponent in Britain was William Morris. Inspired by medieval architecture it was fundamentally anti-industrial and used local material. It emphasised function, need and simplicity, free from ornamentation.

Percy Houfton's octagonal design for Creswell's Model Village, two concentric rows of house built around a central park.

The newly-built Model Village

https://picturethepast.org.uk/image-library/image-details/poster/dcbr000033/posterid/dcbr000033.html

The Model Village as it is today. Originally, a tramway ran along the street to deliver coal and remove night soil from the ash privies.

https://www.geograph.org.uk/photo/4729591

5   *Where there's muck: Birth of a Coal Community*

The front of the houses overlooked the park. At the back, the houses shared a common yard, four houses to each yard.

All the houses were two storeys and comprised a kitchen, living/dining room, a small parlour and three bedrooms. The most contemporary feature was the inclusion of a bathroom. All had running water and electricity and each cottage had its own small front garden. The houses had communal yards where children could play, and washing was hung out to dry after laundering in an outside wash house. Slightly later, The Miners' Institute was built between the houses and the colliery. It housed a reading room, library and lecture room which could seat 400. Creswell miners were fortunate. A branch of the Bolsover Cooperative Society opened a store in the village selling fresh vegetables, meat and fish. At the edge of the village was arable land where the miners could rent allotments for four shillings a year.

Despite the pollution from the mine, overcrowding and poor sanitation were not features of the Creswell development. The state-of-the art accommodation with modern facilities for employees conformed to The Bolsover Colliery Company's philanthropic principles which stood in stark contrast to the cheap, poorly built houses provided in surrounding counties where collieries were still managed by aristocratic owners.

The architectural acme of this design project was York House, an imposing Edwardian mansion complete with typical Arts and Craft features. It was set in several acres of grounds and access was by a sweeping driveway. The grounds boasted ornamental gardens, manicured lawns, a large orchard and walled kitchen garden, all serviced by colliery employees. This was designed to be the residence firstly of Percy Houfton, then the mine managers who followed him. Imposing as the residence was, it was even closer to the pit head than was the model village, so not quite 'living over the shop'.

The village grew as more facilities were added. In 1903 the Drill Hall was built to provide a venue for various recreational activities — flower and vegetable shows and old time dancing. Railway stations, churches, chapels and schools followed in quick succession.

> "The company has tried to make the lives of the workmen as pleasant as possible, and to give them such an interest in the place where they live that they are happy to spend their leisure time in their own village" remarked John Houfton on completion of the housing project.

5 *Where there's muck: Birth of a Coal Community*

The imposing York House was traditionally the residence of Creswell Colliery managers. Along with the defunct pit, it was demolished.

Bainbridge believed that "there was no reason why the miners should not have a village where three things could exist successfully — the absence of drunkenness, the absence of gambling and the absence of bad language."

He was either a supreme optimist or somewhat naïve — *or* he may have remained aloof from his employees. Nevertheless, the local buildings were a fine example of 'state of the art' accommodation. The Model Village was a considerable advance on the ugly, squat rows of back-to-back dwellings traditionally built for miners. The houses were a radical change from the traditional rows of inferior terraced housing of other coal mining areas such as Durham, Lanarkshire and South Wales.

The Drill Hall, Elmton Road (Main Street), Creswell built in 1903 was the centre of a bustling social life in the productive mining days of the village.

http://www.drillhalls.org/Counties/Derbyshire/TownCreswell.htm

Derbyshire miners were said to be 'thrifty' and took pride, not only in their own appearance, but in that of their families. From this account, it appears they were veritable 'models of propriety'. They believed in sickness and benefit clubs, to which many belonged. They were keen on sporting activities with rabbit coursing and pigeon fancying being common pastimes. Gardening was a favourite occupation, raising flowers and vegetables to be displayed with pride at annual village shows in the newly constructed Drill Hall. Cricket and football were very important and catered for by the inclusion of the nearby cricket ground. Nor was education neglected. It was not unheard of for pit boys to work towards and pass public examinations which allowed them entrance to university. What better example than D.H. Lawrence himself?

However, miners' job security remained fickle and beyond their control. Low productivity resulted in less working hours, the consequent less income and the inevitable struggle to make ends meet. In these times families would subsist on a diet consisting mostly of bread, potatoes and weak tea substituted, no doubt, by poaching game from the estate of their neighbouring landowner, the Duke of Portland. Before the advent of coal mining, most colliers had been countrymen. They were reputed to be skilful and wily poachers who saw nothing wrong with taking something from someone who had more than they did. Indulging in this activity, however, must have been a measure of desperation as poachers ran the risk of severe penalties if caught. Conversely, when times were good, miners have been variously described as 'recklessly spending …. on poultry, especially geese and ducks …. occasionally on port wine' which they drank out of glasses and basins. They were also known to 'squander their money … on excursions in carts.'

Around the middle of the 19th century when modern coal mining had its origins, brass bands emerged as a popular pastime which provided a social and cultural outlet for miners. Coincidentally, brass instruments were also beneficiaries of the technological innovation which accompanied the Industrial Revolution. Improvements in design enhanced the sound of the instruments which were then beginning to be produced in greater numbers. Most of the village bands were sponsored by local industrial concerns, none more so than the coal mining industry. 1899 saw the foundation of Creswell Colliery and District Band as it was then known. Achieving national fame in decades to come, the band continues today.

However, to Bainbridge's chagrin, gambling was rife among men *and* women. A large proportion of their wages was spent betting on horse racing and football matches. Even miners' wives would bet sixpence or even a shilling on big races! Nevertheless, Bainbridge would probably have approved of the fact that there appeared to be less drunkenness here than in other parts of the country. Many miners would take their families on outings to the seaside, although the closest coastal towns were on the Lincolnshire coast, about sixty miles away. Also gratifying to Bainbridge was the fact that about a quarter of the population were regular church goers, and of those, mainly Dissenters.

The earliest available photograph of Creswell Colliery Band which was formed in 1899. It went from strength to strength and won many local and National band competitions for many decades and is still in existence.

From the Archives of Creswell Colliery Band;
https://creswellband.webs.com/fromthearchives.htm

The Bandstand where the band would have provided entertainment on Sunday afternoons. It was situated on the 'top' green surrounded by the Model Village.

https://creswellband.webs.com/fromthearchives.htm

5 *Where there's muck: Birth of a Coal Community*

The Miners' Institute, one of the amenities incorporated in the Model Village and traditional home of the brass band.

Despite the impact on the once attractive surrounding countryside, now scarred with black spoilt heaps emitting noxious fumes and a chimney which disgorged carbon dioxide laden fumes into the atmosphere, relaxation was still possible. At opposite ends of the edge of the village two picturesque features survived intact: the prehistoric Creswell Crags with their famous cave art, and the limestone gorge known as Markland Grips where its stream attracts recreational fishing. Along with the lucrative production of coal, the Bolsover Colliery Company had given birth to a thriving community. Villagers worked and played hard.

The Elm Tree Hotel, Elmton. A favourite destination for walkers especially on balmy, light summer evenings

https://www.toopics.com/elmtreeelmton/?lang=en

Markland Grips Nature Reserve, still a pleasant place for a stroll

https://www.flickr.com/photos/respectakp/515180104

5 Where there's muck: Birth of a Coal Community

Quiet footpath through Markland Grips, once popular for fishing, blackberry and hazelnut gathering, still exists. Horse chestnut trees supplied local boys with conkers for autumn contests.

Georgraph: https://www.geograph.org.uk/photo/3551511

Although mining safety had improved when coal mining took on new, large scale significance from the mid-19th century, the hostile working environment did not. In treacherous conditions men often worked in water which reached their waists and still crawled along narrow tunnels. The heat could be intolerable and there was the ever-present threat of explosion, fire or rock falls capable of killing and maiming. Despite government intervention, accidents were still commonplace. Longevity was not an expectation among mining communities. However, hard toil and constant fears for safety engendered closeness and solidarity. There was, at least, equality of lifestyle. The miners worked and played hard, together. Relationships were forged and reinforced around pints of beer in the pub or Miners' nstitute, or in games of football, cricket or bowls on the green outside the Miners' Institute. As in all communities, life went on.

There is ample illustration of the hard life at that time. The harsh lives of the miners are, justifiably, well documented. However, history books provide little information about the lives of the miners' wives. Once young women were married, they invariably endured a life of drudgery revolving around their husbands and the routine of their changing shifts.

> 'Whistle blasts, like the tolling of a monastery bell, announced the miners' work schedules around which family life revolved. The absence of the whistle blasts created a heavy silence in coal towns, for this indicated that the mines were temporarily closed, and the pay envelopes correspondingly empty.'
> D. H. Lawrence (*Sons and Lovers.*)

The women, like their husbands, also forged close relationships with each other. But unlike their husbands, their solidarity was not forged in the public bars.

> 'The stay-at-home mothers stood gossiping at the corners of the alley …. folding their arms under their white aprons. The women, in twos and threes, gossiped … between the blocks. Men, having a rest between drinks, sat on their heels and talked. Washing …. and the constant fight against coal grit which invaded every crevice and covered every surface consumed the women's lives. They married young but aged quickly with frequent pregnancies. Although tired after a day of housework in primitive conditions, and looking after the children, there was still the ubiquitous obligation to put the men's needs first, 'set his breakfast, [rinse] his pit bottle, put his pit clothes on the hearth, set his pit boots beside them, put him out a clean scarf and snap bag and two apples [rake] the fire' before finally going bed, exhausted, herself.' (*ibid.*)

Life was like this for the women of Creswell and it did not vary drastically over time. Meanwhile, for the Creswell community there were regular traditional visits from the Duke and Duchess of Portland. The Duchess was a great lover of animals and was the longest serving president of the Royal Society for the Protection of Birds. She took a keen interest in the welfare of the miners and their families and secured the services of a nurse for the Model Village. In honour of her support, the Nottinghamshire Miners' Welfare Association petitioned King George V and, on the occasion of his silver jubilee in 1935, she was made a Dame Commander of the Order of the British Empire.

Left: William Cavendish-Bentink, 6th Duke of Portland in uniform of the 10th Hussars.

https://en.wikipedia.org/wiki/William_Cavendish-Bentinck,_6th_Duke_of_Portland

Right: Wife of 6th Duke, Duchess Winnifred (nee Dallas York) 1912.

https://en.wikipedia.org/wiki/Winifred_Cavendish-Bentinck,_Duchess_of_Portland

Meanwhile the Duke grew wealthier as coal production

increased. His opulent lifestyle, facilitated largely through the underground toil of the miners, allowed him to feel at home in the company of the crowned heads of Europe. During November 1913, the Portland's entertained, at Welbeck, Archduke Franz Ferdinand of Austria, heir to the Austro-Hungarian throne, and his wife Sophie von Hohenberg. While on a shooting excursion, one of the estate's gun loaders fell causing both barrels of his gun to discharge. The shots narrowly missed the Duke and Archduke. Although history doesn't record the fate of the gun loader, on June 28th the following year, Archduke Franz Ferdinand was assassinated in Sarajevo, an event which has been described as 'the spark that would set light to a continent that was riddled with international tensions' and a contributing factor to the first World War.

During World War l the village remained fervently patriotic. However, on 14 January 1917 a meeting convened by Samuel Smith, chairman of the parish council and well-known pacifist, was held in the Primitive Methodist Chapel. It attracted a large audience, from within the village and surrounding district, composed mainly of patriots who began waving Union flags and singing pro-war songs. Tempers flared on both sides and the meeting descended into disorder. Windows were smashed and eggs (which were then very expensive) were used as missiles. Pacifists denounced the behaviour of flag-waving patriots whose behaviour was described by pacifists as 'hooliganism of the worst type'. A few days later patriots held their own meeting where they claimed that 99% of the villages were in support of the war effort.

However, like all industrial rural and civic communities, Creswell did not shrink from providing support for King and Country, a cause in which it strongly believed. In the mid-19th century, prior to its metamorphosis as a coal mining community, the population of Creswell stood at about 500. By 1900 the number had increased to 2,000. Seven hundred men from the village and surrounding district joined as volunteers or conscripts. This figure carries more significance since, in 1916 coal mining was designated a reserved occupation and miners were exempt from conscription. According to the memorial erected in their honour, ninety-two did not return — a third of them were lost on the Somme.

Welbeck Abbey, 1912

https://en.wikipedia.org/wiki/Welbeck_Abbey2

Countess Schonburg, Major Baker-Carr, Victoria Bentinck, Portland, Duchess of Hohenberg, Winifred Portland, Archduke Franz Ferdinand, Count Schonburg.

Nottinghamshire History: http://www.nottshistory.org.uk/portland1907/portland8.htm

Memorial to Soldiers who died in war, Elmton Road, Creswell.

Elmton with Creswell Parish Council:
https://www.elmtonwithcreswellparish.org.uk/our-history

The year 1914 was also a turning point for the British coal mining industry. As production, exports and employment declined, so began a demise which was to continue for the next seventy years. The need for coal was fickle, and communities built on its supply and demand were vulnerable. The 20th century showed every indication of being as innovative, progressive and turbulent as its predecessor and the coal mining industry, although important *pro tempore*, existing on borrowed time.

6

Cleanliness: Women's Work

We have borne good sons to broken men,
Nurtured them on our hungry breast,
And given them to our masters when
Their day of life was at its best.

We have dried their clammy clothes by the fire,
Solaced them, cheered them, tended them well,
Watched the wheels raising them from the mire,
Watched the wheels lowering them to Hell.

We have prayed for them in a Godless way
(We never could fathom the ways of God)
We have sung with them on their wedding day,
Knowing the journey and the road.

We have stood through the naked night to watch
The silent wheels that raised the dead;
We have gone before to raise the latch,
And lay the pillow beneath their head.

We have done all this for our masters' sake,
Did it in rags and did not mind;
What more do they want? what more can they take?
Unless our eyes and leave us blind.

Joe Corrie

Nan had now left home in every respect. The advent of her adulthood coincided with historical changes in the national environment and the beginning of an exhilarating time for women, especially young women. Living through the Great War had been difficult for her, especially being the oldest child in her family, *and a girl*. Much of the responsibility for household chores and child rearing had devolved on her. By virtue of her 1907 birth, Nan was a child of the Edwardian era and her working-class childhood had been typical of that era. Girls were expected to help their mothers in the endless household chores, which included a considerable amount of child minding. Even as children, girls became weary of motherhood.

Although, by this time, this expectation was beginning to diminish, the inherent bias against educating girls persisted to some extent. The canon that 'excessive mental drain' involved in girls' studies was a precursor to mental, moral and intellectual difficulties and *'an imperfectly developed reproductive system'* still held sway. Undoubtedly, Nan would have wholeheartedly refuted this aphorism. Although she had left school at 15, she was intelligent, and her adult responsibilities had turned her into a pragmatic and resourceful woman. Experience of home and children had embedded in her psyche, at least for the foreseeable future, an antipathy towards motherhood. She had enjoyed her training and excelled in both practical and written examinations. In the then current, post war climate, women such as Nan began to flourish with their new found freedom. Hair was worn short, affordable ready-made clothes were available and designed to free women from the restraint of whalebone corsets.

Women thrived in professions which would previously have been practised by a whole generation of young men had they not been killed on the battlefields of Europe, the Mediterranean and the Middle East. In 1921, Oxford University conferred degrees on women, hitherto only granted to their male peers, despite their having studied the same courses. (Although colleges for female students existed at Cambridge, the university did not allow them to receive their degrees for another twenty-six years.) The attitudes of many future mothers had also been changed by the war. Women who had served in such organisations as army nursing services and Voluntary Aid Detachment and experienced not only the fear of battle but the elation of survival, wanted more for their daughters than the lives which had previously constrained them. Women also tended to talk about their wartime experiences more than their male counterparts.

1920s fashion was more practical and more comfortable than pre-WWI figure hugging clothes which required the body to be constricted in corsets.

Clothes were now ready-made, giving working women the opportunity for a varied, up to date wardrobe.

Changes in Women in the 1920's:
https://demflappers.weebly.com/change-in-women-during-the-1920s.html

Sadly, not all women during this post war period had achieved a state of emancipation. Simultaneously 39,000 women in England and Wales died giving birth — many of which were often unplanned and unwanted. Although products of a coal mining background, both Nan and her parents were able to escape from it. In the coalfields of South Wales, the lifestyle which had sustained people for the last fifty years, continued without remission.

As always in heavy industry it is young fit men and boys who make up the workforce and are most vulnerable to its intrinsic hazards. Such were the risks confronting men and boys who worked at the coal face. Working underground was arduous, dirty and dangerous. Each miner had his own patch from where he dug coal, yet although working separately, the men were united by mutual dependency. They were close-knit and fiercely loyal to each other. This gave uniqueness to the culture of mining communities. Interdependence at work extended to their leisure activities engendering an ethos of gender segregation. Women were excluded from this fellowship and *their* focus of activity became the home with which, primarily, they became identified. Unlike men who were able to separate work from recreation, for their wives and mothers there was no distinction between work and home and they considered themselves to be always at work.

Conditions for these women were demanding. Income was uncertain, depending on the amount and quality of coal their men mined, families were large and the dirt associated with the nature of their men's work made looking after them labour-intensive. For each woman there was the ever-present fear of death or serious injury which meant the loss of the breadwinner. Going off to work at the beginning of a shift was no guarantee men would come home when it was ended.

In South Wales a complex geological formation meant that, rather than occurring in continuous strata, coal occurred in folds making them difficult to work. An associated unbalanced load of superficial topsoil added to the risk of rock falls and roof cave-ins. As with all coal mines, there was the constant threat of explosions caused by the presence of gas. Between 1859 and 1914 there were 23 accidents in the Welsh coal fields resulting in the loss of over 100 lives. There was no sick pay or compensation for the miners injured at work. To improve access to the coal, deeper shafts had to be sunk. Engineering was expensive and to offset this expense for owners, miners' wages were often cut back.

Adding to the uncertainty of obtaining work in the industry, there was the fluctuating demand for coal with the inevitable consequence of lay-offs or short shifts. Strikes and lockouts caused some of the highest losses of income. The highest paid miners — the young and fit — reached their peak earning years in their early twenties. By now women were no longer employed underground.

These mining communities consisted of a greater proportion of men to women. Couples married early — marriage conferred respectability on a woman. Marriage was followed, in rapid succession, by the production of the largest number of children of any occupational group in the early twentieth century. Many of these children did not survive infancy. The 1911 Census shows the typical mining couple had 4.23 children, being significantly above the national average of 3.53. This was not a sign of the miners' fecundity. Children were economically useful assets — particularly male children who, inevitably, would follow their fathers into the pit, often from the age of fourteen onwards, providing a much needed extra source of income. Mining families were dependent upon male providers to a greater extent than other occupational groups in Britain. The fact that it was possible for young men in their early twenties to be paid higher wages in coal mining encouraged the establishment of households at relatively earlier ages resulting, in turn, in higher birth rates.

Group	Births per 1000 men under 55
Clergy	96-101
Doctors	103
Policemen	153
Dock labourers	231
Miners	258
General labourers	438

The work of a miner's wife was never done. Families lived in small, frail rows of terrace houses where the brickwork was blackened by constant exposure to smoke and coal dust. The houses consisted of two small bedrooms upstairs with a scullery, kitchen and small living room underneath. Outside were narrow strips of garden which often opened onto a shed. There was no gas, electricity, running water or sewerage and one lavatory, several metres from the houses, would serve several families. On the wall at the back of the house would hang the tin bath which would be carried through the house in readiness for the men when they returned from their shifts. The small houses, often accommodating up to twelve people, were overrun with children. Forty per cent of the total population of the Welsh coalfields at this time consisted of children. Thirty per cent of households consisted of three children. Few households did not have a child under 15.

Homes were made even more overcrowded by taking in rent paying lodgers to supplement the meagre income, even though it made extra work for the women. Most lodgers paid the equivalent of about 12 to 17 pence a week. Services included washing and, for a higher rent, a modest meal of potatoes and tea. Not all lodgers were strangers. Some were relatives from distant villages who had moved to find work. When the sons of the household reached twelve or thirteen, they usually followed their fathers underground.

With widespread overcrowding, it was not uncommon for men on different shifts to use the same bed as in Arthur Sullivan's comedy *Box and Cox*. But here there was no comedic element. A vivid picture of such conditions in the Lancashire coalfield is painted by author George Orwell in *The Road to Wigan Pier*.

> 'Quite often you have eight or even ten people living in a three-roomed house. One of these rooms is a living room [which] probably measures about a dozen feet square and contains besides the kitchen range and the sink, a table and a dresser.... there are eight or ten people sleeping in two small rooms .... in summer in a tiny stuffy living room where the fire, on which all the cooking is done, has to be kept burning constantly.'

The needs of the men always took precedence over those of everyone else, including the children and governed the daily routine of the home. With so many men and boys in single households, all of whom may be working three different shifts, women's work was never-ending. Preparing baths and hot meals could take all day or all night with the men arriving home at 7 am from night shift, 3 pm from day shift and 11 pm from afternoon shift.

Women were every bit under the control of the mine owners as were the men since the life of domestic labour in the home could be every bit as dangerous as working down the pit. Orwell again:

> 'In such places as these, the woman is only a poor drudge muddling among an infinity of jobs.... There is always something to be done and no convenience and not room to turn round.... No sooner have you washed one child's face than another's is dirty; before you have washed the crocks from one meal the next is due to be cooked.'

Before the installation of pit head baths, men would return home tired and covered in sweat and coaldust. It was the work of their wives (and mothers), to carry in the tin bath and heat up the water on the fire for the men to wash. In addition to being an arduous task, it was also fraught with danger. It took several journeys to and from the fire to ladle the boiling water into the bath in by hand. Women were often scalded, and it was not unheard of for children to die after falling into bath tubs. Since for much of their lives the women were pregnant, the work was made even harder. At the beginning of the 20th century, it was normal for a married woman in Wales to spend around 15 years producing children and hard work often brought on premature labour or miscarriage. Women became prematurely old and haggard by this harsh existence. The death rate among women between the ages of 20 to 45 was appreciably higher than that of men.

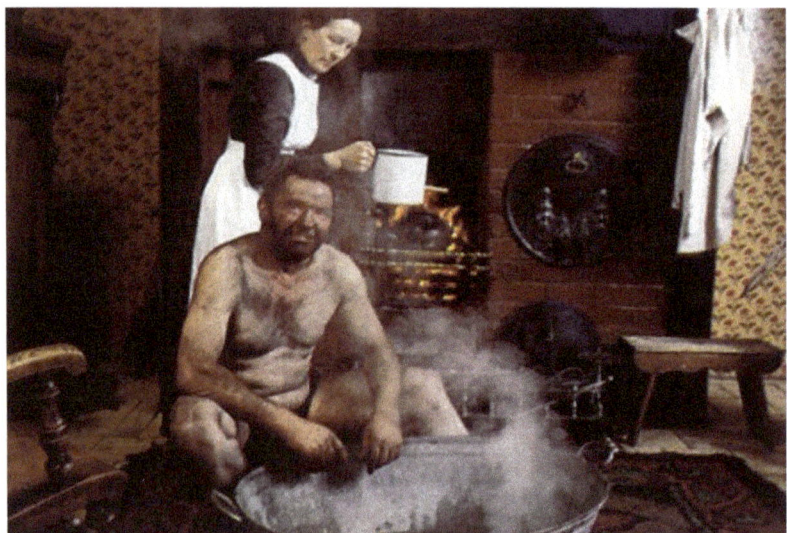

Before the introduction of pit head baths, wives carried out the daily ritual of helping to get their miner clean. Not only did they wash his dirty pit clothes, they also washed the miner.

Grannynar ; http://grannymar.com/2013/04/26/out-of-sight-out-of-mind/

The miners took great pride in their work, and despite difficult living conditions, their wives took an equal pride in their housework although life was a constant struggle against poverty and grime. These were the Welsh 'mams' whose households ran on matriarchal lines. However, their horizons rarely extended beyond their own front doors, and hardly ever past the end of the street. Housing was in short supply and rents were high. It was hard not to become disheartened, yet the women maintained high standards and took pride in their homes. Housework was done to a very high, exacting specification. Floors were scrubbed with great care and pride taken particularly in scrubbing the front doorstep and the edge of the step being outlined with white chalk. Curtains were washed regularly to get rid of ingrained coal dust. Furniture was polished and rugs were shaken. The influence of non-conformism was all-pervasive. Cleanliness came next to godliness and domestic routine was governed by a rigid timetable:

Monday: washing
Tuesday: ironing and bed-making
Wednesday: cleaning upstairs rooms
Thursday: beating mats
Friday: cleaning parlour

The endless routine was often affected by economic hardship which eroded their pride not only in their work, but in their appearances.

Women worked longer hours than the men whose needs took priority. With perhaps a twenty metre walk to an outside communal lavatory, inside the tiny, unsanitary and overcrowded but polished houses inhabited by poverty-stricken people, there was a high rate of child mortality. Epidemics of pneumonia, whooping cough, diphtheria and scarlet fever were common. Infant deaths from diarrhoea came from poor sanitation and other unhealthy conditions.

Rheumatic fever and tuberculosis, closely linked to poor housing, were the most serious diseases. Over half childhood deaths occurred in children under five, 10% of whom died in the first year of life.

Despite pit dirt and poverty, Welsh wives were houseproud.
https://museum.wales/welsh_womens_history/

There were also significant issues for the women with childbirth and family planning. Early deaths among miners' wives, although not as commonplace as with men, were not rare as many women were literally worked to death. Unsanitary, substandard housing, poor nutrition and overwork, combined with a medical service that had to be paid for, made for low standards of women's health. Women became worn out through constant childbirth and domestic labour. Their stoic sacrifice to the welfare of others was accepted without question. In hard times, women frequently saved money by cutting down on their own food which had severe repercussions on their health. But mostly it was the exhausting effect of successive pregnancies which wore out many women.

A young mother and child wait for news after an explosion at Senghenydd pit in Aber Valley, South Wales. The disaster, on 14 October 1913 was the worst ever in Britain and killed 440 men, including a member of the rescue team. The owner of the mine was subsequently convicted of disregarding safety regulations of the 1911 Coal mines Act. He was fined £24, the equivalent of 5½ pence per miner. Sixty of the dead were under 60 and eight under 14. The disaster left 205 widows and 62 dependent parents.

Government enquiry into the 1913 Senghenydd mine disaster: https://museum.wales/articles/2012-07-06/Miners-lives-at-5p-each-The-Government-Enquiry-into-the-1913-Senghenydd-mine-disaster/

7

Every heart deserves a mate: Carys's Dilemma

Meg Pritchard and Gwyn Thomas were both children from mining families who had lived, for several generations, in Rhayenydd, a small mining village in a valley in South Wales. When they were young, they were slightly acquainted yet did not know each other well. Meg was the only girl in a family of boys — three older and one younger than her. Meg's father had been a shot-firer at the local pit but had been killed in an explosion when she was still a child. Thereafter the responsibility for bringing in a weekly wage fell, one by one, to her older brothers. Gwyn's father, and later Gwyn and his brothers, worked underground at the same pit. That was really the only thing their families had in common.

In 1919, just after the end of the war, Meg returned to the village after a five-year absence. She and Gwyn rekindled their acquaintance, became friends, found they liked each other and eventually began walking out together. A short time later, they were married in the Bethesda Baptist Chapel just up the street from Meg's home. It was Meg who had insisted on a chapel wedding. Gwyn's father and brothers had no particular religious affiliation and did not object to a chapel wedding.

As a child, Meg's mother ensured she became a diligent attender of Sunday services, although her solicitousness for their spiritual well-being had not extended to her sons. Meg was often intimidated by the fiery Nonconformist sermons from high up in the pulpit, denouncing the sins of fornication, upholding the sanctity of marriage and the traditional deference of wife to husband. Hell and damnation, they warned, awaited those who transgressed the teachings of Jesus Christ. The content of the homilies, in Meg's case, had fallen on fertile ground shaping her into an upright, rather high-minded young woman.

At the time of their marriage Meg was almost twenty-one, a year younger than her husband and conventionally quite old for marriage in these villages. Most of the girls in the valleys had married during their teenage years and, by Meg's age, had already produced a small brood of children tugging at their skirts. In spite of her age, and the fact that she had had some experience of life outside the confines of her village, when married, Meg was prepared to unquestioningly obey her husband, ceding to him total responsibility for any decision that needed to be made. As far as she was concerned, he would always be head of the family and his wishes would always come first.

During the five years away from Rhayenydd, Meg had worked as a maid-housekeeper-nurse in the home of the ageing Dr Aneurin Jones who lived in another valley twenty-five miles or so from her home. Her financial independence, she reasoned would relieve her family of the responsibility for her upkeep, although it left her mother with the hard work of looking after her sons. Meg was fond of the old doctor and his wife. Mrs Jones had been the victim of a stroke a few years earlier. Her condition had gradually worsened, and she had a second stroke just before Meg's arrival. Mrs Jones was now completely bedridden and, being childless, Meg was employed to help take care of her. It was also Meg's job to look after the doctor as well as their house. The work was hard, yet she liked the doctor and his wife and was happy. A second person was employed to clean the attached surgery and dispensary, although Meg often took messages from patients who wanted to see the doctor.

7 Every heart deserves a mate: Carys's Dilemma

After his wife's initial stroke, Dr Jones had intended to retire and devote his time and attention to his ailing wife, leaving his assistant, Dr Probert, to take over the running of the practice. Dr Probert was young, eager and efficient with impressive London qualifications and experience among the poor in London's East End. He would have been an ideal replacement, even though some of the older patients still insisted on seeing the old doctor. But in 1914, war intervened. Much to the chagrin of Dr Jones, Tom Probert enlisted as a medical officer with the South Wales Borderers and was quickly dispatched to the Western Front. Being one of only two doctors covering a large area, Dr Jones had no option but to carry on his practice single handedly, no longer as the idealistic young doctor he had been when he took up his practice.

Meg had been a boon to the elderly couple. The diligent and caring Dr Jones worked hard and his hours were long which meant he was unable to devote time, attention and love to his beloved, ailing wife. This duty devolved on Meg, whose hours were as long and hard as those of her employer, but hard work was no stranger to her. Shortly before the Armistice, Mrs Jones died. Her husband continued to work until Dr Probert was demobilised and returned to the valley and agreed to take over the practice, leaving the old man free to retire.

Meg returned to Rhayenydd where her life of hard work continued. The household routine was dictated by shifts at the pit, and her mother had aged with the hard work. Meg's mam was grateful for her daughter's help with the endless filling of bathtubs, providing round the clock meals and scrubbing dirty pit clothes. The only variation in the running of the household came with the addition of a sister-in-law, Delyth, the daughter and sister of colliers who knew no other life. More accustomed than Meg to this routine, it was Delyth who became her mother's replacement. Meg felt decidedly displaced and it was then that Gwyn re-entered her life.

Gwyn was from an even larger, but all male family. Some of his brothers had left home to work in different mines. Unlike Meg, Gwyn had not been forced to endure Sunday mornings in chapel. Being active members of the miner's union, their faith lay there rather than in promises of Heaven. Gwyn's home was, like Meg's and the rest of the houses in the village, small and cramped. With the fluctuation in the need for coal after the war, Gwyn's work became precarious enough for him to look elsewhere for employment.

A short time after their marriage, with no home of their own and having had neither time nor reason to accumulate many household goods, they packed what meagre belongings they had and moved to Pontymawr. This was one of the villages in an adjacent valley where Gwyn had found permanent work at the local pit, thanks to an older brother, Gareth, who already worked there. Although struggling to make ends meet in his tiny house with an ever-increasing family, Gareth had invited his brother and sister-in-law to live with him until they were able to find a home of their own. It was hardly an enviable prospect for them but, at least Gwyn, like Gareth, would have regular work.

By the time the rattletrap bus had deposited Meg and Gwyn in the main street, and made its stuttering way further along the valley, it was already mid-afternoon. Although this was the first time they had been to Pontymawr, everything seemed familiar. Rows of squalid little blackened brick houses overshadowed by the huge winding wheel and surrounding dark hills made it, like so many other Welsh villages, a replica of the one they had just left.

People gave them strange looks as they carried their battered suitcases down the street. Men were beginning to tramp home from their long shifts underground, where they had worked since before dawn, their faces black with coal dust. Everywhere there seemed to be the sound of children playing in the streets, shouting, running to meet their dads.

With the help of a passerby they found Gareth's house. Like their own village, everybody knew everyone else. The house, at the end of the street, was a replica of the ones in which both Gwyn and Meg and been raised, scullery, kitchen and little living room downstairs and two little bedrooms upstairs; no gas, electricity or running water and a communal privy at the end of the yard.

As they stood on the worn doorstep, recently scoured with a fresh white chalk line at the edge, Meg's heart sank at the sound on the other side of the flimsy door. She hadn't expected salubrious accommodation but, although she was aware of Gareth's children, neither had she anticipated the din of shrieking, crying children.

"Our mam!" was the cry in response to Gwyn's sharp rap. The battered door was opened slightly by a boy of about 5 dressed in a pair of tattered trousers, obviously those of an adult, the fraying bottoms flapping round his skinny legs. His top was bare, and his head was bald. Both his face and head were a collage of yellow crusty sores and daubed purple stains. A trail of thick, green mucous ran from each nostril.

"Well, our Hugh, ask them to come in."

Meg's heart sank even lower and she swallowed hard as she stepped over the threshold. Her fixation with hygiene, learned during her years of service with Dr Jones, was about to be severely tested. Like Gwyn's, her eyes took a minute to adjust to the dimness as they entered the small, cramped living room. The only light came from a small, yet clean, sash window and a fire burning in the black, polished grate.

Even in the fading light, Meg could see that the room, with its pathetic bits of cheap furniture was, underneath all the paraphernalia of a family of children, clean. But not even the smoke and the fuggy atmosphere, pungent with the smell of unwashed bodies, could cover up the omnipresent smell of the pit.

The frail figure of Gareth's wife, Carys, stood in the middle of the room. She was dressed in a faded pinafore, strands of unruly brown hair escaping from an equally faded headscarf. She came towards them with a shy smile on her face. In her arms was an infant who appeared to be no more than a few months old, while another small child was attempting to stand up by pulling on the hem of her frayed dress. The woman was painfully thin and, her face was prematurely lined. Hugh remained by the open door while a fourth child sat at linoleum covered table wiping jam from her face with the back of her hand. Meg's heart was only prevented from sinking to an even greater depth by the disarming, genuine smile of pleasure from Carys which lit up her thin, careworn face.

"Well now, here you are!' she said gently, "I'd have known you anywhere Gwyn *bach*. The image of our Gareth you are. It won't be long before 'e comes home from the pit. I'm just givin' the children their tea before I put on the water for 'is bath."

Somehow, she managed to disentangle herself from the crawling toddler and kissed Meg on her cheek. She shook Gwyn's hand. Meg recognised this as a genuine gesture of welcome. Carys was obviously pleased to see them although Meg got the impression that the welcome was directed at her rather than Gwyn.

"When Gareth's had his bath, he'll show you round a bit, Gwyn. Might even take you to the Welfare; introduce you to some of the lads you'll be working with."

"You can close the door Hugh, they're here now!" she teased as she began to introduce the children.

Hugh, the oldest, was five. Carys explained, with some embarrassment, that he was at home because he had impetigo or, as she called it, "school sores", and had been excluded from school. Her main concern seemed to be that while away from school, he was missing out on his daily milk and midday meal. The baby in

Carys's arms, a little girl called Mauriel, showed obvious signs of failing to thrive. The crawling infant was introduced as Elwyn, or Ellie — the liveliest looking of all the children. The third little girl, Mared, had now finished eating her bread and jam and was reclining listlessly on a threadbare settee that had been propped up by a piece of wood serving as a fourth leg.

Meg's eyes darted from child to child as they were introduced. At the same time, she did a quick mental calculation — four of them, the oldest one only 5! Meg had had very little experience with children and was taken aback by the feeling of aversion to them which she attempted to quell. Nevertheless, her preoccupation with hygiene notwithstanding, and despite the puny, pathetic looking children, the house, spartan as it was, was certainly clean and well cared for. It met with her approval.

Carys was about to hand the baby to Hugh when, instinctively, Meg stepped forward and took the child who regarded her with a singularly apathetic expression. Carys excused herself and disappeared into the back of the house from where they could hear sounds of heaving and pouring of water. They were both familiar with the sound which Gwyn traced to the scullery. In the centre of the little room was a battered bath which Carys had dragged in from back yard. Steam filled the air and ran in little rivulets down the small window with its limp net curtain. Carys was struggling between the bath and the copper in the corner with a series of buckets of scalding water. The setting was a facsimile of the kitchen at home where his mother had performed this chore the whole of her married life. The water had to be boiling so that the heat would be retained long enough for Gareth to immerse himself to wash off the grime of the pit.

Carys refused Gwyn's offer to help, adding that it was enough just to have someone to mind the children while she filled the bathtub. She was always afraid of accidents when the children were around. The work was fraught with danger. Women were often scalded when ladling boiling water into buckets and carrying them across the room to the bath in front of the fire. Often children got in the way and were burned, sometimes dying as a result. Carys was always careful to avoid this happening to her children. Gwyn returned to join Meg and the children. Gareth, Carys announced, would join them once he was nice and clean.

Left alone with the children an understanding look passed between the young couple. Without speaking each felt the other's apprehension. Yet what choice was there? Gareth was, after all, Gwyn's bother and had offered, not only a chance to find regular work but accommodation, meagre as it was. Blood was thicker than water, and once they had got on their feet, they were sure to find a little house of their own. Anyway, the few shillings they were paying in rent would be of help to Gareth and Carys. Of course, it would be alright they thought, both trying, not very convincingly to reassure themselves.

By the sounds coming from the scullery, they could tell that Gareth had arrived home. Eventually, the door opened and a beaming Gareth, his wet hair plastered to his head, entered holding out his hand to his brother. He hugged Meg. Yes, she thought, slightly reassured, it *might* be alright.

Gareth retrieved the baby from Meg and greeted the other children. She thought she detected a look of sheepishness on his face. Gwyn insisted on returning to help Carys and between them they hauled out the bath, emptied it in the lane just outside the back door and returned it to the large rusty hook in the wall.

Carys had prepared supper of boiled potatoes and cabbage with mugs of strong, black tea. Meg couldn't help noticing that Carys had only served herself one of the potatoes. The children, already fed on bread and jam, didn't eat much. The baby, it seemed, was still being breast fed. No wonder it looked so pinched and disinterested Meg thought, it was obviously suffering from malnourishment. The vegetables, Carys informed them had been grown by Gareth in his small allotment two streets away. Meagre as the meal and the surroundings were, Gwyn and Meg felt that at least they were with family.

Once the meal was over, Gareth gratefully accepted a cigarette from his brother and they sat silently smoking in front of the fire, obviously happy to see each other again. Meg helped Carys to clear the remnants of the meal and then to put the children to bed upstairs. Gareth, Carys and the children would all sleep in one room for the time being. The other tiny bedroom above the scullery had been vacated to accommodate Meg and Gwyn. Four adults and four small children in such a confined space thought Meg, wistfully remembering the room she had to herself when she lived with the doctor.

It would be a tight fit, yet they would manage. Meg would pull her weight with the housework and even help with the children while the men were at work until, hopefully, she and Gwyn could find a place of their own.

The baby whimpered half-heartedly as her mother removed her, once more, from her breast. Three of the children slept in one small bed made up on the floor with the baby in the same bed as its parents.

Once the children were settled, the two women came down the creaking, uncarpeted stairs to rejoin the men. As promised, Gareth went up to say goodnight to the children.

"Oh, please love, don't wake the baby."

Meg noticed again how tired her sister-in-law looked. Although she could only be a couple of years her senior, Carys seemed much older. Her once lustrous long auburn hair was lifeless, already streaked with grey around the temples and there were dusky shadows under her sad eyes. Dark blue knotted veins bulged in her thin calves and swollen feet. Despite the inevitable disruption, Carys seemed glad to have Meg and Gwyn in her home. It was obvious that she looked forward to the female company which Meg would provide.

Gareth returned to the room.

"Love, I thought I might take our Gwyn out for a bit of a walk, show 'im the village, like. He can come with me in the morning when we go to the pit, but it'll be dark then. Thought 'e might like to see where 'ell be livin'" Gareth said self-consciously as the two women entered the little kitchen where the brothers were still sitting in front of the fire.

"Good idea, love. You could show 'im the Institute and the readin' room where you like to go. Perhaps even half a pint as well?" As she said this, Meg noticed that Carys bit her lip slightly, probably unsure if Gareth had any money.

"My treat, brother" offered Gwyn, sensing the same thought. "We've a bit of catchin' up to do, aven't we, boyo? Give you girls a chance to get to know each other."

"Make the most of it while the kids are in bed. Not much chance of 'avin' a chat when *they're* around" Gareth said by way of endorsing the opportunity of spending some time away from the house with his brother. He took his cap from the nail behind the kitchen door and the brothers left, obviously pleased to be in each other's company again

"Poor Gareth; I can't remember when 'e last went out of a night. Do 'im the world of good it will" Carys said wistfully as the brothers departed.

Meg studied her sister-in-law again as they took the men's place by the fire.

"He's right. We don't get much time to ourselves when the kids are around. And I can't think when I last 'ad someone to talk to" said Carys.

"I don't know that many women in the village, not to talk to properly anyway. Both of us are outsiders.

"Gareth's a good husband and father, you know," she added. "Not like most of the men round here who spend the evenin's they're not workin' at the Institute. He likes to use the readin' room there but 'e doesn't get much time."

Meg didn't reply but looked at her sister-in-law encouragingly, sensing that there was more to come.

"'Elps me with the kids, you know when 'e's not at work. Takes them up to the allotment with 'im, sometimes even to the little park at the end of the village."

It was obvious she wanted to say more. Meg waited, smiling.

Carys sensed Meg's silence as invitation to say more. She went on talking.

"Sometimes 'elps me to clear up when the kids are in bed. Not many men around here do that!"

As if on cue, a sudden cry came from upstairs, "Mam! Mam! The baby's cryin' again!" It was Hugh.

Carys rose slowly from her chair. "Better go up or she'll wake the other two", she said wearily.

Meg heard her mount the creaking stairs again. She could hear the baby whimpering through the thin floorboards. Soon the whimpering stopped as she heard Carys humming soothingly. Meg waited apprehensively for Carys to return, uncertain about whether she wanted to hear what she was going to say. Like Carys she too had few women friends in whom she could confide.

After a while she heard Carys's footsteps coming down. She reappeared and returned to the shiny wooden armchair with its straight back. By now it was dark, and Meg had lit the stump of a candle and placed it on the table. Carys threw some lumps of coal onto the fire from the bucket which Gareth had filled before he went out, then stared listlessly as the flames flickered greedily over the new lumps.

"She's hungry you know, the baby," she said in a monotone. "I don't 'ave enough milk, you see."

Through the dim light Meg noticed Carys's face where the flames from the fire were reflected in her moist eyes.

She leaned forward and touched Carys's hand, calloused and bony, chapped and red. She had begun to twist the corner of her faded pinafore and seemed surprised by the physical contact from her sister-in-law. It was obvious to Meg that closeness was not something she had experienced very often, particularly from another woman. She was overwhelmed by this gesture which breached the reservoir of tears causing it to run down her hollow cheeks.

"What is it, Cariad? Meg asked gently, squeezing her hand more tightly.

She had a sense that she already knew the answer.

Carys' shoulders heaved as she began to sob. She tried to wipe her wet cheeks and her runny nose with the back of her hand but that was insufficient, so she covered her face with her pinafore. Between sobs she whispered,

"I'm six weeks gone".

More sobs then, "Looks like I'm expectin', in the family way again. Couldn't believe it then I recognised that sick feelin' again and I knew it had to be true."

Meg remained silent and continued to hold Carys's hand, waiting to see if she would go on. After a few sniffles, "It's so hard, you know. After the baby was born, Gareth was so careful. 'E was really good and for a long time we didn't …. well you know. And even if we did, we never went all the way. Gareth's always taken charge of these things. I mean, it's the man's job, isn't it? 'E said it didn't matter to 'im; 'e didn't want us to 'ave any more children. We've got more than we can afford already and 'e didn't want to make any more work for me. After all, three of the kids are girls, so it's not like they can go into the pit with their dad in a few years, not like our Hugh. It's not like Gareth didn't care for me. He's always been a thoughtful 'usband, not like some of the men round 'ere who only care about themselves. After all, it *is* their right, isn't it? The ministers tell you that at the chapel. It's in the Bible, isn't it? Men always 'ave the last word, isn't it?

"Then one day not long ago I, well stupid really, slipped on the wet floor when I was gettin' 'is bath ready. Luckily our Hugh was in 'ere mindin' the little ones. I didn't really hurt myself badly, just twisted my ankle a bit. Like well, some women can get really badly scalded. Anyway, Gareth was really kind. Worried sick 'e was that it could 'ave been really bad. "E said I should've waited until 'e got 'ome to 'elp but you can't do that can you? All the women know that you 'ave the water ready for when the men come 'ome."

Despite knowing that she would be shocked by what Carys was about to reveal, Meg nodded slowly, hoping it would embolden her to continue, but she didn't need encouragement now, being only too grateful for the opportunity to tell her story. Meg sighed.

"He must still 'ave been worried that night and, well, one thing led to another and, well, Gareth has always been such a gentle, kind man. I knew it was hard for him. I didn't want to take that pleasure away from 'im and I thought well, just this one time couldn't do any harm, could it? And me still feeding the child, I thought it would be alright, see? I thought it would be safe, just this once."

To her horror, Meg realised that she was quite ignorant of such matters. She was newly married and, after living away from home for most of her youth had, like Carys, few close women friends. Her mother had never talked to her about what to expect from marriage. Like Carys and, she supposed, the few married women she knew, she welcomed the thought that her husband would take care of 'those matters'. Besides, Gwyn had told her, in not so many words, that he was prepared to take on that responsibility. She trusted Gwyn. Carys was right, a man obviously knew about these things, whereas she was largely naïve and was happy to remain so and for him to take the lead. She thought that was what he wanted. After an initial conversation about what they expected from marriage, which had been short and, to Meg, embarrassing, they hadn't mentioned that side of their marriage again. She was happy; she didn't want to talk about it; she didn't think it was a woman's place to take an active role. It would be brazen and surely, talking about it would take away all the mystery. It would, Meg thought, be wrong.

Both women were quiet for a while, absorbed in their own thoughts. Carys continued staring into the fire. Her sobbing had ceased. She breathed in; a long, shuddering sigh from her roused Meg from her own thoughts. It suddenly occurred to Meg, "Does Gareth know?"

"I told him last night. I knew it would be hard to tell him when there were other people in the house. The walls are so thin."

"What's going to happen? What will you do?" enquired Meg, concerned for her sister-in-law and, at the same time guiltily relieved that this wasn't her problem.

"I don't know. I thought I might ask some of the women round here. I don't know them all that well, but there's some of the mothers at school might know what to do."

"What to do?" Meg was confused. How could these other women help? Surely it was a problem for Carys and Gareth, and nothing to do with other people.

Carys looked at Meg. She hesitated, worried that she had said too much and shocked her. She was correct in her assumption. Meg, largely ignorant of these matters, had no idea what Carys intended to do. Nevertheless, Carys went on.

"Most of the women round here 'ave been like me at some time or other. Not all of them had the babies though. I've heard them talk. Sometimes they swallow something to make it go away. I've heard them talk about knittin' needles and crochet hooks, even church candles!" At this Meg cringed visibly.

"Oh, Carys! You can't …."

Meg was repelled but was prevented from saying anything further. Almost on cue, the latch clicked, and the door slowly opened. As the brothers entered, Carys gripped Meg's wrist.

"Please" she hissed frantically, "you mustn't tell Gwyn what I said".

It would have been hard for Gareth not to have noticed his wife's red, swollen eyes and flushed cheeks. Although he said nothing, Meg could see that her brother-in-law was uncomfortable. Gwyn seemed oblivious to the tension in the room.

"Well now," Gareth announced, rubbing his hands together with forced joviality, an attempt to cover his embarrassment. "Time for bed isn't it if we've got to be up for work in the morning?"

Carys suddenly remembered that she had forgotten to put out Gareth's pit clothes and boots for morning, nor had she put up his snap for mid-morning; a couple of left-over cold potatoes would have to do. She was grateful for the opportunity to escape and tend to her chores. Meg, still a novice at these tasks, also fetched Gwyn's pit clothes from upstairs and placed them on a chair by the fire the way she had seen her mother do for her father and later her brothers. The four of them took turns, stumbling over the rough yard, to use the privy then quietly went up the wooden stairs.

Meg found it hard to settle. She was glad of the dark. Her cheeks burned. She had been appalled by what Carys had told her, not just about the pregnancy, but the way she had spoken so freely about how she came to get pregnant and how she thought it might be possible to remedy the situation Meg had spent much of her adolescence working away from home, mostly with relative strangers — older strangers. She had never heard anyone talk so freely about such private matters. She was surprised that Carys had found the courage to confide in her.

"One thing's certain" she thought to herself, "there's no way I'll let myself in for that sort of trouble."

She had been prepared for Gwyn to take care of the physical side of their marriage. She hoped she would never find herself in the same sort of trouble that Carys was in right now. Even if being out of work meant they didn't have the shilling or so to pay for the means to prevent it.

"Well" she determined, "If we can't afford it, we just won't do it. Gwyn will have to get used to the fact that I'm not taking any risks."

She looked at Gwyn's sleeping outline in the dim light coming through the curtain-less window. She hoped she would have enough resolve. The thought of her sister-in-law's predicament told her she would.

Long before dawn, there was a barely discernible knocking on the bedroom door, and she heard the stairs creak as Gareth crept downstairs barefoot.

"Time to go, love" said Gwyn as he rolled out of the sagging bed. "Don't get up."

He bent to kiss her head and followed his brother downstairs. She could hear their muffled voices through the uncarpeted floorboards and then the door silently closed. Carys too was still in bed. Meg lay there listening to the familiar tramping of pit boots and the occasional greeting and guffaw as the men and boys traipsed to work in the dark morning, just as they did for six days of every week. Despite the feeling of guilt that she had let Gwyn go off to work while she stayed in bed, she was grateful after her restless night. She rolled into the warm patch Gwyn had left behind. She remembered that her mother had been so superstitious that she never let her husband go off to work in the morning without seeing him out of the door. But one day he did not come home, so it made no difference in the end.

She heard the children's noise from downstairs and, quickly dressing, she joined them. It was a pathetic scene. Hugh was in the kitchen trying his best to feed the two little girls while the baby lay listlessly in a makeshift crib in the corner. Did these children never eat anything else but bread and a scraping of jam?

Before Meg had time to speak, Carys came through the door obviously returning from the privy. "Sorry Cariad, I just feel so sick in the mornings. Just as well I don't feel like eatin'" she said with a wan smile.

From the way Carys avoided any eye contact with Meg, it was obvious she regretted talking so freely the evening before. After seeing the children eating, Meg too had little appetite, but with some encouragement from Carys managed to drink a mug of hot, weak tea.

Hugh's sores still prevented him from going to school and the two women and children passed the day together. Meg helped Carys with the housework and the children, both trying to pretend that the previous evening's conversation had not taken place. In the middle of the afternoon they heard the pit siren announcing the end of the day shift and soon afterwards the tramp and shouting of the men as they retraced their steps home.

The copper was lit in the morning so that there would be enough hot water for two baths. Reluctantly Carys let Meg perform this chore. It was after all not new to her. She had watched her mother trudge between copper and bath. The dangerous, backbreaking work was often the cause of miscarriages among pregnant women. Perhaps this was the reason for Carys's reluctance to let Meg do the work? Later in the evening they all sat down to the usual potatoes and bread washed down with mugs of black tea.

Meg enjoyed the housework when the men were out at work. Not having a house of her own, she loved cleaning this one. Carys, fatigued and lethargic much of the time, did not object. It was almost like being back with the Jones's, sweeping, polishing and scrubbing the front doorstep. She even began to pass the time of day with some of the neighbouring women as they pegged out the washing together. However, unlike her time with the Jones's where there were no children, the pride in her work was short-lived. Some days the two women would walk into the village with the children to buy a few modest rations from the small shop, or pick vegetables, mostly potatoes, onions and some of that year's bumper crop of runner beans from Gareth's allotment. When they weren't working down the pit, Gwyn would often help his brother with the gardening. Women stood in groups at the end of the street, like Carys, wearing pinafores with thin shawls round their shoulders. Carys would sometimes stop and talk to them although they would still nod and look suspiciously at Meg.

This was the routine that developed in the crowded household, only modified by the varying shifts worked by the two men. The women shared the housework and childcare. Meg was happy looking after the toddlers but found it hard to feel anything but pity for the emaciated, mewling baby whom Carys was now trying to wean. Mostly she fed the baby with mashed potato and what milk she could spare. She noticed that Carys had developed the habit of sitting downstairs, not going up to bed until she thought Gareth would be asleep. Although she and Meg became friends, Carys never again confided in her. It was as though their earlier conversation had never taken place. Hugh's sores gradually healed, although he passed them on to each of the girls, including the baby.

On the day Hugh was to return to school, Carys announced she would go with him just to make sure there were no problems. She put her old shawl round her thin shoulders and, on her feet, a pair of even more ancient, down-at-heel shoes. As usual, she wore no stockings. Carys and Hugh left the house. Assuming her sister-in-law would return soon, Meg began the daily routine, glad that the house would be relatively peaceful even for a short while. Gareth had left early for his day shift and Gwyn was asleep upstairs as he was working nights. Meg kept busy, enjoying her short-lived freedom. The house was spotless and even the presence of the little girls was welcome. Mercifully, the baby slept for most of the time. Intermittently, Meg opened the door and scanned the street. There was a small cluster of women at the corner, but no sign of Carys. By the time she fed the girls at lunch time, Carys was still absent and Meg became anxious.

She was sitting by the fire with Mared on her lap when the door slowly scraped open and Carys stumbled into the room. She looked ghastly. Her hair was damp and hung even more limply around her flushed face. She was obviously in considerable discomfort. Alarmed, Meg leaped out of the chair causing the dosing child on her knee to jump and let out a startled cry. This disturbed the other two children who, with a sense of distress, began to cry in sympathy.

"My God, Carys!"

"Privy. Quick! I have to get to the privy".

Carys was moaning and gripping her stomach as she struggled through the scullery to reach the back door.

Meg placed the crying child on the chair and, ignoring the cries of the other two, ran after her sister-in-law, still clutching her stomach with one hand. The other was over her mouth as she tottered uneasily over the rough yard. She barged through the door of the privy, fortunately unoccupied. Meg could already hear the heaving and groaning through the open door.

"Whatever is it, Cariad?" Meg gasped breathlessly as she entered the privy.

The question was answered by another groan as Carys's body, slumped over the wooden seat, heaved and writhed. Evidently the urge to vomit had been the greater impulse. Slumped on the earthen floor, Meg saw that Carys had soiled herself and was lying in a pool of urine and blood. Meg put her hand over her mouth and nose. Although the stench was overpowering, Meg thought she could discern the smell of alcohol. After what seemed ages, Carys lay back against the wall panting and exhausted, disheveled and filthy. She began to whimper.

By now the children's commotion downstairs had woken Gwyn. Ignoring the wailing children, he hurried unsteadily down the yard, pulled up his braces over his vest, his disheveled hair on end. He put his head round the open door. A startled look came into his eyes as he saw the two women huddled together against the wall.

"For God's sake, Meg, what is it? What's going on?"

"Quick, help me to get her into the house."

With a supreme effort Meg managed to keep her voice as even as possible, for some reason, an image of Dr Jones, bag in hand, came into her mind.

"Can you manage, love?" she whispered to the stricken Carys who looked blankly at her. Slowly, she nodded submissively; she seemed barely conscious.

"I done it, you know" she kept murmuring, saliva running from the corners of her mouth; her nose, like Hugh's, running.

"I'm sorry love," Meg mumbled to Gwyn; "it's not very nice."

She put a finger over her mouth in answer to his quizzical look. Between them they lifted Carys from the earth floor and the trio staggered back to the house. The racket from inside and outside the house soon roused the neighbours. Curious women stood on doorsteps looking out of open doors. One or two ventured superfluously, "Everything alright?"

Husband and wife were too preoccupied to reply. Others muttered incomprehensibly or just tut-tutted. Many of the women were familiar with this scene before and understood the reason for it.

By this time, the three children were completely distraught. "Mam! Mam!" The older girl wailed between sobs.

It's alright, love" Meg said in a feeble attempt to reassure her.

Somehow, between them Meg and Gwyn managed to haul the stricken Carys up the stairs, her condition rapidly deteriorating. Despite her filthy state, they put her on to their bed, which was still warm from Gwyn's slumber.

Panting from exertion, Meg said to Gwyn "Can you see to the kids? Then bring me a bowl of hot water, the copper's boiling. I'll explain later".

Gwyn, still bewildered, his sleep having been suddenly and violently interrupted, went obediently downstairs. He had no idea what to do about the children whose sobbing now alternated with loud snivels. Instinctively he thought that Carys's need was greater than that of the children. He filled a large, chipped enamel basin which he found in the sink with hot water and grabbed one of the towels which had been put out for Gareth. Just as he reached the bottom of the stairs, someone came into the room. It was Mattie Price from next door. Even in this situation he was surprised at how much these women resembled each other, the way they dressed, their pinched faces. Mattie took one look at Gwyn, "I'll take them, love" she said pragmatically as she gathered up the three little girls.

Without acknowledging her, Gwyn carried the bowl of steaming water upstairs as carefully as he could. After handing it to Meg and glancing at the wan, bedraggled form on the bed he was happy to retreat. The stench was overpowering. As he went out the door, he shot Meg a terrified look. "My God, Meg, she's not — she isn't going to die, is she?"

Meg's face was as flushed as Carys's was now pale.

"Run for the doctor, there's one at the bottom of Chapel Row, Dr Llewellyn."

Two at a time Gwyn ran down the stairs, slipping on the last one. The door slammed. Meg turned her attention back to Carys whose eyes were already beginning to sink back into her head. She looked deathly pale.

"Listen, love" she said soothingly, "I'm going to try and clean you up a bit and make you more comfortable. Gwyn's gone for the doctor."

At this, a terrified look came into Cary's eyes which seemed to act as a stimulant. She gripped Meg's wrist as she set about sponging her dirty, tear-stained face.

"I can't ... I can't .... I .... Gareth ..." Meg ignored the feeble protest.

"I done it." She repeated. "Sorry Meg, *bach,*" Carys gasped. "Sorry I couldn't tell you".

Almost deliriously she continued, "I went to this house in Osment Street."

Carys told Meg what had happened.

Haltingly, she told Meg that one of the women she knew had given her the name and address of another woman who ran a boarding house in Osment Street who agreed to help her. Meg's heart started beating rapidly, and she could feel the blood pulsing in her temples. She must clean Carys up before the doctor arrived. She tried to keep her talking, that way she felt she would be alright.

"She's helped lots of women like me. She was quite kind and didn't want a lot of money.

"She told me to lie on the bed and put something inside me. Oh my God, Meg, it really hurt. Then she gave me something to drink. I think it might have been gin. Then she mixed some powder with it and made me drink that too.

"When I started to feel ill, she said I couldn't stop there, and it would be best for me to get home as soon as I could.

"It hurt so much …. the pains in my belly, I felt so sick. Oh Meg, I think it's worse than actually *havin'* the baby.

"It was so bad I had to stop on the way home. I went behind a wall. It was awful. Meg, I think the baby's gone. My baby, I feel so empty now. I didn't want to get rid of it, but what else could I do? Do you think God will punish me for what I've done? My head … it feels as though it's goin' to burst."

Gently and firmly Meg removed the putrid clothing and washed the worn-out Carys with firm but gentle strokes, trying to remove the blood and other matter. Both the odour, and the implication of what Carys had done, made Meg feel sick but she carried on. Once Carys was clean, she dressed her in one of her own nighties. Completely exhausted, Carys lay back, too weak now for further narration. She was bleeding profusely, and Meg was afraid the doctor might arrive too late. What if he was already out on a call? She remembered Dr Jones being called out in cases of emergency. Was this why he had sometimes been called so suddenly?

She tore up one of the towels which she took from her suitcase to stem the flow of blood. Finally, she heard the door open and close downstairs. "Thank God" she sighed.

"Carys? Meg?" It was Gareth. Amid the pandemonium she had lost all track of time and hadn't even noticed the noise of the returning miners.

Fear again came into Carys's glazed eyes and she shook her head wearily from side to side.

"He has to know love. Upstairs" she called. At that moment Gwyn arrived back with Dr Llewellyn.

"Stay there!" the doctor snapped at the men as he bounded up the stairs, surprisingly agile for an ageing, overweight man.

The scene which confronted him when he entered the room was all too familiar. "When in God's name will these people learn?" he cursed under his breath as he approached the bed.

A quick examination confirmed he had been right in ordering an ambulance to the house. From his bag he took out a syringe and vial.

"This should help until we can get you to the hospital — if we're lucky." He muttered.

The ambulance arrived and Dr Llewellyn went downstairs to greet it.

"You the husband?" he asked Gareth accusingly. "You'd better go with her. See what she's got to put up with."

Despite the pit grime, there was a discernible pallor on Gareth's face.

There was bumping on the stairs as the ambulance men appeared, carrying Carys on a stretcher. Gareth's eyes appeared even wider in his dirty face. Every door on the street was open now and men and women watched as the ambulance doors were banged and, bell clanging, it sped down the street, leaving a cloud of dust and asphalt in its wake.

Inside the now quiet house, Meg remained upstairs. When Gwyn went up, he found her sitting on the ravaged bed, trembling now that the crisis had subsided. The bowl of dirty, blood-stained water sat on a chair. Filthy wet clothing was strewn across the floor of the room. The nauseating odour persisted but it was now mixed with the faint smell of disinfectant. Gwyn sat beside his wife in the filth and placed a tentative arm around her shoulder. Both of them were shaking involuntarily.

They sat like this for a while, neither speaking. Finally, Meg broke the silence. "What about work, love? You've hardly had any sleep."

"I'll be alright, love. What about you?"

"Oh, Gwyn, I was so frightened. I just hope she'll be alright. I don't ever want to end up like that. I don't want to stay here. Isn't there somewhere else we could go?"

Meg told Gwyn about what Carys had told her that first evening. Gwyn was unaware of Carys's pregnancy as Gareth hadn't mentioned anything. She told him what Carys had said on that first evening about the man's responsibility and how she and Gareth must have been too shy to confide in each other. Meg didn't want her marriage to be like that. She loved Gwyn and knew now that they were equally responsible for what happened to them. It was unfair to expect the man to bear the sole burden of preventing an unwanted pregnancy. They talked for a long time about what they wanted from marriage and where they wanted to be, "Anywhere but here" they agreed.

Then Meg remembered the children. Where was Hugh? Surely school was over now. Together they cleaned up the room as best they could and went downstairs. Gwyn sank wearily onto the threadbare sofa. Meg went next door to retrieve the children, including Hugh whom Mattie had seen coming home from school with her own son and taken into her house with the other children. Mattie was good and said nothing about the events of the afternoon. She understood.

It was dark when an exhausted Gareth eventually returned from the hospital. The children had been fed and put to bed and it was almost time for and Gwyn to go to work. Meg left them sitting by the fire, diplomatically escaping to the scullery to fetch his dinner. She didn't know what to say to Gareth and wanted to be alone for a while. Leaving the brothers to talk, she excused herself, went upstairs and began to clean up some of the mess. She was thoroughly exhausted, physically and emotionally. She had been utterly shaken by the day's events. However, disturbing as the last few weeks had been, she knew they would change her outlook on life and could no longer remain the passive, compliant wife Carys had been. Look what had happened to her.

Although he too was exhausted, and faced the prospect of working through the night, Gwyn without speaking, prepared his brother's bath and stayed with him. Too weary to wash himself, Gwyn helped him. While he washed his brother's back, he told him that he and Meg thought it was best to leave. Gareth understood. Wearily he nodded. Gwyn told him how he'd heard that they wanted miners in the north of England, and he was going to look into it. Anyway, with conditions in the valleys, it would have to be an improvement for them. Gareth remained silent. When he was clean and dressed in fresh clothes, Gwyn brought Gareth to the fire and gave him the food Meg had prepared, then he left for his shift, dog-tired.

Meg was relieved when Carys returned from hospital a week later. She still looked pale and weak. The doctor told her he had done his best and was unsure whether she would be able to have more children. In any case, he told her of the new clinic which had recently opened at nearby Abertillery Hospital. For her own safety, he advised her to go there. Carys was unsure about whether she would. After all, she heard the minister had preached against it in the chapel. Meg felt it was futile to argue and, despite attacks from the pulpit, visited the clinic herself — with Gwyn's endorsement. It was up to Carys and Gareth what they did.

Meg and Gwyn stayed in Pontymawr for a few more weeks until Carys was stronger and able to look after herself, the children, the house and her husband. Then they left and made their way north. Their time in Pontymawr had been an edifying experience for them both. They knew they wanted a home of their own and, only when this happened, and felt secure would they consider starting a family. Unlike their Welsh relatives, they had made it their business to be armed with knowledge of how to make this possible.

Unlike Carys, Meg was not afraid to ask for advice. Her experience in Pontymawr helped her overcome any shyness, and no matter how difficult it might be, Meg was determined that in *their* marriage there would be no such secrets.

8

Godliness and Childbirth: Matters of Fertility

In the 1920s, the rate of maternal mortality in Britain was regarded as a national scandal. The mortality rate in childbirth from all causes in Wales alone was 5.52 per 1000.

This remained unchanged until 1930–1934, albeit with large regional variations, with higher percentages occurring in heavily industrialised regions.

In 1926 the maternal mortality rate in Wales was 4.29% per 1000 in women giving birth and 4.7% in the North of England compared to 3.78% and 3.43% in the Midlands and the South of England respectively. Maternal mortality was, in 1992 defined by the World Health Organisation as:

> 'The death of a woman while pregnant for, or within 42 days of termination of the pregnancy, irrespective of the duration of the pregnancy, from any cause related to or aggravated by the pregnancy or its management but not from an accidental or incidental cause.'

Although not defined in the 1920s, this definition would have been applicable to this era and environment where the majority of births occurred in the home and were either unattended or attended by women who were completely untrained and, in many cases, unfit for this work.

In the mid-19th century the Royal College of Surgeons introduced a Diploma of Midwifery. But twenty years later, when three women applied to do the course, they were refused entry as midwifery training was regarded by the medical profession as a waste of time. Elizabeth Garrett Anderson, the first British woman to qualify as a medical practitioner, presented evidence to the British Medical Association which demonstrated that an increased knowledge of midwifery reduced the number of maternal deaths. She advocated compulsory training in midwifery which subsequently became incorporated into medical training. The 1902 Midwives Act introduced mandatory training for midwives in England and Wales and prohibited the practice of untrained and uncertified midwives. The Act's intent was to gradually eliminate the use of *bona fide* midwives who, although regulated, were untrained. Initially, the required period of training for midwives was a mere three months. Yet by 1926 (just prior to Nan commencing her midwifery training) it was extended to a year.

However, new legislation did not entirely change entrenched ideas or adherence to tradition. Most confinements in depressed areas were still attended by the equivalent of local charwomen, many of whom were illiterate and dangerously unsanitary. Yet, for hundreds of years, these were the women who had delivered the children of working-class women such as miners' wives. Fewer trained midwives, let alone trained obstetricians, were available in these industrialised, unattractive areas of low socio-economic circumstances, so a high rate of maternal mortality persisted.

The most common cause of maternal death before 1930 was *puerperal sepsis*, 'childbed fever', accounting for about half the deaths. The cause of sepsis could often be attributed to the unhygienic practices of untrained midwives who most likely spread infections from confinement to confinement. Although by the late 19th century, antisepsis was being introduced into obstetric practice in hospitals, this was certainly not the case where untrained midwives attended home births. Post and ante-partum haemorrhages, which were more common in women who had already had a number of children, and toxaemia, common in young women giving birth for the first time, accounted for another quarter of deaths. Other causes were obstructed labour caused by a contracted pelvis, often the result of rickets. Ruptured uterus was common as was exhaustion, a sequel to a prolonged labour. Deaths from abortion, spontaneous or induced, were also frequent events. However, unskilled midwifery and unhealthy mothers continued to be the main cause of both infant and maternal mortality. There was no provision for ante natal management for these women. They received poor obstetric care from women who were uneducated with abysmal standards of practice and, living in areas of social and economic deprivation, they were often in poor health and badly nourished.

A division in professional opinion emerged as to the long-term contributing factors to deaths in mothers. While some attributed them to poverty and malnutrition, others believed the cause lay in poor clinical care. One area medical officer of health, with an understanding of poor nutrition and abysmal standards of hygiene, yet believing miners were well off stated:

> "Wages are high and nourishing food plentiful. Poor housing might play a part, but the main reason for maternal deaths was that the women of South Wales were cursed with ignorant midwives who spread puerperal fever from house to house."
>
> (*Deaths in Childbed from Eighteenth Century to 1935*.
> Irvine Loudon: London. *Medical History*, 1986, 30:41)

Elizabeth Garrett Anderson (1836–1917) was the first woman in England to qualify as a physician and surgeon. She graduated in medicine from the University of the Sorbonne in Paris yet, despite excelling in medical studies at the Middlesex Hospital in London, was not allowed to graduate with her male colleagues. In 1866, before she was able to qualify as a doctor in England, she opened the St Mary's Dispensary for Women and Children. Four years later, she became Visiting Medical Officer for the East London Hospital for Children.

In 1872 she transformed it into the New Hospital for Women in London. The hospital specialised in women's health and all the staff were women. It was renamed the Elizabeth Garrett Anderson Hospital in 1918 and continued to appoint only female staff until the 1980s. She lectured at the London School of Medicine for Women for 23 years, continuously advocating better obstetric care. In 1864, alarmed at the high rate of venereal disease within its armed forces, the British government passed the Contagious Diseases Act which essentially enshrined into law the notion that women were responsible for spreading such diseases as syphilis. It gave police the right to arrest any women in ports or garrison towns who they suspected of being prostitutes. Inevitably, many innocent women were rounded up and forced to undergo humiliating, often painful examinations.

Feminists, in disgust, turned to Garret Anderson, then the only practising female doctor in the country, and asked her to condemn the Act. She refused, believing it was a necessary preventive measure. For her stance, she was never forgiven by many members of the women's movement.

National Portrait Gallery: https://www.npg.org.uk/collections/search/portrait/mw242595/Elizabeth-Garrett-Anderson

In the 1920s and early 1930s, the Ministry of Health, convinced that poverty was the primary culprit of the high death rate, presented evidence which showed that, after the distribution of food supplements to poorer pregnant women, there was an associated decline in the rate of maternal deaths from 11.9% in 1934 to 4.0% in 1935. However, the research was flawed as, by this time, there had been a marked improvement in obstetric services.

The choice of food which was distributed was also unusual. Each woman was given:
- 4 ounces of Marmite,
- 6 ounces of extract of beef,
- 8 ounces of Ovaltine egg and milk extract,
- 3 ounces of dried milk, and a pint of fresh milk.

No fresh fruit or vegetables were included and, considering the self-sacrificing natures of these women, how much of the food supplement they gave to their children is unreported.

Despite being illegal early in the 20th century, abortion continued to be a common method of birth control. It was such a ubiquitous means of solving the problem of unwanted pregnancies that it became inextricably identified with birth control, the benefits of which came later to the working class than it did to their middle-class peers. In Britain in the early 1920's induced abortions were responsible for 15,000 female deaths per year.

Working class women had autonomously, and by sharing communal knowledge, made every effort to regulate their own fertility by concentrating on menstruation rather than intercourse. Women knew exactly what remedies were necessary to induce a late period and were able, somehow to procure the means. Nevertheless, there appears to have been an assumption that the *modus operandi* of birth control lay with the men. *Coitus interruptus* was the most used method of preventing pregnancy as was extended breast feeding after each birth — poor diet permitting. Chemical agents were commonly used to induce abortion. There remained an inherent, albeit cursory, adherence to the church's doctrine of sex being for the procreation of children. This supported the belief that if methods were 'natural' rather than 'mechanical devices' (such as condoms and diaphragms), they were not contravening religious doctrine. Difficulties associated with contraceptive methods, and the overarching fear of an unwanted pregnancy, led to partial abstinence from sexual intercourse.

The author A.J. Cronin, also a physician who practised in South Wales, was appointed to the Ministry of Mines to study medical problems in the mining industry. Cronin was familiar with the harsh, drab conditions in coal mining communities. Set in the Durham coal field in 1909, his 1935 novel *The Stars Look Down* represents the hardship faced by Martha, the wife of Robert Fenwick, a striking miner. She, her husband and three adult sons (also miners), inhabit a meagre two roomed hovel. As Robert was imprisoned for inciting an unofficial strike against dangerous working conditions at the mine, they have no income. Her youngest son is 15 when Martha finds herself pregnant and resenting her husband,

> 'Him, again, coming home in liquor, silently, doggedly, in liquor, to have his will of her.'

They have no food and even their clothes and shoes have been pawned to buy tea. After filling the bath for her sons' return from work, Martha goes into premature labour. The next-door neighbour is summoned as there is no money to pay a doctor or midwife. The child is stillborn, but Martha will have no funeral 'since … we can't face the expense'. Her youngest son realises the bitterness of the situation,
'Why shouldn't my mother have food, care, attention, all that her condition demanded? Why was this child not living, smiling, sucking at the breasts?'

In stark contrast, Harriett, wife of the owner of the mine, Richard Barrass, is pampered and neurotic and spends most of her life in bed

> '… she ate well …. her room was surrounded by bottles, tonics, sedatives, liniments, alleviates, antispasmodics, everything — all the physics that had been prescribed for her in the past five years.'
> Cronin A.J. *The Stars Look Down* (1935)

Fertility and Birth Control

In the early part of the 20th century, there was scant, reliable information about fertility control, particularly among the poorer working classes. Paradoxically, a greater range of contraceptive devices, considered to be more 'woman friendly', were available to middle class women who, nevertheless, continued to use abortion as a means of birth control. In 1910, about 1% of the total adult female population in Britain were using contraceptive appliances. By 1930, however, usage by middle-class women had risen to 40% compared to 28% use among working class women. The former were not only more knowledgeable about birth control, they had better relationships with their doctors and so more readily sought information and advice. Although condoms were the most used contraceptive method, they still preferred 'non-manual' methods such as withdrawal and even abstinence. There remained, however, an ingrained reluctance among couples to discuss the topic of sex and birth control.

Marie Carmichael Stopes (1880–1958) was a palaeobotanist with an exemplary academic pedigree. She studied botany and geology at University College, London, where she graduated BSc in 1902, followed by a DSc. She received a PhD in botany from Munich University, Germany, in 1904 and undertook a scientific expedition to Japan in 1907 which included visits to coal mines. During WWI she carried out scientific studies on coal for the British government.

She was publicly opposed to abortion (to which she

euphemistically referred as 'evacuation of the uterus') preferring preventive methods of birth control.

Her interest in providing contraception for the poor was believed to have been an adjunct to her support for eugenics (from *eugenes* - or *well-born*, the philosophy that argues that it is possible to improve the quality of the human race by discouraging reproduction by persons having genetic defects or presumed to have inheritable undesirable traits). She assumed this to have been particularly prevalent among the poor. Whether this opinion is correct or not, it remains the reason for a universally ambivalent regard for Stopes' work.

The Conversation
https://theconversation.com/married-love-the-1918-book-by-marie-stopes-that-helped-launch-the-birth-control-movement-93108

Marie Stopes' *Married Love*, published in March 1918, was arguably one of the most influential books of the 20th century. In colourful prose, her book presented intricate descriptions of sexual activity between men and women. She believed that marriage should be an equal partnership between a man and a woman and her publication brought the topic of intimacy in marriage, including the control of fertility — long a taboo subject — into the public domain so that it could now be willingly and rationally discussed by both men and women.

A year after the appearance of *Married Love* came the publication of *Wise Parenthood*, a 'practical sequel' to its predecessor, which provided information on various methods of birth control. It was 'Dedicated to all who wish to see our race grow in Strength and Beauty' (Stopes, M. *Wise Parenthood*, 1930; G.P. Putnam's: London).

MARRIED LOVE

A New Contribution to the
Solution of Sex Difficulties

BY

MARIE CARMICHAEL STOPES

*Doctor of Science, London; Doctor of Philosophy, Munich; Fellow
of University College, London; Fellow of the Royal Society of
Literature, and the Linnean Society, London*

*With a Preface by Dr. JESSIE MURRAY
and LETTERS from PROFESSOR E. H. STARLING, F.R.S.
and FATHER STANISLAUS ST. JOHN, S.J.*

London: A. C. Fifield
13, Clifford's Inn, E.C.4.
1918

Published in March 1918, after many publishers refused it because of its controversial subject, the preface to *Married Love* states that the intent of the book is to show couples how to enjoy a happy marriage, including 'great sex'. This, she believed, would reduce the number of unhappy people living in failed marriages

In 1921, a 16-page pamphlet *A Letter to Working Mothers on how to have healthy children and avoid weakening*, aimed at the poor, was distributed free of charge. It contained relevant information in a condensed form. The aim of the pamphlet may well have been a way of making amends as Stopes' work had been, until then, directed at the middle class and she was reputed to have little respect, or interest, in poor, working people.

> 'Could there be anything more unreasonable or cruel than to bring into life half a dozen children *doomed from birth* to ill health, poverty, and almost inevitable crime?'
> (Stopes, M. *Married Love* 2013; Scribe: Melbourne p22).

Simultaneously her organisation was renamed the Society for Constructive Birth Control and Racial Progress (CBC). The work of Marie Stopes' has been overshadowed by the fact that she was attracted to the eugenics movement. Eugenicists held the controversial view that by breeding and limiting births, it was possible to improve the genetic quality of the human species, thereby eliminating social problems caused through poverty and overpopulation. Birth control may have been exploited as a means to achieve this end.

Why the need for birth control?

The origins of the need to control reproduction can be found in the 1789 book *An Essay on the Principle of Population* by Thomas Malthus. Its thesis was that, during times of prosperity and growth, populations continue to increase until they outstrip available resources necessary to sustain their growth. Widespread poverty results unless certain 'events' — famine, disease or war which destroy large numbers of life — act as a means of controlling the population, restoring it to a sustainable level. Malthus believed in celibacy as a means of population control and advocated deferring marriage until later in life, thereby reducing the number of reproductive years.

Like all emergent ideologies, Malthusianism was embraced by various schools of thought and adapted to support their ideals. Advocates of Malthusianism were in favour of birth control and actively promoted it through various groups including feminists who, in 1870 coined the phrase 'voluntary motherhood'. Francis Galton, cousin of Charles Darwin and Victorian sociologist and psychologist, was also the founder of the Eugenics Society. He believed that intelligence and delinquency were inherited traits rendering people 'genetically inferior'. Conversely, he believed, their 'genetically superior' peers, should be encouraged to increase their numbers thereby enhancing the calibre of the human race.

As Marie Stopes became more interested in sexual matters, she increased her knowledge of sexual ethics and the physiology of reproduction. Among her formative influences at this time were the works of Havelock Ellis, a progressive reformer who studied human sexuality. A contemporary of Freud, Ellis was in favour of 'non-procreative sex' for pleasure. Ellis was pro-feminism believing that an emancipated woman, free to choose her own mate, would choose one who was 'eugenically sound' thus ensuring a higher quality of a future race. The poor, he believed produced larger numbers of 'poorer quality' offspring which would 'weaken' the race. It was among this group of people, according to Ellis, that birth control was most needed and the way to bring awareness to these people was by widespread education. While Stopes and her contemporaries have been responsible for innovation in contraception, the focus on eugenics is both unfortunate and disrespectful to many women, particularly those from poorer communities.

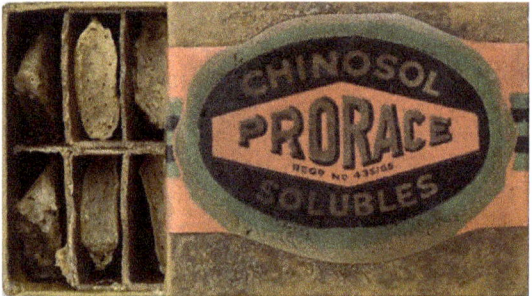

The 'Prorace' brand of contraceptives was developed by Dr Marie Stopes.

Distributed by the Mother's Clinic, which opened in London in 1921, these contraceptive pessaries contain spermicides to kill sperm. They were used alone or with other contraceptives, such as the cap or diaphragm. The pessaries were manufactured by John Bell & Croyden Limited of London. The trademarked 'Prorace' related to Stopes' belief in eugenics. Because it served the poor, Stopes arranged for a company to supply the Abertillery Hospital Clinic with reliable, cheap pessaries for 6d a pack rather than the usual price of 2s 6d.

400 BCE -1965 Vintage Contraceptives: https://mashable.com/2015/06/07/early-birth-control/

However, in 1885, in a Nottinghamshire colliery village surrounded by other pits, the fourth child of an uneducated coal miner was born. The pregnancy was neither planned, nor greeted with enthusiasm. Although the child's mother hailed from a middle-class family fallen on hard times, she became the wife of a coal miner and led the rough, 'hand-to-mouth' existence of a miner's wife. The child, David Herbert Lawrence, became one of the most influential writers of the 20th century. Contemplating his childhood Lawrence said, "If I think of my childhood it is always as if there was a sort of inner darkness, like the gloss of coal in which we moved and had our being." Yet even Lawrence was aware of the dilemma in which women found themselves. In his semi-autobiographical novel *Sons and Lovers*, Lawrence writes of a pregnant Gertrude Morel, the mother of his *alter ego* 'She felt wretched with the coming child …. she could not afford to have this third. She didn't want it.'

Marie Stopes, despite (or perhaps because of) her distinguished position in society, took a huge risk in publishing *Married Love*. Many prominent persons, such as the American, Margaret Sanger, birth control activist, sex educator, writer, and nurse, had fallen foul of the law for advocating birth control, a phrase which she had coined. Stopes became the target of Catholic abuse, and an article appeared in the *Daily Express* calling for her to be sent to prison as the author of an obscene publication. (*Married Love* was already banned as an obscene publication by the US Customs Service and remained as such until 1931.)

Rubber vault cap.

Contraceptive caps are also called cervical, vault or diaphragm caps. They are barrier contraceptives which sit over the cervix and act as a barrier to sperm entering the uterus.

From Wikimedia Commons, the free media repository

In 1922, the Ministry of Health, concerned by the maternal mortality rate, oversaw the establishment of Municipal Maternal and Child Welfare clinics where staff gave advice and information on pregnancy, childcare and contraception. Involvement of the government in public health was then an innovation. Although Marie Stopes' books had brought sex and contraception into the public arena for respectable discussion, there was still an ingrained perception that birth control, and various contraceptive methods, were linked to prostitution.

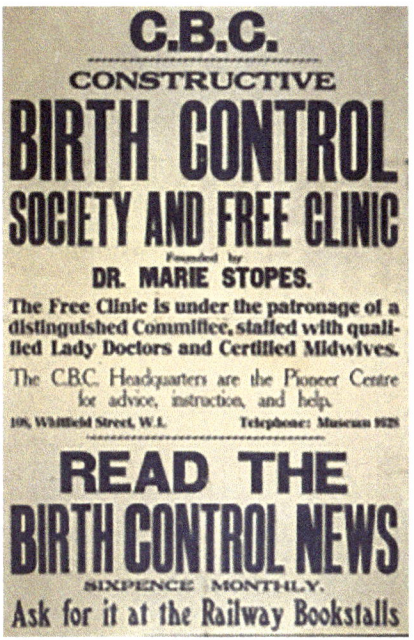

Notice in *The South Wales Gazette* announcing the 1925 opening of the Birth Control Clinic at Abertillery Hospital

Out of the Blue Artifacts: https://outoftheblueartifacts.com/abertillery-birth-control-clinics/

Alarmed at the publicity surrounding Marie Stopes and her work, a delegation of the Catholic Women's League met with the Minister of Health. As a result of this meeting, a directive was issued from his department proscribing the distributing of such information. The penalty for contravening the directive was dismissal. A certain Nurse Daniels from the Edmonton centre in North London was dismissed for continuing to provide information to women in spite of the ban. Women who wanted information on reproductive health, the directive insisted, were to be referred to private doctors or hospitals. Once again this proved a disincentive to poorer women who were unable to afford the necessary fees. Married working class women, who were not themselves employed, were not covered by the National Health Insurance Act. However, in 1930, the government partially gave way to birth control campaigners by conceding that existing Maternity and Child Welfare clinics could, after all, distribute birth control instruction to mothers whose health would be injured by further pregnancies.

At this time there was controversy in Abertillery, a coal mining district of South Wales, which greatly affected the lives of women in mining communities. In 1922, a community hospital was opened in the town. It was partly financed by contributions from local coal miners who were represented on the hospital board. For a further small contribution, women could avail themselves of the hospital's facilities rather than, as previously, travel almost twenty miles to Newport for treatment.

The harsh economic circumstances made the Welsh mining valleys grim places to live and bring up children. People were struggling to survive. Local newspapers were full of reports about maternal and childhood deaths, including one telling of the discovery of the body of a newborn baby thrown into a truck. It was obvious that self-induced abortion was being used as a form of birth control to restrain the ever-increasing population. A cultural reticence to discuss the topic of family planning, at least in public, made this a difficult issue to address. A solution to the problem was badly needed.

In 1923, when Abertillery Hospital had been operating for a year, David 'Dai' Daggar, the miners' delegate from Six Bells Lodge, was elected to the hospital administrative committee as their representative. He was well acquainted with the severity of local living conditions, including the situation of a miner who was evicted for non-payment of rent. (The miner, his wife and nine children had existed on £2 19s 6d eating only bread and margarine for over a year.) Daggar was passionate about improving conditions for the local people and began a strenuous eighteen-month campaign to open a birth control clinic within the hospital to provide information for the married women in the district. His campaign was successful, and he won a mandate from the committee to proceed with the proposal.

Abertillery District Hospital, opened in 1922, was built from contributions by miners of a penny per pound per week. For a similar small contribution, they could also use the hospital's facilities. Abertillery Hospital housed the first ever hospital birth control clinic outside London.

https://en.wikipedia.org/wiki/Abertillery_and_District_Hospital

On Monday 15 June 1925, an advertisement appeared in the town which announced the opening of a 'People's Clinic' for birth control and social welfare at Abertillery Hospital where a qualified nurse would be available to give free advice to married women. All enquiries were to be addressed to the hospital. In September the clinic opened and for a consultation fee of one shilling, married women could receive advice on methods of birth control from 'Lady Specialists'. Apart from the first birth control clinic opened by Dr Stopes at Holloway, North London in 1921, Abertillery was the first official birth control clinic in the country and on 8 November at Abertillery Gymnasium, at a Grand Lecture convened by the Abertillery Constructive Birth Control Committee, Marie Stopes was guest speaker. She also agreed to train prospective staff in the management of the clinic, based on the same lines as the centres in London.

 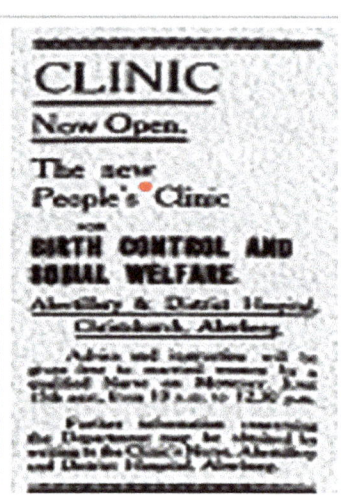

The Abertillery Hospital Constructive Birth Control Clinic opened on 15 June 1925. It was the first ever hospital birth control clinic outside London. Facilities included a waiting room, two fitting rooms, sterilising room, lavatories and two sinks with running cold and electrically heated hot water. Whether or not encouraged by their husbands, the clinic was well attended by local women, although most were ignorant of birth control and often confused abortion with contraception.

Out of the Blue Artifacts: https://outoftheblueartifacts.com/abertillery-birth-control-clinics/

There was, however, reticence on the part of some board members about the venture and considerable active opposition from local religious bodies who dominated the consciences of many of their congregations On 19 June, four days after the opening of the initial clinic, a vitriolic article printed in *The Monmouth Free Press* denounced the proposed clinic, portending a battle for its survival, with the words 'birth control is wrong and evil.'

Although the intervention of Marie Stopes, at Daggar's request, appeared to dispel some residual opposition, fierce sparring between proponents and opponents took place in the form of a barrage of protests and letters to the press. Spearheading the opposition was a local clergyman, Ivor Evans, who together with his fellow clergy, condemned the clinic from the pulpit. The campaign of opposition deteriorated into personal attacks on supporters of the clinic, particularly Marie Stopes. Such a publicly bitter fracas adversely affected the number of clinic attendees, but despite this, and sustained division of opinion among hospital committee members, the clinic remained operative for a further year.

The General Strike of 1926 put an end to financial contributions from miners and the clinic closed that year. However, in 1930 at Pontypridd, fifteen miles from Abertillery, a new birth control clinic was established. It would appear, at least from the point of view of birth control, the religious establishment was no friend of working-class women in general and miners' wives in particular.

The opening of birth control clinics signified a new era. Women, for the first time, were able to take control of their own fertility. Nevertheless, in areas remote from large centres, such as the mining communities of South Wales, many families were still being pushed into starvation and poverty, struggling to feed large numbers of children — many whose births had been unplanned. Class remained a significant issue in sexual politics. Conditions for the poor could only improve when contraception was available to these women and give them the *choice* to accept or refuse motherhood along with the ability to control the size of their families. Unwanted pregnancies and abortions continued as did the pervasive authority of the local church and chapel in regions during economically depressed times. And times were about to become much worse.

Miners vote to go on strike (Theatre Workshop, Scotland 2013)
https://www.redpepper.org.uk/not-forgetting-who-you-are/

9
Not a penny off the pay…

The capitalists gave a mouth to the earth,
To get the black gold out,
Something for the coal miners to cheer about,
Ready the manual workers are to drag coal from dirt.

The miners find both heaven and hell within,
Sustain the toils holding the souls in hands,
Some lose sanity, some bid goodbye to the loved organs,
Some like D.H. Lawrence's father dive into sin.

Yet life like the invincible time goes on,
Yet the children dream of a future better,
But the bitter world loves to conspire,
Against those who barely anything own.

Frustration keeps mocking,
At the labourers as if a burden to carry forever,
Or a virus spreading from one heart to another,
Keeps the handful of peace perishing.

The money mongers don't perceive the sweats and blood,
They like Iago are ruthless creatures,
Only discern the language of the spiralling numbers,
And the miners watch the charitable sky searching for God!

Coal Miners
Md. Ziaul Haque

Coal had propelled 19th century Britain into pre-eminence as a world power and became a symbol for the country's greatness. It had powered factories, mills and furnaces. It had fuelled steam ships which enabled the export trade to boom. Between 1873 and 1913, British coal production more than doubled while exports trebled during the same period. Coal had driven the Industrial Revolution creating enormous wealth for those who owned the mines. Those who laboured underground to produce the source of this wealth were not granted any share of it. By the second decade of the 20th century their living standards were as deplorable as they were at the beginning of the coal-powered boom.

As they reaped the inevitable profits of coal, the colliery owners, whom British Prime Minister Harold Wilson would later describe as 'A harder faced bunch of Gradgrinds never polluted British industry' (Wilson, Harold [1977] *A Prime Minister on Prime Ministers*; p 177) became convinced that it was their business acumen which was responsible for profits. They were deluding themselves. The industry has always relied on a large workforce to mine the coal to create this profit. While the industry continued to thrive and produce profits for the owners there was no reason to invest capital on infrastructure, or even safety. Owners had invested in machinery and equipment only when it became necessary to sustain productivity. Historically, they had only taken action to improve conditions, with great reluctance, when forced by government legislation such as the various safety acts of the late 19th and early 20th centuries.

There were however, as Harold Wilson conceded, a few exceptions. These probably included Muschamp Bainbridge of the Bolsover Colliery Company but, by and large, mine owners showed little regard for the conditions of their employees. Some, the Wentworths of South Yorkshire, for instance, adopted a patronisingly protective attitude to their employees, while others were downright brutal. Miners' pay depended on the quality and quantity of coal they produced. Many owners, to minimise costs, were not averse to having their managers insist that certain coal was of inferior quality and, in some instances, condoned tampering with weighing equipment.

The Subsidised Coal Miner — Poor beggar
Trade Union Unity Magazine, 1925

Although labour was the biggest cost in coal production, there was no shortage of manpower. Seventy-five per cent of the cost of coal production was labour. In 1830, the number of people working in the coal industry (including women and children) was 109,000 and by 1901 it was 1.1 million. Mine owners could reap huge profits since, in many cases, they had inherited land which contained lucrative seams of coal. During temporary slumps in trade, they were able to maintain their profits by cutting prices and lowering wages until conditions improved. Short sighted owners showed little regard or concern for external factors such as the need for coal to drive industry.

William "Billy" Charles de Meuron Wentworth-FitzWilliam, 7th Earl FitzWilliam (1872–1943)

On his succession to the Earldom, he became one of the richest men in Britain, inheriting an estate of land, industrial and mineral-right holdings worth over £4 billion in present terms. His family owned and operated coal mines in South Yorkshire which employed over 2,000 men. He was reputed to have been responsible for ensuring the Fitzwilliam collieries were safe and that his workers received help during economic hardship. However, his sister criticised him saying he had so much while everyone else had so little.

It had been hard labour and the historically low wages of the miners that had contributed to the wealth of families such as the Wentworths and Dukes of Newcastle and Portland, whereas the lives of those who mined the coal were cut short by diseases endemic in coal mining. Those who avoided early death or permanent injury from frequently occurring accidents languished, their lungs damaged by pneumoconiosis. They were blinded by nystagmus, from working long hours in darkness. Their stature became contorted and stunted by years of backbreaking work in cramped conditions. And they lived in tiny hovels which lacked even the most basic facilities. What happened if they were ill? How were their children educated? In these squalid living conditions, it was impossible for wives to keep their homes clean and disease free, let alone clothe and provide an adequate diet for their children. By contrast, the owners for whom they toiled included some of the wealthiest, most powerful and influential aristocrats in Britain who, by the sheer good fortune of owning huge swathes of the British countryside, were able to furnish grand country houses and magnificent residences in London's most salubrious areas.

Wentworth Woodhouse, near Rotherham in Yorkshire, once owned by the Fitzwilliam-Wentworths is considered to be the largest private residence in the United Kingdom. The house has 300 rooms and is surrounded by a 73-hectare park and an estate of 6,100 hectares. It is now owned by the National Trust.

Black Diamonds and how the other half lived: The Guardian, 23 November 2015.

In 1909, when Nan was a two-year-old and her father was still working in the mines, Chancellor of the Exchequer David Lloyd George produced his 'Peoples' Budget'. In pre-budget speeches he attacked social injustice, alluding to the inequitable distribution of the country's wealth. He referred specifically to the oligarchy of aristocratic mine owners for their lack of concern and exploitation of their employees who, toiling in abhorrent conditions, created wealth which supported the owners' extravagant lifestyles. In 1910, 90% of the wealth in Britain was owned by 10% of the population; the top 1% owning just under 70% of wealth in the country (Pikety, T. *Capital in the Twenty first Century*).

Future Prime Ministers David Lloyd George (L) with then President of the Board of Trade, Winston Churchill, promoted the Peoples' Budget of 1909. To fund new social welfare programs, the budget proposed to levy unprecedented taxes on land owned by the wealthy. It was vetoed for a year in the House of Lords and was not brought down until 1910. In 1923, when he was Chancellor of the Exchequer, Churchill had been responsible for returning the country to the Gold Standard.

How Lloyd George towers as a giant who transformed Britain: Wales Online

Fighting for fair wages and enduring harsh working conditions, safety, or lack thereof, has always been an issue in mining. Such conditions fostered an intense sense of community among the miners, especially during times of protest and strikes. Miners knew that in hard times they could rely on the loyalty and support of their wives, friends and neighbours. They were also proud of the work they did. These factors promoted the politicisation of coal. Coal miners had always been at the vanguard of working class struggles and their unions have been the most radical.

The Left of British politics can trace its origins to coal mining areas. In 1888, the Miners' Federation of Great Britain (MFGB), forerunner of the National Union of Mineworkers, was founded and, by 1908, boasted a membership of 600,000. Its intent was to form a national body to coordinate regional miners' unions which, established in the coal producing areas of Britain, had hitherto acted autonomously. In 1890, the MFGB became part of the Trade Union Council, the federation representing most trade unions in the country.

The years 1910–1912 saw a period of industrial turbulence in Britain and the national Coal Strike from February to April 1912 was part of this industrial unrest. Until that time, miners' pay fluctuated with the uncertainty of the coal markets. There also existed a complicated wage structure based on the quality and quantity of coal mined in various districts. The only power the miners had was to withdraw their labour and this they did to secure a universal minimum wage. The ensuing strike lasted 37 days and involved almost a million workers. As a result, the 1912 Coal Mines Act was passed giving miners a minimum wage protection.

During this time of industrial instability, the *Triple Alliance* was formed by the union movement which incorporated the Miners'

Federation of Great Britain, the National Union of Railwaymen and The Transport Workers' Federation. The merger created a large, united organisation which reinforced working class solidarity. Implicit in the amalgamation was the promise of mutual support in the event of industrial disputes and strikes.

Miners and their families in the 1920s were still living in squalid conditions in hovels usually consisting of two rooms which accommodated adults and children. There were no bathrooms or running water and they shared a common outdoor privy with several other families. Malnutrition and disease were endemic.

Britain's 21st century housing bears an eerie resemblance to my childhood: The Guardian, 20 November 2017.

The Alliance was a significant step towards greater unity and ideology within British trade unionism. The onset of World War I, however, curtailed any imminent action by the Alliance. Had war not been declared, it is possible that a general strike would have occurred in 1914.

9 *Not a penny off the pay...*

The miners on strike, 1912

The National Coal Strike was part of a wave of industrial turmoil which occurred in Britain prior to WWI. The strike aimed at securing a national minimum wage began in Alfreton, Derbyshire and lasted almost two months. Almost a million workers took part. Undoubtedly, industrial unrest would have persisted were it not for the war.

https://libcom.org/library/miners-next-step-swmf-1912

In 1913, the British coal industry produced a record 287,000,000 tonnes of coal of which 98,000,000 tonnes were exported. At the outbreak of war in 1914, miners were the largest single group of industrial workers in Britain. Coal was the most important source of energy, and the coal industry was both highly productive and lucrative. This can be credited mainly to the war-time commitment by the labour force to maximising output. Prior to 1914, there had been no *deliberate* government intervention in the development of the coal industry. Production and distribution of coal reflected the demand of a free market economy.

However, in 1914, it became obvious that the amount of coal produced would not be sufficient for the urgent needs of war. Additionally, there was widespread profiteering on the part of the owners. In 1916, labour shortages, due in large part to recruitment to the forces and continued industrial action plaguing the industry, caused the government to take financial control of the mines and responsibility for workplace relations. Outbreaks of industrial unrest continued to erupt throughout the war years in defiance of the 1916 Defence of the Realm Act which forbade strikes and made arbitration compulsory. Those strikes that did take place incurred swift government intervention which saw quick resolutions and prompt returns to work by the miners. It was probably in this environment that Harry, Nan's father, made his decision to leave his secure job as mine deputy, and his family, to volunteer and fight for his country.

The enthusiastic enlistment of young, fit men of Harry's generation was the cause of the dramatic fall in the production of coal after 1916. With fewer remaining miners there was a reduction in the amount of coal produced per shift as the miners who did stay behind to work the pits were neither as young nor as fit as the ones who had gone to war. The industry had lost its most productive workers. However, with the government in control, for those men who did stay behind wages, hours and safety conditions improved. Workers were anxious for the *status quo* to continue, knowing that a return to private ownership would mean a return to harsh conditions and poor pay in order to maximise the profits of the wealthy owners.

However, military victory did not bring industrial peace to Britain. When hostilities ceased it was time for the government to reappraise wartime industrial legislation which had seen unions forego fundamental entitlements such as the right to strike.

Compulsory arbitration was scrapped, and the unions regained their pre-war industrial rights and privileges. Union membership increased and post war unemployment increased union power.

Anticipating a better way of life, the men who returned from the war were inclined take strike action in order to achieve this. Against this uncertain background, and with what appears to be foresight, Harry's decision to leave mining appears to have been a sound one.

In 1919–1920, strikes on the railways, docks, Yorkshire coalfield and even in the police force demonstrated that revolution, which had swept Europe after the war, was possible in Britain. The average number of workers at that time involved in strikes and lockouts was 2,108,000 compared with an average of 308,100 between 1927 and 1939. Fighting in Ireland and India only added to the general disquiet. In 1919, miners demanded a thirty per cent pay rise, a six-hour working day and nationalisation of the mines. When these demands were refused by the government who still, notionally had control of the mines, the Miners' Federation threatened to strike.

In order to avert the possibility of strike action, a Royal Commission into the coal industry was authorised by Prime Minister David Lloyd George. The Commission was led by Sir John Sankey, Labour politician and eminent lawyer. All sides of the industry participated. The Miners' Federation appeared on behalf of their members while the mine owners, protecting their financial interest, were equally well represented. Capitalism and the injustices of the British class system were on trial in a very public way.

" …. the present system of ownership and working in the coal industry stands condemned, and some other system must be substituted for it, either nationalisation or a method of unification by natural purchase and/or joint control." reported R.H. Tawney, one of the commissioners.

Evidence was given during the Commission of the rampant

wartime profiteering by mine owners. Juxtaposed against the obvious wealth of the owners was evidence of the exploitation of poverty-stricken men whose work increased this wealth. Simultaneously, evidence was produced of inflated coal prices which were inflicted on consumers. During the course of the Commission it became obvious that one solution to this unconscionable disparity — to protect the living condition of the miners *and to* prevent high prices for consumers — was to nationalise the industry or, at least, place it under State control.

Sir John Sankey (1866–1948), Labour politician and eminent lawyer, chaired the inquiry to examine the future of the coal industry in Britain. As a young barrister he had worked in Cardiff and, in common with the Prime Minister, David Lloyd George, was fluent in the Welsh language. In 1926 Sankey was appointed Lord High Chancellor by Ramsey MacDonald's Labour Government and was raised to the peerage as Baron Sankey. In 1940 he chaired the Sankey Committee which was responsible for the Declaration of The

Rights of Man (the writer H.G. Wells being the most active member of the committee). The declaration identified eleven fundamental human rights: the right to life, protection of minors, duty to the community, right to knowledge, freedom of thought and worship, right to work, right to personal property, freedom of movement, personal liberty, freedom from violence and right of law making.

https://en.wikipedia.org/wiki/John_Sankey,_1st Viscount Sankey

The Commission delivered four separate reports. Two of them, one signed by Sankey and the other by the miners' representatives, recommended nationalisation; the third one, signed by coal owners and industrialists, recommended the industry remain in the hands of private enterprise while the fourth report, signed by another industrialist attempted a compromise between all the others. By seven votes to six the Commission approved nationalisation of the coal industry.

Sir John delivered his report directly to the Prime Minister who was then participating in the peace talks at Versailles. Knowing that all telephone calls would be monitored and reported, Sankey like Lloyd George, was fluent in Welsh and delivered the message in that language. This confused journalists who, eavesdropping on the conversation, but not recognising the language, called for an interpreter. Eventually they secured the services of a well-known fellow journalist and translator who was proficient in Serbo-Croatian. (Harold Wilson: *A Prime Minister on Prime Ministers* p177.)

Although Sankey and the miners commanded seven out of thirteen votes in favour of nationalisation, the government seized on the lack of unanimity as an excuse for rejecting nationalisation announcing it needed more time to consider the matter. Although it agreed to some reorganisation of conditions in the industry, the miners rejected this, seeing it as a bribe to prevent renewed strike action and the government offer was withdrawn. Wages remained the same; the seven-hour day was imposed by an Act of Parliament and Government control was prolonged. No one was happy with this kind of compromise. As the historian C. L. Mowat put it,

"The bitterness and the troubles of the coal mines for the next seven — or for that matter twenty-seven — years derived in great part from the feeling of both miners and owners that they had been betrayed." (https://caveconspringfield.com/in-tuc-shown-by-the-general-strike-there/)

The owners enraged by the fact that the Government had come so close to agreeing to nationalisation were determined to stand firm and hang on to what they believed was theirs by right. The miners, who had hoped for so much from the Commission, for which they had not asked but had made such an impressive showing at the hearings, felt 'deceived, betrayed, and duped'. All they had achieved from the Sankey Commission was the introduction of a seven-hour day. The Government and the coal owners waited apprehensively for repercussions.

Yet serious trouble did not return to the mining industry until the collapse of the post-war boom in the winter of 1920–1921. In the 1920s coal was the only industry whose exports declined in both value and volume. Unemployment in the coal mining industry fluctuated between 300,000 and 400,000. From January to March 1921 coal prices tumbled. Now anxious to divest itself of responsibility, Lloyd George's Coalition Government announced it would hand back the coal industry to the owners, which it did on 31 March 1921. On regaining control, the owners reacted in a characteristically mean-spirited and grasping way. Although they could have reorganised the industry, they were incapable of agreeing on a suitable plan. They believed the only way to cut production costs was to decrease wages and increase working hours, a deliberate contravention of the Sankey Commission which had recommended the introduction of a seven-hour working day and a wage increase of two shillings per shift.

The owners posted notices at every pithead in the country announcing drastic wage cuts. These cuts, by as much as 49 per cent in regions like South Wales where profits had been hardest hit by the collapse of export markets, were not the worst blow. The new agreement proposed by the owners would destroy the minimum wage agreement achieved by the 1912 strike. And, it would herald a return to the hated system of district rates whereby miners who worked at inferior pits would earn much less than those working on richer seams in Yorkshire or Nottinghamshire.

The vexed question of *national* wage agreements was thus at the centre of the coal crisis in 1921 and the miners refused to abandon the sanctity of such an agreement. The owners argued that pits in the less profitable regions could not afford existing wage rates. The average wage of mine-workers in Great Britain in the first quarter of 1921 was, at its interwar peak, £4 9s 8d per week, and the owners warned that, once they resumed control of the mines, this would have to be cut sharply.

The miners attempted to resolve the dilemma by proposing the idea of a national pool to introduce a levy on every ton of coal produced. This would have assisted the poorest collieries by providing a national fund on which they could draw to cover losses and meet wage bills. If, as the owners suggested, it really was impossible for a very large number of companies to pay a living wage, then the only alternative to closing pits or cutting wages, the miners suggested, would be to accept the national pool proposal as a means of equalising wages.

The owners proved intransigent and rejected the proposal.

Unsurprisingly, the miners rejected the idea of lower wages and, on 1 April 1921, All Fools Day, they were locked out of the mines. A week later the Triple Alliance called a national rail and transport strike in support of the miners. The strike was due to begin on 15 April and more than two million men were expected to stop work. The backlash, which had been threatened since 1919, was about to take place.

At the last minute, on a day which became ignominiously known as 'Black Friday', the railway men and transport workers withdrew their support, citing the fact that, although the miners expected their support, they had not included other unions in their arbitration. The excuse given was that the miners had failed to exhaust all possibility of negotiations with the owners! Once more betrayed, the miners went on strike — alone.

On the Government side, preparations for the threatened national strike were far more forceful than in 1919. Lloyd George declared a state of emergency, called up eighty-thousand special constables and made some ominously effective military preparations, placing machine-gun posts at some pitheads. Playing to public fear and exaggerating the threat of violence, he announced plans for calling up the Reserve and forming a Volunteer Defence Force.

An enterprising tradesman's signs during the 1921 coal strike.

9   *Not a penny off the pay...*

The Government garnered support by emphasising the revolutionary nature of the proposed strike. The right-wing Organisation for the Maintenance of Supplies was established to provide volunteers in the event of a strike. A state of emergency could be proclaimed by invoking The 1920 Emergency Powers Act. Writing in the government newspaper The British Gazette, Prime Minister Stanley Baldwin declared :

"Constitutional Government is being attacked. Let all good citizens whose livelihood and labour have thus been put in peril bear with fortitude and patience the hardships with which they have been so suddenly confronted. Stand behind the Government, who are doing their part, confident that you will cooperate in the measures they have undertaken to preserve the liberties and privileges of the people of these islands. The laws of England are the people's birthright. The laws are in your keeping. You have made Parliament their guardian. The General Strike is a challenge to Parliament and is the road to anarchy and ruin."

The General Strike of 1926: A nine day wonder that forged Great Britain; Anglotopia for Anglophiles

The miners fought on alone for three months throughout the summer of 1921 before hunger forced them back to work on far worse terms than before Black Friday. Their average pay fell from £4 9s 0d a week in the first quarter of 1921 to £2 18s 10d in the fourth quarter — a drop of 34 per cent in nine months.

Salvation Army food kitchen, 1921 miners' strike.

The coal industry had now been firmly returned to private enterprise and, by the end of the year, it was clear that Black Friday had set a pattern: union solidarity had been breached. Wages fell heavily in every industry during the 'employers' offensive'. What the miners, and indeed the entire labour movement needed desperately after 1921, was a display of unity to wipe out the shame of Black Friday. It came four years later on 31 July 31 1925 — 'Red Friday'.

Throughout these events, and precipitating them, there was economic turmoil in Britain which was experiencing a decline in its global economic status. The financial cost of the war, plus the loss of so many lives, had put additional pressures on the economy. Unemployment was, and would remain for some time over 10% and the situation, especially for miners, was about to get worse.

Above: Arthur J. Cook, Secretary of the Miners' Federation of Great Britain addresses striking miners.

The General Strike of 1926 was initiated by the Trades Union Congress (TUC) in support of the British coal miners in their dispute with the mine owners for increased wages and improved conditions.

Lasting nine days, from 3 to 12 May, 3,000,000 out of

5,000,000 British workers stopped work. Nothing moved without the agreement of the workers and, by end of the first day, builders, printers, iron and steel workers and heavy chemical workers had joined dockers and transport workers in a demonstration of solidarity.

Although it was expected to be successful, the strike failed in its main purpose, which was to force the government to satisfy the miners' demand to bring back the wartime subsidies it had recently withdrawn.

On 12 May the TUC called an end to the strike. The miners had gained nothing.

The British Strike: https://libcom.org/history/articles/british-general-strike)

In April 1925 there was a return to the Gold Standard, which had been temporarily abandoned at the start of war in 1914. The Gold Standard is the monetary system by which a county's currency is tied to the amount of gold it possesses. In 1925 it was fixed at pre-war parity but, because the country's gold reserves had been depleted by the cost of the war, the currency was artificially high. As a result, every export industry was affected, especially British coal which became so expensive that it was unable to find an export market.

The situation was made worse by the fact that French and Belgian troops who, under the terms of the Treaty of Versailles had occupied the Ruhr-centre of Germany's coal industry, were now withdrawn leaving it free to export its coal to the rest of Europe. In addition, Poland was now producing cheap coal. British coal was unable to compete in overseas markets. Despite the feasibility of using capital to invest in modern technology, colliery owners refused to consider any remedy other than a policy of reducing miners' wages and returning to an 8-hour day.

'It would be possible to say that the miners' leaders were the stupidest [sic] men in England if we had not had frequent occasion to meet the owners...' remarked arch contemporary Tory politician, Lord Birkenhead.

After steadfastly refusing to intervene, the Conservative government, led by Prime Minister Stanley Baldwin who had succeeded David Lloyd George as Prime Minister in May 1923, finally agreed to the demands of the Miners Federation and announced a nine-month subsidy to maintain current wages and hours. The original amount of the subsidy of £10 million amounted, eventually, to £23 million. Labour declared victory. This proved to be a humiliation for Baldwin who, at the end of the nine months, took his revenge.

The report of the subsequent Samuel Commission, established in March 1925 to again examine the mining industry, produced further recommendations which were accepted by the government. These included long-term reforms which were considered necessary for the restructure of the industry but, in the interim, the commissioners agreed that owners were justified in demanding a reduction in wages and an increase in hours. Although the mine owners were delighted at the recommended wage cut, neither the owners nor the miners were impressed with the rest of the recommendations. The response from the Miners' Federation came with the slogan 'Not a penny off the pay, not a minute on the day'.

Half-hearted attempts by the government to review their decision proved futile and the TUC General Council declared that, unless satisfactory terms could be reached with the government by midnight on 3 May, there would be 'coordinated industrial action' in support of the miners. Negotiations continued between the TUC, the government, the owners and the miners but they were futile. On 30 April 1926, the owners issued a lock out notice. The pits were closed and would remain closed until the miners accepted wage cuts. The government declared a state of emergency.

The aim of the strike was to force the government to act to prevent mine owners reducing miners' wages by 13% and increasing their shifts from seven to eight hours. On 12 May 1926, the TUC General Council visited 10 Downing Street to announce its decision to call off the strike if the proposals worked out by the Samuel Commission were respected and the government offered a guarantee there would be no victimisation of strikers. The government stated that it had "no power to compel employers to take back every man who had been on strike". However, the TUC agreed to end the dispute without such an agreement. The miners struggled on alone but, by the end of November, most were back down the mines working for less pay and longer hours. Others remained unemployed for many years.

Playing to public fear, some of the measures employed by the government in the event of the 1926 General Strike going ahead included calling up 80,000 special constables, many from universities and public schools. Armed vehicles were placed at strategic sites as a deterrent.

The Special Committee of the General Council of the Trades Union Congress convened in 1925 to work on the dispute in the coal industry to avoid a national strike and visit Downing Street for discussions with Prime Minister Stanley Baldwin. The protracted negotiations, which lasted a year, proved to be futile and in 1926 the General Strike went ahead.

Over the next two days negotiations intensified and on 2 May, when it seemed as though agreements were possible, Baldwin abruptly ended negotiations, probably in retaliation for the humiliation of the previous year. He cited the fact that notices for a General Strike had already been distributed by the unions. He also accused the unions of 'overt acts interfering with the freedom of the press'. Leaving the TUC dumbfounded, he thanked them for their efforts before taking his leave with the words, "Goodbye. This is the end."

When the General Strike was terminated, the miners were left to fight alone. Arthur J. Cook appealed to the public to support them in the struggle against the Mine Owners Association: "We still continue, believing that the whole rank and file will help us all they can. We appeal for financial help wherever possible, and that comrades will still refuse to handle coal so that we may yet secure victory for the miners' wives and children who will live to thank the rank and file of the unions of Great Britain."

https://todayinlaborhistory.wordpress.com/2015/05/04/may-4-1926/

9 *Not a penny off the pay...*

A General Strike was declared by the TUC in support of the miners although they knew it was doomed to failure. The strike began at one minute to midnight on 3 May 1926. Three million dockers, transport workers, engineers, foundry workers and general labourers downed tools and Britain came to halt. The strike lasted for nine days.

On 12 May 1926, the TUC General Council caved in and visited 10 Downing Street to announce its decision to call off the strike if the Samuel Commission's proposals were respected and the government offered a guarantee there would be no victimisation of strikers. The government stated that it had 'no power to compel employers to take back every man who had been on strike'. However, the TUC, albeit in the absence of a consensus, chose to end the dispute.

The miners had achieved nothing. Alone, they remained on strike throughout the summer of 1926 and into the following autumn. As the weather grew colder, miners and their families, barely affording to subsist, could be seen picking through pit spoil heaps for scraps of coal to keep them warm.

Right Hon.
STANLEY BALDWIN, M.P.

Stanley Baldwin, Prime Minister at the time of the General Strike said, "...one day there came a great strike in the coalfields. It was one of the earlier strikes, and it became a national strike. We tried to carry on as long as we could, but of course it became more and more difficult to carry on, and gradually furnace after furnace was damped down; the chimneys erased of smoke, and about 1,000 men who had no interest in the dispute that was going on were thrown out of work through no fault of their own, at a time when there was no unemployment benefit. I confess that that event set me thinking very hard. It seemed to me at that time a monstrous injustice to these men, because I looked upon them as my own family, and it hit me very hard—I would not have mentioned this only it got into the Press two or three years ago—and I made an allowance to them, not a large one, but something, for six weeks to carry them along, because I felt that they were being so unfairly treated. But there was more in it really than that. There was no conscious unfair treatment of these men by the miners. It simply was that we were gradually passing into a new state of industry, when the small firms and the small industries were being squeezed out. Business was all tending towards great amalgamations on the one side of employers and on the other side of the men...We have to see what wise statesmanship can do to steer the country through this time of evolution, until we can get to the next stage of our industrial civilisation."

https://www.agefotostock.com/age/en/Stock-Images/Rights-Managed/MEV-10009637

When the strike was over King George V wrote in his diary,

'Our country can well be proud of itself as during, the last nine days, there has been a strike in which four million people have been affected, not one shot has been fired and no one has been killed. It shows what a wonderful people we are.'

Historian A.N. Wilson is of the opinion that, rather than showing how wonderful the British people were, the strike demonstrated the selfishness of the middle classes and the power of their wealth. In 1927, the Conservative government introduced the Trade Union Act. The act banned all strikes which attempted to coerce, either directly or indirectly, the government by inflicting hardship on the community. Also banned were mass picketing and the proscription of civil service union from affiliation with the TUC.

10

Isn't it marvellous?

Miners walk away at the end of their shift (Painting by G. Palmer)

Mrs. Evans fach, you want butter again.
How will you pay for it now, little woman
With your husband out on strike, and full
Of the fiery language? Ay, I know him,
His head is full of fire and brimstone
And a lot of palaver about communism,
And me, little Dan the grocer
Depending so much on private enterprise.

What, depending on the miners and their
Money too? O yes, in a way, Mrs. Evans,
Yes, in a way I do, mind you.
Come tomorrow, little woman, and I'll tell you then
What I have decided overnight.
Go home now and tell that rash red husband of yours
That your grocer cannot afford to go on strike
Or what would happen to the butter from Carmarthen?
Good day for now, Mrs. Evans fach.

Mrs. Evans fach, you want butter again.
How will you pay for it now, little woman
With your husband out on strike, and full
Of the fiery language? Ay, I know him,
His head is full of fire and brimstone
And a lot of palaver about communism,
And me, little Dan the grocer
Depending so much on private enterprise.

What, depending on the miners and their
Money too? O yes, in a way, Mrs. Evans,
Yes, in a way I do, mind you.
Come tomorrow, little woman, and I'll tell you then
What I have decided overnight.
Go home now and tell that rash red husband of yours
That your grocer cannot afford to go on strike
Or what would happen to the butter from Carmarthen?
Good day for now, Mrs. Evans fach.
The Angry Summer,
Idris Davies, 1926

"The multiple face of patriotism exhilarated him - undergraduates at the docks, young women driving cars, shopfolk walking cheerfully to their work, the swarm of 'specials', the general 'carrying on'. Even the strikers were good-humoured." (Galsworthy, J. *Swan Song*, (1967, Penguin: Harmndsorth.)

The first issue of *The British Worker* on 5 May 1926 was published by TUC for the duration of the strike.

It was printed on the presses of the *Daily Herald*.

https://libcom.org/history/ten-days-class-war-merseyside-1926-general-strike

Although the strike was, as anticipated by the TUC, a failure for the working class who had hoped for so much, it was a bitter defeat and hardly the cause for, nor should it have been the object of, such patronising nonchalance as the above remarks. Written by John Galsworthy, they were uttered by his character Michael Mont, Tory MP and son-in-law of Soames Forsyte of a wealthy solicitor *cum* property millionaire.

For the duration of the strike, factories, mines and power stations were idle. Armed soldiers patrolled the streets and the police force was augmented by the swearing in of special constables. When the strike was announced, whoops of glee could be heard from the salons of the well-heeled of Mayfair as the aristocracy took the bit between its teeth and, with the spirit that had made the Empire great, came to the aid of their country, now being threatened with the same fate as the one that had befallen Russia in 1917. Society delighted in the opportunity to perform their civic duties. A good time, it seemed, was about to be had by all.

Swan Song is part of *The Forsyte Saga*, the best known work of John Galsworthy, which was published between 1906 and 1921. It chronicles the events and history of three generations of the Forsytes, a large, wealthy upper class English family, aware of its status of 'new money'. The main character is Soames Forsyte, a successful lawyer and art connoisseur who personifies the book's theme of the acquisition and inter-generational transfer of capital. *Swan Song* is set in the 1920's and deals with the general strike from an upper class perspective. Soames' daughter, Fleur, married to an upwardly-mobile young MP, volunteers to run a canteen for strikebreaking volunteers.

Aristocratic ladies and debutantes queued up, eager to volunteer to work as telephonists or run canteens, washing dishes and serving meals to the army of bankers and stockbrokers who, cheerfully and freely, offered their services to work in transport and industry.

Enthusiastic Oxford undergraduates drove buses on which they had scrawled such slogans as 'Flappers are welcome!' Some threw 'strike parties' and the satirical weekly magazine *Punch* published cartoons about appropriate attire for such work.

"My word! Look at the lorries. It's marvellous, isn't it?" utters a young passenger of Soames Forsyte. "Mad thing, this strike making everybody do things they weren't accustomed to do", says Soames, referring to his spoilt society daughter, Fleur Mont. "This canteen ... I'm enjoying it frightfully …. I hope the strike lasts", gushed Fleur in a hurry to wash off the grime of the day before heading out into the night for another evening of cocktails and dining. (Although *Swan Song* deals with the General Strike from an upper middle-class stance, Galsworthy did express sympathy with the plight of the miners describing it as 'heartbreaking'.)

Society ladies were eager to volunteer their services, while still having fun, to keep the country going during the 1926 general strike. Across the country, volunteers flocked in their thousands to join organisations to help provide essential services.

https://www.pinterest.com.au/adrianjmatthews/general-strike-1926/

Jeanne Malcolm (later Lady Jeanne Malcolm), wife of Conservative John Malcolm MP, and Edwina Mountbatten wife of Lord Louis Mountbatten, 'working' as volunteers at Hyde Park canteen during the General Strike of 1926.

University of Southampton Special Collection

Strike breakers, with the protection of the police force, ensure public transport is not disrupted.

https://www.agefotostock.com/age/en/Stock-Images/Rights-Managed/ MEV-10579658

10 Isn't it marvellous?

The multiple faces of capitalism. Students, *inter alia*, did their best to ensure essential services were not disrupted by the strike. Although it is generally believed that many volunteered their services in the interests of preserving the capitalist system from being undermined by the workers, most of these men were probably fulfilling their childhood dreams of driving buses or trains.

https://www.pinterest.com.au/adrianjmatthews/general-strike-1926/

In her book *Black Diamonds*, Catherine Baily chronicles the rise and fall of the Fitzwilliam Wentworth dynasty whose fortune was made from coal mines in South Yorkshire. There appeared to exist a somewhat symbiotic relationship between the 7th Earl, Peter Fitzwilliam, and his employees. Possibly it was a pragmatic show of gratitude on behalf of the miners, whose employment could be precarious. From various accounts they held him in high esteem for the considerate way he treated them and the good order in which he maintained his pits. Yet the Earl, Baily informs, depended on his miners as they created much of his wealth.

Baily applauds the Fitzwilliam's *noblesse oblige* that drove them to take care of the miners and their families, while simultaneously preserving the feudal master/servant *status quo*. The Fitzwilliams owned a fifty-room house in London's Mayfair and vast estates in Ireland in addition to the Wentworth Estate. Nevertheless, while the they led their opulent lifestyle, life in the pit villages revolved around the struggle to survive.

For the duration of the miners' lockout, which outlasted the General Strike, Earl Fitzwilliam undertook to provide the children of mining families with one midday meal *per week*. With help from the miners' wives, 1300 children were fed 'water gruel, tea cakes and sandwiches' in huge marquees erected in the grounds of Wentworth House. The provision of meals was supervised by the Earl's sister, Countess Maud. Most of the women wore white aprons over their shabby dresses whereas Countess Maud, attired in clothes of fine fabric in pale, spring colours, was highly visible in the crowded tent. Reportedly, the families of the miners remained in awe of the family to whom they were grateful for this act of practical altruism. When her hours of supervising the communal feeding were over, the Countess probably repaired to her Wentworth House apartment, bathed, dressed in more fine clothes and dined sumptuously, the scouring of the gruel pans, no doubt, being left to the scullery maids.

In support of the miners' industrial action, 4 million British workers came out on strike for nine days. Generally, they respected requests from their leaders to avoid violent and disruptive behaviour. This was not wholly true of some members of the upper and middle classes who, believing the end was in sight for their privileged existence, volunteered to take the places of the workers for the duration of the strike. Although their behaviour had every appearance of a university rag, it was subversive and undermined the seriousness of the strike's intent. Volunteering to keep essential services operating also enabled the government to protect the interests of big business.

Countess Maud Wentworth-Fitzwilliam
https://www.pinterest.co.uk/pin/637892734699459431/?nic=1

One of the features of the 1926 Strike and lockout was the critical level of destitution and starvation which eventually forced the miners back to work. Families were forced into debt which, even after a return to work, took years, if ever, to repay. With erratic and unpredictable small amounts of money available to them it was impossible for the wives of striking miners to make provision for their families and they frequently had to resort to the Relief Office for meagre handouts just to subsist. The burden of how to feed the family fell squarely on the women. Although the men were out on strike, work never stopped for the women. The overarching concern of the miner's wife was for her family and how they would be fed and clothed. This anxiety was enough to make many women natural antagonists of the strike. While some wives remained resolutely silent, others attempted to convince their men to return to work.

* * * *

Within most mining communities during the strike the role of women was ambivalent. Were they victims or opponents of the strike or were they heroines whose courage was as strong as the men's? Were they defiant, or were they passive? The answer seems that they were all of those. While some women appeared to remain enslaved to their domestic routines and subservient to their men, it was their astute household management that helped to maintain morale and was, in a roundabout way, a means of supporting their men during this time. For other women the strike provided the opportunity to break out of the home to fight defiantly for the causes of socialism and feminism.

There was, traditionally, a strict gender division of labour in coal-mining communities; men were the breadwinners and women the wives and helpers. For those women who took part in organised action during the strike, their involvement was usually in a complementary capacity. For the duration of the strike and lockout, however, there was frequently a crossover of roles.

Women were the facilitators of solidarity and cohesion within mining communities. While their men forged and strengthened their relationships with each other in the pit, the pub, club and Union Lodge, the women formed spontaneous, strong and supportive networks among themselves. They shared much in common — early marriage, large families and endless skivvying which revolved around their men, the pit and shift work. Apart from domestic service, employment for those women outside the home was virtually non-existent.

Miners and their wives were reduced to foraging for coal, combing through soil heaps for fuel that was barely combustible

https://flashbak.com/the-story-of-british-coal-in-photographs-1900-1930-48814/

Miners forged close relationships at work, based on mutual trust and reliability. This closeness continued outside their working hours in social activities such as sport and drinking at the local miners' institute. Their wives, whose lives revolved around a domestic routine, formed informal relationships closer to home.

https://www.pinterest.com.au/littleimadden/wales-cymru-am-byth/ *****

This lifestyle was replicated in such communities throughout the country and Nan's mother, Emily, would have been part of such a matrix in her small Yorkshire village. Women inadvertently cultivated lasting, mutually supportive relationships as they gathered to gossip on street corners or hung out their daily washing together. Women had traditionally united the community. What little they had, they shared. Yet during the precarious times of the 1920s, there was a growing divergence between female roles. Wartime upheaval had irrevocably altered these roles. More women now worked outside the home in a greater variety of occupations. Once the war had ended, the fight for universal enfranchisement resumed. Change infiltrated ordinary communities where newfound female militancy began to evolve. Despite industrial action many women continued to live lives which revolved around domestic routine, but just as many marched defiantly behind banners and made their voices heard in the public arena, broadcasting their sympathy for industrial action.

In Wales, 'White Shirting' was a public shaming ritual, developed by the miners' wives, aimed at undermining the masculinity of the strike breakers. The practice involved seizing a 'scab', or 'blackleg' and pasting him with whitewash. He was then forced into a white shirt and strapped into a wheelbarrow before being ceremoniously paraded through the streets then ignominiously ducked in the river. In a further attempt at humiliating blacklegs they were taunted with poles strewn with women's clothes in an obvious disparagement of their masculinity.

Many women in mining communities were politicised during the lockout. Many became increasingly involved with the Labour and Communist parties as they did their utmost to support and promote solidarity with men. The Women's Committee for the Relief of Miners' Wives and Children was formed by Labour women to combat the effects of the strike. They supplied food, clothing and boots to families whose poverty was aggravated by the strike. In a further effort to relieve the stress on families, the committee arranged prolonged holidays for over 2,000 children, hosted by families in and around London. In addition to providing temporary relief from the daily grind of poverty, it also created bonds between people of the coalfields and city dwellers. Most of the children had never seen a town or city before and, for most, it was the first time they had been on a train.

Without the women, it is conceivable that the lockout would have collapsed much earlier than it did. Herbert Smith of the Miners' Federation reported that half the attendees at his meetings were women "and they were always the toughest half". Women such as Lil Price campaigned against relief cuts and were active in picketing to prevent the slow gravitation of men returning to work. Lil was a miner's wife, yet not a member of any political party. She helped in communal soup kitchens, was active in leading demonstrations against strike breakers, and later jailed for riotous behavior.

The Communist Party was then very active in coal communities and although initially committed to a platform of sexual equality, became highly gendered as industrial policy at that time tended to exclude women. Although women were able to join the party, membership was mostly restricted to the wives of male members and even they were unable to participate at the same level as men. The paramount anxiety was the struggle over mining pay and conditions and, since their place was mostly seen as restricted to home and domestic responsibilities, their roles within the party were relegated to organising fund-raising activities such as socials and bazaars.

There is evidence of the attempted involvement in the strike of the Women's Guild of Empire (WGE), a conservative organisation which was vehemently opposed to strikes. They attempted to urge the miners' wives to publicly express their disapproval of the actions of the striking men. In fact, seventy-five women from coal communities in South Wales, wearing Welsh national costume, attended a London rally condemning the strike. Their action was roundly criticised as 'betray[ing] their men in their fight for a decent existence'. This criticism came from Elizabeth Andrews, another woman who came to prominence at this time. Urging her fellow supporters not to get involved with the WGE, she denounced the Guild as largely consisting of 'shopkeepers, parsons' wives, squires' daughters and colliery management womenfolk'.

Overall, women found the Labour Party more accepting of them as equals, and in 1925 there is evidence that women with Communist sympathies were active within the Labour party. Socialist women supported the General Strike and promoted equality between men and women. Behind the militant miners were many equally militant women. Some of these women were experienced suffragettes, able to draw on their well-honed campaigning skills which they used in support of the strike. (Ironically, it was another two years before women under thirty were allowed to vote in Britain.) Typical of their commitment and foresight, one of the women's groups organised a speaking tour for Stella Brown, the birth control advocate.

However, for the duration of the lockout, women were mainly represented as victims of a male struggle, starving while the government reneged on its responsibility. Because they had voted not to work, locked out miners were not eligible for poor relief. Their wives, however, were granted ten shillings a week and dependent children between two and four shillings, based on whether or not they received school meals. Because there were so many barefoot children, poor law authorities and other organisations donated money to pay for shoe repairs. Shoeless, and in some cases scantily clad, many children were unable to attend school. There are stories of women cutting up their own underwear to clothe their children and some mothers even carried unshod children to school.

During the weeks and months of the lockout, miners, together with their wives, engaged in a variety of voluntary work. They cleaned, painted and decorated public buildings. They maintained chapels and schools and, for most of the time, spirits were high. There are even reports, albeit apocryphal, of football matches between mixed teams. As much food as possible was home grown in small garden plots and allotments, men and women working side by side at cultivation. Often, they worked together to prepare and serve food in the communal kitchens. Until then, shared work was uncommon.

An extensive network of soup kitchens for miners providing communal eating was established across the South Wales coal fields during the months of the Lockout.

People and Nature: some socialist ideas about society and their interaction. https://peopleandnature.wordpress.com/

Nevertheless, during the strike, women suffered disproportionally to men, always working, always going hungry so their families could eat. It was common practice for men and boys to be fed first, women eating afterwards — if there was enough food. Maternal mortality rate and deaths from tuberculosis among women increased. Girls were often below weight and poorly dressed, indicating that they were expected to follow their mothers into a life of self-denial. It was said that women bore the brunt of the strike with an associated increase in still births and neonatal deaths. It is obvious that the absence of trained midwives, let alone medical intervention, was a feature of childbirth here. Overall the women focused on maintaining solidarity of class with their men rather than advancing the feminine cause.

Women protesting about local parish councils cutting off payments to striking miners.

(Adiwell Heritage recording the History if a West Lothian Village)

Yet the 1926 lockout proved a catalyst which propelled many women, either willingly or reluctantly, into public life. Many women represented their communities by public speaking, fundraising and protesting. Many, mostly anonymous, were arrested. All were women with young children. Of the two hundred and one women arrested during the lockout, one hundred and sixteen were sent to prison, thirty were bound over and thirty-five were acquitted. By far, most women however, galvanized by a sense of belonging to, and the common values of their communities, were driven to informal and 'traditional' forms of protest. For this reason, they remain, despite their effectiveness, anonymous.

In November 1926, with the advent of winter, the Miners' Federation finally conceded defeat and called for negotiations with the owners. There were no prior conditions. The miners were eventually forced back to work with no alternative but to accept reduced wages and increased hours. They had achieved nothing by going on strike. It was a humiliating failure with wages and condition worse than they had been 1914. The workers had been virtually starved into submission. Some of them never worked again.

In the aftermath, a feeling of antipathy developed where the strike had devastating economic effects on the non-mining, as well as the mining, communities. Many local small businesses were bankrupt and most local councils were also in debt.

At the end of the bitter dispute, the camaraderie and convergence of gender roles, which had lasted for the duration of the dispute, quickly dissipated and there was a return to the pre-existing state of affairs. Most wives, mothers and daughters retreated to their former lives of poverty, grime, hard work and subservience to their husbands, now with the added burden of crippling debts accrued during seven months without pay. The men resumed their traditional status of authority, recreation at the pub and miners' institute, fishing and working in the allotments. Those children who had been sent away returned home.

Some of the wives, who had loyally supported their husbands, angrily challenged the role of the mining unions during the dispute and its action on behalf of the miners. As a result of the strike, wives in some of the coalfields of Britain formed a women's section of the MFGB with the aim of allowing them some say in affairs affecting mining communities. However, they were never allowed access to male dominated union meetings and never achieved public recognition.

The crisis in the coal industry deepened during the Great Depression of 1929 and in 1932, the industry reached its nadir when unemployment was recorded at fifty-three per cent. Visits by the

Prince of Wales and other society identities highlighted their plight and brought some relief.

The Road to Wigan Pier, George Orwell's 1937 account of his travels in the depressed industrial North of England itemises the weekly expenditure of an unemployed miner, his wife and two small children on a weekly allowance of thirty-two shillings. The miner's wife provided Orwell with the following list of expenditure exemplifying the still existing hardship of the bleak living conditions where unemployment was rife.

	s	d
Rent	9	0½
Clothing Club	3	0
Coal	2	0
Gas	1	3
Milk		10½
Union Fees		3
Insurance (on the children)		2
Meat	2	6
Flour (2 stone)	3	4
Yeast (the women made their own bread)		4
Potatoes	1	0
Dripping		10
Margarine		10
Bacon	1	2
Sugar	1	9
Tea	1	0
Jam		7½
Peas and cabbage		6
Carrots and onions		4
Quaker oats		4½
Soap, powders, blues etc.		10
Total		£1/12/0

(Orwell, G. (1985) The Road to Wigan Pier, *Penguin: Harmondsworth p 83*)

The disastrous period came to an end with the outbreak of World War II in 1939. Mass unemployment declined and there was again a demand for coal. Work in light industry became available for women, largely through government initiated schemes and ordnance work. However, a female workforce was regarded merely for the duration of the war rather than a major permanent restructuring of gendered employment.

The miners had a deservedly 'good war', gaining the gratitude of the nation for maintaining coal and energy supply for the duration. Nationalisation followed the war in 1947. By 1950, the generation of miners who had lived through the horrendous ordeal of the lockout of 1926 was fading and with it the entrenched attitudes of class hatred and acrimony. This situation was to last until the 1970s but, uncannily, history has a habit of repeating itself.

It is an inevitable fact during industrial disagreements that wives share equal involvement. Their homes and lives revolve around their men. Keeping them clean and fed while providing a comfortable home to return to at the end of varied shifts is a full-time job and often to their own detriment. Again and again, women deal with the frustrations caused by strikes, layoffs, and mine closures. Behind the solidarity with their men is an acceptance of their circumstances and an appreciation of the politics of mining and of the communities in which they live.

Despite the hardship, associated with the Miners' Lockout, many women in affected mining communities found strength in adversity. Many were transformed into activists, effective fundraisers and community leaders. They developed the art of public address, making a profound impression on their audiences, speaking from personal experience of the hardships inflicted on their communities. Sadly, many of these women have remained anonymous but, from this harsh background, they are represented by some of the most influential political activists of the century who were themselves miners' wives.

Special Women

Elizabeth Andrews OBE, 1882–1960

Elizabeth Andrews, nee Smith, was born in 1882 in Penderyn, in the Rhondda Valley coal mining district of South Wales. She was the third of eleven siblings born into a Welsh speaking mining family. Although forced to leave school at twelve to help in the home, when seventeen she spent a year away from home learning to become a needlewoman and soon owned her own workshop.

Hidden Heroines https://www.bbc.co.uk/programmes/profiles/38Q6q4s1KJ4bZKr9dZMn5W/elizabeth-andrews

Elizabeth was aware of the inherent dangers in mining and the constant anxiety experienced by families for the men's safety. In 1885, her father had escaped an explosion which had killed eighty-one men and boys at the Maerdy Pit in the Rhondda. As children, Elizabeth and her siblings were captivated by their father's frequent retelling of the story of this event which he even illustrated with chalk drawings on the floor of the kitchen. His narrations became almost ritualistic and this led Elizabeth to focus on the miner/father role, not in an economic sense as breadwinner, but as the archetypal compassionate, heroic figure who, knowing the dangers of mining nonetheless undertook the work. Her father died aged 57, as did two of her siblings, from silicosis.

Mining communities such as the one in which she grew up, were, at that time, known for large families with high maternal death rates which influenced her decision to work to improve conditions for women.

In 1904 Elizabeth joined the Women's Suffrage Movement in support of votes for women and, in 1910, after her marriage to Thomas Andrews, a founder member of the Rhondda Independent Labour Party, she became increasingly active in Labour politics establishing a local branch of the Women's Cooperative. Although a formidable organisation, it provided women and girls with a forum where they could discuss and debate their rights. Elizabeth also organised political campaigns on women's issues including health and suffrage. Founded in the 1880s, in the 1920s the Women's Cooperative working class base formed an alliance with the Labour Party. Women's rights and universal pacifism were the Cooperative's core values enabling women to represent themselves in workers' movements.

Andrews became a member of the Women's Political and Social Union fighting for women's right to vote in public elections. The Representation of the People Act was passed in 1918. It gave enfranchisement to all women over the age of thirty who were either resident in their constituencies or occupied land or premises with a value of over five pounds. (Simultaneously the local government franchise was extended to women over the age of twenty-one on the same terms as men.) Also, in that year, women and men were given the right to individual membership of the Labour Party. In 1919, Elizabeth Andrews was elected to the Rhondda Labour Party Executive, was its first female political organiser for Wales and remained in this post until 1947. One of her early tasks was to translate leaflets from English to Welsh encouraging women to use their newly won vote.

Elizabeth Andrews book, *A Woman's Work is Never Done*, was published in 1957. A lifelong socialist, she campaigned for women's rights supporting such causes as childcare, improvement of maternity care and universal suffrage.

South Wales Miners' Library https://minerssite.wordpress.com/2018/03/07/international-womens-day-educate-agitate-organise-elizabeth-andrews/

By the end of the 1920s, women, mostly married women, formed half the membership of the Labour Party. Although politically they had been active since the 1880s, women were, by now, working as local councillors, Justices of the Peace and local magistrates. Their focus was largely on health, education and welfare reforms such as the provision of public baths, school meals and infant and maternity clinics.

In 1919, Elizabeth Andrews together with two other miners' wives were the only women to give evidence before the Sankey Royal Commission's investigation into the working conditions in pits. She described the lives of women in coal mining areas as slavery, telling of their gruelling work including the dangers of boiling and carrying water through the house for their husbands to wash away the ingrained coal grime. As a miner's daughter, she spoke from the heart. She successfully managed to persuade the Government and mine owners of the dire need for pit head baths for the miners. Eventually a special fund, administered by the Miners' Welfare Committee, was established in 1926 to build pithead baths. By 1952 more than 400 of them had been installed at British pit tops.

Before the installation of pit head baths miners went home covered in the filth and grime from working underground. At home, they would wash in zinc bathtubs brought in from the back yard, usually by their wives, who had boiled and filled the tubs with water which had to be carried through the house. This chore was fraught with danger. Many of them were badly scalded in accidents which, in overcrowded little houses, often involved and proved fatal to, children.

https://www.flickr.com/photos/36844288@N00/3948726106

But Elizabeth was interested in much more than baths. She cared desperately for the plight of the people around her and was a staunch advocate for miners and their wives and children. She vowed to, and did, change the lives of miners' wives and mothers. Her book, *A Woman's Work is Never Done*, describes their lives of hard labour and poverty living in squalid housing where lack of sanitation provided breeding grounds for typhoid and dysentery and were responsible for the unacceptably high death rate among children.

She demonstrated the contribution made by working-class women in fighting for political change knowing from personal experience of the hard lives they led. Throughout the 1920s and 1930s, Elizabeth Andrews wrote articles for the women's page of *The Colliery Workers' Magazine* about strikes and food shortages. Specifically addressing women, she argued that they were the ones who bore the heaviest burden in the fight for better pay and working conditions. She highlighted how the survival and management of their households was also an important part of the struggle for improvement and was inseparable from that of their menfolk claiming, "The children of today, who will be the men and women of to-morrow, will have cause to be justly proud of their mothers who helped so nobly in this fight".

For the whole of her life, Elizabeth Andrews worked tirelessly to improve health and education services for the people of Wales. In 1948 she was appointed a member of Glamorgan executive health committee by Aneurin Bevan, future Minister for Health and architect of Britain's National Health Service.

Elizabeth Andrews died in 1960 aged 77. She was a miner's daughter who never disclaimed her roots. She lived in mining communities which survived strikes and lockouts, fighting all her life for the rights of women in mining communities and lived up to her motto: 'Education, Aggravation and Organisation.'

Beatrice Green, 1885–1927

Beatrice Green, nee Dykes, was born in 1885 in Abertillery, a mining community in South Wales. She was one of seven children whose father was a tin maker and who, when Beatrice was five, became a coal miner.

Beatrice took an active role in the local Ebenezer Baptist Church Sunday School and, after a County (later Grammar) School intermediate education in Abertillery, became a school teacher. She was renowned as having 'brilliant gifts' but, on her marriage in 1916 to Ronald Emlyn Green a miner she was forced by the then marriage bar, to give up her job. Over the next ten years, Beatrice and Ron had two sons. Beatrice remained very politically minded but being a miner's wife meant she already had a full-time job. She was, however, unusually fortunate in that her husband's parents were prepared to undertake the responsibility of taking care of her children thereby allowing Beatrice the opportunity to immerse herself in Labour Party activism and pursue her interest in public work.

Although not advocating the reversal of gender roles, she did, like many of her female Labour cohort, believe that women should be responsible for their own lives and have control over certain issues which most affected them as women, particularly issues of fertility control. She also maintained that women should be able to engage in public work on equal terms with men.

From its inception, Beatrice worked assiduously as secretary of the Abertillery Hospital League which raised funds to buy and launder linen for the hospital. In 1923, the League decided to introduce a membership subscription thus transforming into a social club with regular events for its members. As the League's representative on the hospital's board of management, Beatrice was consulted by Dai Daggar about the proposal for a birth control clinic for the hospital. Beatrice was a fervent campaigner in favour of birth control, not then a particularly popular issue in Abertillery, and through her work became a close friend of its chief advocate, Marie Stopes.

In 1926, Beatrice Green became president of the Monmouthshire Labour Women's Council which raised funds to provide milk, food, blankets and clothing for pregnant and confined women. During the 1926 Strike and Lockout, she raised funds on behalf of the Women's Committee for the Relief of Miners' Wives and Children, adamant that they should not be starved into surrendering to the demands for increased hours and decreased wages which were being pressed by the mine owners. Together with Elizabeth Andrews, Beatrice Green travelled to London to help organise the temporary fostering of about 2,500 vulnerable children from the coalfields thereby relieving the financial burden on their families. For those who remained behind, she helped organise and run soup kitchens and school dinners, ensuring that the 1,600 people of Abertillery were fed each day for the duration of the lockout.

By now, Beatrice was becoming well known nationally, in demand as a public speaker, regularly addressing meetings and rallies in London and raising funds for local charities. She publicised the dreadful plight of the strike bound people of Abertillery which, like many towns in south Wales, had very little employment except for mining, so that the entire town was plunged into economic misery as a result of the strike and lockout.

This work required enormous sums of money and, although much came from fund raising campaigns, international contributions were also received. Canadian miners who had survived an equally vicious industrial dispute against short hours and reduced wages understood their Welsh brothers' dilemma and were generous donors. Equal generosity was matched by the solidarity of the coal miners of the Soviet Union who organised a levy from their own wages which they donated for the relief of the Welsh miners.

Many women's delegations visited the Soviet Union in the 1920s.

https://warwick.ac.uk/services/library/mrc/explorefurther/digital/russia/visitors/

As a gesture of thanks, and to strengthen ties between British and Soviet trade unions, a nineteen strong delegation visited the Soviet Union in August 1926. Six women, representing miners' wives in different coalfields, of whom Beatrice was one, were part of the delegation. Their trip lasted almost two months, during which time, travelling mostly by train, they covered huge distances visiting schools, hospitals and workplaces, meeting men and women and seeing all aspects of Soviet life. Stopping at stations along the way they were given ceremonial welcomes. Miners' Unions pledged continuing support for the plight of Welsh miners. The whole experience was an act of bravery for these women who, having previously regarded a trip to London as a significant event had never before left the shores of their own country. Although not herself a Communist, Beatrice was impressed by what she saw. "One of the greatest marvels accomplished by the Russian revolution," she wrote, "is the complete emancipation of women. Today in Russia women possess an absolute equality of rights with men. She has economic independence and equal political, moral and social rights."

Meanwhile, the lockout was gradually breaking down, the miners and their wives and children no longer able to hold out against the draconian directives of mine owners without national support. Finally, at the end of November 1926 they were, as Beatrice had feared, deprived and starved into submission. They accepted defeat and returned to work. The Women's Committee for the Relief of Miners' Wives and Children raised the huge sum of £313,874 over the course of the lockout.

Despite the ignominious defeat of the lockout, Beatrice Green maintained her activism. She continued the prodigious production of articles for Labour Women in which she offered warm, practical advice on childcare. In September 1927, she presided over a conference of Monmouthshire Labour women which attracted over 800 delegates. She was a tireless worker and seemed set for an outstanding political career. Sadly, on 19 October 1927, at the age of forty-two, she died of complications associated with ulcerative colitis leaving a husband and two young sons. Beatrice Green was buried at Blaenau Gwent Chapel, Monmouthshire.

Politically and socially Beatrice Green was a woman ahead of her time. As socialist and feminist she campaigned indefatigably not only for the miners but their wives, of whom she was one, but also their children. Modern research has provided evidence to show a connection between ulcerative colitis and stress. Her short life of hard work for the benefit of others may have adversely affected her health and been the cause of her early death.

Still with its rows of houses, present day view of Abertillery

Dr Marion Phillips 1881–1932

Although neither the wife nor daughter of a miner, of the working class nor even British, Dr Marion Phillips deserves acknowledgement in any account of the 1926 Lockout.

Marion Phillips was born on 29 October 1881 in Melbourne, Australia, the youngest of seven children. Her father was a solicitor who, together with his wife, believed firmly that girls should receive an education

Women's History Network https://warwick. ac.uk/services/library/mrc/explorefurther/ digital/russia/visitors/

equal to that given to boys and had their daughter educated at Presbyterian Ladies' College in Melbourne.

Marian matriculated in 1898 before gaining admission to

Melbourne University where, in 1902 she was awarded the Cobden Medal for political economy in addition to several scholarships in history, philosophy and logic. In 1904 she graduated BA, and in July that year, went to England on a scholarship worth £50. There she resumed her studies in history and economics at the London School of Economics. In 1909, she was awarded DSc in economics.

In 1906, while studying at the London School of Economics, Marion Phillips met Beatrice and Sydney Webb, co-founders of LSE. She initially worked for the Webb's before being employed by the Royal Commission on the poor laws as a research assistant inquiring into public health, poor-law medical relief, and the treatment of destitute children. She continued this work until 1909. In 1907 she had become a member of the Fabian Society, a socialist organisation whose goal was to advance the principles of democratic socialism by gradual reform rather than by revolution. She also joined the Independent Labour Party, becoming a member of the executive committee. She joined the non-militant National Union of Women's Suffrage Societies acting for a time as its secretary during 1910.

In 1912, Dr Phillips was elected a Labour councillor for the London borough of Kensington where she campaigned for public provision of baby clinics, school meals, improved council housing employment schemes, prohibition of sweated labour and better medical inspection and treatment for school children.

During World War I she served on the Consumers' Council of the Ministry of Food as secretary of the standing joint committee of industrial women's organisations. Marion was inclined to be abrasive and did not suffer fools gladly but according to Beatrice Webb, although she was not liked by fellow prominent Labour women, she was well respected by the grass roots female membership for her hard work.

Ella Wertheimer was from a Jewish family who, as a result of being the object of anti-Semitism had changed the family name to Winter. She knew Marion Phillips when they both lived in Australia and when she later moved to London resumed her friendship with Phillips of whom she said, "We all admired her extravagantly — her brilliant mind and effectiveness as a speaker, her activities as suffragist, pacifist, labour organizer... It was a red-letter day for us all when Marion came. She was striking-looking, with black hair, small hands and feet, intense brown eyes and a stout, uncorseted, ungainly body, which one forgot in the acute discussions she always brought into being."

During the 1920s, Marion Phillips antagonised many of her fellow female activists by strongly opposing the Labour Party's policy on birth control. She believed that the party's stance on birth control would alienate the Catholic working class thereby losing their votes. She believed that 'sex should not be dragged into politics' and that promoting birth control could potentially 'split the party from top to bottom'.

During the 1926 Miners' Lockout, Marion Phillips, as secretary of the Standing Joint Committee of Industrial Workers' Organisations, headed a national fundraising effort and helped establish the Women's Committee for the Relief of Miners' Wives and Children (of which Beatrice Green was also a member) to provide assistance for pregnant and nursing mothers. This was the only organisation to be officially sanctioned by the Miners' Federation of Great Britain to raise funds on their behalf. It collected and distributed more than three hundred thousand pounds to assist the needy. The then Secretary of the Miners' Federation of Great Britain, Arthur Cook, praised the efforts of the committee declaring, "It is the women who made the great sacrifice. Therefore, we shall never forget how, led by Dr Marion Phillips …. The Labour women all over the country …. set themselves the task of …. combatting the cruel effects of an industrial war of attrition carried on against women and children."

After raising almost a third of a million pounds, the WCRMWC was discontinued. However, a crisis such as the one the women had experienced, inevitably and inexorably changed lives and, during these cataclysmic months, the mining women had shown that they were a force to be reckoned with.

Marion's work during the General Strike brought her into close collaboration with the women of the Durham coalfield and in 1926 she was nominated by the Durham Women's Advisory Council and the miners of Monkwearmouth as a prospective Labour candidate for the multiple-member constituency of Sunderland. Despite its largely working-class population, a growing middle-class in the constituency led to the seat being held by the Conservatives. However, she accepted the nomination. In the 1920 general election, Marion Philips was returned as the Labour member for Sunderland and Durham, the first Australian to be elected to the British parliament. Already ill with cancer, she died in 1932 without ever returning to her native Australia. As an MP, she continued to champion working class issues, including paid holidays, unemployment schemes and training for women workers.

Unfortunately, she occupied the seat only for a short time. The election coincided with a downturn in the economy and rising unemployment which continued to worsen under then Prime Minister Ramsay MacDonald. In October 1931, another general election took place and was a disaster for the Labour Party. Only 46 members retained their seats. Phillips, along with all the other women MPs, was one of those defeated.

Sadly, by this time, Marion was suffering from stomach cancer. Three months after the election, on 23 January 1932, she died in

London and was buried at Golders Green Cemetery. Tributes to her life and work poured in. During her relatively short life she had lobbied tirelessly for the rights of women, particularly working women such as those in mining communities and was described as one of the best all-round women Members of Parliament.

In September 2019, 90 years after her election, Marion Phillips was commemorated by a blue plaque in Sunderland.

11

Solo Once More

Twenty years after she had finished her training and anticipating a rewarding career, Nan was travelling in the cabin of a removal van with her belongings stowed in the back. She resented every mile which took her further away from her clean, newly built house. The house had become a cocoon, where the confidence and security she had lost in the maelstrom of the last few years had been gradually restored. Despite her loneliness and distress she had begun to feel more secure and confident with a sense of achievement in having secured a hearth of her own. Although she regretted leaving behind her network of caring friends in Scotland, she had proved to herself that she was after all an independent woman. A feeling, perhaps, that events of the last few years had helped to undermine. Despite missing the support of these friends, she no longer regretted her decision. Her only obligation now, she considered, was to her children. She would do her utmost to make amends to them for the loss for which they had not been responsible and from which they too had suffered. From now on she would, as far as she was able, be both father and mother to them.

When she had sat by her fireside with the children, she had almost begun to feel optimistic about the future. The house, *her* house, had helped her to feel this way. She knew that the children sensed this security. These times would soon become a soothing memory to which she would return for solace when doubts about her ability would inevitably infiltrate her thoughts and undermine her confidence. Her little family could rest here for the time being, thriving on that sense of stability, although Nan knew, it may only be temporary.

Each mile closer to her destination only increased her feeling of doom. How could she survive in this ugly village? The landscape was scarred by smouldering spoil heaps, dominated by winding wheels and a huge chimney belching smoke and grime which settled everywhere like grubby snowflakes. Her stomach churned with nervous anticipation and dread. The need to work had become imperative after her marriage to Jack, an officer in the merchant navy, ended in separation in 1945 leaving her with the sole responsibility of rearing two children. Her husband's agreement to pay a small amount of alimony was an informal rather than a legal arrangement and could stop at any time. In any case the amount would not be enough to raise two children *and* provide them with a home. Nan's mind began to wander into the past as the van trundled ever closer to her destination,

In 1930, as memories of the General Strike were passing into history and Britain was still suffering from another economic downturn, Nan, now a qualified State Registered Nurse and State Certified Midwife, was about to embark on a career for which she had been well prepared. The National Census of 1931 showed the population of Great Britain to be 37,559,045 of which 138,670 women and about 15,000 men listed their occupation as nursing. Eighty-eight percent of the female nurses were, like Nan and her training school peers, unmarried.

During her three-year training in Ashton-Under-Lyne, Nan had formed a small, yet close-knit group of friends, the closest of whom was René, daughter of a large Lancashire family of Jewish cotton manufactures with a family home in Manchester's Cheetham Hill. René's father, as the youngest son, spent much of his time travelling on the Continent as a salesman seeking orders for the family business. René's family welcomed Nan into their home and, after her sparse, rowdy upbringing in a large family of children, she loved the calmness, comfort and welcome extended to her. René and Nan, having forged a musical partnership in the nurses' home, would perform duets for the family. René sang in a somewhat reedy soprano voice accompanied by Nan on piano. *Drink to me only* had become their signature tune.

René had a younger sister, Annie who, after a prolonged labour, was born with the aid of forceps and sustained considerable brain damage. Even in those days, births attended by expensive obstetricians were not without risk. Although she lived at home during her childhood, Annie's erratic behavior tended to upset the family's equilibrium. During adolescence and early adulthood, she began to suffer from outbursts of violence. During lucid intervals, she realised she would never be able to lead a normal life and made several suicide attempts. She was eventually admitted to an exclusive nursing home in Manchester where she lived for the rest of her life, punctuated by the occasional visit home, but discouraging visitors except for her immediate family. Despite her excellent training and because of the unfortunate circumstances surrounding her sister's birth, René did not have the confidence to practise midwifery, fearing a mishap similar to Annie's.

Other friends in their social group moved away or returned to their home towns to work. One friend met and married a local businessman from Ashton and remained there. The group would remain friends for a long time, despite rare reunions. However, Nan or Nancy (as René called her) and René remained close friends for the rest of their lives.

Ashton-Under-Lyne General Infirmary staff, c.1930.
Nan is standing on the extreme left of the photograph and
René Lawton, standing, sixth from left.

After their final midwifery exams, the pair returned to the District Infirmary in Ashton-Under-Lyne, René to nurse male surgical patients and Nan to work on the children's ward. After a while René began training and working as a district nurse in a Lancashire mill town where she stayed for the next thirty years. Diligently, every Sunday afternoon, she visited her sister.

Nan spent a further few years working at Ashton District Infirmary in various specialties including the operating theatre, and a year as a supervising night duty staff nurse. Her special love was paediatric nursing and many years after she had nursed the last of her young patients, she could recall some of their histories. Most children were admitted from extremely poor homes in the district, suffering from conditions such as rickets — weakening of the bones as a result of vitamin D deficiency. Often this was the result of infants lying in cots or prams inside houses all day without exposure to sunlight while they waited for their mothers to return from work at local mills. Vividly she recalled the case of two little boys who, prior to 5 November, had been playing with fireworks. They thought it would be fun to see what would happen when they placed a lit firework underneath an inverted terra cotta plant pot. Excitedly, they lit the blue touch paper and stood back to watch the result of their handiwork. The plant pot exploded and the boys were admitted to hospital, their faces pockmarked by embedded fragments of terracotta. Another infant was admitted with badly scalded legs. His mother had filled the bath with boiling water and, before she returned with cold water, the child had already stepped into the bath.

During this period of her life Nan returned home as often as she could, although her hours were long, and she was only allowed one day off duty each month. The cost of a bus ticket was often a drain on her meager budget as wages were poor. Nursing was regarded then, as it would be for many years to come, as a 'vocation' with the associated assumption that large salaries would attract 'unsuitable' people to the profession. In 1931, nurses in provincial hospitals worked 119 hours a fortnight and, in London hospitals 117 hours. It was mandatory for nurses to reside in hospitals living in nurses' homes. They had their own rooms, there was a common sitting room and meals were eaten together in a large dining room. Although the homes were usually comfortable with facilities such as tennis courts and sometimes a swimming pool, there were many restrictive rules and regulations governing the resident nurses.

One of Nan's rare visits home when she worked in Ashton, no doubt taking a short cut on her two mile walk to and from the bus stop.

Life for Harry and Emily was still hard, although Emily preferred working on the farm to staying indoors doing housework which, with her large family was, in any case rather futile. She was thrifty and self-sacrificing and, unknown to her husband, amassed quite a large sum of money through her scrimping and saving. Nan's parents had by this time moved to a larger farm which Harry could afford to purchase. When they were both forty-seven, they unexpectedly produced another son, their last child. Evidently, even at that time, Marie Stopes' influence had not spread as far as the Pennines. Nan didn't particularly enjoy her visits home. Her parents were always busy and she resented the intrusion of her small brother whose presence, with the indignity of youth, she blamed on her father's lack of self-restraint. The farm was also very isolated and public transport unreliable. Although Harry would sometimes meet her in his horse and trap during milk rounds, often she would walk from the bus stop to the farm. Nan often spoke of her mother's indifference towards her children — the memory of a solitary kiss from her mother evoking the softness of her mother's skin — so it was particularly moving for her when, on taking out her purse to give up her last few coins for the return fare, she often discovered that Emily had placed a few shillings there.

In the mid-1930s Nan was appointed night sister at Shire Hill Hospital, Glossop, a market town in the High Peak District of Derbyshire, close to the borders of Cheshire and Yorkshire. At this time, nurses were still obliged to work 119 hours a fortnight for a very small salary, particularly

Nan sets out on her long walk to catch the bus back to the hospital.

considering the amount of responsibility the position carried. Despite this, and the fact that she only had one night off every month, she remained at Shire Hill for over a year enjoying, when time permitted, a healthy social life — mostly revolving around the hospital. On one occasion, when the hospital held a fancy-dress ball, while masquerading as a ghostly apparition, wrapped in sheets borrowed from the hospital laundry, she startled the night porter. She was also a keen tennis player and played during the mornings after finishing her night shift. Her fund-raising, however, was possibly not received very warmly — nor encouraged — after she bought a cheap aluminum saucepan to make toffee for the sweet stall. The lining of the saucepan melted into the toffee and formed solid little balls resembling tooth fillings. Some of her happiest Christmases, she recalled, were spent working in hospitals.

From Glossop, she moved to the mining village of Whitwell in Derbyshire where she was employed as a district nurse, caring for the sick and elderly in their own homes. Since this preceded the advent of the National Health Service, her salary of about £30 a year would have been administered by the local Parish Council who raised the requisite money from various sources — fundraising (bazaars, fetes), endowments and small contributions (a few pennies per week) from patients who could afford to pay. In addition, she was allocated money for her uniform and various medical requirements. She was billeted with a family, the Bennetts. Transport was provided in the form of a bicycle, but she walked everywhere to make house calls in the village even to those outside the village boundary as her education had not included learning to ride a bike. After several attempts by Mrs Bennett to teach her, lessons were abandoned in the interest of safety. It was a skill she never mastered. Occasionally she caught an infrequent bus or relied on the good nature of villagers who obliged by offering transport, sometimes motorised, more often horsepower.

Enjoying the sun, and rhododendrons in Clumber Park, on one of her precious days off from district nursing in Whitwell.

She was happy in Whitwell. She liked and got to know the village environs and made friends among the villagers. Although it was a mining village and only two miles from Creswell, it was a much more attractive village as the mine was, unlike Creswell, outside the village. However, after two years she resigned to take up a position in charge of a female surgical ward at Worksop's Victoria Hospital. Worksop was another market town about five miles from both Whitwell and Creswell. Unknowingly, this move determined the course of events of the rest of her life.

Nan Jackson would become a close friend and helper for the next 20 years, although her friendship with the younger Nan was, at times, tumultuous.

She made the move to Worksop in 1937 and, in the course of her work, formed what would be another lifelong friendship with one of her patients whose name coincidentally was also Nan, Nan Jackson. Nan Jackson's husband, Harry, owned a local bakery and the couple, who had never had children, lived in the picturesque Pear Tree Cottage in the village of Carlton-in-Lindrick, also a few miles from Worksop. Nan became a regular visitor to their home and, although Nan Jackson and Harry were closer in age to Nan's mother and father, the three became very close. Nan and Harry Jackson provided the comfort and warmth, and probably affection, which Nan felt had been lacking in her own home.

The two Nans begin their Norwegian Odyssey mid 1939

Ship-board romance blossoms, but Nan Jackson is determined not to be left out.

In the spring of 1939 both Nans travelled by ship from Hull bound for a holiday in Norway. While on board Nan met and fell in love with the second officer, Jack Stewart. On 1 September, war with Germany was declared. Knowing the extent of Jack's involvement in the hostilities, they arranged a hasty war-time marriage during one of his last-minute weekend leaves. She was married from Nan Jackson's house and the wedding service took place in the Saxon church of St John's Carlton-in-Lindrick on 30 September 1939. The only members of the wedding party, apart from the bride and groom, were Nan's father, Harry, Jack's mother who travelled from the family home near Glasgow, Nan Jackson and her husband and Nan Jackson's elderly uncle, who lived with the Jacksons. The wedding breakfast was a small afternoon tea party in the garden of Pear Tree Cottage before the newlyweds departed for Seaton Carew, a small seaside resort near the North Sea port of Hartlepool, to honeymoon for the remainder of the week end. Presumably this destination was chosen as it was close to where Jack would rejoin his ship.

Married in haste? Wedding day 30 September 1939
St John's Church Carlton-in-Lindrick, Nottinghamshire.

As with all wartime weddings, Nan and Jack's was arranged in a hurry. There was some doubt as to whether Jack would get weekend leave for the ceremony, so an alternate plan was made to be married at the Flying Angel Mission for Seafarers in Hartlepool where Jacks' ship awaited him. In the event, all was well. An impromptu wedding breakfast for the handful of guests was held in the garden at Pear Tree Cottage before the newlyweds departed for their two-day honeymoon. Although Nan's mother did not attend the wedding, her father did. Jack's mother, Grannie Stewart (on right of picture) travelled from Glasgow to be present. Between Nan and Grannie Stewart is 'Little Granddad', Nan Jackson's uncle.

Nan continued to work at the hospital in Worksop. As it was wartime she was not, as a married woman, obliged to resign. As with many wartime couples, the newlyweds saw each other intermittently. For much of the war, the ships which Jack commanded had been converted into hospital ships with a complement of medical and nursing staff. Although their meetings were infrequent, Jack did at least get back to Britain at times during the war, unlike many troops who were stationed abroad for the duration. Whenever possible, often at short notice, she would usually manage to get leave to travel to various parts of the country to meet Jack when his ship was in port. She saw quite a bit of the London blackouts when his ship docked at Tilbury and the Strand Palace Hotel became their regular rendezvous.

Nan and Jack met occasionally when Jack's ship docked in Britain and they enjoyed the occasional rendezvous. However, because they had spent so little time together before or since their marriage, there was always an initial awkwardness to their meetings. When they did begin to feel comfortable in each other's presence, it was time to part again.

This photograph was taken during a short break in North Wales after Jack's ship had docked in Liverpool.

In May 1940, Nan became pregnant with her first child yet continued to work for the first few months of her pregnancy. Jack and Nan decided, probably for the sake of safety and, because it would be close to her mother-in-law and sisters-in-law, to buy a house in Troon, an attractive holiday resort on the Firth of Clyde in Ayrshire. Nan was introduced to the Houston family, distantly related by marriage to Jack's family. She became a close friend to the eldest daughter, Minnie, who managed a tea shop and bakery in the town. On 5 February 1941, in the house in Troon, while Jack was away at sea, she gave birth to her first child, Ian, delivered by family friend and local GP, Dr McCulloch. Sadly, the baby was badly deformed by myelomeningocele and spina bifida, defects of the spine and spinal cord, and when only a few days old, Ian died.

This was a heart-breaking experience for Nan, made even harder as it occurred while Jack was at sea and none of her family was there to provide comfort and support. Although she had Minnie, she faced the grief alone. She again commenced work as a district nurse working closely with Dr McCulloch. Using her midwifery training, she assisted him with home deliveries and after care.

Later that year to her delight, at the age of 34, she again became pregnant and in May 1942 a healthy son, Alistair was born. A third child, daughter Elizabeth arrived in February 1945. At thirty-seven, Nan was deliriously happy with her two healthy children and, after the birth of her baby daughter, felt she must be the happiest woman in the world.

After a few months, Nan's happiness was violently shattered and her marriage ended when she discovered, while packing Jack's trunk at the end of yet another shore leave, a cache of letters at the bottom of his trunk. The letters were from a woman who was a nurse on board his ship. She and Jack had been in a relationship for the previous two years. The letters disclosed that the woman was pregnant with Jack's child. Nan confronted Jack and a violent quarrel erupted. Jack returned to his ship and the marriage was over. Alistair was three and Elizabeth a few months old. None of them ever saw Jack again.

Troon 1942. Another shore leave shared with some Troon friends. Minnie Houston, was a significant part of Nan's life as was Nan Jackson, who is at the front holding Alistair, her godson. 'Uncle' Harry (husband of Nan Jackson) is next to her. Grannie Stewart and Grannie Houston middle back row. John and Jennie Brown, next door neighbours, are at the right of the picture.

Together as a small family with Alistair in Troon 1942.

Nan was distraught and, in her distracted state of mind, decided it would be best for the three of them to leave Troon and return to England. She had loved living in Troon and had made a large circle of friends both through Minnie and through her work. Despite advice and pleading from her friends not to act rashly, she was adamant and could not be persuaded to change her mind. She remained in Troon for a further year until the house was sold. As the house was purchased during the war, Jack had insisted that only Nan's name be on the deeds in the event of his not surviving. He also added, albeit tongue-in-cheek, the caveat that should she sell it without consulting him, the marriage would be over. It already was and she sold it without compunction. The proceeds of the sale were her only means of income. Like a hurt child, she longed for home and the comfort of family.

Harry and Emily had agreed that the three of them could stay at the farm until other accommodation could be found. The furniture was packed and dispatched south by rail to be stored until a new home was found. In the aftermath of six years of war, chaos prevailed and the railway carriage containing the furniture was shunted onto a railway siding where it remained for several months. That was the least of Nan's concerns. By now she had lived apart from her family for twenty years and had very little money. Apart from the money from the sale of the house, Jack had agreed to pay her a small monthly allowance of fifteen pounds. He continued to pay for the next thirty years and the amount remained the same. Resentment at Jack's disloyalty and anticipation of a life of financial hardship meant she had no qualms about retaining the proceeds of the sale of the house. She was, therefore, reluctant to use the money for day-to-day living expenses, intending it as a deposit for a new one.

The sojourn at the farm was not a happy one. In hindsight, moving south to be near her family was a bad mistake. She had little in common with her siblings now, married and living in the vicinity of their parents' farm. Nan had not seen her parents together for several years, and although they visited her in Troon, it was always separately. Their estrangement was evident as Emily had become withdrawn and even more distant. She was obsessed by fundamentalist religion. In retrospect, Nan realised that Emily was suffering from depression, but she was so weighed down by her own misery that she failed to recognise the symptoms in her mother. Harry didn't even bother to disguise his impatience with his wife nor his disgruntlement with the presence of his eldest daughter and her two small children who seemed to be constantly under his feet. Nan felt like an unwanted guest. In the post war environment, prospects for her obtaining a home of her own were grim. She realised that she loathed farm life. As a child she had hidden away when calves were taken from their lowing mothers and sent to market. Even now she tried to block her ears against the mournful lowing sound. She missed the companionship of her friends, Minnie especially. *And* she missed her husband, wondering if she had been too hasty in calling an end to the marriage. Perhaps after all, the two of them could have reached a compromise about the future. Now it all seemed too late.

It was almost the end of the year and Nan and the children had been at the farm for several months. Winters in the Pennines are long, dark and cold. One foggy December afternoon when it was almost dark, Alistair was sitting in front of the kitchen fire talking to Emily when she suddenly got up and went outside. Nan and Elizabeth were resting upstairs. After a while, Harry returned, having finished his work for the day. There was no sign of Emily and no sign of a prepared meal. They waited, and waited. When they finally thought of asking Alistair if he'd seen his grandmother, he told them that she had gone outside. Both Harry and Nan realised that something was amiss. Emily's coat and outdoor shoes were still in the vestibule of the farmhouse and a search of the outhouses revealed no sign of her. Harry called neighbours who helped in a frantic search of the surrounding fields, calling her name which only seemed to echo in the damp, foggy night.

After several futile hours the police were called and, together with the neighbours, they continued the search. In the early hours of the next morning, Emily was found in the field of a neighbouring farm. She had apparently tripped and fallen on her face into a puddle of water where she had drowned. Although the possibility of suicide was raised, a subsequent inquest returned a verdict of death by misadventure. The fall was most likely the result of a heart attack.

After the funeral and a miserable Christmas, during which her father seemed even more taciturn and resentful of her presence, Nan decided that the New Year would be the time to take some positive action. However, the winter of 1946–1947 was harsh, meteorologically and economically. Harry's farm was almost a thousand metres above sea level. There were heavy snowfalls which formed drifts up to three metres high, roads were blocked and no supplies could get through. January temperatures plummeted to record lows. February was the dreariest on record. The cattle were brought into the barn; the sheep were left to fend for themselves and many failed to survive the bitter cold. Harry was unable to make his milk deliveries and vegetables froze in the ground. Although they were reasonably self-sufficient, they were reliant on travelling tradesmen for staples — tea, and flour for bread making — which were, in any case, rationed. Coal deliveries were impossible.

Nan fulfilled her mother's domestic role as best she could. The claustrophobia of the isolated farmhouse, the long dark nights and her dwindling bank account took its toll. She felt more alone than ever and could confide in no one. Even more she resented her younger brother whom she really never got to know. Although he was grieving for his mother, she was unable to offer much solace. In her irrational emotional state, she unfairly blamed him, along with their father, for Emily's death. Nan too was mourning her mother and regretting the chasm which had formed between them during the years they had spent apart. She missed her own home, she missed her friends and, most of all, she missed having a husband to turn to. She realised she was still in love with Jack.

After the middle of March, the days began to lengthen and, with the arrival of warm air, the snow began to thaw. The sight of a solitary motor bike rider driving past the farm on a road as high as the dry stone wall was greeted with great excitement and in early April, in time for Easter, snowploughs managed to open the roads so they were able to replenish their depleted larder. Harry took stock of the winter and was able to resume his livelihood. Most importantly, to Nan, that spring brought with it the hope that a normal life for her and the children could resume.

The immediate post war General Election had ushered in the Labour government of Clement Atlee with an outright majority. Could people now dare to feel optimistic even in this age of austerity? Despite a military victory, economically Britain was in dire straits. She had lost export markets and was heavily in debt to America for war loans. Rationing of food and other commodities, now in even shorter supply, would remain in place for several years. The harsh 1946–1947 winter exacerbated Britain's fiscal vulnerability causing a 10 percent drop in industrial production in the first post war year. There were fuel shortages and power cuts were commonplace.

At the end of the war, Britain faced its worst housing shortage of the 20th century. Thousands of houses across the country had been lost to German bombs and many more were badly damaged. During six years of war, no new houses had been built and it was estimated that 750,000 new homes were required in England and Wales in 1945 to provide accommodation for families. With much accommodation in large cities destroyed and the influx of returning troops, either to young families or with the intention of fathering them, an ambitious program of house building was taking place. Frustratingly the frozen ground was followed by widespread flooding as the snow melted. House building came to a standstill — not a promising omen for Nan. Nevertheless, she felt she could wait no longer. Taking the children, she set off on a home-hunting expedition.

Nan and Harry Jackson had remained close friends and continued to be supportive of Nan. As she still had close ties to Worksop she decided to concentrate on that area in her search for housing and the possibility of work. Nan Jackson still lived in the same Carlton-in-Lindrick cottage and, at her invitation Nan made it her headquarters during her search. Although initially the reunion was sweet, with no children of her own, her friend soon became irritated by the swollen household. She was inordinately fond of Elizabeth but, unused to boys, had little tolerance for Alistair. This hurt Nan and caused friction in the house so that, even more acutely, she felt the desperate need to be in a home of her own. The three of them had been nomads now for almost two years, dependent on the hospitality of others.

After a particularly tense morning when rain prevented the children from playing outside, Nan, now feeling even more an imposition than ever, dressed the children and the three of them went out. Alistair walked by his mother's side and Elizabeth was in a pushchair.

They walked past the old Saxon church where, eight years previously, she and Jack had been married. They continued walking until they reached the nearby weir. Nan was desolate. She had no husband, neither home nor money and, clearly, no immediate prospect of obtaining either. She was completely dependent on the help of others. But what had the children done to deserve this? The rain continued to fall and she contemplated the body of water in front of her as a possible means of escape from the turmoil that was now her life. Then she thought of her mother, alone on that foggy December night. She looked at the children. They were not responsible for the present situation, why should they be made to share the ultimate cost of what seemed like a solution to all her problems? Shuddering she turned and quickly walked away.

Her return route took her once more past the church. The three of them went up the slippery path and into the church porch, the scene of her solitary wedding photograph. Even in her current state of mind, the irony struck her. The door was unlocked, and the little family trudged wearily inside. The interior, with its whitewashed walls was peaceful and dry. They walked towards the altar and Nan left the children sitting in a pew and went to look at the huge bible resting on the brass lectern. She never divulged what she read but when she returned to sit with the children — strangely quiet as though they sensed the gravitas of the moment — she had become calm. She lost track of time and had no idea how long the three of them sat there.

Eventually she started. By the diminishing light she realised that it must be quite late. The children, who seemed to have been drawn into Nan's surreal, almost hypnotic state began to show signs of restlessness. They were hungry, and by now, cold. Nan remained in an uncharacteristic state of tranquillity. The episode had strengthened her determination that the three of them could and *would* survive. Things would be alright. Her reverie was further interrupted by the church door opening and the entrance of her friend's husband. Harry had been pressed into the role of peacemaker. They all returned to the cottage. No lasting damage had been done to the friendship.

Her strengthened determination to find a home was, shortly afterwards, rewarded. She found a house near completion in a new housing development on the outskirts of the town, only a few miles from Carlton-in-Lindrick. Reserving enough from the sale of the Troon property for monthly mortgage payments, Nan put down a deposit on the house which was due for completion by the end of summer, not exactly ideal timing but manageable. New factories were opening nearby and in an interview with one of the managers she learned that plans included the installation of a medical centre which would require the services of a registered nurse. The future suddenly seemed a little less bleak. Alistair, now five, was enrolled in school in Carlton.

Obtaining a mortgage was another unforeseen hurdle. Although women had proved themselves capable of doing men's work during the war, they were quickly banished back into the home when the men began to return. At that time women were not allowed to take out a mortgage independent of their husbands. Even joint bank accounts were non-existent. Lone women entering restaurants or hotels were regarded with disapproval whereas, in some 'polite' circles, divorced women were openly shunned. Nan was neither a wife nor an ex-wife.

To secure a mortgage, she had to prove that she was no longer in a relationship with her estranged husband and that financially, she could service a mortgage. For this she had to engage the services of Mr Mead, a very helpful local solicitor. To his credit, Jack cooperated and provided as much assistance as possible — although stopping short of financial help. The outcome was successful, and Nan was able to purchase the house.

Although there was little money left after they took up residence, with the small allowance from Jack, frugality and some help from her friends, particularly the Jacksons, by the autumn of 1947 Nan and the children had begun their new life. The familiar furniture was finally brought out of storage; they were home again. To celebrate the beginning of their new life, she planted a small Monterey Cyprus tree in the garden outside the front door. Nan decided to defer her search for work until Elizabeth was old enough to start school. She would be home every afternoon to meet Alistair from the school bus. This, she considered, was the least she could do to restore some sort of stability to their lives after the loss and turbulence of the previous two years; and with stringent management it seemed that this would be possible.

Although she enjoyed the security of again living in her own home and the satisfaction of caring for the children, on whom she now poured all her love, she was lonely for close adult companionship. Her attitude to Jack was ambivalent. She missed him dreadfully, but she also resented him for his betrayal, not just of her, but mostly of the children. 'Daddy' she realised sadly, would never be part of their childhood vocabulary.

Although it was one of the legacies of war, single motherhood was still not the norm it is in present-day society. There was a noticeably ambivalent attitude, especially among other women, to her single mother status, then a novelty. Nan was also aware that, unlike war widows, if she did meet another man, she was not free to re- marry. Although having ample grounds for divorce, she recoiled from the prospect.

Despite a post-war increase in the divorce rate, since couples had married in haste followed by long periods of absence, there remained a residual stigma and shame associated with a failed marriage. Divorce cases were publicly reported in titillating detail for people to read about in the press. But deep down, Nan still loved

Jack and possibly even still harboured the thought he may eventually return to her life. She decided it was better, at least for the time being, to dismiss any notion of divorce.

At the time, and outside Nan's domestic sphere, two major social reforms of the Atlee Government came into force. Created the previous year by passage of the Coal Industry Nationalisation Act, on 1 January 1947, the beginning of that harsh winter, the National Coal Board came into effect and the government took control of all mining activities in the country.

The following year saw the launch of the National Health Service (NHS) promising a free, comprehensive range of health services for all residents of Britain. Allocation of these services would now depend on the health needs of the individual without regard to wealth or social status. Delivery of community services included hospital, general practitioner and maternity services.

It would be safe to assume that the announcement of the formation of the National Coal Board (NCB) on 1 January 1947 failed to arouse any elation in Nan. Yet these reforms were to play significant roles in her future. Circumstances conspired, however, to raise in her an awareness of both schemes.

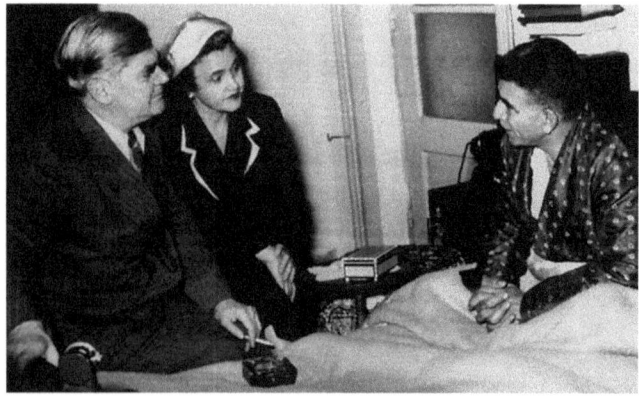

Aneurin Bevan was Minister for Health in the post war Labour government and architect of the National Health

Service. He was born in 1897 in Tredegar in the South Wales coalfield, the son of a miner. At 13 he left school to work down the pit before winning a scholarship to study in London. He is seen here with his wife and fellow MP, Jenny Lee visiting a hospital in the early days of the NHS. Note that not only is he smoking a cigarette as he sits by the bedside, someone has very obligingly supplied an ashtray!

In what some have described as a forerunner to the NHS, the Tredegar Iron and Coal Company formed, in the 19th century, the Tredegar Workmen's Medical Aid Society, a visionary and comprehensive health scheme to serve the health needs of its workers. Compulsory deductions were taken from workers' wages to pay for a doctor's salary.

Eventually the scheme was enlarged, employed more doctors and increased its services. In the 1920s, reminiscent of events in nearby Abertillery, the scheme was extended to include non-mining members. Five doctors, one surgeon, two pharmacists, a physiotherapist, dentist and district nurse were employed to provide a wide range of medical services which included X-ray, provision of spectacles and dentures and fitting of artificial limbs.

Paying for health care: life in Britain before the 'free' NHS; History Extra
https://www.historyextra.com/period/20th-century/nhs-history-pay-healthcare-free/

She had committed to devoting the next three years to being at home and providing much needed stability to her family as she derived enormous pleasure and satisfaction from her domestic role. However, lack of money was a recurring theme which was to be integral to the rest of her life. She also missed her work and the companionship of colleagues. She had spent most of her adult life working in a professional environment in positions of authority. She was well trained and experienced and, although a little premature in her planning, she knew that eventually she would have to return to work.

NHS community services covered the provision of hospital services, general practitioners and maternity services where health visitors and midwives were the responsibility of local authorities. Nan had gained considerable experience in home delivery during her work with Dr McCulloch in Troon and she had excelled in her midwifery training at Birch Hill. She decided to take the plunge and apply for the advertised position of district midwife employed by the neighbouring Derbyshire County Council. Her application was successful, and after a mandatory period of extra training, she was appointed to the position in Creswell the mining village five miles away. With the job came a three-bedroom council house. She accepted the position and, reluctantly, sold her house in Worksop and made the momentous move to the dreaded pit village of which she had pre-war memories. Coal, it seemed, had entered *her* life.

12

Taking off the 'L' plates

A replica of Nan's Car, a 1947 Ford Anglia.
http://clubs.hemmings.com/NAEFR/photo.htm

The decision to sell the Worksop house — the first home that Nan had bought by herself — was not easy, but necessary. The post war housing shortage worked in her favour as she sold the house quickly and made a modest profit. Apprehensively she began to plan the move. Although happy about the prospect of resuming her working life, and the greater financial security it would bring, Creswell was certainly not on her list of preferred places to live. She had memories of the village built around the pit with its grime and stench. She still held fond memories of neighbouring Whitwell which, compared to Creswell, had managed to retain some of its rural pre-industrial charm. She would be a stranger in Creswell, a single parent who knew no one. It wasn't just herself for whom she felt apprehensive, she would also be exposing the children, the two people she loved more than anyone else, to an upbringing in an environment which she herself dreaded. They were totally dependent on her and taking them there would seem almost like an act of betrayal.

If the last few years had taught her anything it was that, from now on, all important commitments in her life would continue to rest squarely on her shoulders. She had no one in whom she could confide her fears about the future which she now faced alone. She crossed her fingers and hoped that she would be capable of making a good job of it. Once more their belongings were packed and moved. In this case, the journey was short — at least as far as the crow flies — and in the autumn of 1948, Nan made her hesitant way to a new life. She felt as though she were moving to a different universe.

At the time of Nan's arrival, Creswell had become a thriving colliery community, and the population had grown to about five thousand. The village had survived six years of war, although not without loss. As in the previous war, many of the miners had joined the armed forces and among those who enlisted, thirty-two had been killed.

Coal was an essential commodity during World War II as it still provided power for industry, rail transport and shipping. It was also necessary to keep people warm on the home front and, in 1941, mining was again designated a reserved occupation, which exempted miners from military service. This caused considerable resentment among some miners who wished to enlist and fight. By 1942, again in a reprise of the earlier wartime era, the industry was under the control of the government. Nevertheless, there was still a shortage of mining labour. In order to remedy the shortage of both manpower and coal, the government decided to call for volunteers of conscription age to work in the mines. The call was met with apathy so that, in 1943, the government began to draft men of military age into the mines. Such conscripts were called 'Bevin Boys' after Ernest Bevin, Minister for Mines and National Service in the wartime coalition government. (During the industrial tumult of the 1920s, Bevin had been General Secretary of the Transport Workers' Union.)

One in every ten men called up for military service was conscripted to work in the mines. Most of them resented and were displeased by this. They were provided with suitable pit clothes, boots and helmets and sent to centres in various collieries where they received six month's training. Creswell was one of these centres. After completing their training, the men worked down the pits alongside experienced miners. Like their peers who were drafted into military service, they were thrown together and housed in military style dormitory accommodation. Nissen Huts, basic single storey concrete buildings with corrugated iron roofs, were hastily erected on waste land which became known, predictably, as 'Bevin Hostels'. Bevin Boys were often resented by the local people whose sons and husbands were fighting in various theatres of war. However, unlike their compatriots in the armed forces, Bevin Boys were not awarded medals for service to their country.

> Like their counterparts drafted to the military services, Bevin Boys were drafted into coal mines for the duration of the war. Like the military, they were housed in barrack style hostels.

Most were inexperienced at this type of work and resentful. Unlike their peers in the military, despite the necessity for continued coal production, and the inherent dangers in coal mining, Bevin boys received no official commendation for their service to the country.

Bevin Boys at Creswell, 1944.
(The forgotten conscript: The story of the Bevin Boys; theforgottenconscript. co.uk/bevin-boysllery/)

The scheme ceased in 1948, just prior to Nan's arrival in the village, but the hostels remained (and still do). They were used as cheap accommodation by some of the villagers and to provide homes for newly displaced persons arriving from fractured post-war European countries. The immigrants included a small number of German prisoners of war, as well as refugees from Communist regimes in Eastern Europe and Baltic states.

Creswell, despite its vital role in providing coal for the war effort, had not been a target of wartime bombing. However, it is only 26 kilometres from the Sheffield. With its heavy industries, principally steel works and war time armaments factories, Sheffield was in the Luftwaffe's cross-hairs. Between 1940 and 1943, the large industrial centre was regularly bombed with huge losses of lives and homes. Nevertheless, this failed to disrupt industrial production. Although not the target of air raids, Creswell was the recipient of the occasional stray bomb courtesy of planes reducing their loads while returning to Germany after bombing raids on large industrial centres. Probably the only other wartime incident involving airpower was the crash of a Wellington Bomber while on a training flight from a nearby airfield. All five of the Canadian crew were killed.

At the outbreak of war in 1939, the largest concerted mass movement of people in British history took place. Almost three million, mostly children, were evacuated from their homes in areas considered vulnerable to enemy air raids and relocated to places which were safe. Like items of luggage, labels were attached to children who, separated from their parents, were dispatched to various parts of the country for their protection. One such town considered to be unsafe was Lowestoft, a port in Suffolk on the east coast of Britain. During the war Lowestoft was a naval base and was relatively close to German U-boat activity in the North Sea. It was *per capita* one of the most heavily bombed towns in the country. Creswell was thus inducted into the war effort being compelled, for the duration, to accept evacuated children from this port. Although there are numerous historical accounts of evacuated children being mistreated, it is unlikely that many, if any, received anything short of a warm welcome from the mothers of Creswell in whose homes they were billeted. Many close and lifelong relationships were formed between these children and their host families and many maintained contacts after the war had ended. However, the influx of children did put a strain on local school facilities so that it became necessary for alternate classes to be arranged at schools. Evacuees attended in the mornings while village children were taught in the afternoons.

When Nan arrived in the village both economic and social conditions were relatively buoyant. Creswell had always been a highly productive colliery and, unlike many other pits, spending on infrastructure had not been neglected. The colliery was, like other coal mines in Britain, now under the control of the newly established National Coal Board, acquired by the Government from the Bolsover Colliery Company in 1947. The colliery remained the major source of employment for the village.

Clothing and most food, including bacon and bread, were still rationed in 1948. The harsh conditions of the 1947 winter had destroyed most vegetable crops, including the staple potato, which was also rationed. However, most miners were industrious outside their working hours and their wives were resourceful. The allotments built at the time of the model village and augmented by further conversion of land for this purpose elsewhere in the village, were still very much in use. Miners needed no government motivation to 'Dig for Britain'; they took pride in their horticultural prowess, growing their own supply of vegetables and some fruit. Many also kept pigs and hens on their allotments (or gardens if they had them) to further supplement their food supply. Many of their wives made their own bread. Petrol rationing was reintroduced in 1948 but, since most people in Creswell didn't then own a car, it was no great hardship for them.

A two-year period of National Service, peacetime conscription, was still in place when Nan arrived and would remain so until 1960. Even though coal mining had been classified as an essential service, there were still many local lads in army, navy and air force uniforms.

Church and chapel were still well attended and there were now three schools in the village — infant, junior and secondary. Those who were successful in passing the eleven plus examination went on to grammar schools outside the village. A pre-war building program by the Derbyshire County Council had produced an estate of 'council houses' providing additional, reasonably priced rental accommodation to the Model Village for the growing population.

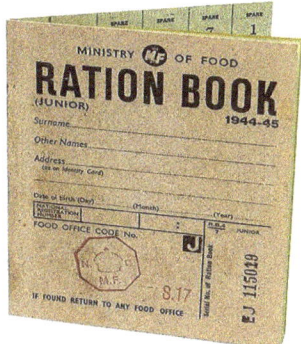

Before World War II only about 30% of British food was produced locally, hence a heavy reliance on imports. Potential wartime enemy attacks on merchant shipping would result in food shortages so food rationing was introduced in Britain on 8 January 1940. Although people continued to pay money for goods, every member of the public was issued with a ration book containing coupons that shopkeepers cut out or signed when people bought food and other items. Ration books were issued in various colours ensuring that people received the right amounts of food.

+ Buff coloured ration books were issued to most adults.
+ Green books were issued to pregnant women, nursing mothers and children under 5 allowing them a pint of milk per day, a double supply of eggs (normally 1 fresh egg or a quantity of dried egg per week), first choice of fruit (which was limited).
+ Blue ration books were issued to children between 5 and 16 who received fruit, half a pint of milk per day and full meat ration (equivalent to two chops per week).

Rationing continued until 1954, nine years after the end of the war. However, children were delighted when restrictions on sweets were lifted in 1953.

'A fair share for all': Rationing in war time Britain. https://www.findmypast.co.uk/1939register/rationing-in-britain-ww2/

A strong communal spirit had persisted and, in fact, now seemed enhanced after the strain of six years of war. The Drill Hall, no longer used for practising military drill, became the venue for the weekly 'hop' where couples could demonstrate their skills performing the 'Jive' and 'Bee Bop', dance routines imported by American GIs who were stationed in Britain from 1942 until the end of the war. Newfangled dance routines, however, were not able to displace the Old Time Dances. The Veleta, Military Two Step and the Progressive Barn dance still provided hours of fun for intergenerational families and friends, men partnering women, women dancing with each other and children, all gliding along the specially polished wooden floor. There were ambitious, professional and amateur dramatic and operatic society productions, accompanied by live orchestras and regular garden and flower shows where miners exhibited prize specimens from their allotments and small gardens. Their wives formed a floral art society and held annual shows. Beauty competitions were held where hopeful belles vied for the title 'Coal Queen'.

There was a very active unit of the St John Ambulance Brigade and, of course, the famous Creswell Colliery Brass Band, made up mainly of colliers. As old as the colliery itself, the band was formed in 1899 and achieved great success in band competitions which were then popular. The band had performed for royalty during a visit to the northern coalfields in 1912 by George V and his wife, Queen Mary. During and post war the band performances were regularly heard on the wireless and performed at London's spectacular Albert Hall. No formal occasion in the village was complete without a performance by the band, many of whose members also donned dinner suits to perform as part of the orchestras to accompany operatic society productions.

A hierarchical social structure remained in the village. With the nationalisation of the mine, at its apex, instead of a representative of the Bolsover Colliery Company, was the colliery manager and his wife, holding quasi gubernatorial roles. Their presence appeared to embody the now defunct Lord and Lady of the Manor, the Duke and Duchess of Portland. Forelock-tugging, it seemed, was part of the genetic material of the mining community. The local vicar, minister, doctors and teachers were ranked in pecking order according to the esteem in which they were held and were called on whenever there were bazaars or flower shows to be opened. The highlight of the summer season was a garden party in the grounds of York House which, even after nationalisation, had remained the residence of the mine manager. In November, the grounds of the house were again thrown open for a communal 5 November celebratory bonfire and fireworks. Over the years, traditional rivalry had developed between opposing gangs of children from Top and Bottom Model Village who, during the weeks preceding 5 November built huge pyres of wood and branches to see who could build the bigger bonfire.

This was the industrial and social milieu that awaited an apprehensive Nan as she arrived as the new midwife. However, she had made her bed and now it was up to her to try and lie comfortably in it.

According to Edith Funell in the 5th edition of *Aids to Hygiene for Nurses*:

'The position of midwife is a very vital section of the Health Service.'

Nan's position as District Midwife had the bonus of subsidised accommodation — a three bedroomed house, part of the pre-war council housing estate. She arrived in the village alone. Nan Jackson had agreed to take the children while she went to Derby to complete the mandatory two-week intensive training on the administration of Entonox, a mixture of equal parts nitrous oxide and oxygen. Its use was pioneered into midwifery practice in the 1930s to replace chloroform, then known to be potentially noxious.

Prior to the 1930s, limited analgesia was offered to women in childbirth. In the early 20th century there had been contention among obstetricians that certain groups of women suffered relatively little discomfort when giving birth, while 'over-civilised' women were more sensitive to pain. (There was even a racist view that assumed certain ethnic groups had smaller heads which made childbirth easier and relatively pain free.)

However, by the 1940s, conventional medicine began to question assumptions about childbirth and pain. In fact, the women who did receive adequate analgesia were usually those who could afford it. The question, "If a man wants a tooth out, he has to have gas or cocaine, and when in great pain, has morphine …. But a poor woman in the throes of childbirth, what does she get?" was posed in the *Gloucester Echo* in 1942.

As late as 1946, 68% of women were giving birth with no relief from pain. When women began to lobby for pain relief during delivery, within a decade, this figure had halved.

The gas and air mixture was delivered via a portable apparatus carried in a case about the size of an airline bag and weighing several kilograms. It was part of the equipment which Nan carried to each delivery. In addition, she carried a bag containing scales, dressings and various medications. Nan was a woman of slight stature so this would have been hard work for her. To maintain asepsis during deliveries she wore a gown and facemask to avoid breathing germs on the patients. All of these had to be laundered at home. She was also responsible for cleaning her instruments. When attending a patient, hands had to be washed frequently. Women giving birth at home were provided with plenty of sterilised dressings and cotton wool supplied free of charge by the county council and delivered by the midwife.

Mini gas and air analgesia apparatus, England 1943–1960.

Even in 1948, life for the domiciliary midwife was hard. On call 24 hours a day, gas and air apparatus weighing several kilograms had to be taken to each delivery with a bag containing instruments and dressings.

The appliance consisted of a rubber bag which was connected to a small portable cylinder of nitrous oxide. When fully expanded with nitrous oxide, the bag then lifted a metal plate which prevented further expansion and, therefore, overdosage. The gas was inhaled by the mother via a rubber face mask attached to the bag by a second, corrugated rubber tube. The analgesic effect was felt within about 30 seconds after the first few deep breaths. The gas was filtered through the mother's lungs, and not absorbed by the unborn baby thus ensuring it was safe.

https://collection.sciencemuseumgroup.org.uk/objects/co76125/minnitt-gas-air-analgesia-apparatus-england-1943-1960-anaesthetic-machine

When Nan Jackson delivered the children to their new home, all the furniture was in place and their bedrooms allotted. Fortunately, the house was similar in size and design to the Worksop house, so everything fitted in well. As a talisman the Monterey Cyprus tree which had been planted when she first moved into the Worksop house, was transplanted into the council house garden. Alistair relocated to the local school, but it would be another two years before Elizabeth could follow him.

Disappointingly there was still little government support for the provision of nurseries and certainly there was no prospect of this happening in Creswell where working mothers were, at that time, an exception. The only available option was to find a live-in maid or housekeeper to maintain some sort of equilibrium for the children as Nan would be on call day and night. Most of her meagre salary would go towards paying the wages of these girls — three in quick succession, two of whom were reluctant to leave but did so for better wages.

During the hours she was on call, it was essential that Nan could always be contactable. She had to leave messages stating her whereabouts. Although a telephone was installed in the house, these were the days well before the advent of mobile 'phones. The maid was allocated days off which coincided with Nan's, leaving virtually no free time. During her days off duty she would be relieved by Gertie Cooper, a warm-hearted, chain smoking midwife from Whitwell. The fact that Nan retained fond pre-war memories of Whitwell, where she still had friends from her pre-war days, probably went some way to diminishing the antipathy towards her current surroundings.

Transport posed a further dilemma. Her practice included, in addition to the village, outlying farming hamlets. Her hours were erratic, and her delivery bag, gas and air apparatus and cylinder were not inconsiderable weights. Clearly a bicycle was no use to her, even if she were able to ride one, and she had reached the conclusion that cycling was a skill she was never going to acquire.

Using some of the money from the sale of the Worksop house she purchased a black Ford Anglia. However, like riding a bike, driving a car was also not then part of her repertoire so she employed the services of Mr Gilbert, a local garage owner from whom she purchased the car, to teach her to drive. Until she passed her driving test Mr Gilbert had to be present in the car which meant accompanying her to each delivery. History doesn't record how he felt waiting in the car for her to reappear but he certainly resented being called out at two in the morning — not an unusual time for babies to choose to enter the world.

Eventually, she became confident enough — or perhaps she was unable to face yet another tirade about being dragged out of a warm bed at some God-forsaken hour– to remove her learner's plates and sit on them while driving through the night. This caused some confusion with the local police constable who, while on his nightly foot patrol, would often wave cheerfully to his nocturnal co-worker — only to see her, at a later date on her way to take her driving test, learner plates *and* Mr Gilbert *in situ*. Not surprisingly, she passed her test. After all, she had logged quite a few solo driving hours by then.

Once she commenced working, Nan found it exhausting, yet also exhilarating. Her rigorous Birch Hill training had put her in good stead. At the end of a gruelling day the luxury of debriefing, especially after a particularly stressful delivery, was then unheard of. Equally hard for her was the fact that there was no understanding partner waiting for her at home, with whom she could discuss events of her day.

Although women were able to choose whether to give birth at home or in hospital, medical suitability and lack of overcrowding permitting, about one third of all births at this time took place in the home and were considered safe. The maternal mortality rate was then thirty-five in one thousand births and falling. Nan was responsible to the County Supervisor of Midwives and she attended all normal births, including breech births. In the event of an emergency she would call one of the local doctors. In those days there was little, if any, demand in Creswell for private maternity homes. Occurring in the home, childbirth in this era was usually a gentler experience. It often took place in the presence of family members rather than in the impersonalised atmosphere of a hospital where it became a medicalised event and where, instead of lying in their own bed, women lay on their backs, their legs fixed in stainless steel obstetric stirrups.

Yet Nan lived in fear of attending an abnormal birth or one with an adverse outcome. Fortunately, this never happened to her although she admitted that she never went out to a delivery without uttering a silent prayer that everything would be safe. The women were strong, healthy and not unused to adversity themselves.

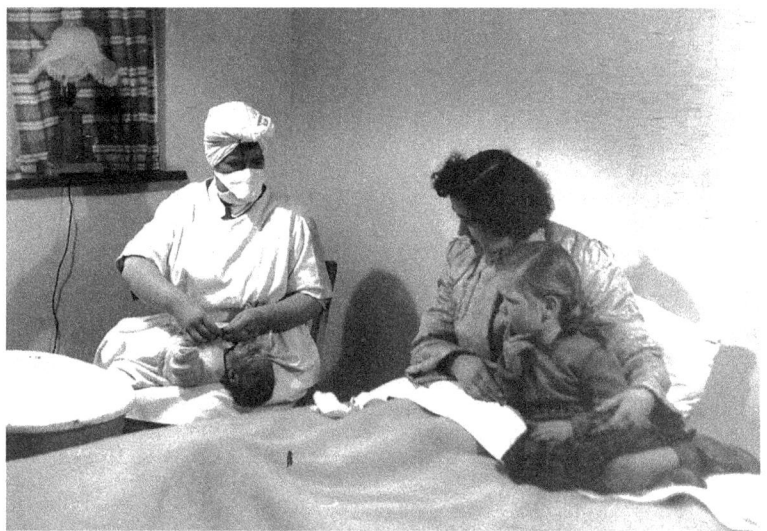

A special bond developed between midwife and patient when births occurred in the familiar surroundings of the home and normally free from medical intervention. In emergencies, the family doctor was called to assist. Aseptic practices were strictly observed. The midwife was responsible for sterilising the instruments used, and laundering her own gowns.

Home birth in Middlesex: Nursing Notes April, 1950, Midwives chronicle and nursing notes.
https://rcmheritage.wordpress.com/2013/04/03/nursing-notes-and-midwives-chronicle-april-1950/

Normally the midwife was a formidable person, a presence to be feared, as she had a lot of authority. However, this was not Nan's persona. Since she was the only midwife in the village, the women got to know her well and she them. She also got to know their husbands and families. She had an eclectic cohort of patients, mostly miners' wives, whose stoicism and hard work she admired. There were also the wives of local shopkeepers and farmers.

She would meet the women prior to delivery and would attend antenatal clinics with the local doctors with whom she also developed a good working relationship. They, in return, respected her hard work, professionalism and skill. At that time, for reasons of hygiene, midwives shaved the pubic hair of women about to give birth. Nan could see no logic in this and abstained from this procedure in the interests of the women's dignity. She would continue to visit mothers and new babies for the fourteen day 'lying-in period' after the birth, after which their care passed to the local health visitor.

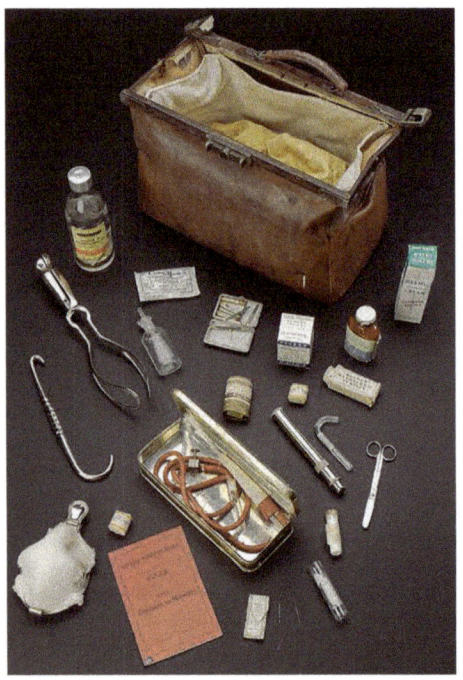

Contents of midwife's bag.
https://rcmheritage.wordpress.com/2013/04/03/nursing-notes-and-midwives-chronicle-april-1950/

In the immediate post war era, there was no central heating or the luxury of washing machines and tumble driers. There were no supermarkets and village shops were not brimming with food. Family cars were practically non-existent. Instead, there were coal fires burning in the grate, ration books and, by this time hopefully, a flushing toilet and running hot and cold water. Most of the women Nan attended were collier's wives who had already had multiple births and whose husbands, if not at work, were present in the house during the deliveries. Invariably there would be the additional sturdy support of a female neighbour or relative. Anxious husbands often paced up and down the footpath immediately outside the front door, smoking cigarette after cigarette. On one occasion a father-to-be was roused from his fireside chair by Nan yelling from upstairs, "Get Doctor Wood, quickly! Bang on his door and say PPH*, he'll come." He did, in double time. These were everyday issues she dealt with — and dealt with well.

Some of the time, the deliveries were reminiscent of A.J. Cronin novels and not all the babies were eagerly anticipated nor welcome and not many had handsome well-sprung carriages awaiting their arrival. Most babies on their maiden outing were placed in an ancient perambulator which had been used to transport a succession of offspring — frequently all at the same time, with toddlers perching on the rim and groceries stacked underneath. Frequently, little or no preparations were made for the arrival of a new baby. Instead of linen sheets, there were sometimes only grey old army blankets, or overcoats on the beds.

Many of the homes Nan worked in were squalidly situated houses around the base of the pit tip. The Bevin Hostels, which once housed conscripted miners and now served as makeshift housing, were also part of her round. Arriving home from these pitiful homes, it was not uncommon for Nan to find a tablet of Lux or Palmolive soap, then still rationed, put into her delivery bag by a grateful patient — a luxury they could ill afford. Rarely, she was offered

---

*   PPH = *post-partum* haemorrhage

money but always declined, suggesting instead that they put it into a money box for the new baby.

There was at least one occasion when she stripped one of Elizabeth's dolls of its clothes, old ones the children had worn as babies, for a new-born child for whom no preparations had been made. The smallest baby she recalled delivering at home weighed a mere three pounds (about a kilogram and a half. The baby, a girl was, to the bemusement of the father and older brother, nursed in a shoebox by the hearth. The baby grew into a heathy child.

Despite the proximity of the pit and its noxious smell, most homes were spotlessly clean, the families happy and babies welcome. As she got to know the miners and their wives she recognised and admired their tenacity, loyalty and humour. The men battled hard for little reward in one of the hardest, most dangerous and poorly paid jobs in the country and Nan enjoyed their cheeky banter. Their stoic wives were their strongest supporters.

During the two years she worked as a midwife Nan made many friends, including a local solicitor who proposed marriage. She declined as she was, after all, still a married woman. Whether she was lonely is debateable. She developed a fairly busy social life, but her work was demanding and stressful and the hours were long. Domestic arrangements were often fraught, and she resented the fact that work obligations were frequently an impediment to the commitment she had made to provide a secure environment for the children. When called out on the middle of the night it was not uncommon, when backing the car out of the driveway to look up and see a distraught child banging on the window. She would then get out of the car to come back and comfort the child, all the time knowing that she was needed elsewhere.

The 'maids' also posed problems. The original one, Nancy, was a delight and Nan's complete confidence in her kindness and integrity was not misplaced. The children were frequent visitors to Nancy's family home where they mixed well with her younger siblings. However, her wage was a pittance and the hours long. Reluctantly, Nancy resigned and resumed her former work in the village sweet shop where, at least, she earned decent money. Nancy, it appeared, was irreplaceable. Her successor, although efficient was taciturn and not able to cope with being left alone with two children, often for several consecutive nights, and resigned after only a short time. Job applicants were few and far between and the third one was lazy and spent much of the day gossiping with neighbours, either in their homes, or in Nan's house. Although Alistair was at school, Elizabeth was still only four and, in this girl's charge fared none too well. There was an additional worry for Nan. The girl's boyfriend became a frequent visitor to the house during Nan's nocturnal calls and the girl left abruptly when she became pregnant. Nan was left in dire straits with no replacement in the offing. By this time, the strain of her working hours with barely any free time became too much. Once more it was time for her to take stock. It was 1950. Elizabeth, now five, was old enough to go to school.

Fortuitously at that time, a new position became vacant at the pit, now under the auspices of the National Coal Board. A nurse was required to take over the running of the medical centre, responsible for the health of the hundreds of men who worked underground and on the pit top. Nan applied for the position. To attend the interview, she took time from work and was still wearing her midwife's uniform when she arrived at Sherwood Lodge near Mansfield, local administrative headquarters of the NCB. At the end of the interview she was offered the position.

Returning to the village, either the elation at her success or confusion at Mansfield's one-way road system caused her to get lost. Finding herself behind a brewer's lorry she decided to follow it in the hope that it would lead her out of the town. It did, straight into the brewery yard. The site of a midwife in a Ford Anglia driving into a brewery yard was somewhat surprising for the brewers. After the laughter had subsided, she was given explicit, reliable directions to her destination.

She gave up her midwife's uniform and equipment. In honour of her surname, her two-year tenure as village midwife became known, colloquially, as *The Stewart Era*. One of her legacies was a legion of little boys who bore her name. For the rest of her life in the village she would proudly point out sturdy, grown boys and girls, confiding, "That's one of my babies".

* * * *

Yet again Nan had made a momentous decision which called for more disruption and further planning. A new midwife was appointed to replace her, and in the interim, Nan remained in the council house. Around this time, Nan and Harry Jackson, with no family of their own in England, made the decision to emigrate to Australia to be near Harry's only niece. While working as a midwife Nan had encountered a woman called May Clarke. May was about Nan's age. Her husband, Fred, had previously worked underground but, because of an accident, now worked at the pit top. May was a typical miner's wife — a robust, salt-of-the-earth woman who, in her brusque manner, would do anything she could to help others in need. Nan had first met her during a particularly protracted labour and had been grateful for May's involvement.

No doubt May recognised in Nan someone who could benefit from some occasional support herself. Although, outwardly from opposite poles, Nan and May found mutually recognisable qualities. Fred was born and bred in Creswell, but May had moved from a neighbouring village when they were married twenty years earlier.

They had been through hard times together, especially at the time of Fred's accident when there was doubt about whether he would ever work again. Fred and May had two children, a son and a daughter, who were slightly older than Nan's children. They also all lived in a house in the Model Village, a stone's throw from the pit and, literally around the corner from Nan's new medical centre. Fred and May were to play a significant role in Nan's life in the village for many years to come. After Nan retired and left the village and Fred had died, May and Nan remained friends.

The first and most important decision was to find a new home. Nan assessed her financial situation. She still had some residual money from the sale of the previous house and her salary over the last two years had been sufficient to live on without drawing on this amount. After selling her car she would have enough money to put down a sizeable deposit on another house. Since she had already obtained a previous mortgage, this time it was a slightly less complex procedure. (Regrettably she was unable to retain the services of the solicitor from the previous occasion, the man whose proposal of marriage she had refused. Nan was unsure if her refusal influenced his decision to give up the legal practice and become a minister of the church.)

Although local councils were then engaged in ambitious building of subsidised housing, there was still a dearth of private housing on the market and there was a deadline to vacate the existing house for the incoming midwife. Again, her timing was good. Nan found a detached, three-bedroom house in a quiet street well away from the pit. It had a large, but overgrown, garden complete with a small orchard of apple and pear trees and a small concrete air raid shelter, later used by Alistair as a mushroom farm. The house had been built around thirty years earlier and was in sound condition although badly in need of redecoration. It was within walking distance of the schools (Elizabeth was due to start in September at the beginning of the new school year). The children loved it — especially the large garden and the air raid shelter.

With Fred and May, she spent the long summer evenings cleaning, painting, stripping and replacing layers of old wallpaper while the four children ran amok outside and made friends with the neighbouring children. Nan looked longingly at her garden, and anticipated weeding and planting. There was ample room for a vegetable patch, perhaps even a greenhouse. At last the house was ready for habitation. Once more the furniture arrived at a new destination and was accordingly arranged. The Monterey Cyprus tree came too, and was planted outside the front door. It survived the move and flourished.

After two years she began to feel a strange sensation. She realised that she was starting to feel at home, probably for the first time in her life. She was meeting new friends, forging a successful professional career and being treated with respect and warmth by her fellow villagers. She had now, without reservation, thrown in her lot with the mining village she had previously detested and feared.

Something else occurred by this time on the national stage. At last there was acknowledgement of the dangers of coal mining. Safety was now in the hands of the state.

13

Dirt and Dust: Miners' Safety, at last.

An old Miner, sits by the fireside,
Thinking back over the years,
The memories, drift upon him,
Of the toil, the sweat and the tears.

He started work as a young lad,
He wanted to follow his Pa,
There was nothing else, the money was good,
And he thought it would get him far.

But now nearly fifty years later,
After working that big black hole,
His lungs are scarred with the memory,
Of the dirt and the dust from the coal.
The Miner's Tale
Jayne Davies

During her formative years, when Nan was growing up, there had been much activity regarding health and safety in the coal industry. Had this not taken place, the position to which she was eventually appointed would have remained non-existent. In 1947, after decades of struggle, nationalisation had finally been achieved — although it is arguable that it may have come too late to save the industry and improve the lives of the workers and their families. As late as 1946, only 21% of miners were over the age of 50 and their average age was 39.1 years compared to 35.7 years in 1931. Clearly mining aged these men. However, when out of the hands of private enterprise, the process of reform had accelerated with enhancement of miners' safety being one of the most significant benefits. Nevertheless, beneficial changes had occurred, albeit for most of the first half of the century, at a grindingly slow pace.

Between 1850 and 1914 at least 90,000 miners died in British coal mines — an average of one every six hours and accounted for 25% of all occupation related deaths. In that same period, every two hours a miner was *seriously* injured and *badly* injured every three minutes. Even today the work involved in mining is among the top ten industries with high injury and fatality rates. Health and safety, it seems, were irrelevant in the scramble for increased profits.

Long before safety in mines became an issue for government, miners began to demand safer and less arduous working conditions. Toward the end of the 19th century, Beatrice and Sydney Webb made reference to a 1662 petition from miners to King Charles ll requesting, *inter alia*, that owners provide better ventilation in mines.

The management of mining safety appears to have followed a somewhat haphazard course. By and large it was not regarded as a serious issue by mine owners. Various legislation was enacted in response to catastrophes (the 1842 act was prompted by the Huskar disaster) and *ad hoc* Royal Commissions were established in the wake of various other mining disasters. The stimulus for the formation of a Royal Commission in 1907 had been a disaster in a French coal mine where an underground fire, ignited after an explosion of coal dust, had claimed the lives of one thousand men. In 1908, during that Commission's sitting, a further ten men and boys were killed in a mining accident in Somerset where there had been no organised rescue teams and a party of volunteers, including the mine manager, searched for ten days in a futile attempt to locate survivors.

The long-awaited Coal Mines Act of 1911, the most effective to date, was a culmination and enhancement of various other statutes enacted during the 19th century regarding conditions in the coal industry. It was the first *major* legislation governing mines since the superseded act of 1887 which had mainly addressed the danger of explosions, the most common risk in coal mines, and had assigned the responsibility of mine safety to mine management. While the 1911 act reinforced the provisions of its predecessor, particularly in relation to safety, the intent of the new legislation was to improve safety and health as well as the actual overall management of mines. One of the beneficial outcomes of improved safety would be a healthier workforce which would inevitably, it was claimed, increase productivity.

Among the significant recommended changes to the existing law, the 1911 Act made the installation of safety stations at various points underground compulsory. It also became a legal requirement for management to employ teams of trained rescue workers equipped with breathing apparatus. (Although these provisions were *recommended* in the 1887 Act, they had never been enforced). To minimise the risk of underground fires, precautionary measures to prevent explosions of coal dust would now also be a legal requirement as was the sealing of disused and abandoned mines. In addition to enforcing directives for improving mine safety, the Act mandated an eight-hour working day for miners.

The following year, 1912, further legislation was passed requiring mine owners to provide ambulances. Owners were also made responsible for installing rescue stations to be situated within sixteen kilometres(ten miles) of every mine which employed a hundred workers. Training teams of rescuers to keep and maintain safety apparatus became requisite. This ruling, strictly adhered to, resulted in a noticeable increase, not only in the number of rescue stations staffed by full time trained rescuers, but in the supplies of rescue equipment such as breathing apparatus.

A 1912 Act established the Mining Qualifications Board to ensure colliery managers and under-managers, firemen, deputies and shot firers who were responsible for mining safety were suitably qualified and in possession of certificates of competence. Under the terms of the same Act it became obligatory for mines to be supervised daily by a manager and an under manager. Mine safety was at last being taken seriously.

Interestingly, the 1911 Act saw the introduction of canaries into coal mines as a safety precaution to detect carbon monoxide and other toxic gases. Their use is credited to John Scott Haldane, who was known as 'the father of oxygen therapy'. Haldane's research into carbon monoxide led him to recommend the use of canaries. Like other birds, being vulnerable to airborne poison, they are good early detectors of carbon monoxide. Far from contravening animal rights, there are reports of miners treating the birds as pets and whistling to them as they worked. Whether on animal welfare grounds or not, in 1986, canaries were finally retrenched, to be replaced by electronic detectors.

Hazardous working conditions and long hours had become a working-class phenomenon since the advent of the Industrial Revolution when small scale artisanal occupations were replaced by large scale industry. Resulting sickness and injury posed a threat to productivity. Only when it was apparent that workers' health was affected by the conditions in which they worked — operating heavy, often dangerous machinery, handling chemicals — did occupational health become an issue.

As early as 1775, Percival Pott, a surgeon, was the first scientist to identify a connection between working conditions and ill health, specifically between the nature of work and carcinoma. In Pott's day it was the practice to employ young boys as chimney sweeps. Being small and nimble they were able to negotiate winding Victorian chimneys. Pott noticed a high incidence of scrotal cancer among these boys which he attributed to exposure to carcinogen laden soot particles in the sweat which ran down the boys' bodies. The particle-charged sweat accumulated in the skin creases of the scrotum where it generated a carcinogenic reaction. *Chimney Sweeps' Cancer* was claimed to be the first recorded occupation-related cancer.

The use of canaries as a means of warning against the presence of firedamp (methane, a particularly flammable gas) in coal mines. They are suited to this because they are small and portable and because their anatomy makes them vulnerable to airborne poisons. Birds are continuously inhaling. This is what helps them to fly. Miners would take the birds into the mines with them and would whistle to them while they worked. In 1986, 200 canaries were made redundant in British coal mines and replaced by electronic detectors.

https://www.pinterest.com.au/pin/313915036517452986/?lp=true

Two hundred years before Pott's discovery, Georgius Agricola (1494–1555) lived in Saxony and founded the discipline of geology. He was also a physician who attended miners in Joachimsthal, now part of the Czech Republic. In addition to documenting mining related accidents, Agricola recounted instances of miners working with heavy metals in fetid, cold and wet conditions. He described the respiratory diseases to which they frequently succumbed, diseases which he attributed to dust penetrating 'the windpipe and lungs producing, difficulty in breathing.... the disease which the Greeks call asthma [which] eats away at the lungs and plants consumption on the body'. Agricola had discovered silicosis and pneumoconiosis, still common ailments among miners.

Another early researcher into occupational health was Philippus Theophrastus Aureolus Bombastus von Hohenheim (Paracelsus), who was a contemporary of Agricola. Paracelsus (1493–1541) was one of the most influential medical scientists in Renaissance Europe. His fields of research included alchemy and metallurgy. Reputed to be the father of toxicology, Paracelsus was a pioneer of the Medical Revolution, a movement based on ancient Greek and Roman theses. Associated with the progress and development in existing medical knowledge, it laid the foundations of modern medicine.

Paracelsus visited many mining sites in Austria and Moravia where he noticed a correlation between the amount of dust, ash and fumes present in the mines and impaired lung function in miners. Observing [that]

> 'mountain consumption and sickness [was associated with] miners, smelters, samplers, moneyers, goldsmiths and alchemists coming into contact with the poisonous air found in the earth.' He identified 'mountain consumption'

as a disease of the lung, 'a swelling of the body, an upset stomach …. Such sick are those consumed by the mountain.'

What Paracelsus described were pulmonary tuberculosis and lung cancer, both associated with coal mining.

Paracelsus, recognised the high toll exacted by the earth in return for surrendering its riches, and concluded that

'a very good thing, worth to be acquired, has first to be separated from the bad. The art is such, that nothing good can be acquired without a price …. To get what you want, you must face also that you do not want'.

During the 19th century there was a rather ambivalent attitude among the non-working classes towards occupational welfare of working people. Long, hard hours of work inevitably resulted in a high rate of accidental death and injury. This, in turn, led to numerous orphans and widows who subsequently became a drain on the state. Hard work, it was believed, also drained workers of physical *and* moral energy, thereby preventing them from leading good Christian lives. The contemporary *laissez-faire* economy seemed to resolve this conundrum by regarding any attempt to improve the lives of the rank and file as an imposition. (The literal translation of *laissez-faire* 'let go' implies non-involvement in the activities of others.)

At the time when coal mining was making Britain an industrial success, the men who mined the coal were the object of conflicting opinions within the Victorian populace. As their numbers increased with the development of the industry, they became easily distinguishable by the effect of their arduous work. Miners developed stooped, stunted bodies. Their sallow complexions, once the grime had been washed away, and their swollen eyes and eyelids from working in the dark, further defined them. However, because they obviously possessed the stamina required to able to perform such physically demanding work, they were regarded as examples of robustness. Ironically, because the filthy work required them to bathe regularly (regardless of the circumstances under which these ablutions occurred they were considered, to have a higher standard of personal hygiene than was the norm for their class. Bathing, it was considered, also improved their general health.

It was not only their distinctive stature which defined them. The work brutalised them. Their facial shapes, features and expression, it was said, reflected this brutality giving them a savage appearance. Disturbingly, this led some to regard miners as racially 'degenerate'. Many cited as evidence the fact that these men lacked sensitivity. How else were they were able to tolerate excruciating pain of physical trauma frequently caused by the inherently dangerous nature of their work? Their wives were not immune from this slur. Mining communities were small and closely knit. Men and women married from within their own community. With innuendoes of incest, miners' wives were not spared these abhorrent insults. Complacent prejudice may well have hindered early innovative medical care in coal mines.

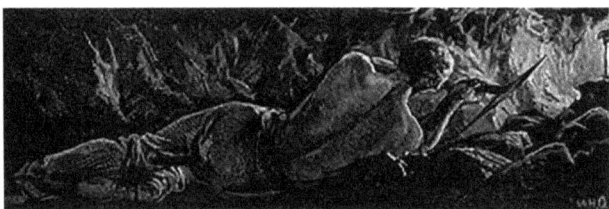

Long, narrow tunnels made it necessary for coal miners to work for an average of twelve hours a day in extremely confined conditions. Unsurprisingly their physical stature became permanently stooped and deformed and made them easily recognisable in the community.

Trappers, Hurriers and Hewers: Working in a Coal Mine:
https://thoroglove.wordpress.com/2015/03/12/trappers-hurriers-and-hewers-working-in-a-coal-mine/

13 Dirt and Dust: Miners' Safety, at last.

The foundations of occupational health and safety legislation had been laid down as early as the first Factory Act in 1833 with the appointment of inspectors responsible for improving the working conditions of factory workers. However, coal miners, with their perilous work environment, were largely ignored by the Act. Although the Mines and Collieries Act of 1842 had prohibited women — and children less than ten years of age — from working underground, it ignored health and occupational welfare, and in no way improved working conditions *per se*. As mining was a much older occupation than factory work its inherent dangers, it seems, were acceptable.

Being unable to work because of injury or work-related illness invariably meant loss of income. There was no compensation or sick pay as miners' wages were proportionate to the amount of coal they dug out each shift. Failure to work a full shift was reflected in the amount of money received. Added to this dilemma, in smaller and remote communities, hospital services were few and far between. In the absence of professional health care, people in crises — births, injuries or even death — turned to untrained persons who, unfortunately, dealt in ineffective, 'quack' remedies. Most injured miners were treated in their own homes with the help of their wives or other family members and friends.

Organised resources to manage underground accidents remained limited and uncoordinated with injured miners left, largely, to fend for themselves. Although hospital facilities existed in the larger towns and cities, they were not affordable to most workers as few 19th century employers provided welfare or medical services for their employees. Treatment, if any, was given by a local doctor, possibly assisted by a nurse or midwife — provided a pre-paid contribution had been made.

The famous mustard makers, Colman's, employed at their factory in Norwich possibly the first industrial nurse. Philippa Flowerday was appointed on 17 November 1872. Her duties included helping a doctor each morning with clinical examinations and taking supplies from the works kitchen to the sick at home, a duty which entailed about forty-five visits a week. She assisted the Colman's Sick Society, administering a clothing club. For these duties she received a salary of twenty-six shillings a week. When she married in 1888, she was succeeded by a Sister Quarry.

In 1872, aged 32, Philippa Flowerday was employed by Colmans and became the first industrial nurse. She provided care for the employees of the Carrow Works factory by helping the doctor each morning and taking supplies to the sick at home. It is thought that she made over 45 visits a week. It was the first post of its kind to be established in Britain.

In 1872, Philippa Flowerday became the first known industrial nurse in Britain. Employed by Colman's in Norwich to care for employees at their Carrow Works factory, her duties included helping the doctor with morning clinics and delivering provisions to sick workers in their homes.

In the latter part of 19th century Britain, the St John Ambulance Brigade was formed, largely from mining communities, with almost every mining community having its own division. Communal first aid classes became popular, both socially and educationally. Conscious of the need to train employees in first aid and safety measures, coal owners were very supportive of local divisions of the brigade and, in many collieries, training in first aid was given to all new entrants to the industry before they could be employed underground. In what probably reflected medicine at this time, the following instructions for treatments of various work-related medical events were given in a first aid manual:

Treatment of wounds:

'After the first manifest danger from loss of blood the most urgent claim of a wound is to make it a place that cannot be invaded by the Pus Germ, and so become suppurative or matter forming. This germ is practically everywhere — in the air, in dust, in dirt, on the skin, the clothing, or the implement causing the injury. It must be dealt with as perpetually lying in wait to attack broken surfaces, and the gospel of opposing it is summed up in the phrase Absolute or Surgical Cleanliness. First Aid, is to thoroughly lave the wound with plenty of fresh water and a clean cloth, then fix a First Aid Dressing comprised of new lint dipped in pure water or half and half whiskey and water above it, and so seal it against the atmospherical attack of germs.

Treatment of Burns and Scalds:

The first is caused by dry heat, the latter by moist. Treatment: Keep out the air. Cover with flour and cotton wool, or Carron Oil, Olive Oil, Vaseline, or Lard.

For Electricity Burns:
Clean Loaf of Bread and pure water poultices, frequently renewed.

The St John Ambulance Brigade was created in 1887 by the Venerable Order of St John. Its primary purpose was to teach first aid to industrial workers so that they could provide assistance in workplace emergencies. They often formed in mining communities where they provided first line treatment in accidents. Almost every colliery village had its own division. Training was taken very seriously, and mine owners often supported the Divisions by becoming Presidents. They became the forerunners of medical services in mines. When Nan began her work at the mine, she worked closely with them and valued their skills and experience.

St. John Historical Timeline https://stjohnwa.com.au/about-us/our-history/st-john-historical-timeline

Before the development of large-scale government and employer health insurance and other financial services, rudimentary workers'

13 Dirt and Dust: Miners' Safety, at last.

health schemes, like friendly societies, began to emerge in the late 19th century. Although most were initially concerned with workers' financial well-being, many of them also offered medical resources for their members. There also emerged at this time the provision of medical assistance for coalminers via workplace schemes. Demonstrating an awareness of the dangers in mining and the need to provide medical care, mines appointed doctors to provide health services for their employees and miners became the first among the working class to receive medical treatment from qualified doctors. Compulsory donations withheld from wages went towards paying for the doctors' salaries. Appointments and/or dismissals remained the prerogative of the employers. Coal miners, however, believed they rarely got value for their hard-earned money and decided, around 1900, to take matters into their own hands to improve the quality of their care. Voluntary contributory medical associations were introduced and miners paid a weekly subscription of sixpence to be part of an association.

In the 1920s, such schemes as the one in Tredegar (See earlier chapter), employed doctors at set salaries and any surplus funds were used to extend medical services. Such innovative schemes expanded to include the provision of service for non-mining personnel and often allowed access to dental, pharmacological and physiotherapy services in addition to medical treatment. Convalescent and maternity homes augmented available services, providing treatment for children and dependent wives. The schemes were based on socialist ideals where paid workers subsidised the healthcare of their less well-off peers.

Again, A.J. Cronin, writer and medical practitioner, provided a fine example of such a scheme. He was employed in mining communities in South Wales in the 1920s and did, at one time, work in Tredegar. His fifth novel *The Citadel* written in 1937 describes not only his working experience and local living conditions, but the procedure involved in his appointment. During his employment by The Tredegar Medical Society, Cronin conducted research into the association between the inhalation of coal dust and lung disease. The Tredegar Medical Society became, eventually, the archetype for the National Health Service established by noted Welsh Labour minister, Aneurin Bevan.

By the mid-1920s, suitable accommodation was being provided at coal mines for the treatment of injured miners. This resulted in the appointment of a recognised first aid attendant, a member of the local St John Ambulance Brigade, to be available at all times, although usually he had additional duties to perform.

However, as with much innovation, advancement in the growth of industrial health was driven by war. During World War I, the Ministry of Munitions established medical departments in their factories to provide advice on hygiene, health and welfare, possibly because, for the first time, increasingly large numbers of women were being employed. As a result of their war time experience, doctors and nurses were appointed by some enlightened employers to work in the field of industrial health. Their cumulative knowledge and experience contributed to the emerging specialist practice of occupational health.

Although interest and improvement in this developing branch of health care was bolstered during World War II, the introduction of the National Health Service in 1948 created even greater momentum. At the time the service was established there was a national shortage of doctors and nurses in primary medicine, and therefore a disincentive on the part of the government to duplicate services by expanding into industries, especially the newly nationalised ones such as the National Coal Board. In 1949, Prime Minister Clement Atlee commissioned the Dale Enquiry 'to examine the relationship' between preventive and curative health services and to examine how various services could be used to greater advantage. In 1951, the twelve-member committee, which included two nurses, concluded there was no overlap in services and that industrial health services provided a separate and necessary role. The committee also pointed to the wide range of services already being offered by some of the larger industries, with the widest being offered by the National Coal Board. These services, however, were basically no more than first aid. Consequently, there was a government increase in resources available for further development of industrial health services.

Forty-six years after the landmark legislation of the 1911 Coal Mines Act, under the auspices of, arguably, the two greatest government reforms of the 20th century, the passage of a National Health Services Act and the Coal Nationalisation Act, a government-controlled service for the health and safety of miners was established.

In the 19th century there was a an awareness of the dangers involved in the mining of coal and a recognition of a duty of care on the behalf of management to their employees which began to coordinate previously haphazard medical responses to mining accidents.

Although not the centre at Creswell where Nan worked (which together with the rest of the pit has now been demolished) the one on the right bears a structural resemblance.

http://www.raggyspelk.co.uk/washington_pages/photo_gallery/pg_01.html

As an example of how far mining medical and safety services have progressed, the following job description appeared on *Seek* (an Australian job search site) for the services of an occupational health nurse for a mine site in Queensland. The specialised nature of caring for miners at work is now paramount.

About the role

A rewarding opportunity exists for a Queensland Registered Nurse to join our OHST Team at Carpentaria Gold. The position offers a competitive salary package as well as an attractive 8 days on and 6 days off shift roster. This position reports to the OHST Manager and supports our Mining and Processing operations as well as the local community.

Key Aspects

The key aspects of this role are:

- Provide emergency medical treatment and first aid as required
- Maintain the site medical clinic and medical supplies
- Maintain medical records
- Conduct drug and alcohol testing
- Develop and promote health and wellbeing programmes
- Co-ordinate the management of workers compensation claims and injury management
- Conduct fitness for work assessments
- Provide front line support to site emergency rescue teams
- Conduct site medicals (audiometry, spirometry, ECG)
- Conduct on site vaccinations as required
- Dispense approved Medications (Schedule 2, 3, 4, 8)
- Foster continued relationships with RFDS and QAS
- Coordinate pre-employment medicals with external providers and provide advice on medical assessments and fitness for work
- Provide emergency medical assistance to the local community
- Skills and experience

To become part of this dynamic team you must possess the following qualifications, skills and experience:

- Must be Qld Registered Nurse qualified (must be currently registered)
- Minimum of 5 years experience
- Emergency response experience highly regarded
- Regional or remote experience

- Experience in injury management
- Immunisation qualifications
- Rehabilitation & Return to Work Coordinator qualifications highly regarded
- Well-developed written and verbal communication skills
- Genuine desire to help people and achieve solid outcomes
- Must have a current manual drivers licence
- Ability to work in a semi-remote environment
- Proven experience to work successfully within a dynamic team and work environment
- Conditions of employment will be discussed at the interview.

https://www.seek.com.au/job/39874991?type=standout&searchrequesttoken=96f2fff1-7fe4-424d-90a1-54dc89e9c654

14

Pit Boots, Sutures and Foreign Bodies.

Miners at Creswell Colliery in 1947 — Nan's constituency.
Alamy. https://www.alamy.com/stock-photo/miners-working. html?blackwhite=1&page=3

In 1947, Area Medical Officers were appointed to National Coal Board medical centres which were Staffed by State Registered Nurses, assisted by St John Ambulance Brigade trained first aid attendants who had, prior to 1947 staffed the centres. To encourage an interest in first aid, and to enhance this service, a scheme was introduced to train volunteer miners. On completion of the training each man received a certificate and badge depicting the eight-pointed cross of St John, inscribed with the motto 'We Give And Take Care'.

In Creswell about 85% of the village labour force was exclusively reliant on the mine for employment. Of these, 50% were miners who dug the coal, 10-20% pit labourers and 11% were tradesmen (painters, electricians and fitters). The remaining, approximately 20%, consisted of 'non-manual' staff — office clerks, canteen workers and nursing/medical staff. Operations both above and below ground were supervised by mining officials. In the close interlocking community, each layer of management held a unique position in the social hierarchy, the manager being accorded the status of local squire. Dependence on one industry made for an uncomplicated social structure. Born into families where mining had been the traditional occupation for generations, miners knew little other than mining, nor the existing social order in which they had grown up.

It was in this environment, in early 1950, that Nan began her employment with the National Coal Board as a Registered Nurse managing the medical centre at the Colliery. She continued to work there until her retirement in 1967.

Her appointment was one of the first in that division of the National Coal Board and, shortly afterwards she was joined by colleagues appointed to the same positions in neighbouring pits. Helen Skelton was employed to run the medical centre at Whitwell pit. Nan had known Helen's family in her pre-war years as district nurse and she and Helen became firm friends for the next thirty years. Like Nan, Helen had a chequered career. At sixteen she had left home to work as a nanny to an expatriate family living in Argentina and, after training as a nurse, had spent most of the war as part of the Queen Alexandra's Royal Imperial Army Nursing Service serving mainly in North Africa and Middle East. Like Nan, she brought to the position years of experience and knowledge.

Facing a post war nursing shortage, the Ministry of Health encouraged men as well as women to join the profession. A one-year training course was introduced for men leaving military service to accelerated entry into the nursing profession. Many of these men had gained excellent experience during the war working in medical units.

Their front-line experience in a very male environment rendered them ideally suited to the type of nursing work in a heavy, male dominated industry such as coal mining. This was not a problem for Nan and her female colleagues, and their new roles brought them into frequent, mutually supportive contact. Ironically, Nan's predecessor in Creswell had been a man who, after only a short time in the job, had resigned.

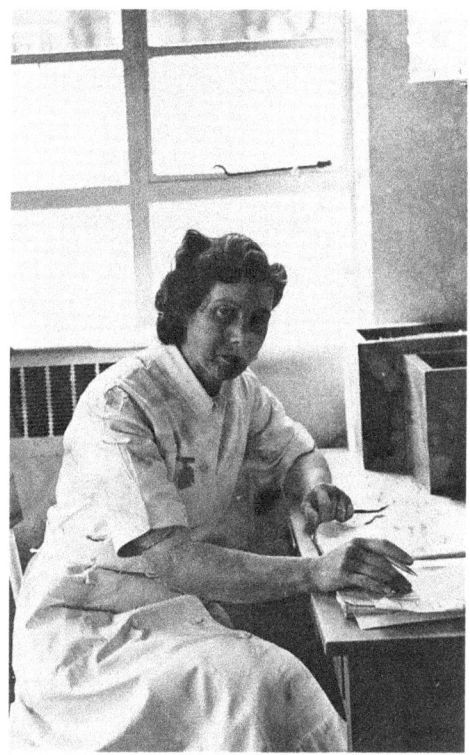

"What's your check number?"
Nan writing her report at conclusion of a clinic visit, c.1951

However, there was a significant bone of contention, namely, the disparity in pay for equal work. Male nurses received a higher rate of pay than their female colleagues who, in many cases, had much more nursing experience and responsibility. This disparity was, presumably, based on the assumption that men were usually the single breadwinners in the family with household expenses such as mortgages. Although many of the female nurses were married women with husbands also receiving a wage, this was not the case with Nan. This did not sit easily with her!

Historically, mining hazards fell into two groups: accidents and industrial diseases. Both demanded cooperation between employer and employee to minimise the risks. Risk management was, therefore, a key requirement of Nan's job description. In addition to attending accidents — life-threatening or otherwise — she was responsible for ensuring that safety regulations were in place *and* adhered to. Knowledge of treating and preventing the impressive inventory of diseases associated with coal mining was an important part of her expertise. Nan, being responsible for the health and welfare of three thousand men, continued to put her profession first and, as in the past, approached her new role with total commitment.

Although her working hours were more compatible with rearing two young children than they had been in her previous position, they were still long. She worked from 9am to 5pm from Monday to Friday and from 9am until 1pm on Saturday, and the work was still demanding. Both children now attended village schools and were able to get to and from school independently. Her attendance at school open days often proved precarious. Yet family life was, as she had intended, 'normal' given that theirs was not a conventional family at that time.

In 1950, when Nan arrived, the medical centre was still staffed by the three first aid attendants who had worked there since its inception and whose working hours reflected those of the miners' shifts — day, afternoon and night. As can be imagined, there was a 'settling in' period for the newly arrived person in charge. The day attendant, George was a mild little man, helpful, but sadly lacking in confidence, efficiency and competence. Chris, the afternoon worker was affable, helpful and more than happy to relinquish some of his control to Nan. He had spent his whole life in the village and was a very reliable source of information concerning the backgrounds of most of the men whom Nan hadn't already encountered. Frank, the night attendant was altogether a different kettle of fish and, encountering Nan at each morning's handover of shift, was resentful and sullen.

Of the three men who had worked alongside Nan's predecessor, Frank was the one most trusted by the miners which allowed him the advantage of undermining Nan's authority. He jealously guarded his patient load and made appointments for them to be seen by him either late in the evening or early in the morning outside Nan's working hours.

After a few weeks Nan arrived at work one morning, breathless as usual after cooking breakfast, supervising bed making and seeing two children off to school before hanging out the washing. She encountered, sitting in the waiting room, a man with one eye heavily bandaged. As she entered her office, Frank awkwardly rose from the chair behind her desk. With obvious difficultly, he swallowed his pride and suggested that this man should wait and see Sister. Nan always had a particular interest in ophthalmic nursing with considerable experience, both adult and paediatric. For over a week the man had been seeing Frank who treated him with antibiotic eye drops in the belief he had conjunctivitis. Nan brought out her favourite, newly acquired piece of equipment, a binocular loupe. She could see immediately that a foreign body had lodged in his eye and was the cause of the infection. Skilfully the offending fragment was removed, antibiotic drops inserted, and a clean dressing applied. The man subsequently recovered and there was no residual damage to his eye.

Undoubtedly, without her intervention, and Frank's ability to swallow his pride, the man would have been in serious trouble, at worse losing his sight and facing extended time off work. Working underground requires perfect eyesight. Nan had gained Frank's respect. During her years at the pit, both George and Frank retired and were replaced by younger men. Surprisingly, it didn't take long for Nan to become good friends with Frank and his family.

Despite 'regular' working hours, Nan was still on call day and night, weekends included. No telephone was installed in her house and, if needed for an out of hours emergency, a messenger was sent to bring her to the pit. This was not infrequent. Emergencies, when they arose, were serious and many of the accidents she attended were horrendous.

One of the main responsibilities of a mine's medical service is to advise and organise efficient first aid facilities above and below ground. Prompt, effective assessment and treatment can mean the difference between life and death, or permanent disability. There were first aid stations underground, and miners specially trained in first aid were rostered onto each shift. Part of Nan's responsibility was to ensure these stations were well stocked and maintained. Stocks included sterile dressings, blankets, carrying sheet and splints as well as access to sandbags in case of spinal injuries. Men suffering from fractures faced long jarring underground journeys before receiving specialist medical treatment. Many men worked a thousand metres underground where the distance by man-carrying locomotive was often several kilometres. On-the-spot first aid attendants had to be capable of administering effective pain relief, frequently morphine in pre-loaded ampoulettes. Communication about the injured man's condition, emergency treatment and administration of any medication had to be accurate. Ultimately, the responsibility for training men to carry out this task was Nan's.

She made frequent trips underground in the event of accidents to ensure that the injured men were in a stable condition before being moved. Wearing overalls and heavy boots she would scramble along the ground for considerable distances to reach the patient, medical emergency kit in her hand. The kit contained Morphine an opiate to relieve severe pain, and Coramine (Nikethemide) a central nervous system and respiratory stimulant. Most of the accidents occurred at the coal face, and as temperatures in some parts of the mine were 30 degrees Celsius, she soon became acquainted with the working conditions of the men in her care. However, these subterranean excursions took their toll and each one would leave her feeling exhausted for the next few days. Unlike the miners, her descents were sporadic and not frequent enough for acclimatisation.

Much of her work involved routine treatment of conditions such as beat knees (bursitis) and elbows caused by the strain of repetitive work, eye injuries, ear infections and dermatitis. Often, in the course of meticulous history taking and recognition of symptoms, she was able to summarily diagnose various conditions which were appropriately referred for further investigation. Nan was also conscientious about increasing her knowledge in her field of work. Personal development was encouraged and facilitated by the area superintendent of nursing. Whenever time away from work permitted, she and her colleagues spent working days with various medical specialists at Chesterfield, Sheffield and Worksop hospitals.

She was responsible for performing medical examinations on cadet miners who went to nearby Markham Colliery for a mandatory period of training prior to commencing work underground. On at least two occasions, while testing the eyesight of new recruits, she discovered boys who were unable to read. This prohibited them from employment at the pit as, among other problems, they would be unable to read safety warnings signs. The boys were referred for remedial reading lessons.

She was instrumental in introducing the visit of a mobile X-Ray screening unit to the colliery to detect and diagnose chest ailments such as silicosis and lung cancer among the miners. In a demonstration of solidarity, she joined the queue of men, waiting her turn. She even joined the ranks of men who were required to undergo further investigation as Nan's X-Ray revealed a partially collapsed left lung. Although not considered to be a serious health threat, it was thought to be a side-effect of Spanish 'flu virus she had endured as a young girl.

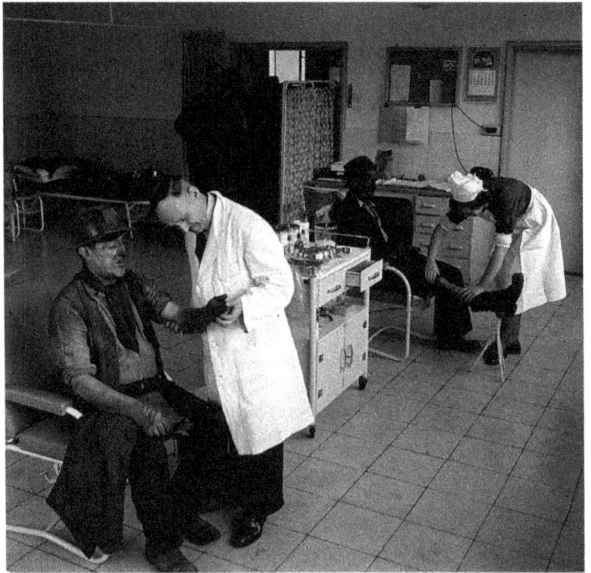

Medical attention for miners

https://www.mirror.co.uk/news/uk-news/gallery/amazing-peek-inside-britains-coal-11045179

The accidents she attended were always serious. Sometimes a doctor was summoned, but invariably Nan and trained underground first aiders were the first on the scene. After assessment, and any necessary emergency intervention, the injured man was safely transported to Chesterfield Hospital in the big, navy blue NCB ambulance, Nan in the back with the injured miner and the experienced Wally in the driving seat clanging the bell to warn other road users to make way.

Modern emergency transport for injured miners, c.1950.

The author remembers, with acute embarrassment, one occasion when Nan had safely delivered a patient to hospital in Chesterfield late one afternoon when she realised it was school 'home time' at her daughter's school. Thoughtfully, she and Wally drove round to collect her, thus saving an hour's bus journey. The ambulance was very prominently parked among the shiny cars waiting to collect other girls — as was Nan in her, by then, unkempt uniform. The hardest part was trying to think up excuses for the following morning!

The nature of the accidents would have been familiar to those received by field dressing stations in theatres of war. The dangerous nature of the work was reflected in the seriousness of the accidents sustained. Fractures were frequent and, undoubtedly, the worst ones were spinal fractures, many caused by collapsing roofs. Often the spinal cord was severed. In any case, strict care was essential to prevent hemi or total paraplegia. Nan encountered a shot-firing accident where a detonator had been wrongly placed, hitting one man in the face with the full force of the explosion. Although the man survived, he was never able to work underground again.

Not all accident victims survived. One of the miners carrying out maintenance work on the pit shaft fell to his death. Machinery intended to increase coal production also changed the nature of accidents. A short time after Nan's arrival the trepanner, a coal cutting machine, was introduced into the pit. It consisted of a cylindrical drum used to cut the coal as it rotated horizontally along the seam. On the top of the drum was a wheel of steel pegs which spun rapidly and cut the coal into small pieces. Despite safety precautions and adequate warning of the trepanner's approach, one of the miners failed to heed the warning and the top of his skull was sheared. These were the type of dangers miners faced daily and the scenarios which confronted Nan every day in the course of her work.

There were medical emergencies, not wholly related to the work, such as sudden heart attacks which could occur in any workplace. Nan regarded all the men as *her men*, and she felt deeply for every one of them. Whenever an accident occurred, she never failed to visit the miner's wife to explain the situation and the nature of the accident. She also made time to listen to their concerns and fears, often summoning extra help if needed. However, in the wake of any trauma she came up against, there was in those days, no subsequent debriefing or counselling available. She and her first aid team just carried on with their work.

Trepanner, coal cutting machine consists of a large rotating steel drum equipped with tungsten carbide picks that scrape coal from the seam. It can mine up to 14 tons a minute, more than non-mechanised mining of the 1920s would produce in an entire day. After the coal is removed from the seam, it is transported along conveyor belts from the coalface to the base of the mine shaft.

On one occasion when treating a man with chronic back problems she was appalled to see his scarred back. It was, he told her, the result of, 'birching', punishment inflicted on young male offenders by beating with a birch pole. (Birching was discontinued in 1948). There were, however, interspersed with these sad and tragic events, some light-hearted relief. The design of the medical centre was an elongated circle approached by a surrounding path. Nan claimed that she could always tell, not only if one of the members of the band were approaching, but also his chosen instrument by the individual musical sounds they made as they approached.

Trumpeters and cornet players rather than hum, sang "pap-pap, pap, pap, pap", whereas tuba and euphonium players emitted a sound like "poom, poom, poom-boom". Trombonists were identifiable by the unmistakable "whaaaaha, whaaaaha".

Nan was adept at inserting sutures. One of the more unusual cases with which she was confronted was an injured black and white mongrel dog which belonged to some local children. The dog had a nasty gash in its side. Vets were few and far between in Creswell at that time and, anyway, the children had no means of transport. Their pleas for help did not fall on deaf ears. Nan obliged and sewed up the wound and the only time the dog whined, she recalled was when she injected local anaesthetic. For the next few days the dog was seen running around the model village with an ever-increasing trail of, by then, grubby bandage. The dog survived.

With her home-making skills, Nan made her medical centre as attractive and welcoming as the pit top environment allowed. Naturally, cups of tea were a ubiquitous panacea for soothing many traumatic events. One of the 'perks' of her job was an allowance for crockery. Apart from being aesthetically pleasing for visiting nursing and medical officers, it must have proved both comforting and therapeutic for her patients to sip tea from fine Indian Tree china, together with soothing Wild Woodbine cigarettes — also routine issue.

The fact that she had worked in the homes of many of the miners, delivering their children and taking care of their wives was an advantage to Nan who was trusted and respected in the village although, being a single woman in a predominantly male work place did imply a certain vulnerability. For this reason, she endeavoured to maintain a statutory professional distance between herself and the miners. This never detracted from her popularity and she was always treated with affection by both the miners and their wives.

Accordingly she was granted a significantly high status in the village hierarchy.

Just the thing!

Before smoking was known to cause lung cancer, cigarettes were standard issue. Since most coal miners were smokers, and provided they weren't badly injured, a Woodbine was offered as an accompaniment to a soothing cup of hot, sweet tea. Woodbines were cheap and popular in the 20th century with the working-class.

http://www.cigarety.by/brand.php?n=10&l=22&p=0&w=WILD+WO ODBINE+

https://picclick.co.uk/Vintage-G-W-Sons-Queens-China-Indian-223470510834.html

Initially her participation in the social life of the village came from invitations to engage in quasi work-related activities. Sacrificing one of her valuable evenings at home, each Tuesday she became an instructor with the enthusiastically organised local division of the St John Ambulance Brigade. In addition to the usual bandaging, splinting and attending to fainting people, she introduced into the curriculum basic toxicology and pharmacology. Until then the Holger-Nielsen technique had been used for artificial respiration but was, in about the mid-fifties, replaced by mouth-to-mouth resuscitation. Nan obtained a "Resusci Anne" mannequin to demonstrate and practice the new method which extended to training sessions above and below ground for first aid attendants.

The Derbyshire Miners' Holiday Camp at Skegness on the east coast of England was opened, in May 1939, after campaigning by trade unionists, to provide an annual holiday for Derbyshire coal miners and their families. In those days it was probably the first chance available to them to enjoy a holiday, let alone one by the sea. In the early 1950s, a purpose-built block was constructed to provide facilities for the many paraplegic miners injured in the course of their work. For two weeks each year, the injured miners and their families were able to use this facility, free of charge. For several years, Nan accompanied them, not exactly a holiday for her, as she was required to be available in case of any untoward events — which did occur and would occasionally require transfer to the local hospital. Nevertheless, these sorts of commitments strengthened her ties with the miners and their trust in her.

DERBYSHIRE MINERS HOLIDAY CENTRE, SKEGNESS

The Great Exhibition of 1851 organised by Prince Albert of Saxe-Coburg and Gotha, husband and consort to Queen Victoria, was a celebration of then-modern industrial technology. It provided a stage for Britain to demonstrate to the rest of the world everything it had achieved. Britain led the world in industrial technology. Over five months, the Exhibition was visited by over six million people and was evidence of why Britain was thoroughly deserving of the epithet *Great*. A hundred years later, six years of war had left the county on the brink of bankruptcy. Much of the country, as a result of intense enemy bombing, was still in ruins. Food and other commodities were still rationed, and an air of austerity and gloom persisted. The Government's remedy was to hold The Festival of Britain opening in May 1951, the centenary of the original festival. The theme of the 1951 Festival was *looking towards the future* and provided an opportunity to showcase, *inter alia*, modern architecture and town planning in the rebuilding of the nation. Although centred on the capital, London, it was a nationwide event. As an antidote to dismal war years, the Festival was a success. Throughout the summer of 1951 events took place all over the county as part of the celebration and an estimated 49 million British people took part in some way. Creswell was no exception.

The village had always enjoyed an excuse to celebrate. It was adept at producing parades and processions, beauty competitions and gala days led, as always, by its brass band, eager as ever for an opportunity to show of its musical talents. A key event of the Festival in Creswell was a grand parade of lorries and horse drawn drays, each depicting a particular English theme. Nan's nursing colleagues in the village, the district nurse and the district midwife who had succeeded her, made an enthusiastic contribution to the festivities. Their chosen theme was the newly fledged National Health Service and the amenities it provided. They procured the services of a large horse drawn dray and set to work to produce a shameless display of propaganda. The dray was fitted with a framework consisting of four corner posts and cross beams, reminiscent of a four-poster bed. Round these were twined red, white and blue ribbons to which were pinned posters advertising various medical and nursing services. Nurses' children, augmented by a couple of their friends, were co-opted as actors in their pageant. Three little girls in perfect miniature uniforms represented hospital, midwifery and industrial nursing services. General practice and dental services (together with 'patients') were on display and Alistair appeared with a blackened face, wearing a miner's helmet and carrying a miner's lamp — not hard to guess which service he represented. Oblivious to the effect of celebrations elsewhere in the country, the 1951 Festival of Britain Gala Day in Creswell was a resounding success.

A pat on the back for the National Health Service and a shameless exercise in patriotism. Creswell celebrates the Festival of Britain in 1951

There was a strong ethos of community and culture where the countermeasure for traditional hard work was concentrated in creative and congenial pastimes. Social events appeared to follow the calendar and made good use of the local Drill Hall. During the winter months there were various very professional productions of plays, pantomimes and musicals — *Blythe Spirit*, *Dick Whittington* and *Oklahoma*. The opening night of *Rose Marie* took place on a particularly cold night in January. When the hired costumes failed to arrive after a particularly heavy fall of snow blocked approach roads, cast and production team were not to be deterred. Instead of scarlet jackets, Mounties wore the black and gold uniforms of the bandsmen — many of whom played in the accompanying orchestra. Improvisation and talent were in plentiful supply.

Florist to the stars: Constance Spry, guest of the ladies of the Creswell Floral Art Society

https://www.thetimes.co.uk/article/the-surprising-life-of-constance-spry-sue-shephard-vqjnfvp90dlpry

Displays by the Floral Art Society (one-time host of a demonstration by Constance Spry) heralded spring. Summer was busy, not only with the shows of roses but the ever-popular baby competition. Nan, much to her chagrin, was always asked to judge. She disliked the idea intensely, believing that every baby was beautiful in his or her mother's eyes. She also felt that it was an exploitation of non-consenting infants. Nevertheless, she was by now such a fixture in the village that it would have been churlish to refuse. Securing the assistance of the other two village nurses and her Coal Board colleague Helen Skelton, she set to work to write to various manufacturers of baby foods and products to request donations of goods to be used as consolation prizes. Many working evenings were spent, with the help of the children, and yards of pink and blue ribbon and wrapping paper (donated by local shopkeepers), until she had enough prizes to give one to every baby who participated.

The October half-term school holiday was designated 'potato picking week'. Miners' wives clad in overcoats, men's cast off trousers and headscarves, shod in wellington boots and armed with aluminium buckets, would gather in groups at appointed street corners, most accompanied by their children, similarly shod, waiting for lorries to arrive. They would clamber aboard and be transported to nearby farms where they spent back-breaking days pulling up potatoes. Each evening, in the autumn dusk, they would be returned by the same means of transport. Although lacking the Arcadian allure of the annual migration of London's East Enders to the hop fields of Kent, potato picking week no doubt provided a welcome break from routine as well as companionship — and some welcome extra cash.

Autumn was always Nan's favourite season and was marked by the local vegetable show when the produce of a year's hard work in their allotments was proudly displayed by the miners. Nan was a proud exhibitor and loved the show. It gave her a chance to prove that she was more than the equal of the men. She was fond of her large garden and proved to be a skillful gardener. The garden backed onto a large field which, by then, had been converted into more allotments to supplement those used by the miners around the Model Village.

On long summer evenings when the children had been put to bed, she would often spend an hour or two working in the garden. She could frequently be seen in conversation over the fence with allotment holders who were generous with tips on various plantings. On their advice she dug a celery trench which yielded a profuse harvest. She grew raspberries on canes while gooseberry and black currant bushes flourished. Yet her pride and joy, which she had brought to perfection independently, was a small apple tree which produced a maximum of four apples each autumn. They were enormous and were deservedly awarded second prize at one of the shows. However, the real feather in the cap of the organising committee was to host an edition of the BBC's *Gardeners' Question Time* when gardening queries and advice were broadcast nationally.

During the time Nan worked at the pit, the National Coal Board allotted a concessionary coal allowance to its employees. One ton was delivered to their houses each month. Where there was more than one miner per household the allowance was made to the elder. Nan although employed by the NCB was naturally not a member of the National Union of Mineworkers and did not receive this allowance. For the first few years of her tenure at the pit she paid for her own fuel. The miners somehow became aware of this and decided unanimously to each donate a fraction of their own allowance so that she received the same yearly amount as they did. Coal was, in those days, delivered to the footpath outside the house so that Nan still had to shovel it into a wheelbarrow and transport it to a coal house adjacent to the house. This was hard work, especially since, for part of the year, she would have to do this in the dark at the end of her working day. Disused wooden pit props sawn into small logs were also delivered to the house to be chopped up for kindling for the ubiquitous coal fires. Each Christmas, without fail, she received a larger than usual 'Yuletide log' on which was written in chalk 'Merry Xmas Sister'.

Almost twenty years after her apprehensive arrival in the village, seventeen of them at the pit, Nan's feelings for the village and its inhabitants remained ambivalent. She used to say that the best, and most secure, time of day was when she entered the driveway of her house and closed the gate behind her. She had made many friends among the vibrant mining community, friends who, although she addressed them by their first name, unfailingly called her 'Sister'. Despite the intervening years, she retained a subliminal feeling that she wasn't really one of the community. By this time the children had completed their schooling and left the village to pursue tertiary education. Although she had also been alone during school holidays when the children were young and they had spent time on her sister's farm, now she was permanently on her own. She could not envisage spending the rest of her life alone in this village and had a strong desire to be close to her siblings.

With mixed emotions she anticipated her retirement. By this time a new, larger medical centre closer to the pit top had been opened. The young, enthusiastic men who had replaced the original first aid attendants had all benefitted from Nan's knowledge and experience. The miners wanted to arrange an official leaving ceremony to be held in the Miners' Institute across the road from her old medical centre and sent one of their representatives to determine her feelings on the matter. She knew there would be valedictory speeches and the band would play as part of her farewell. Politely and sensitively, she declined the offer, admitting that the experience would be too emotionally overwhelming for her. After all the years, she felt that a public display of emotions would be unprofessional and undignified. When the house was sold and a new one purchased elsewhere, she left the village as unceremoniously as she had arrived.

She was now sixty and, except for a few years as a married woman, she had worked since she was fifteen. Retirement seemed an appealing proposition and she could leave with the village with impunity, knowing she had served the community well. During her time in Creswell, as midwife and 'pit nurse', she had shared the ups and downs of daily life with the rest of the community, but it was now time for the next phase of her life. Despite the communal high and low times, there was, however, one momentous experience that had bound her to the village and its people for the rest of their lives.

15

Fire!

A gentle Kiss to say goodbye
He sees the love within her eyes
Please be careful she always says
Don't worry dear, it will be okay
He holds her tight and shows no fear
She holds him tighter, holds back the tears
Now out the door to earn his pay
    She sits head bowed begins to pray
She watches his tail lights go out of sight
In early morning or late at night
She never knows when he will come home
    The work is hard, the days are long
She tries so hard to hide her tears
Keep the children safe and neat
God bless her heart to make her tough
    With a will so strong and a gentle touch
A special woman to share a life
God's special gift, a miner's wife.
Miners' Wives, Megan Allen.

Monday 25 September 1950 was the 268th evening of the year. Summer, such as it had been, was over. The month had been particularly wet, and this day was no exception with its heavy rain and accompanying thunderstorms. Not only had rainfall been higher than average that summer, temperatures had been lower, particularly night-time temperatures. The Meteorological Office had issued a forecast for cool and damp conditions for the following day as over a thousand miners set out from their homes that evening to work a nightshift underground.

Like all collieries in Britain, Creswell had been nationalised on 1 January 1947 by the Labour government led by Clement Atlee, which was swept into power after the landslide victory of the 1945 general election. (Although the Labour Party had been returned to government in February 1950, it was only by a very slim majority.)

Nationalisation had been a hard-won victory for miners and there was now an air of optimism in the coal industry. In the period immediately following nationalisation the production of coal soared, although the majority of mines were not, unfortunately, in good shape by this time given the history of the coal industry which had, for decades, been plagued by neglect and frugality of private ownership. Creswell Colliery, however, had been an exception. Formerly owned and run by the now defunct Bolsover Colliery Company and opened as late as 1899 it had been, throughout its existence, well equipped and maintained.

Significantly, 25 September 1950 was the eve of an event which will be long remembered in the village. As part of the reorganisation of nationalisation, Creswell Colliery was, in 1950, part of the No. 4 Sub-Area of No. 1 Area of the East Midlands division of the National Coal Board. The manager, George Inverarity, had been appointed in November 1946, having, previously, been employed by Bolsover Colliery Company as a relief manager. The undermanager, George Payton, had formerly worked as safety officer at Creswell colliery. The manager and undermanager were assisted by six overmen, a safety officer and several deputies. In compliance with the 1911 Coal Mines Act, both Inverarity and Payton held first class Certificates of Competence.

Creswell Colliery was built over the Barnsley or Top Hards coal seam, the most important seam in South Yorkshire and is the source of half the coal produced in this area. The name of the seam is derived from its thickness. The upper layer consisted of bright, soft coal; the middle layer of dull coal — 'the hards'; the lower layer of further bright soft coal. The 'hards' were used for powering locomotives and steam ships and the soft, mixed with other coal, was used in the manufacture of coke. The seam was up to three hundred metres (almost 1000 feet) underground and laid down over 300 million years ago.

Many years of coal production lay ahead. Despite the advent of oil as an alternative power source, coal was in 1950 still valued for its energy content for use in domestic heating and lighting and for powering heavy industry. Since Roman times the work of extracting coal from surrounding rock has advanced from manual digging and tunnelling to a highly mechanised industry using sophisticated hydraulic devices to dislodge the coal, aided by conveyor belts to transport it below and above ground. However, throughout the industry's evolution, the common factor has remained the miner and his constantly dangerous, backbreaking work. The history of mining contains a litany of disasters which have claimed miners' lives in large numbers.

Despite the thrifty intransigence of private ownership, by the mid-20th century, mechanisation had become an important part of coal mining. In Creswell, in 1950, there remained only one district of the pit where coal was cut and dug out by hand. Throughout the rest of the colliery a Meco-Moore cutter loader, or 'long wall cutter' — a combined cutter and conveyor system — was used. The cutter, fitted with two horizontal rows of tungsten carbide 'jigs', or picks, travelled along the base of the coal seam, cutting and shearing the coal. The coal was cut and loaded directly on to a conveyor system in one single procedure. This system was among the first to combine cutting and loading of coal which put an end to the laborious work of shovelling coal into tubs. It was also safer as it left walls, ceilings and floors more even, requiring less support. Enabling six men to do the work which had previously been done by twenty, the Meco-Moore could cut, break and load five hundred tons of coal in one shift, significantly improving productivity. Conveyor belt systems replaced the tubs or 'skips' which, a century earlier, had been laboriously dragged along narrow passages by women.

Preparing to go underground. Miners collecting their lamps from the lamp cabin at commencement of shift. National Mining Museum

15 *Fire!*

*https://www.ncm.org.uk/system/uploads/image_content/image/1046/
P11288_miners_picking_up_lamps_and_batteries_in_the_lamproom.jpg*

The Meco-More coal cutter was in use at Creswell Colliery at the time of the 1950 disaster. Being 16 feet long and 3 feet high, the Meco Moore cutter moved at 27 inches per minute. The machine was connected to a conveyor belt which carried the cut coal from the coalface to the mine entrance, one of the earliest machines to do cutting and loading. It was first used in Britain in 1934 and increased both safety and productivity.

http://www.healeyhero.co.uk/rescue/individual/Phil_Wyles/Meco-2.html

A conveyor belt is, basically, very wide belts, usually consisting of two or more layers of rubber to allow it to safely carry a heavy load. The belt forms an endless loop attached around two or more pulleys, or drums, rotated by motors. As the drums rotate, so does the belt because of the friction between the belt and the rotator wheels. Both wheels move in the same direction, either clockwise or anti-clockwise. The conveyor belt at Creswell colliery was about a meter wide of 7-ply construction with rubber facings and, driven mechanically at a speed of about 100 meters an hour, could transport the coal over large distances.

The Creswell conveyancing system was made up of a series of tributary belts which carried the coal from outlying districts. At various stations it was transferred from the tributary belts to the major or trunk, conveyor belt. The trunk belt then carried it to the pit bottom from where it was hauled to the surface. Although mostly loaded mechanically, coal was sometimes loaded on to the tributary belts by hand, usually by men working on the afternoon shift. Repairs and maintenance of the belt were carried out on all three shifts, but chiefly the night shift.

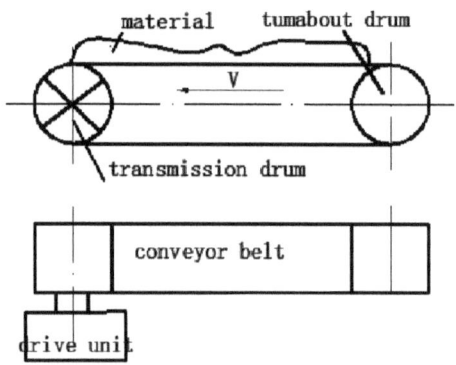

Working principle of conveyor belt.

Researchgat: https://www.researchgate.net/figure/Working-principle-diagram-of-belt-conveyor_fig1_322215601

In September 1950 at Creswell Colliery 1,144 men were employed underground and 355 at the pit top. Between June and September that year 14,000 tons of coal was produced, most of it mined in the South West District of the pit. It is this district which is the focus of this account.

Leading in and out of the various underground districts were two roads, *in-bye*, leading from the pit shaft to the coal face and *out-bye*, leading in the opposite direction, from the coal face to the mine entrance. Of the two roads leading in and out of the South West District , one was occupied by a tributary conveyor belt to transport the coal, the other road carried men to and from the pit bottom by means of a paddy, a small train on rails which was also driven by an endless rope haulage mechanism. The two roads were about eighteen metres apart but converged to about nine metres as they approached the pit bottom.

Freshly dug coal carried by underground conveyor belt c.1950.

Conveyor systems use wide belts and pulleys, supported by rollers, along their paths. They allow large volumes to be rapidly transported over considerable distances making them less expensive and more efficient then manual labour. Belts made from rubber are commonly used to move items with sharp, irregular surfaces such as cut coal. To transport goods over sloping surfaces or around bends, toughbed conveyor belts are used.

https://www.alamy.com/stock-photo/coal-mine-underground.html

Miners travelled over distances for several kilometres to their work at the coalface. 'The Paddy' saved time and energy.

Picture National Mining Museum https://www.ncm.org.uk/learning/learning-resources/image-bank

During the day shift, a complement of 93 men was usually working in the South West District, 163 men worked the afternoon shift and 122 men the night shift. On the night of Tuesday 25 September, of a total of 232 men working underground, 131 were working in the South West District, extra men having been transferred from elsewhere.

15 *Fire!*

Underground roadway with conveyor carrying coal underground.

At the time of the Creswell Colliery disaster, there were two roads leading in and out of the area where the fire occurred: one for transporting men (previous page) and one to carry coal (above).

https://sunnewsreport.com/msha-in-quest-to-improve-mining-safety-equipment

Good ventilation is essential in all mines to enable miners to breathe and rid the mine of gases, dust, humidity and heat. Fresh air passes into the mine while contaminated air is removed. The primary system of mine ventilation consists of *intake downcast* (fresh air) and *exhaust upcast* (used air). The correct flow rate of air must be sufficient to meet effective ventilation requirements. Since air follows the path of least resistance, large fans are installed to control and maintain the flow. *Toppings*, solid fireproof walls, allow the air to be effectively channelled thereby maintaining effective ventilation.

Creswell Colliery was reputedly well maintained with adequate lighting and ventilation. Firefighting equipment, including fire hydrants, were installed and water was supplied by a main pump. As the pump in the South West District was run only during the night-shift, arrangements were made to feed water into the main pump from surface tanks during the day and afternoon shifts. In addition, another pipe was used to supply water via the upcast shaft into the fire-fighting mains. Fire stations were situated at regular intervals and examined regularly. Firefighting plans were in place and regular drills took place in compliance with fire and safely regulations. For greater effectiveness in the event of underground fire, work was currently in progress to install water pipes with a wider bore.

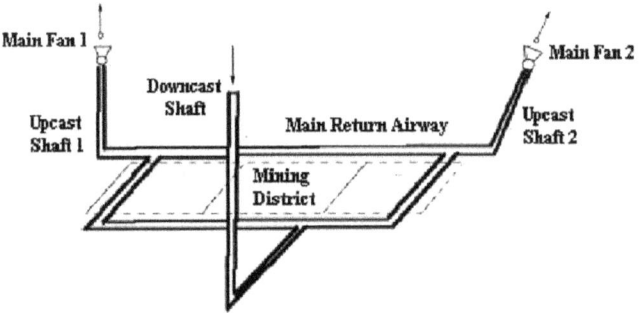

Fig. 3. Configuration of the mine ventilation system

https://www.semanticscholar.org/paper/Reliability-evaluation-of-mine-ventilation-systems-Miao-Wang/a2bcecd86ec105973a47db6e1d57617eb281827f/figure/2

An underground telephone exchange, manned by a permanent switchboard operator, provided necessary communication within the mine and the pit surface. In the event of an emergency call being received during the day and afternoon shifts there were normally men working nearby who acted as messengers relaying calls for assistance, thereby allowing the operator to remain at his post. When, and if, an emergency arose during the night shift, the night switchboard operator had to deliver the message himself.

This was the work environment early that Tuesday morning

when two hundred and thirty-two men were working at Creswell Colliery, almost a kilometre underground.

On Monday 25 September, one of the men working on the afternoon shift noticed the appearance of grooves on the No. 2 tributary conveyor belt which passed through the South West District. The belt was stopped and an examination carried out by the belt maintenance person. He noticed that one of the grooves — about 15 centimeters from the side — extended for 90 metres along the belt. For a short length the groove had penetrated about two-thirds of the thickness of the belt, but at no point did the belt appear to have been completely cut through. Despite examining the entire length of the belt, he and another maintenance, man could find nothing to account for this. The belt was subsequently restarted, and inspections were carried out at regular intervals throughout the remainder of the shift, the final inspection taking place at about 8.30 pm.

A full shift of coal was transported without mishap. Nevertheless, arrangements were made for the maintenance men to work overtime in order to repair the damaged belt. For some reason this arrangement was cancelled by the overman, a senior miner responsible for the daily work including coal output. Believing that insufficient coal had been cleared, he gave instructions for the belt to continue running until all the coal from the day shift had been cleared.

With the arrival of night shift workers, the belt attendant at one of the other transfer stations again examined the No. 2 belt. He discovered that the existing groove had, in the intervening time, extended to almost 200 metres — more than double the original groove — and, over a length of about six metres, the belt was completely cut through, wide enough for him to push his hand through the gash. Quite clearly, the damage had worsened. Increasing damage notwithstanding, instructions were once more given to restart the belt.

It continued to operate without any problems until just after 3 am when it tore completely and began to trail on the ground. The transfer attendant sent a telephone message to the motor attendant at the pit bottom informing him of what had happened and requesting that No. 2 belt be stopped. However, despite an additional request it continued to operate until, after a further order, it was eventually switched off. The motor attendant, belt attendant and transfer point attendant then set off from opposite ends of the belt to carry out another inspection. After about 400 metres outbye, the motor attendant encountered smoke and, a little further along, noticed flames along the roadway coming from one of the transfer chutes. A further 50 metres along the roadway, the belt attendant noticed a mangled heap of belt which then burst into flames. The belt attendant immediately returned to the No. 2 station from where he sent an urgent telephone message to the underground telephone exchange requesting to be put in touch immediately with the overman responsible for the South West District. The power was immediately turned off and further help was summoned. The time was 3.45 am.

As the nearest fire station was on the other side of the fire it was inaccessible. By now the belt was well alight. An urgent message was sent to the undermanager and the manager while men from the nearest firefighting team arrived on the scene with portable fire extinguishers. Unfortunately, one of the extinguishers was out of order and the other one was ineffective against the fierceness of the blaze. Telephone messages were sent to bring more firefighting teams and equipment from other parts of the pit and the manager and undermanager were informed by telephone of the magnitude of the emergency.

Simultaneously urgent requests were sent to the Central Rescue Brigades from Chesterfield, about 15 kilometres away, requesting them to attend. Senior National leaders of the NCB, HM Inspectors of Mines and officials of the NUM were also informed. Above ground, while the village slept, the Creswell Colliery Disaster Plan was set in motion. The time was now 4 am.

When the under manager arrived underground, he went immediately to the scene of the fire, having been told that the affected miners were on their way out. He met with the firefighting teams who had arrived from other areas of the pit and who, on coupling their hoses were dismayed to see only a thin, ineffective trickle of water leaking from the hoses. Despite intervention by the undermanager, there was no improvement in water pressure. Critically, on that night, for the first time in many years, the main pump which fed the branch pumps had failed to start at the commencement of the night shift. An examination of the pump showed it was unable to be repaired that night and, despite the arrival of the engineer, emergency repairs came too late to help fight the fire had which had, by that time, spread even further. The restored water pressure which had been ineffective in extinguishing the fire was used to cool down smouldering wood and other material.

More portable fire extinguishers, together with stone dust, were collected and brought to the scene in the hope these would control the blaze. This action appeared to be successful, and a message to that effect was relayed to the surface. Unfortunately steam and smoke which had filled the roadways obscured visibility and concealed the magnitude of the situation. The fire had, in fact, spread a considerable distance along the road, exacerbated by the burning belt which had now snapped completely. The time was 5.15 am.

At 5.20 am, the rescue team arrived from Chesterfield but with persistently low water pressure and poor visibility were unable to help extinguish the fire. Leaving the mine firefighting team to contend with the blaze, they put on breathing apparatus containing liquid air and attempted to push ahead of the fire in the hope of preventing it from spreading further *inbye*. Their attempt was thwarted by the intense heat. Further attempts to reach the fire were frustrated by deteriorating roofing conditions and, although temporary roof supports were brought in, they were of little use. The fire had travelled about 100 metres in an hour and a quarter.

Meanwhile, amid this frantic activity, several men who had been working in the South West District began to emerge, having made their way through the main return airway. Shortly afterwards another, solitary miner appeared, having walked along a similar route. He was extremely distressed and told rescuers that, on his way out, he had opened a door and seen the inferno beneath. He said that more men were following behind him, also attempting to get out. It became apparent that it was now impossible for the main contingent of men working in the area to escape. Rescue teams were immediately despatched to explore the main return airway.

After almost five hundred metres they found the first body. There was no response to attempted resuscitation. A further two bodies were recovered, and rescuers reported that they had seen another ten bodies in the airway where the air was so thick with acrid smoke it was extremely difficult to see anything. Despite the appalling conditions, exploration of the return airway continued. Throughout the night 200 rescuers, working in relays, began the grim work of recovering the bodies. By morning an additional 44 bodies had been recovered. At 10 am a further notice was issued to the effect that exploration had revealed the fire was even more extensive than had been predicted. Except for the continuing exploration of the main return airway, a decision was made for all other rescue work to be temporarily suspended. Further exploration was deemed to be futile.

At the pit top, a conference involving representatives of the National Coal Board, National Union of Mineworkers and mine inspectors was hastily convened to assess the current situation and decide what further action could be taken. Unanimously they concluded that, since there could be no survivors from the inbye (closest to the coal face) fire and, since the precarious condition of its roof now made the airway impassable, sealing off the entire district was the only available recourse if the fire were to be completely extinguished and an explosion prevented. Two sites were identified in which to place the seals and arrangements were made to immediately haul necessary equipment and material to the area.

Before the sealing operation was commenced, a further inspection of the scene of the fire was carried out. It appeared that the smoke in the main airway was suddenly less intense and the outbye side definitely seemed to be cooler. However, because the damage to the roof was so extensive, it was impossible to establish the condition of the area closer to the coal face where the miners, presumed dead, were trapped. A subsequent inspection confirmed that the smoke was less dense, and a decision was made for one further attempt to recover the bodies. More bodies were found in the main airway and brought out and, while the slight improvement in conditions prevailed, more rescuers were dispatched to explore the smaller slit airways. However, conditions there were still so bad that the rescuers had to be withdrawn and, to prevent the possibility of an explosion, the work of sealing the area was commenced immediately.

Explosions in coal mines require a combination of several elements: fuel, heat and oxygen together with (typically) methane gas, frictional ignition and air. To prevent explosions, installed seals need to be solid and airtight and placed in tunnels and airways, thereby cutting off the supply of oxygen which accelerates the fire. Effective sealing is a means of ensuring both the prompt containment of an underground fire and preventing potential explosions. For them to be effective, however, rapid construction is essential, and time was running out at Creswell Colliery.

Two teams of rescue men wearing breathing apparatus worked simultaneously in two-hour shifts to seal off the intake and return airways. They built two stoppings about 1,000 metres from the coal face. Constructed from sandbags, the intake stopping was two and a half metres long and the return airway stopping was two metres long. Each stopping was fitted with 2 inch diameter (5cm) steel sampling tubes and 10 inch diameter (25 cm) steel ventilation pipes. At one stage, the teams were laying sandbags at the rate of eight hundred an hour. During the construction of the stoppings a metre square tunnel was formed to maintain ventilation for as long as the work took place. When the work of effectively stopping both tunnels with sandbags was completed metal plates were, again simultaneously, bolted over each end of this tunnel. After this final sealing, the mine was evacuated for forty-eight hours. At the end of this time the seals were inspected and proved to have been effective. Air pressures were tested and shown to be balanced. The outbye ends of the stoppings were reinforced with brick walls a metre thick and constant testing of atmospheric pressure behind the stoppings was begun.

The bodies of forty-seven miners were recovered and a further thirty-three remained behind the seals. An immediate inquest into the deaths of the forty-seven miners was held at the Miners' Institute at the colliery on Thursday 28 September. Evidence of identification and statements from doctors were taken before the inquest was adjourned until an official enquiry ordered by The Ministry of Fuel and Energy could be completed. The established cause of death was poisoning from carbon monoxide, very large quantities of which were found in blood samples.

15 Fire!

Stoppings are used to control and direct the ventilation air flow through underground coal mines to dilute and render harmless methane, coal dust, and other contaminants to prevent explosions. They are substantial seals placed in underground tunnels intended to contain any explosion occurring within the workings. In cases where active mine fires are being fought, they are intended to prevent any explosion from being ignited by the fire by quickly sealing it off. During the fire at Creswell colliery sandbags were used as stoppings to facilitate rapid construction.

https://www.cdc.gov/niosh/mining/UserFiles/works/pdfs/eeomv.pdf

The small party of miners who had escaped via the airway, and considered themselves lucky to have survived, told the story of their escape. The first intimation of danger was at about 3.30 am when the power was cut. When, after a short time, it had not been restored, one of the men decided to investigate. After walking about thirty metres he encountered a thick cloud of black smoke which he somehow managed to penetrate. Then, after crawling a short distance on his hands and knees, he lay down on the ground. Much to his surprise, he was approached by a man who informed him that there was a fire at one of the transfer stations in the conveyor belt system. The atmosphere was extremely hot. Other men who were following this man in groups of twos and threes had by now caught up with him. Taking off their shirts, they doused them in water and placed them over their mouths and noses. The thick smoke made it impossible to see and they had to grope for the paddy train rails along the floor to guide them. All of them emerged from the airway together. Each described this as the worst experience he had ever encountered. It was then that they realised they would never see the rest of their workmates again.

Funeral arrangements had to be made for the forty-seven recovered miners. A conference was held between the local church vicar and chapel ministers and a roster of burial times was drawn up. The burials took two days to complete and were held the following Friday 29 and Saturday 30 September. For two days, in pouring rain, cortege followed cortege as the miners were laid to rest, once more under the ground, each after an individual service. At the end of two tortuous days of funerals, there was an ecumenical memorial service on the Saturday evening in which the colliery band accompanied the singing. Telegrams of condolence were read from the King and the Prime Minister. There was not enough room in the parish church for all the attendees, so the service was relayed to congregations who had gathered in the local schools. The original intention to hold an outdoor service so everyone could attend was abandoned as the rain had not eased for the entire two days. Hardly a household in the village was unaffected by the tragedy.

During the time the burnt-out area of the pit was sealed off, over a thousand air samples were analysed. At one stage, samples were taken every fifteen minutes, day and night, so that it became necessary to convert one of the pit top offices into a temporary laboratory.

15 *Fire!*

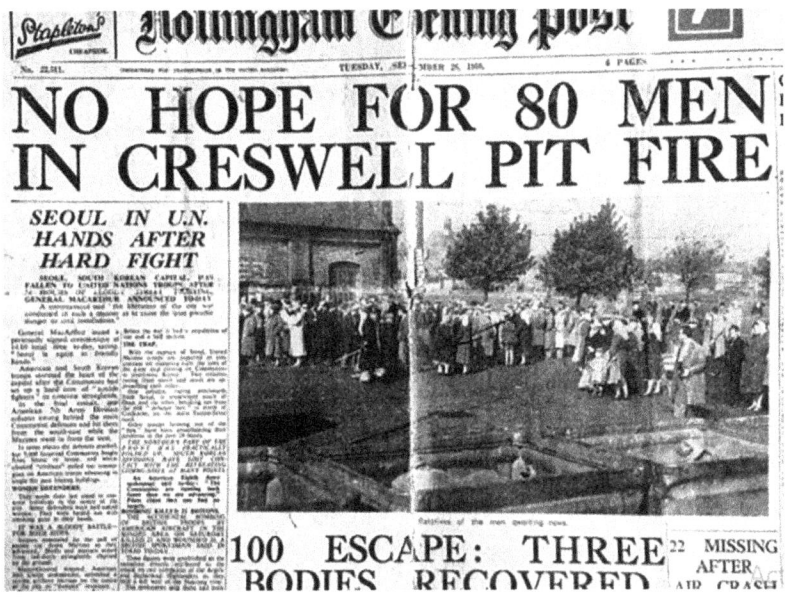

Front page of Nottingham Evening Post, Tuesday 26 September announcing the grim news.

http://www.fennerdunlopeurope.com/ir/fenr/marfleet/pdf/150yr_Anniversary_Brochure.pdf

Volunteers work to fill the thousands of sandbags needed to seal off the fire and anxious families wait in silence for news of their men.

https://www.alamy.com/stock-photo-creswell-colliery-fire-106111038.html

In the evening of Tuesday 26 September, when the of the magnitude of the disaster was revealed, over 2,000 people, many of whom had been there for over twelve hours took part in an ecumenical service.

Church of England Vicar, Rev Branson read a telegram from the King who sent his "heartfelt sympathy to the wives and families of those who have lost their lives."

Arthur Horner, General Secretary of the NUM delivered the following words: "Blood is on coal today, as it always has been. Let those who criticise the miners, and the cost of coal, now realise the price of getting it."

At the end of the fateful week came two gruelling days of funerals.

Shutterstock: https://www.shutterstock.com/editorial/image-editorial/coalmine-disaster-at-creswell-colliery-1950-church-memorial-service-held-at-the-pit-head-1344639a

Eventually air sample analyses showed the cessation of all combustion activity beyond the seals and, in the following December, planning began with a view to reopening the affected district and restoring it to working order by the following Easter. The intervening period would allow ample time for the layers of affected rock to cool down and minimise the risk of the fire reigniting. The proposed date of reopening was 22 March 1951, the beginning of the Easter holiday weekend, almost six months to the day of the fire. With this date in mind, preparations for reopening began.

As soon as it was considered safe, rescue teams re-entered the fire-damaged area. In addition to equipment and materials necessary for the work of broaching the seals, they carried a grim cargo of lead-lined coffins.

The men cautiously began their task. As the gas behind the seals would contain a large amount of methane, temporary seals and stoppings were built at selected points so that the gases could be removed in stages. Carefully controlling the amount of air entering the affected area would limit the methane content and keep it below the lower limit of flammability, thereby decreasing the risk of explosion and further fire. A large specialised fan was used specifically for the purpose of preventing gas-contaminated air into the atmosphere.

Gradually the seals were removed and the area was cleared. Events went according to plan until further progress was disrupted by the condition of the fire damaged access roads in which airflow had been blocked by fallen debris from the original fire. In addition, a sudden drop in surrounding air pressure triggered a release of gases which interfered with the ventilation. Further work and exploration ceased, and the roadway was resealed although, by this time, a further twenty seven bodies had been recovered.

The positioning of the new seals allowed for limited inspection of all fire affected areas, and repair of the conveyor road, so that safe ventilation would be available for the final clearing of the working panels. This was completed on 10 August, 1951, when the final six bodies were retrieved. They had been entombed for almost a year

The limited exploration was able to confirm that the fire had begun at the No. 2 transfer station and had travelled almost seven hundred and fifty metres outbye. The conveyor belt was a heap of burnt wreckage and No. 2 transfer station charred with blistered paintwork. Much of the debris was removed and sent to the Mines and Safety Station at Buxton for forensic examination. There was over seven hundred kilograms of damaged belting. Evidence pointed to the fact that the fire had started in one of the feeder chutes. From various experiments at Buxton it was concluded that a small piece of ironstone, wedged against the belt, would have caused it to eventually cut through the casing.

An inquiry into the disaster, conducted by mining engineer Sir Andrew Bryan was presented to Parliament by the Minister for Fuel and Power in June 1952. Examination of the remains of the fire revealed an area strewn with the debris of torn, burnt belting and charred wood, but there was no *conclusive* evidence as to the actual cause of the fire. Various specimens were forensically examined. It was theorised that a heap of stones — shale and ironstone, debris from the rock surrounding the coal seam — found near one of the transfer stations, had got trapped in the belt driving mechanism. Subsequent experiments using ironstone demonstrated that it had the ability to tear the belting to a considerable depth. It was thought that a piece of the stone may have settled at the top of the transfer station and become wedged against the belt with which it would have been in constant contact. This would have been sufficient to cause the long deep laceration through several layers of the belt's composition. Once the stone had completely cut through the belt, it would have come into contact with the steel delivery drum. The constant friction caused by that contact could have created a spark igniting the fire which, it was estimated, would have occurred in about 10 minutes. The report concluded there were several factors involved in the high death rate, including telephones being too far from the coal face, repair work being done on the paddy, inadequate air shafts and low water pressure in the fire hoses. It was noted that there had been a delay in contacting the men in the South West Division. The report recommended:

"Where the lives of men are endangered by a fire, a responsible official should be charged with the sole duty of seeing that the threatened men are warned without delay and that everything possible is done to facilitate their escape …. There should be included in the code of signals used on telephone systems a distinctive signal to indicate that a state of emergency exists which requires the immediate withdrawal of men. It would be an advantage if this alarm signal could be heard by as many as possible of the men threatened by the danger."

Sadly, the safety of these men appears to have been overlooked during the ensuing melee. There was no evidence to suggest that a message urging the immediate withdrawal of the men was ever received. In his final paragraph, Sir Andrew pays tribute, *inter alia*, to:

> "…. the heroism of many, known and unknown, among the work*men*, officials, management and rescue teams during the many distressing hours immediately following the fire."

A concrete memorial bearing a bronze plaque naming each of the dead miners still stands. A national disaster fund was opened for the survivors. No memorial bespeaks the loss of so many men to a small community which came into being and was sustained by the mine which claimed these men's lives.

> *Towards this little village our sympathies are sent*
> *The mine again has taken toll, and claimed its savage rent*
> *Full eighty gallant human souls have gone to meet the cost*

"The Price of Coal" have gone to join 'The Legion of the Lost"
In Creswell Village, vale of tears, with every home bereaved
Some father, husband, brother, son, some loved one deeply grieved
And once again, as in a flash, the price of coal is paid
But broken hearts they leave behind, when in the churchyard laid
And as before, these tales are told — The Annals of the Mine
Such tales that fill us all with pride, unselfish and Divine
Of one who could have saved himself, but turning back to find
He lost his life, to warn close mates he couldn't leave behind
And others could have made the grade, but stopped to finish off
The job that they had set themselves, twas honesty enough
The old, old tale of British grit, that never lets us down
It's the history of the coal mines, and this little mining town
Their women waited up above, and as they hoped and prayed
For God a miracle to work, tho' heartsick and dismayed
But as the weary hours dragged by, and as their hopes grew dim
Beyond all doubt at last they knew, the issue lay with Him
The rescue teams who risked their lives, all miners, picked and fit
They worked with all their hearts and souls along that fire-swept pit
In that inferno well they knew their mates they wouldn't find
With heavy heart, at last they left the pals they loved behind
So once again the bell was tolled, at what a tragic cost
The mine again has taken toll and eighty lives are lost
Black diamonds dug by sweat and blood embowelled in the earth
How can we speak in terms of cash, how can we price its worth
Its price is far beyond our ken, away from mortal eyes
It's God who knows and counts the cost, away beyond the skies

Walter Oxley J.P.
Creswell, 1950

16

Sweetheart and Wife: Freda's Story

A miner was leaving his home for his work
When he heard his little child scream
    He went to his bedside, his little white frame
"Oh daddy, I've had such a dream
    I dreamed I saw the pit all afire
And men struggled hard for their lives
The scene then changed and the top of the mine
Was surrounded with sweethearts and wives."
"Don't go down the mine, Dad
    Dreams often come true
Daddy, you know it would break my heart
If anything happened to you.
Just go and tell your mates
And as true as the stars that shine
Something is going to happen today
Dear Daddy, don't go down the mine."
The miner, a man with a heart good and kind
Stood by the side of his son
    He said "It's my living, I can't stay away
For duty, my lad, must be done."
The little one looked up, and sadly he said
"Oh, please stay today with me Dad
But as the brave miner went forth to his work
    He heard this appeal from his son.

> "Don't go down the mine, Dad
> Dreams often come true
> Daddy, you know it would break my heart
> If anything happened to you.
> Just go and tell your mates
> And as true as the stars that shine
> Something is going to happen today
> Dear Daddy, don't go down the mine."
> **Robert Donelly and Will Geddes 1910**

It was the evening of Tuesday 25 September when Owen kissed Freda before reaching for his cap.

"So long love, back in time for breakfast.

"Bye, Mam" he called to his mother.

As usual, by this time in the evening, Meg was dozing in her upright Windsor chair by the fire. Superstitious as ever, she refused to go to bed until her son had left for work, even then, it was always a restless night when she knew he was working far below her.

The days were already getting noticeably shorter and tonight, as he closed the kitchen door and stepped out from the warmth of the kitchen into the damp yard, Owen could feel the chill of autumn. The smell of coal fires and the reek from the tip were even more pungent in the misty night air.

It was this familiar, stifling miasma he had noticed when he returned to the village after a three-year absence. The gap had been long enough to forget how oppressive it could be. At least the rain had stopped — for the moment. The chill in the evening air reminded him that in only another three months it would be Christmas. He was really looking forward to Christmas this year. Davey would be two and the thought of the boy excitedly ripping open his presents made Owen smile to himself. Freda had joined

Mrs Harper's Christmas club earlier in the year and had just about paid off the lovely little wooden train set she'd had her eye on for a while. Owen felt a thrill of childlike excitement as he imagined himself on Christmas Eve, while Davey was asleep in bed, fitting the little rails together on the rug in front of the fire. He could already see Davey's eyes light up with excitement when he was brought downstairs on Christmas morning.

Suddenly Owen felt a slight pang, and a frown creased his forehead when he thought of Davey. Strange the little lad had been so upset that night. Owen had always put Davey to bed, no matter what shift he was on and, after a song or two, and perhaps a story, the boy's eyes would close and he'd be fast asleep in no time. But tonight, Davey didn't seem to settle when Owen bent to kiss him goodnight. He clung to his father.

"Stay daddy", he pleaded.

Owen lay on the bed beside the child. Perhaps they'd been a bit hasty moving him into a single bed and he probably missed the security of his cot.

Eventually Davey fell asleep, Owen tiptoed out of the room and down the creaking stairs. Now it was almost time to leave, so not much time now for a chat with Freda. However, tonight was the last night of his nightshift roster. Freda would be up when he got home in the morning and they could talk over breakfast while Meg and Davey were still in bed. Later he would take the boy for a walk and perhaps go and see the pit ponies, now enjoying their retirement in a nearby field. Owen could stay up all day tomorrow, and they could have a swing in the park. He would laugh as Davey squealed with delight as Owen pushed the swing higher and higher. He loved it when he and the boy were out together.

"Ay-up lad, not so fast." Lost in his thoughts, Owen hadn't heard the heavy footfall of hobnail boots approaching from behind as he came out of the Bottom Park and on to the approach road to the pit.

"Oh, evenin' Ted, I were miles away."

"Penny for 'em, lad" said Ted, but before Owen had time to answer they were joined by another couple of men heading in the same direction.

"Evenin', by God, it's a bit nippy tonight lads."

"Aye, nights is really drawin' in now."

It was almost nine-thirty and Owen, as usual, had eaten sparingly. Freda knew that he didn't like to go to work at night on a full stomach. After a life in the pit, and his time in the army, he had grown used to shift work and turning night into day had become second nature to him. Anyhow, if he knew Freda, she would have put a nice piece of her moist fruit cake wrapped in wax paper in his snap tin with a little bit of cheese she had saved from her rations. Owen recognised his good luck. Lots of men weren't so fortunate. They had to make a detour to the canteen for some thickly cut bread and margarine — not much of a meal for the hard work that lay ahead. How fortunate was he to have married a woman like Freda!

As they approached the pit top, the damp air reverberated with the loud ringing of hob-nailed pit boots on the concrete. Men in groups, almost in step, were marching to this gigantic hole in the ground, like mythical lemmings. Only, these men were more like moles. On they trudged, past the Miners' Institute. Band practice would be over for tonight, Owen remarked to himself, and they'd be well into their second pint by now.

"Be there next week" he thought to himself. Although he wasn't much of a drinker, he enjoyed being with the lads in the band trying out new pieces on his cornet.

The medical centre on the right was dimly lit. Sid Hopkins, the night first aid attendant, would be on duty, probably having a lie down on the examination couch in Sister's office. Poor little Sid, with a permanent dewdrop on the end of his nose, would have been waiting on his plump little wife all day and now trying to catch up on a bit of shut-eye, anticipating a quiet night ahead. That was one good thing about night duty, there was never much to do and anyway, if anything major happened, they'd call for Sister to come.

On they lumbered, past the cricket pitch on which the goalposts had been put up in readiness for the football season, and on towards the pit head baths for a quick change into their grimy pit clothes before heading to the lamp cabin to get helmets and lamp batteries. Only another eight hours and then he'd have a few days off; time to spend with his little family. He never went to bed after getting home from his last night. He saved that pleasure until night time when 'normal' people went to bed. Once in bed, even if he fell asleep straight away, he savoured the pleasure of snuggling into the warm sheets with darkness outside — luxury! Why waste one of his precious days off sleeping?

Emerging from the lamp cabin, Owen and his six mates, together with a group of other men, handed over their identity discs to the banksman who counted them in as they entered the cage that would lower them to work. The six friends were joined by others who would be working in the same area. They knew each other well. The whistling, joking and teasing belied the loyalty they all shared with each other. Tonight, there was talk of the coming election.

"As long as we don't get that posh bugger Churchill again", remarked Spike Williams vehemently. Spike was an armchair socialist.

"Bloody Churchill — 'e's never been no friend to t' bloody miners."

Frank Rushton's son had told him that when Churchill's corpulent, baby-like image had appeared on the Warner Pathe News at the children's matinee last Saturday, the whole place erupted with such spontaneous booing that the manager threatened to stop the program. They all guffawed as he retold the story. Owen smiled his warm smile. His quiet personality made him different from his mates, but he was still one of them, and when they were at work, they had complete trust in each other. Their lives depended on it.

The gate clanged shut. The headgear whirled and they were lowered into the abyss, warm air whooshing past them, their jokes echoing round the brick lined shaft. They saw, through the strong metal grill of the cage floor, the circle of lights as the subterranean village came towards them — the village under the village.

Suddenly, they were deep in the underground cavern, handing over their second discs to the underground banksman. Both discs would be collected on the way out in the morning once they were all safely out of the pit. All that was left now was to make the journey to their district to begin work for the night. When they were busy, the night went quickly, but Owen still looked forward to morning. After bathing at the pit head baths, he would bundle up his dirty work clothes for Freda to wash and, along with his mates reverse the route he'd taken the night before.

After Owen had left, Meg remained dozing by the fire while Freda cleared the table and began to wash the dishes in the scullery.

"Freda!" she called, suddenly roused. "The boy's awake again."

"That's not like him", Freda said as she pushed aside the heavy velvet curtain guarding the little vestibule at the foot of the stairs.

"You'll only make 'im worse. Let 'im cry hissself to sleep. Makin' a rod for your own back, it is" counselled her mother-in-law, her sing-song Welsh lilt, still as noticeable as ever after all these years.

"No, I'd better go up. This isn't like him at all. Something must be worrying him".

As she entered the little bedroom, she could see the child was distressed.

"Want daddy" he gasped between sobs.

It was obvious Davey wasn't going to settle. The child was usually a little out of sorts when Owen worked nights. Today he'd missed his outing to the park and Freda had been tense because the children next door were shouting in the yard when they came home from school for their dinner in the middle of the day. She was always afraid their noise was going to disturb Owen. Yet Owen was a heavy sleeper, a throwback to his time in the army.

Freda wrapped Davey in his little eiderdown and carried him down the narrow staircase ignoring Meg's look of disdain.

"Spoilin' 'im, that's what you're doin'. Well, I'm goin' up. Time I was in bed even if *he's* stayin' up all night" she muttered through gritted teeth.

She struggled arthritically out of her chair.

"Night duck, see you in the morning", Freda said fondly, looking up.

Freda noticed the table. While she was upstairs with Davey, Meg had laid it for morning, even placing the rashers of bacon in the big black frying pan on the side, ready for Owen's breakfast. She had brought the washing through from the scullery and placed the wooden clothes horse in front of the fire to air. Despite her all but useless hands, now contorted with arthritis, it was hard for her to break the habits of a lifetime.

Freda sat down in front of the fire settling Davey on her knee. She began to rock him back and forth as she hummed. Although she was fond of Meg, she had always felt a little intimidated by her brittle Welsh manner, especially when Owen wasn't there. Freda knew that Meg resented the fact that, as his wife, she was now a more important part of Owen's life. Once she heard the creaking stairs and muffled footsteps overhead, Freda began to relax. The child began to settle. Freda gazed into the glowing embers of the fire just as she and her sister Chrissie used to do as children, making up stories, seeing images of fairy castles in the spaces between the glowing coals. As Davey fell asleep, her mind wandered.

Freda had spent her whole life in this village. She and her family were an integral part of the community whose lives revolved around the pit. Round the clock shifts had become part of their genetic material. All the villagers were well aware of the time of day by the blaring of the pit buzzer announcing the end of one shift and the beginning of the next. Freda had seen how her mother's life had centred on her father, Joe's, work at the pit by keeping the girls quiet during the day when he worked nights, washing his grimy pit clothes, heating the water and scrubbing his back in the tin bath in front of the kitchen fire well before the advent of the pit head baths. Joe King had started work at the pit as a boy of fifteen, just after it was opened. He would tell his daughters how, after his last day at school, his dad had taken him to the Co-op to buy a brand-new stainless-steel snap tin. His clothes and boots had belonged to his brother who had since outgrown them. Joe told them of his excitement at being woken up early in the morning, long before it was light, waiting for his first shift to begin with a mixture of fear and exhilaration as, with his dad, he crossed the pit yard to the cage. He was packed in with the other miners, his dad's arm resting reassuringly on his shoulder. His stomach turned as they descended into the dark. Joe had worked his way up to become undermanager and had retired a few years earlier. He and his wife Vera still occupied their larger 'villa' in the Model Village to which they had moved after Joe's promotion. The house was slightly more imposing than those of the miners, but a little less imposing than the ornate Victorian villas upon which it had been designed. Freda now lived in the Bottom Model, diagonally opposite the park from her parents' house which she could see through the window of her front room. She had never contemplated a life anywhere other than a little house in the mining village into which she had been born and raised.

Freda had come to live in this house as a bride, almost ten years ago. It was what brides did in those days. It never occurred to her that she and Owen would move into a house of their own. Besides, Owen would never leave his mother to live on her own. Meg had never wanted Owen to work in the pit. She had more ambitious plans for him, but they were dashed when it became obvious that the boy failed to shine at school. He was affable, smart even, but completely lacking in ambition. He took life as it came, like Freda. He did, however, readily agree to music lessons and, as it turned out, he was very musical. Since they could not afford a piano, Owen chose to learn to play the cornet, a slightly smaller version of trumpet. He had an innate Welsh love of music and loved nothing better than to sit outside the Miner's Institute on summer evenings listening to the band practising energetic, throbbing marches, sometimes alternating with mournful, lilting melodies which filled the air. When he passed the audition and became part of the band his chest swelled with pride.

Owen's parents had known hard times in the Welsh Valleys at the end of the Great War. As newlyweds they had no home of their own and had moved to Pontymawr a few miles away in the next valley. They moved into the house already occupied by Gwyn's older brother, Gareth, his wife and four children. That was not unusual in those days. Gwyn and Gareth had worked together at the Pontymawr pit for a while. Surrounded by hardship and faced with no prospect of an improvement in their standard of living, Meg and Gwyn decided to leave their roots in the Welsh Valley and, with many other Welsh miners, moved north to where the pits were more profitable and, Gwyn had heard, better managed and the miners treated fairly.

A few years after they had left the valley Gwyn's fourteen-year-old nephew had joined his father down the pit. Gareth's youngest child, a little girl, had died, just after her first birthday, succumbing to one of the frequent outbreaks of scarlet fever, although she had never been a healthy baby. Meg supposed the household, in the shadow of the Welsh pit had, like mining communities everywhere, remained unchanged — one of unceasing round-the-clock travail, a regime which was dictated, like all mining households, by the varying times of the men's shifts, and by the routines of feeding, bathing, washing and sleeping.

Compared to her life in those early days, Meg considered Freda's life to be one of luxury. Although Meg had wanted a child of her own, finding herself pregnant so early in her marriage would have given rise to a feeling of dread rather than the joy it should have been. She had seen too much heartache caused by unplanned pregnancies. Early on she was often beside herself with worry. But she and Gwyn had been careful. Bringing a child into a squalid environment like the one they'd left behind would have meant a move from the already overcrowded house to some other equally flimsy hovel. The thought was anathema to her. She had seen what happened to other women on whom this misfortune fell and was determined it wouldn't happen to her.

They had never left the valley before and, grim as life had been for them, it was still a wrench when they left their home and families and, with very few possessions and heavy hearts, arrived in Creswell in 1920. The decision to migrate had been the right one for both, and they seldom looked back on their life in Wales with any fondness.

It didn't taken Gwyn long to find work at the pit and eventually they moved into their own house in the Model Village; after the overcrowded Welsh hovel it seemed almost palatial. A year later, Owen was born in the house.

Throughout the strike of 1926, and the ensuing lockout in his native Wales, Gwyn repeatedly thanked his lucky stars they had come to this Derbyshire village. He was never out of work and fitted in well with his mining mates among whom he made some close friends many of whom, like him, had migrated from the South Wales coalfield. Meg was less outgoing and seemed content cleaning and polishing her smart little house and the few pieces of furniture they had started to accumulate. Unlike Gwyn with the men, Meg was never really part of the matrix of neighbouring colliers' wives. She wasn't unfriendly but she never visited their homes and seldom invited them into hers. Besides, some of them were known to imbibe in the odd drink in the Institute on a Friday night. She'd heard them — men *and* women — singing at the tops of their voices when they returned home after closing time. Some of the women even enjoyed the odd flutter on the horses when they had the money. Meg had imported many of the puritan values hammered into her psyche as a child on Sunday mornings sitting on the hard pews of the local chapel. No, she was quite content with her own company and that of her small child as she waited at home for Gwyn to return from his work — always with a hot meal ready on the kitchen table and clean, warm clothes airing in front of the fire.

Then, when he was barely forty having worked underground since he was a boy, the pit eventually claimed Gwyn's life. After years of what was thought to be a smoker's cough, he was sent to the local chest hospital and diagnosed with pneumoconiosis — black lung. Meg nursed him at home for the short time he had left. When he died there was no option other than Owen taking his place as breadwinner.

After Gwyn died, Owen and Meg remained in their house in the model village. Gwyn Thomas, like Freda's father, had gone to work down the pit as a boy of fourteen. Although Owen had completed his secondary education by the time he took his father's place, it had always been a source of regret to Meg that her son had been obliged to follow in his father's footsteps and work down the mine. She had once harboured dreams about a better future for him.

By the time they were married, Freda and Owen had known each other for almost twenty years. They had played together in the park joining in the gangs scavenging in the local woods for the communal 5 November bonfire. There was a traditional rivalry between the children of the Top and Bottom Models as to who could build the biggest and best bonfire. Sentries were even posted at night to guard against enemy raiding parties which tried to steal branches to add to their own pyres. The two had started at the infants' school on the same day and were always in the same class as they progressed through infants and the local junior and secondary schools. Owen had been a quiet, thoughtful lad, an avid reader who had cut his literary teeth on Richard Compton's *Just William* series, later progressing to *Tom Brown's School Days* or escaping to the world of *Raffles*, cricketer and gentleman thief. He was, like his mother, always a little aloof from the rest of the class. Yet he was somewhat of a dreamer and, although different from the other boys, they made allowances for his idiosyncrasies and always regarded him as one of them.

Freda and Owen remained friends after they left school and later occasionally went out together; not on 'dates' like the other lads and lasses who hung around outside the Drill Hall during the Saturday night dances, Owen was much too serious for that sort of thing. A couple of Christmases in a row he had taken Freda to the City Hall in Sheffield to hear performances of Handel's *Messiah* and, when the whole village travelled by coach to support Creswell Colliery football team play an away match against Accrington Stanley, Owen and Freda had gone over to Manchester to hear the Halle Orchestra and choir performing *The Dream of Gerontius*. Although it had all been a bit over Freda's head, she wouldn't have dreamed of hurting Owen's feelings by telling him so.

Owen had a deep-rooted sense of social justice, always siding with the underdog, a trait he had no doubt inherited from his father, a staunch Labour man who had been hardened by the events of 1926. Gwyn had never made a secret of his poverty-stricken origins nor the contempt he held for the reprehensible treatment the miners received at the hands of wealthy pit owners. Years of living in cramped hovels with no guarantee of a proper wage at the end of the week, had fostered resentment of the power of the greedy bosses. He remembered hearing how his brothers and their families had suffered during the lockout, starved back to work and burdened with debts which would never be repaid. At least that was something he and Meg and the boy would never have to endure.

After the war had dragged on for three years, Owen felt it was impossible to remain disengaged from the struggle against the forces of fascism. Despite his reserved occupation and the thought of leaving his widowed mother, Owen, unlike many others, stuck by his principles. He enlisted in the army and was posted as an infantryman to the 2nd Battalion, Sherwood Foresters. To those who knew him, this didn't come as a surprise. What did surprise them was that he asked Freda to marry him before he left.

Freda was a tall, well-built girl, not unattractive, but with all the appearance of one destined for spinsterhood. Whereas Owen, like his father, was considerably shorter and stocky with sandy, thinning hair. His hallmark wire framed spectacles gave him the appearance of an intellectual. He looked, and was, different from the other miners who were mostly bemused by him. Since his days at school, his demeanor had never detracted from his popularity among his school friends nor later, the men with whom he worked.

There had been the usual hurried war time wedding — clothes and reception all on a shoestring to comply with stringent rationing. "England's last 'ope" some people had remarked rather cruelly when it was announced that they were going to be married. Meg, who had always doted on Owen, was unsure which made her feel more uneasy — his going away to war or his having chosen to marry.

Owen was special to his mother, and she had reared him in a hot-house atmosphere. His talent and liking for music had been encouraged, although, unlike his father, he wasn't blessed with a fine Welsh tenor voice. Owen had a fondness for classical music which was one reason he enjoyed being part of the village brass band. It had been easy for him to switch between trumpet and cornet, stirring renditions like Hubert Parry's *Jerusalem* and the mellifluous *All of an April Evening* thrilled him to the marrow. Although his relationship with his mother deepened after Gwyn's death, Meg, who remained an obsessive polisher of furniture and beater of rugs, found it difficult to accept Owen's decision to join the war effort. She also couldn't imagine why, on the eve of his departure for active service, he should want to take a wife. This was the setting in which Freda, no slip of a girl herself, left her villa home for the smaller miner's cottage across the park and she never regretted her decision. Luckily for Freda, although another bone of contention for her mother-in-law, was the fact that, because 'there was a war on', she was able to carry on working as manageress of the local grocery store.

After Owen left for training camp, Meg and Freda rubbed along although Meg still found it hard to share her home, especially with a woman who, she considered, had usurped her place in her son's affection. She was determined to remain mistress of her own house where she could continue to clean and sweep to her heart's content.

Freda was oblivious to all this and carried on with her daily working life as before, at the local Co-op. Dealing with petty squabbles and the daily rationing-related issues was like water off a duck's back to her. That some people believed that Freda was more responsible than Lord Woolton for the shortage of food she found quite amusing and even Meg found it difficult to suppress a wry smile on listening to Freda's anecdotes over high tea in front of the fire.

Then, at the beginning of 1943, Owen came home for a short embarkation leave before setting out with his regiment for North Africa. Meg cried a lot, making it hard for Owen and Freda to find time alone together. Owen was not only a husband going off to war, he was also an only son. After a frustrating and unsatisfactory few days for the three of them, Owen left and the two women resumed their lives, together but apart. Although Freda was easy going, her Welsh mother-in-law couldn't have been more different; she was as intense as she was house-proud.

After fighting in Tunisia, Owen's battalion was sent to Italy where they took part in the Anzio landings. Remaining for a further year, they fought all the way through Italy suffering heavy casualties in what was some of the fiercest fighting of the war. From there he was sent to Palestine where he stayed until the cessation of hostilities. When the war ended Freda, feeling rather self-conscious, had gone to Chesterfield to meet him from the train. It had been a tough war for Owen, and he had lost many friends. Outwardly, he seemed unchanged, the same easy-going Owen. He and Freda had travelled back to the village by bus, reunited but feeling rather like two strangers who, having known each other since childhood, had barely spent time together as husband and wife, having shared few experiences of married life. His memories of the war, harrowing as they must have been, were never divulged.

To add further to people's bemusement (including Owen and

Freda's), shortly after Owen's demobilisation and return, Freda became pregnant. Meg greeted the news with outward indifference, no doubt remembering the circumstances surrounding her own 'planned' pregnancy. If the baby were a girl, she would be displaced even more in Owen's affection. It didn't occur to any of the three that the domestic arrangements of the trio would be altered by the new baby's arrival.

Contrary to the advice of her friends who had been off to give birth at the local maternity hospital, Freda, who was considered rather mature for a first time mother, elected to have the baby at home. This was probably the first decision she had made which met with Meg's approval. The house was suitable since it was clean and warm, had running water and a proper lavatory, albeit across the communal yard. That Owen was determined to be at her side when the time came, certainly did *not* meet with his mother's approval. After all, this was women's business and no place for a man. Their decision didn't cause a problem for the midwife. She was an outsider, without the hidebound ideology of her disciplinarian predecessor, and was a mother herself. Davey's arrival was greeted by both parents, an anomaly at that time. Owen's presence at Davey's entrance into the world created a special closeness between father and son. Even Meg softened when she saw the baby for the first time.

Suddenly Freda was roused from her reverie by Davey who gave a deep sigh in his sleep. Still on his mother's knee, he was trying to turn over but, cocooned in his eiderdown, it was impossible. It seemed safe now to return him to bed. Freda decided to do likewise. She glanced at the clock on the sideboard as she crossed the room and it was well after midnight. Owen would be home in a few hours, and she would have to be up busying herself with breakfast — the nicest meal of the day when Owen worked nights. There he would be, safely home once more and, while Meg and Davey were still asleep, the two of them could share the intimacy of the meal and smoke a cigarette together. They treasured these few-and-far-between intimate occasions.

At 3 o'clock, Owen checked the time on his father's old watch. He was now more than half way through his shift and just one of over two hundred men working in the South-West Division of the pit that night, a thousand feet underground. Freda and Davey would still be fast asleep. It was Tuesday already. He checked the time again — 3 more hours to go.

At 3.45 Freda was woken by a sudden cry from Davey's room. This *was* unusual. Although as a baby he had taken a while to settle, he had been sleeping through the night for weeks now. Wearily, Freda sat up and groped for her slippers.

Just at this time word was beginning to spread stealthily through the village that all was not well at the pit. In earlier days there had been an informal village telegraph whereby news of trouble at the mine was communicated from house to house by wives banging on the back of the fire grate with a poker. By 1950 this had been superseded by a more sophisticated technique which was, if not more effective, just as frightening. Wives and families were beginning to jump out of warm beds hastily pulling on coats over their night wear, oblivious to the cold night air as they sped to the mine. The ominous clamour of the bells of vehicles carrying rescue teams signalled that something was gravely amiss. Those living closest to the mine had been woken by the noise of feverish activity. Instinctively they knew the cause. After generations, they needed no extra sensory perception to alert them to disaster.

Trying to comfort the distraught child, Freda heard the racket. When she opened the window of the stuffy little room people were already running towards the pit. Their cries filled her with horror. Subconsciously, a lifetime in a mining village had conditioned her to accept the inevitability of such a moment. For hundreds of years mining communities had faced occasions such as this.

"Pit's on fire! Pit's on fire!" was the mantra repeated by the stampeding families.

Meg, also in possession of this inbuilt extra sense, was already at the top of the stairs, a look of horror on her face. She had Freda flung coats over their night gowns and, with Davey still wrapped in his eiderdown, raced toward the pit, stumbling, picking themselves up again and willing themselves to get there as fast as they could, all the time being overtaken by others sharing the same sense of panic.

When they arrived, panting, at the pit yard, they thought they must be the only ones there. It was dark and there was no sound. As they walked in they brushed against others. What they saw startled them. They were surrounded by hundreds of others, all with racing hearts, wrenching guts and heads about to explode. Not a sound was heard. Children stood among them, they too were waiting for news of their fathers, uncles, grandfathers. No one spoke — there was no need. They stood in silence, waiting, their shivering not caused solely by the cold night air.

Freda was vaguely aware of someone gently lifting Davey from her arms. She let him go, too preoccupied to object to him being removed.

"I'll take 'im love." It was Edie Cullen, her next-door neighbour.

Edie had been through all this already when she was made a widow by the mine. It had claimed her first husband's life before the war. Also roused by the pandemonium, she had been swept along on the tide of frightened families. She knew that Owen was working in the mine that night. Freda, mesmerised and oblivious to the hundreds of others, stood and waited. Meg, her heart pounding, stood with her daughter-in-law. Silently they all waited — and waited.

Their vigil lasted for the remainder of the night and well

into the following day. Eight hours after the start of the fire, an announcement was read, relating the events of the night and finally, telling everyone what they dreaded to hear. All hope of finding further survivors had been abandoned. Freda and Meg stood in silence, unable to move. Then they heard a dismembered voice announcing the names of the dead men. Freda dared not look at Meg.

Owen was among the second group of men brought to the surface. He had been sitting with a group of twenty other men, mostly the friends he'd joked with on the way down, all apparently waiting to be rescued.

The two women stayed among the crowd of relatives, continuing their vigil throughout the afternoon, oblivious to the passage of time. It grew dark. Still they waited, transfixed, with hundreds of other families. All were now numb with exhaustion and shock. Leaders of the local church and chapel arrived to join them. Already mining officials had joined the crowd, standing in silent support. Other miners and rescue workers, still wearing their grimy, smoke-stained clothes stood with them. With the winding wheel turning above their heads they sang hymns and prayed together, *Oh God our help in ages past … Abide with me*. There was a minute's silence and, unwillingly but wearily, they quietly dispersed, making their hypnotic way back to their homes. Still no one uttered a word.

Freda had little memory of the next few days through which she moved in a trance. The day-to-day tasks of caring for Davey were performed automatically. She held the child close to her heart. Davey was strangely quiet and composed, sensing the loss and despair around him. He was all that was left of Owen. She felt indifferent to Meg's silent lonely sobbing in her cold bedroom, impotent and unable to comfort her.

Throughout his years abroad facing the brutality of war which, she considered, was completely incompatible with his docile personality, Owen was never out of Meg's thoughts. Despite all the odds, he had survived and come home to her, but now she realised his return was only a loan. Like the thousands of women who had married coal miners, she had lived her entire marriage with the constant fear that the mine would claim the life of her husband, just as it had claimed her father all those years ago. She had prepared herself for the loss of a partner but never a son and for this, she could never forgive the pit.

Owen was buried on the first day of a two day melancholy funereal marathon. Arrangements seemed to have been made mysteriously without Freda being aware of what was happening. Somehow she managed to survive the ordeal, retaining only a dim memory of the event. The rain poured down their faces, or was it tears? In the days following the funerals, as the rain continued, Freda sat in front of the fireplace which, instead of burning coals, contained only white ash. It made no difference to her, whatever she did she felt cold. She would always feel cold without the warmth of Owen's body beside hers. Her heart was broken, and the pain was exquisite. Not even the substitute warmth of Davey's little body next to her heart could ease it. Subconciously she persisted with Davey's routine and, at night, they shared the big bed that she had shared with Owen. She slept on Owen's pillow which still bore the lingering scent of his hair. Meg's only wish now was that she would not live any longer as all she wanted was to be united with both her men. Freda was incapable of any thought beyond her own pain. The pain which filled each woman left no room for words of comfort for each other.

Memorial to the 80 miners who were killed in the Creswell Colliery disaster on 26 September 1950. The memorial is inscribed with the names of the dead. Together with a memorial garden, the memorial stands in the Skinner Street Cemetery where many of the men are busied.

http://www.healeyhero.co.uk/rescue/pits/Cresswell/cres.htm

But Meg *did* survive as did Freda. They were able to glean some comfort from the fact that they had, at least, been able to give Owen a proper burial. Many men still lay underground, their bodies sepulchred where the fire had burned, sealed off until it was safe to bring them home. In time the two women found consolation in being with other dispossessed families. Although feelings were shared, healing was an individual process. Their wounds were still raw when, six months later, the underground seals were broken, and more men were bought out of the mine to be buried. A few remained and, the following August, the remaining men, interred for almost a year, were brought home and finally allowed to rest with their comrades. Only then could the process of healing genuinely begin, a universal process gloomily familiar to mining communities. Sadly, but inevitably, the process will be repeated again and again wherever men go down the mines.

Davey got his train set for Christmas, but it was Joe, his grandfather, who put the rails together and constructed the little station for him — Joe who, against so many odds, had survived his whole precarious working life

Unlike Meg, at least one of Freda's wishes came true. Her son never went down the mine to work.

17

1984 — Beginning of The End: Losing the Battle.

Tweedledum and Tweedledee
Agreed to have a battle;
*   For Tweedledum said Tweedledee*
Had spoiled his nice new rattle.
Just then flew down a monstrous crow,
As black as a tar-barrel;
Which frightened both the heroes so,
They quite forgot their quarrel

On 12 July 1946 the Coal Industry Nationalisation Act of 1946 received Royal Assent. Under the terms of the act, the 'great experiment in Socialism', the National Coal Board was created. Its members were appointed by then Minister for Fuel and Power, Manny Shinwell. On 1 January 1947, Vesting Day, all mines with over 30 employees came under its authority.

> "The coal mines now belong to the nation. This act offers great possibilities of social advance for the workers and indeed for the whole nation. If …. workers, National Coal Board and government shoulder their duties wisely, these great advances will be assured."

After Attlee's speech announcing Nationalisation, many coal mines held celebration ceremonies where the blue and white NCB flag was hoisted above the pit.

(Picture: The Coal Research Establishment. https://www.photomemorabilia.co.uk/FBC/CRE/tn_CRE_flag.jp)

Spoken by Prime Minister Clement Richard Attlee on Vesting Day, the words appear to optimistically herald a golden future for the coal industry which, after decades of contention, striving and frustration on the part of the miners, was now *safely* in the hands of the nation. The optimism was validated by an immediate increase in coal production. In 1946–1947 Britain had experienced a freezing winter, so severe, in fact that the whole country closed down and, as a result, Shinwell was replaced as Minister by Hugh Gaitskell. There was also a post war international shortage of coal which lasted until 1957. It seemed an apt time for the government to take over the industry and attempt to increase production.

From that day, blue and white National Coal Board flags were flown on offices and headgears of the country's 1,000 pits. Many collieries held small inaugural ceremonies to hoist the flags with the famous statement: 'This colliery is now owned by the people, worked by the people on behalf of the people'.

Unfortunately, the optimistic celebrations may have been somewhat misguided given the given the history of the coal industry over the preceding fifty years. The intransigence of private ownership with its reluctance to invest money at the expense of profit had always hampered the industry. With hindsight, Attlee's words appear to be not only optimistic but bullish and anachronistic. After decades of support and industrial action by miners to achieve nationalisation of the industry, it may have come too late.

Under New Management

This cartoon appeared in *The Daily Worker*, January 1947.
https://www.nationalarchives.gov.uk/education/resources/attlees-britain/new-management/

One thousand six hundred and forty-seven collieries, formerly owned by private companies, were nationalised by the NCB after paying £164,660,000 in compensation to former owners. Of this number, about half were run down and in need of considerable investment to render them viable. A further £550 million was spent on improvements in infrastructure and welfare. New machinery to increase productivity and facilities such as pit head baths were a boon to miners who, after wage increases, became among the highest paid workers in the country. Simultaneously, their working week was shortened to five days. However, the overriding aim of the government was not merely to reward the workers but to make a profit. Sadly, history was not on the side of the newly nationalised industry and public ownership did not fulfil the long-held hopes of the miners.

Although this book is primarily about women and the coal industry, it would be incomplete without mention of the Miners' Strike of 1984–1985. Almost sixty years after their heroic activism and solidarity in support of the 1926 General Strike lockout, the fighting spirit of these women once more came to the surface.

In 1984, many grandparents and even parents of striking miners and their wives had links to the 1926 General Strike. Comparisons and contrasts have been made between the two greatest industrial disputes ever to have occurred in Britain and have been the topic of numerous theses. In 1926, miners came out in strike against pit closures. The strike had the support of 100% of miners and their union. It was an all-out strike in which the country came to a standstill. It lasted for 9 days.

Fifty-eight years later, miners once again came out on strike against pit closures. This strike lasted 358 days. Unlike its predecessor, it was *not* largely an example of restrained behavior. Trade unions were not unanimous in their support of the strike and it divided the country. Both disputes ended in failure.

The 1984 Strike occurred in response to the government closure of twenty pits with an estimated loss of twenty thousand jobs. What followed was a massive demonstration by miners in their own defence. At its core, the reason for striking was not seen as purely economic but about the right to work. Under the slogan *Coal not Dole*, the 1984 miners' strike was a watershed in relations between the government and the unions and a last stand by the miners to fight for their livelihoods and their communities. Unfortunately, the strike culminated with the death knell of both.

By the beginning of the 1950s, the decade following nationalisation, there was a transformation in the global energy market. Oil began to replace coal as a source of energy. North Sea gas was discovered in the 1960s and its production soared in the 1970s. The demand for coal plummeted. By the 1980s the coal industry was reliant on government subsidies for its survival, and the decision by the Government of the day to end the subsidies was followed by the closure of twenty of the country's most unprofitable mines. This was the catalyst for, arguably, the most acrimonious industrial discord in British history. Yet the origin of the end of the coal industry, as discussed in Chapter 9, can be be traced back to 1913, often regarded as the industry's zenith. From then the industry began to decline and the downturn continued until its eventual, but inevitable, obsolescence eighty years later.

The British miners' strike began on 6 March 1984 and lasted until 3 March 1985. Led by the National Union of Mineworkers' (NUM) General Secretary, Arthur Scargill, its intention was to withdraw labour from coal mines to overturn the Conservative government's policy on pit closures.

Described as 'the most bitter dispute in British history', the 1984 strike was the worst industrial crisis to hit the nation since 1926 and the closest, since that time, that the country had come to civil war. At its height the 1984 strike involved 142,000 mineworkers, 38,000,000 lost working days, 9808 arrests in England and Wales, a further 1504 in Scotland and the death of at least 3 people. By the end of the strike 5,653 miners had been tried for alleged offences. Around 150 to 200 strikers were imprisoned — 42 for eighteen months or more. The two miners held responsible for one of those killed received life sentences. The NUM was fined £200,000 for its activities, and the estimated cost of the strike to the country was £2.4 billion. There are several predisposing events which culminated in the dispute of 1984–1985.

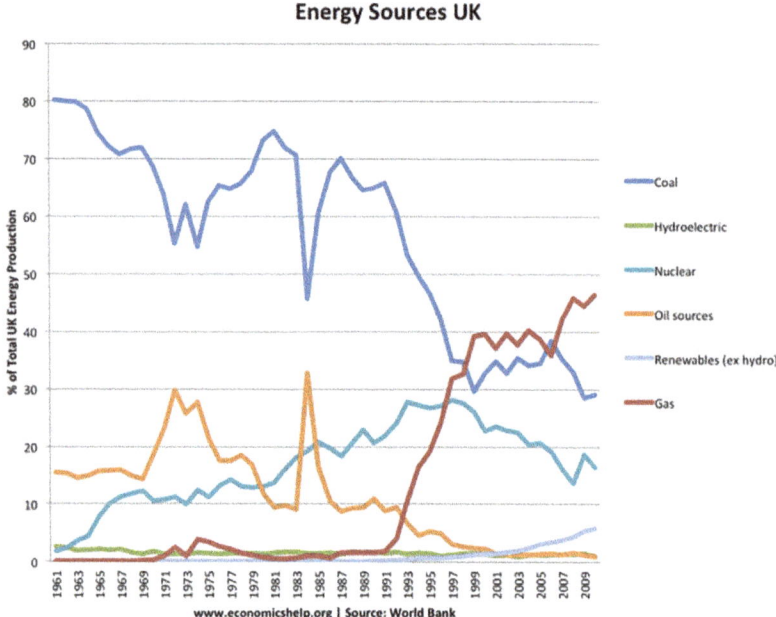

The decline of the British coal industry started after World War I but was accelerated after World War II when alternate, cleaner forms of energy became available.

The decline of the UK Coal Industry: Economics Help
https://www.economicshelp.org/blog/6498/uncategorized/the-decline-of-the-uk-coal-industry/

Prior to 1973, low oil prices decreased the demand for coal. This heralded the closure of 223 pits between 1967 and 1970 by Harold Wilson's Labour government. However, in October 1973, the Arab-Israeli (*Yom Kippur*) War ended in an Israeli victory. In retaliation, members of the Arab Organisation of Petroleum Exporting Countries (OPEC) proclaimed an oil embargo against countries,

17   1984 — Beginning of The End: Losing the Battle.

including the United Kingdom, which had supported Israel. As the supply of cheap oil ended, the emphasis returned to the production of coal to supply industrial and domestic demands. Government money was re-invested in coal mining and, consequently, the power of the NUM increased.

Throughout the 1970s, the British economy experienced high rates of inflation prompting the then Conservative Prime Minister, Edward Heath, to introduce a wage freeze in both the public and private sectors. The freeze affected all workers. Despite this, the National Union of Mineworkers which had become a very militant organisation, at its national conference passed a resolution calling for a 35% wage increase for its members. A counter offer by the National Coal Board was rejected by the NUM as insufficient. A national ballot in favour of strike action ensued, but was lost. In its place, an overtime ban threatening power supplies, was implemented.

At the end of 1973, to conserve electricity and coal stocks, avert a currency crisis and maintain business continuity, a number of measures were introduced by Prime Minister Edward Heath's government including the Three Day Work Order. As its title suggests, this restricted the working week thereby limiting commercial electricity consumption to three consecutive days. Even BBC and ITV broadcasts were subject to these restrictions so that each organisation was only allowed to air until 10.30 on alternate nights. Most pubs were closed.

Also, in January 1974, most NUM workers, having rejected the lower than expected NCB offer of a pay increase, now voted by an overwhelming majority to strike. Government threats to use the army as strike breakers did not eventuate and the strike commenced on 5 February 1974. Two days later, Edward Heath called a general election which was held on 28 February using the ambivalent slogan '*Who governs Britain?*'

The election resulted in a hung parliament. Although the Tories won the popular vote, Labour secured more seats in the House of Commons. Failing to secure support from the Liberal and Ulster Unionist MPs, Heath resigned and Harold Wilson again became Prime Minister, albeit leading a minority government. Two weeks later, the full working week was restored, and miners received their 35% wage increase (with a further 35% the following year). In a second general election held in October 1974, Labour was returned with a three-seat majority.

1974 in Britain did not have a happy beginning. At midnight on 31 December 1973, Prime Minister Edward Heath introduced a 3-day working week. Its introduction was an attempt to conserve diminishing fuel supplies and lasted until 7 March. Above, a telephonist works by torchlight.

1974: The Three Day Working Week: The Guardian
https://www.theguardian.com/politics/gallery/2009/apr/16/past-conservatives

After the defeat of the Heath government, Margaret Thatcher assumed leadership of the Tory Party in 1975 and, with Thatcher at the helm, the Conservatives regained government in 1979. They commenced a radical program of industrial restructuring known as *'Thatcherism'*, a belief in free markets and a small State with non-involvement of government in the planning and regulation of people's lives. In a rejection of the post war welfare state and nationalisation, except for the National Health Service, Mrs Thatcher was determined to give free rein to privatisation and free market economics. To achieve this goal, it was imperative to destroy the trade unions, and the NUM was a prime target.

In 2010, cabinet papers released under the 30-year rule exposed the scale of Margaret Thatcher's long-held ambitions to crush the power of Britain's trade unions in general, and the National Union of Mineworkers in particular.

> "We had to fight the enemy without in the Falklands. We always have to be aware of the enemy within, which is much more difficult to fight and more dangerous to liberty."
> (Margaret Thatcher's speech to the backbench '1922' Conservative Private Members' Committee, July 1984).

The term 'enemy within' referred to the union movement, specifically the NUM. 'Strategic principles and practical measures' drawn up *apropos* the NUM were, arguably, designed to be provocative. Chancellor of the Exchequer, Nigel Lawson described preparations for the approaching industrial action as 'like re-arming to face the threat of Hitler'.

In the wake of the defeat of Edward Heath's government in 1974, right wing, free marketeer and Conservative MP Nicholas Ridley produced, in 1977, *The Ridley Report*. Ridley believed in halting the power of trade unions and was convinced that it impeded market forces, consequently causing inflation. In his report he described how the Conservative government could fight *and* defeat a major strike in a nationalised industry. He made several recommendations to deal with strikes, including hiring of non-union labor, adapting power stations to burn oil *and* coal (which would be imported from non-union foreign ports) and increasing the stockpile of coal supplies. The report proposed cutting off money to those on strike so that they would have to be financed by the unions. It also recommended training and equipping a large, mobile squad of police. Like Thatcher, Ridley believed that union power should be checked to prevent it destroying future governments. Nicholas Ridley's recommendations were, to the letter, the blueprint to which the Thatcher government adhered during the events which were to follow.

Bearing in mind the feminist maxim 'the personal is political', and with the scene set for the most spectacular political contest for almost 60 years, it is probably pertinent at this point to elaborate on the major protagonists in the unfolding drama.

Scottish-born tycoon Sir Ian MacGregor was appointed chairman of the National Coal Board in 1983 by the Thatcher Conservative Government. At an annual salary of £59,000 (current value around £200,000) his appointment was described by then Shadow Energy Minister John Smith as "extraordinarily stupid".

*On this day: BBC Home\
http://news.bbc.co.uk/onthisday/hi/dates/stories/march/28/ newsid_2531000/2531033.stm*

Ian McGregor was born in Kinlocheven in the Scottish

Highlands in 1912. After completing an engineering degree at Glasgow University, he became, very early in his career, involved in confrontation with trade unions over striking crane drivers. This resulted in driving cranes himself for two weeks, thereby attracting the attention of his managing director. Macgregor was marked out for early promotion.

During World War II, McGregor worked for the Ministry of Supply before transferring to the Ministry of Aircraft production from where he was sent by Minister Beaverbrook to work in the US. He remained in the US during the term of the 1945 Labour government, having a dislike of its policy of nationalisation.

While in the US he maintained his disdainful confrontational attitude towards trade unionism and at one point, his car, with him inside, was overturned by union pickets. He went on to forge a successful business career in the US before returning to Britain in 1977, ironically at the behest of Labour Prime Minister James Callahan, to take over the running of the ailing British Leyland car company.

Following the election of the Thatcher Conservative government in 1979, Macgregor was appointed the following year as Chair of the nationalised British Steel Corporation. In 1980, British Steel employed 166,000 staff producing 14 million tons of steel a year, but was running at a loss. MacGregor embarked on a ruthless program of plant closures and redundancies and, by 1981, had reduced its staff to 71,000. In addition to increasing unemployment, this action effectively destroyed traditional steel working communities. His *modus operandi*, besides earning him the *sobriquet* 'Mac the Knife', made him an ideal candidate to implement Margaret Thatcher's economic policies *vis-à-vis* the coal industry. Following his successful tenure at British Steel, the government appointed him to head the National Coal Board.

On 28 March 1983, MacGregor took over the chairmanship of the NCB from Norman Sidall, a mining engineer who had begun his working life at the Yorkshire coalface. MacGregor was seen by the government as a supporter of *Thatcherism*. Having begun his NCB incumbency by informing the Yorkshire miners that they were less productive than their American counterparts, he applied the same 'slash and burn strategy' used during his time at British Steel by cutting jobs, closing unprofitable mines and scaling down the coal industry in the belief (and intent) that pit closures would provoke a strike for which the government would be well prepared.

'The Iron Lady' was a title bestowed on Margaret Thatcher by a Russian newspaper. She was fond of the name by which she became ubiquitously known as she also considered herself to be strong.

Margaret Hilda Thatcher was the first female Prime Minister of the UK, and held that office for longer than any other British Prime Minister in the 20th century. Strong and successful, loved and hated in equal measure, she is also considered to be one of the most divisive.

Picture: Stand for America
https://www.standforamericanow.com/general/countdown-our-10-favorite-margaret-thatcher-quotes/

17 1984 — Beginning of The End: Losing the Battle.

Margaret Hilda Thatcher, the longest serving British Prime Minister of the 20th century, was born in Grantham, Lincolnshire in 1925, the daughter of a grocer. She was educated at the local girls' grammar school and, after reading chemistry at Somerville College, Oxford, trained as a barrister. She joined the Conservative Party in the 1940s and, after several unsuccessful attempts, was eventually returned as Conservative Member of Parliament for Finchley, London in 1959.

When the Conservatives lost Government in 1974, Margaret Thatcher replaced Edward Heath as leader and, after the Tories regained power in 1979, she became Britain's first female Prime Minister. Belief in a free market economy underpinned her radical policies which became known collectively as 'Thatcherism'. A free market economy is based on two essential tenets: a belief in a market where prices for goods and services (including wages, the price of labour) are based solely on supply and demand where, in due course, equilibrium is achieved without government intervention and, secondly, the doctrine of the *small State*, a rejection of State ownership. To these ends, Thatcher introduced policies to privatise state owned industries — British Telecom, British Airways *and* the National Coal Board. Implicit in its economic policy was the government's abandonment of a commitment to full employment, affirming that this was the responsibility of employers and employees.

Margaret Thatcher was a dogmatic politician who attempted to humanise her policies and beliefs in 'Victorian values' by comparing herself to a 'thrifty housewife'. Her beginnings as the daughter of a grocer, she claimed, had instilled in her the value of hard work. Union leaders, she affirmed, were the stumbling block to economic progress.

Arthur Scargill was the son and grandson of Yorkshire coal miners. He became president of the NUM in 1981 when he was already a forceful adversary of Margaret Thatcher. Despite the failure of the 1984–1985 Miners' Strike, Scargill remained popular with the majority of miners and, after the strike, was elected lifetime president of the NUM. In 2002 he resigned the leadership to become Honorary President.

Picture: Business Insider Australia, April 12, 2013
https://www.businessinsider.com.au/arthur-scargills-thatcher-text-2013-4

Margaret Thatcher's nemesis, Arthur Scargill, was born in 1938 in Worsbrough Dale, a coal mining community near Barnsley in Yorkshire, the son of a coal miner. Scargill left school at 15 to also work as a coal miner at Woolley Colliery where he remained for the next nineteen years. At 17 he became a Marxist, joining the Young Communists League in 1955. In 1961, Scargill became Compensation Manager with the National Union of Mineworkers and was highly regarded for his work in this position. It was during this time that he graduated from Leeds University with a degree in Economics, Industrial Relations and Social History. The year 1973 saw him become Yorkshire Head of the NUM where he played a critical role in bringing down the Conservative government of Edward Heath.

Scargill led an unofficial pit strike in 1969 which had started in Yorkshire but soon spread nationally. The militant stance and the use of pugnacious tactics during this strike were pivotal in the way the NUM would conduct itself in future industrial events. The strike saw the introduction of 'flying pickets' involving hundreds of miners who could be bussed, very rapidly, to different areas to close down working pits. It was Scargill who led the NUM in the 1984 strike, claiming that the Thatcher government's provocative policy of closing a number of pits each year, which it regarded as unprofitable, was the root cause of the conflict. Although the Government denied this, Scargill was eventually proved correct.

In 1945, The National Union of Mineworkers (NUM superseded the Miners' Federation of Great Britain (MFGB as the miner's union. Strongly supportive of the Labour Party, the NUM took part in strikes in 1972, 1974 and 1984–1985. When Arthur Scargill assumed leadership in 1981, the union boasted a membership of 170,000. After the failure of the 1984–1985 strike, it became considerable smaller and by 2015, membership had declined to about 100 members.

Picture: National Union of Mineworkers
http://num.org.uk/

The National Union of Mineworkers (NUM) was formed on 1 January 1945. It became the successor to the Miners' Federation of Great Britain (MFGB) which had represented discrete miners' unions in various areas. (It was the MFGB secretary Arthur Cook who had coined the General Strike slogan 'Not a penny off the pay, not a minute on the day'.) The evolution of the NUM was accompanied by a congenital schism within the union. Miners from Nottinghamshire, Leicestershire and the Midlands (and, until 1960, Yorkshire) formed the right wing of the union whereas those from Scotland and Wales, closely aligned to the Communist Party, were on the left. Despite its traditional support of the Labour Party in the 1950s, the NUM was overwhelmingly a right-wing union.

Although representing all mine workers in Britain, each area retained autonomy with its own headquarters, president and general secretary. With a decentralised regional structure, certain regions were more militant than others. Although individual areas could call strikes initially, a national strike required a two thirds majority vote of all members. Since this was practically impossible, this figure was decreased to 55% and in 1984, to 50%.

Although post war economic policy allowed for closures of unprofitable pits, it only did so with the proviso that miners agreed to the closures and that they were guaranteed economic security. Enforced closures which left redundant miners with limited re-employment alternatives were not tolerated. In March 1984, in protest against the pit closures, and without a national ballot, Arthur Scargill, National President of the NUM contravened NUM rules and declared a national strike.

A month later, in April 1984, the NUM convened a Special National Delegates Conference to decide whether it should hold a national ballot in favour of a strike. Delegates voted 69 to 54 against the motion. Separate ballots were then held in each area. Miners

17 1984 — Beginning of The End: Losing the Battle.

in Nottinghamshire, Leicestershire, South Derbyshire, North Wales and parts of Lancashire voted to continue to work. In the absence of a *national* ballot in favour of striking, it was ruled illegal. Consequently striking miners were ineligible for strike benefits.

From its beginning the 1984 Miners' Strike was reported in the media in militaristic language: it was a *war* between the Government and the NUM; the *battle* of Orgreave; miners *fighting* for their rights. Arthur Scargill was described as *a dictator* by one daily newspaper. Mrs Thatcher had declared the mines to be the *enemy within*. Such hawkish metaphors helped to shape public opinion on the strike which was, by and large, hostile towards the miners and the NUM.

War on the picket line: how the British press made a battle out of the miners' strike: *The Conversation*.

https://theconversation.com/war-on-the-picket-line-how-the-british-press-made-a-battle-out-of-the-miners-strike-60470

The National Association of Colliery Overmen, Deputies and Shot Firers, NACODS, held a vote to strike in support of the NUM, but the vote failed to reach a two thirds majority. There was an existing arrangement between the union and the NCB that, in the event of NACODS members facing aggression and/or intimidation from NUM pickets, they would be allowed to stay off work with pay. As picketing activity escalated, the NCB defaulted on this agreement stating that they expected NACODS members to cross the picket lines to supervise those miners who chose to work.

A second ballot in favour of strike action ensued which secured the necessary majority and, for the first time in its history, the NACODS members voted to strike. However, after further negotiation with the NCB who threatened to replace their deputies with non-union labour, their strike was called off. Ian MacGregor later conceded that, had NACODS gone ahead with its planned strike action, the NCB would have been forced to compromise their stance on the striking NUM, a move which would probably have saved pits and jobs.

There was provocation from both major protagonists. Arthur Scargill declared "The policies of this government are clear — to destroy the coal industry and the NUM." Margaret Thatcher continued to label NUM members as "The enemy within". Scargill believed, as Attlee had, that the miners should have a share in the profits of the coal industry.

Thatcher's belief, in line with her classic liberal principles, was that the industry should accede to the power of the market. In many respects, the Miners' Strike of 1984–1985 was an ideological conflict between the forces of Left and Right. Against the background of a division of opinion within the union, and hostility between the union and the government, in March 1984 more than 187,000 miners came out on strike.

17 1984 — Beginning of The End: Losing the Battle.

The press described the strike as 'Scargill's Strike' and Arthur Scargill was accused of seeking reasons for a strike ever since he had taken over leadership of the NUM. Tactically he was criticised for calling the strike before summer as winter may have been more effective. Scargill later criticised the Labour party, under opposition leader Neil Kinnock, for its lack of support. Even without the benefit of hindsight it was evident that the coal industry was doomed. With new, cleaner sources of energy requiring less manpower, coal mining would soon be consigned to oblivion. What is manifest is the blatantly provocative nature of the strategy employed by the government to manipulate events towards the inexorable sequel.

Seeking to avenge the miners' 'victories' of 1973–1974, Margaret Thatcher, on commencing office, remarked to then Home Secretary, William Whitelaw, "The last Conservative government was destroyed by the miners' strike. We'll have another and we'll win". Her reference to Arthur Scargill and the striking miners as 'the enemy within' implicitly compared the power of the mining union to the sinister regime of Argentinian dictator General Galtieri whom she had vanquished in the jingoistic Falklands War two years previously. Thatcher's intention was to shatter the aura surrounding the NUM and with it the acknowledgement of the dangers faced daily by its members working underground. The power base of the NUM lay in the closely-knit mining communities; *their* demise was to be collateral damage. *'When you close a pit, you kill a community'* became a commonly heard slogan.

Former Prime Minister Harold MacMillan, by then Lord Stockton, arguably the last of the 'old Tories', referred in his debut speech to the House of Lords, to the people of these communities thus:

> "It breaks my heart to see — and I cannot interfere — what
> is happening in our country today. This terrible strike, by

the best men in the world, who beat the Kaiser's and Hitler's armies and never gave in. It is pointless and we cannot afford that kind of thing."

In November 1984, after almost a year of striking, he again revealed his feelings for the miners,

"My heart is broken by this terrible strike of the best men in the world."

MacMillan's words evoked the sentiment he had displayed in April 1926 when he wrote to Winston Churchill (no friend of the miners in 1926) of the 'appalling' conditions endured by his constituents. (His constituency of Stockton was at the heart of the Durham coalfield.) The divisive nature of so much of the news reporting of the 1984–1985 miners' strike, and media concentration on picket line violence, meant that there was often little coverage of the remarkable solidarity shown by the international trade union movement.

The strike was not just a conflict between the government and the NUM. In the first half of the 20th century over a thousand collieries were operating in Britain. By 1984, that number had dropped to 173. From one million in 1922, the number of miners had decreased to 231,000 in 1982. These numbers are stark, but even starker are the fates of the communities wholly dependent on coal for survival. In many households more than one person depended on coal mining for a living. Whole communities had sprung up around local pits which had been the sole source of employment for generations. The future of these communities, their beliefs, values and traditions were at stake as well as the future of their families.

Once the strike was underway 'flying pickets' travelled away from their own pits to convince their non-striking colleagues not to

17 1984 — Beginning of The End: Losing the Battle.

cross picket lines. Police were employed to protect the miners who continued to work. In most cases picketing was orderly and peaceful but violent clashes did break out between police and striking miners.

The miners gathered outside the Orgreave coking works to prevent supplies of coal reaching the plant and, in the ensuing melee, stones were thrown, there was a charge by mounted police and 93 pickets were arrested. Orgreave was the most violent clash, not only of the 1984 strike, but ever witnessed in the history of British industrial disputes. It determined the hostile nature which persisted throughout the strike and the public's antipathy towards the miners. It was a well-orchestrated confrontation in which thousands of miners faced thousands of police, some of whom were mounted, and all armed with batons and riot shields. As a result of the fracas, 55 miners were charged with riot, then punishable by life imprisonment.

The Enemy Within? Frightening confrontation between striking miners and a more than adequate police force.

The Screening Museum
http://www.cinemamuseum.org.uk/2019/screening-of-still-the-enemy-within-2014/

On Monday 18 June, one of the most violent clashes in British industrial history took place at the coking plant at Orgreave, a small village near Rotherham in South Yorkshire.

The Telegraph
https://www.telegraph.co.uk/news/politics/margaret-thatcher/11137412/Margaret-Thatchers-miner-speech-inspired-by-Methodist-hymn.html

"The scandal of Orgreave": *The Long Read*, 18 May 2017

https://www.theguardian.com/politics/2017/may/18/scandal-of-orgreave-miners-strike-hillsborough-theresa-may

A year later, during the trial of the first fifteen of those charged, evidence given by police was held to be 'unreliable' and the trial subsequently collapsed. In the opinion of the defending solicitor, the case revealed a failure of the South Yorkshire police rather than the guilt of those charged. It was reported that some police officers had given false testimony, and some had even committed perjury. No police were charged for their actions. Thirty-nine miners were later paid £425,000 in compensation by the South Yorkshire police force for wrongful arrest, unlawful detention and malicious arrest. Despite the evidence of malpractice, and the collapse of the trial, the Government opposed any inquiry.

For the duration of the strike the miners received no wages. Without a unanimous vote the strike was illegal and striking miners were denied state benefits. However, benefits were paid to their families, but £15 pounds was deducted from each payment to take account of strike pay and families were denied 'urgent needs payment'.

The strike, lasting exactly one year, was contentious and schismatic, not even having the universal support of NUM members. While there was almost unanimous support in the North East, South Wales and the Kent coalfields, miners in North Wales and the Midlands were less enthusiastic. Although miners in Lancashire objected to the strike, they never crossed picket lines.

There were various attempts to overturn strike action. During the first few weeks the NCB obtained an injunction limiting picketing at Nottinghamshire pits but was prevented from invoking the ruling. Various challenges to the strike's validity were issued by groups of miners who continued to work. Miners in North Yorkshire whose branch had voted against the strike argued that, in the absence of a national ballot it was, in fact, illegal. In Nottinghamshire, where the NUM had voted in favour of striking, most members continued to work. In many communities, households were divided between men who wanted to strike and those who wanted to work. Almost three decades later, many of these divisions still exist. Nevertheless, the strike did change people's lives, notwithstanding loss of communities. During twelve life-changing months, people changed the way they thought and behaved towards each other. They found collective strength, particularly the women who were on strike by proxy, every bit as committed as the men.

Although there had been widespread sympathy within the community for the miners who had lost their jobs, there was also disapproval of the actions of Arthur Scargill and the NUM. Their action in calling the strike without a national ballot was seen as high-handed. It was alleged that NUM officials had travelled to Libya to collect funds for the strike. Coming six months after the murder of a British policewoman by Libyan agents outside the Libyan embassy this caused a public outcry. (These allegations were later proved untrue.)

The National Coal Board mounted a propaganda program in which they claimed (falsely) that hundreds of men were returning to work each day throughout the strike. However, by January 1985, after months of deprivation and a cold winter without heating, there was, in fact, a sharp increase in the number of miners returning to work. Their action was met with little opposition from persevering strikers. The returning miners had not ceased to believe in what they were fighting for, but they had little choice. Their homes were being threatened with repossession, their marriages were failing under the strain and their children were being deprived of food and clothing. On 3 March 1985, almost a year to the day since it began, the longest industrial dispute in 20th century Britain came to an end when Arthur Scargill and the NUM executive voted grudgingly, 98 votes to 91, to return to work. Like its 1926 precursor, the strike had failed.

17   1984 — Beginning of The End: Losing the Battle.

At the end of a hard year and the most violent, acrimonious industrial dispute in Britain, defeated, but still defiant miners were accompanied by their wives and families as they marched back to work.
"Miners' strike 30 years on: I fought not just for my pit but for the community": The Guardian
https://www.theguardian.com/politics/guardianwitness-blog/2015/mar/05/miners-strike-30-years-on-i-fought-not-just-for-my-pit-but-for-the-community

Surrounded by the women and children who had supported them throughout the year, defeated but still defiant, striking miners, many in tears, returned to work. Carrying union banners, many were led by the music of their own brass bands. At some pit gates they were presented with carnations — the symbol of defiance — by women.

Margaret Thatcher led the Conservative Party to a landslide victory in the 1987 General Election but, after a factional coup, she was forced to relinquish the leadership to John Major in 1990. As Baroness Thatcher, she died in April 2013. Ian MacGregor died of a heart attack in 1998. To Margaret Thatcher he had 'brought a breath of fresh air to British industry'. To Mick McGahey, NUM president at the time, he was "an anti-class person and vicious anti-trade unionist." The union movement had been significantly weakened. Despite the controversy surrounding the NUM decision to strike, and the failure to prevent pit closures, Arthur Scargill was elected lifetime President of the NUM, resigning in 2002 to become its Honorary President. Scargill, now 82, is divorced from his wife Anne, a passionate activist. He is said to be living a semi-reclusive existence although still a fervent supporter of extreme left wing causes. He has acquired an ambiguous reputation. While being exalted by many of his supporters to hero status in bringing down the Tory government in 1974 and his militant stand against Thatcherism, his detractors believe that he became enamoured with the trappings of power during the 1984–1985 strike.

During a Parliamentary debate in December 1973, eleven years prior to the strike, Roy Mason, MP for Barnsley South, former Minister of Power and a former miner, proclaimed:

'Working underground in a coal mine is not a life for any man. It is not fair on his wife. It is not fair on his family. It is a pity that we cannot close all the mines tomorrow — but we cannot. The nation depends upon them. That is why we must pay the miners, and pay them well, until that day of the final closure gloriously arrives.'

In 2015, the days of final closure arrived when the last British coalmines ceased operations, Hatfield Colliery in June, Thoresby in July, and Kellingley in December. The history of deep-coal mining in the UK had come to an end.

17 1984 — Beginning of The End: Losing the Battle.

The metaphorical war-like language persisted throughout the strike's duration.

War on the picket line: how the British press made a battle out of the miners' strike: The Conversation.
https://theconversation.com/war-on-the-picket-line-how-the-british-press-made-a-battle-out-of-the-miners-strike-60470

18

The Aftermath

Life after coal: *The Guardian*
https://www.theguardian.com/politics/2015/dec/20/coal-kellingley-miners-easington

While the turbulence of 1984 was wreaking havoc in Britain, Nan was far away from it all. Following her retirement from the pit in 1967, both children were now living away from home. Elizabeth had moved to London to train as a nurse at one of the 'big five' hospitals. Alistair, married and with a child, had moved to Zambia to take up a teaching position. Nan bought a house in a small Yorkshire village to where she moved, again to be near her remaining family of origin. Again she had deluded herself into believing they could be a close-knit family. With their own adult families and grandchildren, the siblings were even further apart than during her previous attempt at closeness twenty years earlier. Prophetically, even the Monterey Cyprus, again transplanted as a talisman, failed to survive in its new home. This was one move too far.

Shortly after her arrival in Yorkshire, sibling relationships were severely tested when Nan received news that Alistair had been killed in a car accident. He was returning home from Ndola after a trip to the capital, Lusaka, travelling along was aptly called 'the Hell Run'. The car, in which he was a passenger, hit a pot-hole and collided with another vehicle. Alistair and the driver were killed instantly, as were the occupants of the other car. In her grief, Nan was inconsolable and no one could foresee that she would recover from the loss of a second child. Support from her family was constrained and again she turned to her ageing Aunt Mary who once more proved her mettle. Nan stayed one more year in Yorkshire and, feeling that she had little more to lose, sold the house. Furniture and household effects were loaded into a container for their longest journey ever, and she moved, with Elizabeth, to Australia.

It was from over sixteen thousand kilometres away that she watched sadly, the nightly news bulletins of hardship, violence and divisiveness tearing apart what she had finally come to think of as 'her community'. Creswell was one of the collieries where the miners had voted to work through the strike. It was still a lucrative pit. Nan never expressed a political opinion for, nor against the strike. To her it was a cause of sadness that the community she had come to know was becoming so lacerated. Although she saw no recognisable faces in the news bulletins, many of the players in this tragedy were known to her. Many of them were still 'her babies'. They were known to her, and she to them. Although they never met, one of the militant women who appeared on her television screen was probably Annette who appears in the following chapter.

> *Ah'm a picket*
> *A Yorkshire picket*
> *We confront our friendly bobbies every day*
> *Ah'm a picket*
> *A Yorkshire picket*
> *What we do for love, they're doing for th' pay*
> *But when we're standin' side by side*
> *And singin' 'Here we go'*
> *Or 'Arthur, we'll support you evermore'*
> *That feeling of true brotherhood is one they'll never know*
> *Those overpaid, blue Bastions of the law.*
> **Jean Gittens, 1986.**

19

Annette's Memoirs, 1984

Sunday December 18 1983

https://thatchercrisisyears.com/2013/01/20/when-thatcher-caved-in-to-the-miners/

These were the headlines that greeted us each morning. No wonder Christmas 1983 seemed strange. Usually the build-up was the best part. Putting up the tree; cards coming through the letterbox and landing with a plop on the wooden floor in the hall; dark by four and a big coal fire; fridge bulging with food. Ever since I was a child, the excitement and preparation were the nicest things about Christmas. When it arrived, it was usually a bit of an anticlimax. Except last year — it wasn't a good time then. Watching the news every night, waiting for Steve to finish his shift and come home, each day seeing trouble approaching and knowing that by the time Christmas arrived we'd be that much closer to it, gave me an awful sensation in the pit of my stomach. I had this awful feeling, like butterflies, not wanting to eat for fear of being sick and yet feeling empty all the time. Each morning I'd be awake long before it was time to get up, almost as if I'd pressed the pause button for a few hours' sleep only to have the worry flood back into my mind the minute I was conscious. Steve lay snoring beside me, yet I knew he was worried too. We didn't talk about it much. Men and women seem to see things differently.

Trouble had been brewing for a while. Maggie Thatcher and the government closing all these pits. The writing was on the wall. She was spoiling for a fight and it looked as though Arthur Scargill and the union were going to oblige. The papers said that the government had been putting aside huge amounts of coal so that industry wouldn't go short if the strike came. The ban on overtime seemed just like a rehearsal for the real thing. Steve, like all the other miners, was worried about his job. He was almost forty now and didn't know any other work than mining. He had worked down the pit since he left school at sixteen. I'd never had a job since we got married and we were totally dependent on Steve's wages.

It was the kids I felt sorry for. Justin was fifteen at the time and Janine just eleven. Instead of a week in Wales that year, now the kids were a bit older, we'd been planning to redecorate the front room– buy a new carpet and some decent furniture. There would be no hope of that now. We'd need to hang onto every penny we had.

The union was expecting a real fight, and probably a long one too — but we never expected it to last so long. Just as well, as I don't know how I would have felt if I had known. "It's them or us", Steve used to say. There was even talk of the army being called in. It was almost as though they were talking about war again. Damn it! We were both in our 40s. In another few years the kids would have been off our hands and we should have been able to start taking it easy.

Oddly, once New Year was over, I seemed to worry less. If it was going to happen there was nothing I could do about it, so we just resigned ourselves to the inevitable.

Despite all the worry we had a nice Christmas — almost as if we knew we didn't have a lot to look forward to in the New Year. We thought, "Well, if we're in for a bad time, we might as well make the most of what we've got before it comes." Steve says I always go halfway to meet trouble, but I think most people in the village felt the same as I did, at least all the women I knew did.

On Christmas Day, Mam and my stepdad, Melvin, came for dinner. My real dad died of leukaemia when I was only six. He'd always worked at the pit until he wasn't well enough to go there anymore. He was an electrician, so he was able to keep working for quite a while, even after he got sick. Mam said sometimes he used to come home from work really tired and she'd put a blanket over him while he had a rest on the sofa in front of the fire. More often than not, I'd crawl under the blanket beside him and go to sleep too. I can remember that.

After he died, Mam got a job in the pit canteen, so we were able to keep living in the pit house. It was hard work managing the shifts but, between her sister and my grandma, we managed. I think that's one reason I've never gone out to work — I wanted to be there for the kids. Mam used to get on well with most of the men at the pit, but it could be difficult sometimes as she didn't have a husband. Some were a bit cheeky, though most of it was good-natured and she could give as good as she got. Her dad was a miner too, so she's never really known anything else.

When I was about nine, she met Melvin. I think he'd had his eye on her for a while and she'd noticed him at work because he was always quiet and polite, not like some of the other men. Melvin was from Gloucestershire and had worked in the Forest of Dean coalfield. He'd come up to Yorkshire in the 1960s when the pits there were closing down. He used to play the E flat tuba in the band. When Mam and Melvin got married, he came to live in the house with us. My sister, Kathleen, was born when I was 11. Melvin was a good dad to us both and treated me just like his own daughter. He'd retired by the time of the strike, and, although he didn't say much, he was very much against how the government treated the miners. He never forgot what it had been like to lose his own job when he was in his 40s. I suppose you could say mining's in my blood, just as in Steve's.

Steve's from Derbyshire. His dad worked at the pit as a fitter and turner. He never wanted to work underground. Steve's grandad had been killed down the pit and when Steve's dad and uncle were teenagers, their parents were both killed in a car crash, so they went to live with his father's brother, Uncle Tommy and his wife, Auntie Jenny. Tommy and Jenny only had one daughter. They'd had a son, but he died when he was a baby. After he died, Jenny lost all her hair. It never grew back, and she wore a wig until she died. I think Steve always felt he should be fending for himself so, when he was 15, he left school and came up here to get a job in the pit.

Tommy and Jenny still lived in the same village at the time of the strike, but they're both dead now. Steve's older brother, Jeff, didn't work at the pit. He became a surveyor and lives in Nottingham. Steve and Jeff were never very close, and we never saw much of him, especially when the strike started. Jeff never agreed with the strike and I shouldn't be surprised if he votes Conservative. It's odd really, because Tommy was such a staunch Labour man. He was well-read and could talk about almost anything.

Justin and Janine were really good. They knew they weren't going to get much for Christmas that year. We really had to tighten our belts. Like most people, we had hardly any savings to fall back on.

Finally, in March, it happened. I remember Steve coming home after his last shift and telling us how they'd put in some special safety measures underground just in case they were out for a while. They were thinking a week or two, perhaps even a month! Actually, when the strike started, it was quite a relief. At least we knew what we were up against — or so we thought. The unions called a vote. Steve and the lads from Yorkshire were all in favour of industrial action and voted in favour of striking. They've always been very militant around here. The union was very much divided about the strike. All the lads here voted for it, but the pits in the Midlands — especially where Steve was from, were all against it. They said their pits were still making a profit and were good places to work. The pits there always had lots of money spent on them — new machinery and stuff like that. The miners there also felt very bitter because Arthur Scargill refused to hold a national ballot so they could all have their say. They all voted against the strike and said the union's decision to go ahead with it wasn't democratic. Personally, I used to think Arthur Scargill was a bit scary. Not that I had any time for Margaret Thatcher. Still, what did I know?

At first Steve really threw himself into the strike — up early in the mornings and off with Brian and his other mates while the kids and I were still in bed. Sometimes he would go late in the day and be out all night. It was always late when he got home, and it was difficult to explain to Justin and Janine what was happening. The good thing was that most of their friends' dads were involved too. Justin wasn't much younger than his dad was when he first went to work down the pit. He could see why his dad was fighting against closing the pits, but he said he could also see that, eventually the pits would have to close as they weren't profitable. Justin never had any intention of working at the pit anyway. He always wanted to go to university. Janine was just like any other 11-year-old, it was all Prince and Madonna.

I always seemed to be on my own in the beginning. I still wanted to be at home when the kids came home like when Steve was working shifts. Apart from the fact that I didn't have to organise my work around different shifts, life wasn't all that much different from usual — except for no pay packet on Fridays. I cleaned the house from top to bottom; it helped to keep my mind off what was happening. Money was very and tight and we still had two kids to feed and clothe as well as ourselves. Steve used to keep telling me everything would be all right but, somehow, I knew it wouldn't. We were luckier than a lot of people. At least we lived in a pit house and didn't have a mortgage. All our stuff was paid for — except for the car.

Steve always seemed to be worn out when he got home. There were always a lot of police waiting for them no matter which pit they went to join the pickets. The police weren't too bothered about how roughly they treated the pickets either. He said some of the miners' wives had started to picket too. If the miners crossed the picket line they could be arrested for trespassing and sacked. They couldn't sack the women because they didn't work for any of the pits. I couldn't imagine how women could do that and anyway, in those days Steve wouldn't have wanted me to. The men said the police were just as rough with the women as they were with the men. They used to call them awful names, just to provoke the miners into fighting back. Most of the police weren't local. Steve said a lot of them were brought up from London — you could tell by their accents.

Then one day in April, a lad was killed at Ollerton in Nottinghamshire. He was a Wakefield lad and had been there on picket duty. A lot of pickets had been brought in to persuade working miners there to come out on strike, but the police had been waiting for them. A local lad threw a stone which hit the Wakefield lad in the neck. Although they rushed him to Mansfield hospital he died soon after. Everyone was very upset. On the same day, Steve had been picketing at a pit close by.

They waited until the night shift came on. Hundreds of police were there too, wearing helmets and carrying riot shields and batons. The police just kept lashing out with their batons, pushing and manhandling people, beating the striking miners, but they fought back. Steve had obviously been shaken by all the violence. He said one man who crossed the picket line to go to work later had his house windows smashed. I hated all the violence.

Usually when Steve got back, the three of us would already be asleep. At first it used to upset the kids as they could go days without seeing their dad, but at least when Steve wasn't there, I only had to make food for the kids. I used to manage with a cup of tea and sometimes a slice of toast. It seemed strange not having to stick to meal times with Steve not working, but he still got to spend time with his mates down at the institute or at the union lodge. Of course, he had no money for beer but, apart from this and not working shifts at the pit, his life seemed to go on as usual. Sometimes I thought they enjoyed the novelty of it, and I seemed to see less of him than when he was working.

Life really went on the same for me — looking after the house and making sure the kids were alright. I seemed to be the one who worried most about the future and how we were going to manage. I remember I used to wake up at four in the morning, petrified about what was going to happen to us, and Steve would be fast asleep. He would have neglected the allotment if I hadn't kept nagging him about it. Thank goodness the really cold weather was over. At least the allotment kept us going with salad and vegetables. Justin used to take some little sacks and go with his friends to collect what bits of fuel he could from the slag heap. It didn't burn very well but it was better than nothing. I didn't light the fire until night time and not at all if it wasn't really cold. I did what I could, but began to feel guilty and useless just staying at home.

There was no money for anything. Because I didn't work, we got supplementary benefits — but even with family allowance and strike pay, all we had coming in was less than twelve pounds a week. Like most of my friends, I still supported the strike wholeheartedly. Most of my friends were married to miners. Everyone knew everyone around here. The village had grown around the pit, the miners' institute, the band, dramatic society and flower shows. We knew that, if the pit went, there would be nothing left.

All the newspapers were against the strike, not that we bothered much with them. We couldn't afford them anyway. Even on television, every night they kept saying how the wives didn't want the strike and were nagging the men to go back to work. That's what Mrs Thatcher wanted, but it just wasn't true. Strike, strike, strike and all that violence! They didn't seem to get it. They couldn't understand how the women could support the strike. No matter how hard things got, I would never have given in and I don't know of any wives who would.

One night in May, when I was watching the news on telly, there were reports about a big rally and a march by miners' wives in Barnsley in support of the strike. Thousands of women were there including Arthur Scargill's wife, Anne, who led the march through the town. It made me think, "Here's me sitting here trying my best to make ends meet, worrying myself sick about what's going to happen, *I* could do something like that. At least I'd be doing *something*." I got so mad and then suddenly remembered that a woman near here, one of the miner's wives whose husband was a union official and who had done some picketing, had called a meeting at the institute. She was asking for anybody interested in volunteering to attend. I made Steve take me down there. He wasn't very happy about it, so when we got there, I told him to go home and I'd make my own way back.

It was really good! I've never known anything like it. There were so many women there, some I knew, but a lot I'd never seen before. Pam, the woman who called the meeting, spoke and told us all about the people she'd met in Barnsley. They'd started a group and were calling themselves Women against Pit Closures. She was trying to form the same sort of group in our village. We just talked and talked, and it felt good to be among these women who were all going through the same thing.

I felt as though I wasn't alone anymore. I've never made friends very easily but, after the last few weeks of feeling that we were the only family in trouble, I felt so much better. It seemed to put things in perspective. We talked until well after midnight and decided that we would try to set up a centre and cook meals for families who couldn't afford any food — which was just about all of them. Some of the women said they were going to picket with the men. I didn't feel that I could do that, but cooking? That sounded really good — what could be dangerous about that?

Some of the husbands were a bit doubtful when they heard what we planned to do, but at least they didn't try to discourage us. Most of us hadn't worked since we were married, and we weren't sure that we could manage such a big venture. We soon showed them!

The vicar gave us permission to use the church hall which was already equipped with trestle tables and enough chairs. That was a good start. Although the kitchen was small, at least it had a working gas cooker with six burners. First, we needed to get some crockery and cutlery as well as some big saucepans. The union gave us some money to start up, but it wasn't very much, so we had to beg for the rest.

We went doorknocking. People here couldn't afford to give us much money but promised to donate what little food they could spare, especially those with gardens and allotments. Everybody was supportive and enthusiastic. The butchers supported the strike and were very generous. So were the bakers, whose union supported the miners, and they donated bread.

We went on outings to places like York, Liverpool and Chester collecting money. Some people weren't willing to give, and some were quite rude, but surprisingly, mostly people were very generous. As well as raising money we used to enjoy having a day out! We held jumble sales and raffles — we used to write to big companies and stores asking them to donate prizes. By that time, different groups of people all over the country were donating money to the strike — holding benefit concerts, collecting money to support us — even donations of clothes and shoes came in and it felt good to know that not everyone thought the miners were in the wrong.

Most people were unaware of the help we got from trade unions on the Continent. It wasn't reported in the press, they probably thought it would weaken the government's stand against the miners by making them look even meaner. There was a lot of respect for the NUM in countries like France and Germany. They were solidly behind us and, for the whole of that year, sent truckloads of food and clothing as well as making financial donations. Margaret Thatcher didn't hold all the aces.

The aim of the kitchen was to give everyone who couldn't

afford it, at least one hot meal a day. We drew up a roster. I worked Mondays, Wednesdays and Fridays. We had set meals for different days of the week — casseroles, cottage pie and meat and potato pie — anything that was filling and cheap to make. Some of the women who didn't like cooking volunteered to help with the washing up and the serving. Others volunteered to take charge of the money and keep the books. However, I must say that the union wasn't very helpful. They wanted us to put the money into their funds. Luckily, we had a strong committee who stood up to them and refused.

Once we got going it was very good, and very busy. Everybody pulled their weight and we all helped each other. During the school holidays, Janine sometimes came with me to help. Justin hung around with his friends and sometimes worked with his dad in the allotment. We didn't get to spend much time together. It seemed funny that I was now out working.

Some people stayed away from the centre because they felt ashamed to be accepting charity. Mining people can be very proud. So we started putting together food parcels for those who couldn't come to the centre. We tried to look after each other *and* those who found it hard to look after themselves. At least if people knew where the next meal was coming from, it was one worry less. Those are the principles Mam and Melvin and my grandma instilled into us as kids. If the government thought they were going to starve us back to work, we were determined to prove them wrong.

Although we didn't always agree with each other, the closeness we felt was one of the best things that happened to me. It was as though it was us against the rest of the world, and when we were together, we felt we were strong and capable enough to face anything. We seemed to be able to say things to one another which we would never have previously dreamed of. Some of the girls were saying how they hadn't had a period since the strike began when some joker piped up, "At least that'll save you a bit of money!" We all cracked up.

At times I used to get fed up with never being able to get dressed up — I mean, not properly dressed up as if I was going somewhere special. I just wanted a change from old jeans, jumpers and trainers. I used to get sick of wearing clothes that wouldn't get spoilt by grease and food scraps. As for hair — one or two of the girls had been hairdressers and used to do our hair for free. Others just let their hair grow long and tied it up. As time went on it got more and more difficult to take pride in your appearance.

Apart from at the kitchen, we used to meet regularly, sometimes with groups of women from other areas. At one of the meetings there were two miners' wives who'd been demonstrating at Greenham Common against nuclear weapons. They talked about what it had been like there, especially their experiences with the police. They said the behaviour of the police to the miners' wives who were picketing was worse than it was at Greenham Common — probably because the women there were usually more middle class. Actually, these Greenham Common women were very good to us and helped us with donations of food as well as advice. They really boosted our confidence.

After that meeting, I was talking to some of the women who've been picketing with the men and I decided that I wanted to give it a go. Although Steve was against it, he never tried to stop me. I think he wanted to try to protect me, but seeing what I did with the kitchen and all the fundraising made him see me in a new light. Besides, I felt it was unfair to leave all the risky work to others. I still felt very nervous though.

The first time was really frightening, and I wondered if I'd made the right decision after all. About a dozen of us went in a minibus down to Nottinghamshire. There were police road blocks at the county boundaries and all vehicles were stopped and searched. As a rule, it had been easier for smaller groups of women to get through than it was for the men. Sometimes, women picketers were used as decoys to draw the attention of the police away from the men picketing somewhere else, but mostly the women picketed to show solidarity with the men.

When they talked about police violence, they weren't joking. I've seen women being thrown into the back of police vans, being punched and threatened with arrest. I don't think there was one woman who didn't encounter aggressive behaviour from the police who deliberately provoked a lot of the violence by name calling and insulting the women. They taunted and even propositioned women, setting out to humiliate and demean us. They yelled things at us like, "Fucking miners' wives, they like it rough." "Fuck off back to your fucking filthy hovels", and "Filthy slags". I have to say, I've never heard any miners use that sort of language — not in front of women anyway. We used to wonder how they treated their own wives and how they'd feel if they saw them being treated the way they treated us. We saw police beating groups of men, waving £10 notes in front of the miners' faces, yelling at them "When did you last see one of these?", bragging about all the money they were getting for overtime. A lot of us didn't believe they were really policemen. Surely British policemen wouldn't have behaved like that.

Even then, police violence was never really reported in the news — they made out that all the violence came from the miners. We got to really hate the police and the way they treated us — worse than they would treat animals. But I think the thing that shocked me most was the way *I* hated *them*. I hated the way they made me feel so angry so that I wanted to be violent to them in return. I've always hated violence. I remember once as a child going into town with Mam and there were two men fighting at the bus stop. I was so upset that I cried. I'd always told the kids not to fight back, just walk away. And here I was, hating the police so much I think I could have killed one of them. This was my biggest problem, and it frightened me. That's why I decided not to go to the picket lines again.

In August there was a huge rally in London in support of the miners. Our women's group all went by coach and travelled through the night. Steve stayed at home with the kids. I hadn't been to London many times. The first time was when I was about ten and I went with Mam to meet my Godparents when they came back from Australia. There was such a fantastic, exciting feeling at this rally and so much support from people in the streets and other unions who marched with us. There would have been about 25,000 and a lot of us signed a petition saying we were in support of the strike which was later given to the Queen. Lots of the women made speeches, including Pam from our group. All the way down on the coach she was nervous at the thought of speaking in front of so many people. Then, once she'd finished, she said she felt so good she could have done it all again. It was wonderful. We all felt so happy travelling back home and we just couldn't stop talking about it.

It was early in the morning by the time I arrived home, just getting light. I tried to be as quiet as possible, not wanting to wake Steve and the kids. I remember, when I opened the door there was this unusual smell — not an unpleasant smell, just unexpected. I once heard someone on the radio saying that the nicest smell a working woman can experience when she comes home from work — even nicer than newly baked bread — is the smell of bleach, because she knows the cleaning lady's been. We never had a cleaning lady, but it was definitely bleach that I could smell. It got stronger as I crept upstairs and into the bathroom and turned on the light. It was spotless! "My God", I thought, "he's been cleaning!" Steve was still awake when I went into the bedroom. "Justin's at Alan's and I sent Janine round to your Mam's. I've cleaned the house." "You never have", I said. He had! The only problem was that it had taken him so long he never got to bed! I remember thinking, if this is what the strike can do, it can't be all that bad!

By then I'd stopped picketing. I wasn't *frightened* of the violence, I was *disgusted* by it. More than that, I was shocked at the feeling it aroused in me. I decided to concentrate on helping with the welfare side. We organised for people to help with advice about how to get various Social Security allowances. They also gave financial advice and helped people to make arrangements for various payments. The Citizens' Advice Bureau was very good, and we had lots of volunteers. We helped with clothing and shoes, especially for children. Soon the schools would be back, and the kids would at least get a free midday meal. Life was very hard for us all living on next to no money. It was autumn now, my favourite season. That also meant that the cold weather would soon be back and I worried about how we were going to keep warm.

Then I saw on the news how Princess Di had had another baby — a little boy. Like Mam, I've always loved the Royal Family. Mam got our first television in 1953 just so we could all watch the Coronation. There was the Princess standing next to her husband outside the hospital holding the baby, a big car waiting to take them home. I thought, "I bet she doesn't have to worry about what she's going to have for her dinner tonight or how she's going to keep the new baby warm". It seemed so unfair, this young girl who had probably never done a hard day's work in her life, with all that money and husband in a secure job. And here's me, pushing forty, don't own my own house and terrified that the washing machine or the Hoover's going to break down and can't be replaced. It was like rubbing salt into a wound. I could see the police good naturedly holding back the crowds, grinning and sharing in the good news, not a baton in sight. When I thought about what the police had said to us and the way they treated us all, honestly, I could have thrown something at the telly.

By this time the nights were just beginning to draw in and there was a chill in the morning and evening air. We all thought with dread of the coming winter. There was still no end in sight after six gruelling months. People felt depressed and many started to get sick. Food was short, as was fuel for heating, and there was no money for medicines. You could tell that people were starting to lose heart and many of the men were beginning to talk about going back to work.

In October they said the strike had cost the country over six billion pounds. By now about two thousand miners had already gone back to work. You can't live on fresh air. I continued to support Steve and the lads who were determined to carry on. All the same, I wasn't like a lot of the women. Despite all the hard work and fighting, putting myself in harm's way, I couldn't help feeling sorry for people who were so desperate that they went back to work. I could see why they had to. The weather was getting colder and wetter, food was scarce and there was no heating. I remembered how I'd felt the previous year in the lead up to the Christmas and the strike. I had been right to be so worried. We were still going with the centre. If it hadn't been for that and the other women, I think I too would have been losing heart by now. We kept going by sheer determination and encouraging each other.

In November all the kids collected branches and bits of wood, anything that would burn and made a huge bonfire — just like we all used to do when we were young, only instead of Guy Fawkes, they burned two effigies — one of Margaret Thatcher (complete with handbag) and one of Ian Macgregor. At least it gave us all a good laugh and lifted our spirits. It meant a lot to the parents to see that

19 Annette's Memoirs, 1984

the kids were behind us. We'd all had a rough year and deserved a bit of fun. Yet more and more men were drifting back to work.

Steve and I didn't talk too much about it. We each knew how the other felt. Anyway, we didn't see a lot of each other by then. I was out a lot of the time and, as well as working in his own allotment, Steve had helped others convert their gardens into vegetable patches. He had also, surprisingly, taken on the responsibility of looking after the house. Looking back, I'm sure he was depressed but didn't say anything. I think he felt guilty about all we'd been through as a family and, apart from the fact that he wasn't working, he wasn't all that certain that he would ever work again — even after the strike.

Round about that time there was another disturbing incident. A taxi travelling along a motorway in Wales was taking a non-striking miner back to work when the car was hit by a lump of concrete that was dropped from a foot bridge by some miners. The driver was killed, and two miners were charged with his murder. This really turned people against us, and we started to lose a lot of public support. Things really looked bleak for us all — and the cold November weather certainly didn't help.

Christmas 1984 was another Christmas I won't forget. Toys came from France and Belgium by the truckload. Denmark sent hundreds of chickens and Afghanistan, of all places, sent sultanas. Children had been invited abroad to stay with some of these European miners and their families. It was the children I really felt sorry for. They'd never asked for any of this hardship. I suppose we could have said we were doing it for their future, but a lot of them didn't want mining as a future — boys like our Justin. I think most of us realised that surely the writing was on the wall for the strike, so we decided to go all out and make the best of the Festive Season.

Our woman's group decided to hold a communal meal in the

early evening so that families could spend the day together. The week before Christmas we filled hundreds of plastic shopping bags with 'special' Christmas food for those who couldn't or didn't want to come to the centre on Christmas Day. Some of the men delivered the parcels in an old van. No one was going short if we could help it. Some men did a deal with the Forestry Commission who let them go into the local forest and clear the dead wood for people to burn. They got us a lovely big Christmas tree for the centre and, after school broke up for the Christmas holidays, we got the younger kids to bring round decorations from home and they trimmed it. That communal spirit was something none of us had experienced before. We'd all been through such a rough year we felt we owed this to ourselves.

Ho, ho ho! Christmas cards 1984 show how beaten the miners felt.

https://www.mirror.co.uk/news/uk-news/miners-strike-30-years-on-4851732

19 Annette's Memoirs, 1984

Mam and Melvin came to our house again for Christmas Day and brought food with them. The worst thing was that we couldn't afford presents for Justin and Janine. Mam said it was like when they were little and they used to get an orange and some nuts and perhaps, if they were lucky, a little toy in their Christmas stockings. In the afternoon after they had left to go to my sister's, the four of us went around to the centre and we all got busy. The place was absolutely packed. It was a wonderful evening — a good chance for people to let their hair down and enjoy themselves, something they had rarely done in the last few months. After a while Janine and Justin and their friends all wandered off together and, after we'd all helped to clear up, Steve and I, despite being knackered, decided to walk home. I remember, there was a lovely moon and it was a clear, crisp night. Nothing but a cold house awaited us. The firewood had well and truly gone by then.

This was probably the first opportunity we'd had to be together and talk for a long time. We talked about how we'd both changed. For most of the year we seemed like ships passing in the night — going to bed and getting up at different times. You can imagine what that did to our sex life, not that we had neither the energy, nor the inclination most of the time. I think Steve felt like a failure — as a husband and a father. Yet, in a way, the strike had changed him for the better. As the year drew to an end, he had become quieter, more introspective and, as he had spent more time with the kids than before, more considerate about the rest of the family. He didn't mind doing things around the house which he would never have thought of doing before. In fact, he admitted he quite enjoyed it. In the early days he was angry. He had always believed that, like his dad and grandad, he would work down the pit — barring accidents — until he retired. All that certainty had been taken away. He'd begun to look ahead, as much as he dared, to a life which didn't include the pit, considering what possible options might be available to him while he was still young enough to change.

The opposite had happened to me. I thought I'd always been happy with my lot in life. I'd left school at sixteen and gone to work in the local supermarket. Saturday nights were spent out with friends and then I met Steve. Because he wasn't from round here, I suppose that's what made him more interesting than the other lads I'd gone to school with. *And* he was a miner, so I felt comfortable with him. I'd never known nor expected to a live any differently from the way my Mam and grandma had lived.

Marriage and children were all I ever expected from life. All my friends were the same. We did everything together. I had always relied on Steve. He brought in the weekly wage, I asked for his help if I needed it *and* his opinion on what I should do, even what I should wear. Not that I always took notice of him, but he was always like a backup for me — more like the other half of me. That year had taken that security away and I had been forced to reassess how much my way of life meant to me, especially when it seemed possible that it could be taken away. It wasn't possible to take anything for granted anymore.

I began to make decisions for myself, to function independently of Steve, although it was a hard way to learn. 1984 taught me that I was stronger than I thought I was. I began to look around at other people — women in my position — and saw that others had changed too, not all of them in the same way I had changed, but changed none the less. These, I think, were the positive things to come out of that year. I wasn't sure whether I wanted my old life back or not, at least, not the way it was.

Then 1985 arrived. If anyone had told us the strike would last so long, we'd never have believed them. It was a cold, depressing start to the year and we knew we were on a downward slope. On the first day of the year 80,000 men returned to work.

I never got over the violence that the strike aroused in people — on both sides. I'd always loathed and feared violence, regarding it as a lack of self-control. In some situations, anger was understandable — but not violence. The miners were, literally, fighting for their lives, their security, and their role as providers and protectors of their families. Their wives fought to support their men, fighting for their children's right to a decent home and education, fighting for their villages and communities. It was a collective unconsciousness which had existed in these communities as long as pits had existed and men (and women) had worked them. That's what outsiders didn't understand. Thatcher didn't understand — or refused to admit it. For most, this fight was triggered by fear which came from people's core. There had always been a love/hate relationship between the women and the pit. They hated it because of its harshness and cruelty, but the thought of it closing spelled the end of the community. If the pit went, there would be nothing left. But I still don't condone violence and never will.

The behaviour I *cannot* and *will not* forget nor forgive is the organised, institutionalised violence shown by the police — the British police. These were the men (and they were mostly men) who had come to our school to teach us about road safety. They were the local bobbies who walked our village streets looking out for us. Remember the old slogan 'If you want to know the time, ask a policeman'? *I* wouldn't give the *policeman* the time of day now, even if my life depended on it. I've lost all trust in and respect for them. The only civil words I ever heard uttered by one of them that year came from a middle-aged sergeant who said, in a northern accent, "Why don't you get off home and see to your husband's dinner love? Let me stand here and shout 'scabby bastard' for you." The rest of them would smash you over the head with a baton or pin your arm up behind your back and bundle you into the back of a police van as soon as look at you.

The other thing that disgusted me (and I probably shouldn't say this) was the way families were split by the strike. For most of the men who went back to work it was a hard decision. Those who had never voted for the strike, how democratically were they treated?

My sister had a friend whose husband went back to work. His wife had been diagnosed with breast cancer just after the strike started and had to have surgery. She was only thirty and they had two little children. She lost all her hair, couldn't afford a wig and had to travel to the hospital every day for six weeks for treatment. How else was he to afford petrol and pay for someone to help with the little ones? He had two brothers who were on strike and neither of them would have anything to do with him after the strike. This man made the decision to go back to work to save his wife and family, knowing that it would cost him his friends and family.

I heard a lady talking on the radio. Her husband had worked all through the strike and had received many death threats. All the windows in her house had been smashed and throughout the strike she felt like a prisoner, unable to leave her house. She was a woman supporting her husband too. The strike caused lots of bad things to happen. When Maggie Thatcher was asked after the strike if rifts like this could be healed, her reply was, "Those who go back to work in the pits, and the managers, they will do their level best to heal it." She didn't know miners.

February was more dismal than usual, and not just because of the weather. Still more and more men were going back to work. While many of the wives remained as resolute as their striking men, many others, and I include myself in this group, carried on with the work but the heart had gone out of it. They were cold, hungry and could see no future. Debts were piling up and they had no idea how, if at all, they would be settled.

On Sunday 3 March 1985, at NUM headquarters in London, 98 members voted to abandon the strike against 91 who sought to continue the struggle. Steve and I were in the house alone when we heard the news. We shared identical feelings about it. We were dumfounded but, at the same time, couldn't help feeling relieved. We were also very unsure about the future. I hadn't seen Steve cry very often, but we were both in tears after the announcement was made. For the rest of the evening we felt too exhausted to speak much to each other. It was depressing to think that, after all we'd endured and sacrificed, we had been defeated by a government for which no one we knew had voted. I suppose that *is* democracy.

However, the feeling of companionship and living hand-to-mouth with others made us appreciate what a valuable commodity that comradeship was. The car had gone, and we owed money, but at least Steve and I had each other, where many other families had failed to survive intact. The kids had come through it with us, and the experience would be one they would never forget. Nothing is permanent and nothing can be taken for granted. All I know is that the four of us were different people from the ones who had greeted the strike a year earlier.

20

We are women, we are strong.

Why don't the wheels go round, mam?
Why don't the wheels go round?
Our fathers fought, and their fathers too
For an industry that we'll leave to you
Just remember lad, it's not them, but you
That makes Britain's wheels go round.
Jean A. Gittins, miner's wife and poet from Kippax, Leeds, 1986.

http://www.bbc.co.uk/southyorkshire/content/articles/2008/12/17/
women_against_pit_closures_christmas_cards_feature.shtml

Much has been written about how the 1984–1985 Miners' Strike affected men. Women also played a major role in this watershed time. Although not employed in the industry, their role was not merely ancillary. What is remarkable is the level of participation by the miners' wives and the role they played in supporting *and* maintaining the strike. Often absent from the gaze of the media, the women fought alongside the men. Their defiant presence on the picket lines has been acknowledged in the public's memory and recorded in newsreel footage. Their fund-raising skills and public displays of tenacious support and solidarity with the men demonstrate what, until then, had been untapped talent.

Women have not always occupied an auxiliary, supporting role in the development of the coal industry. During the 17th century when coal was obtained from more superficial seams, it was dug out by men but it was women and children who carried it out of the mines. Until mid-way through the 19th century, women continued to work underground, and their working conditions became, like those of the men they worked alongside, every bit as brutal as they helped to supply the coal needs of the Industrial Revolution. This was brought to an end by the 1842 Act prohibiting them from working down mines. The coal industry then became dominated by men. Traditionally gendered roles remained entrenched in mining communities well into the second half of the 20th century. Women were largely 'airbrushed' from the mythology which developed around the male miner. Only *he* had the stamina necessary to perform the work.

Following the social upheaval of World War 1, when women had filled jobs of men sent into battle, male and female roles again became stereotyped. After the 1918 Armistice, men were happy to return home and resume their work. Many women (by and large) were happy for them to *be* home but still more were unhappy to relinquish their work to the returning men. Although many communities returned to the gender *status quo*, in most mining communities there had been few traditionally male jobs which could be done by women.

Women of mining communities, typically, rarely received much more than a basic education. The majority leaving school at 15 without qualifications, drifted into local factories, shops or hairdressing to earn a living until an early marriage. This was shortly followed by a succession of pregnancies and, invariably, a day-to-day existence in a small, colliery-owned terrace house, fighting a never ending battle against smut and coal grit which invaded their homes, homes, permanently infused with the inescapable sulphurous stench of burning pit detritus. These women endured the wait until Friday when the men collected their wages and they could buy food to put on the table — and, if invited, have a few drinks later that evening in the pub or miners' institute.

Any variation to their daily routine was dictated by the hours of their husband's shift work, keeping the children quiet during the day while he slept, making sure there was a hot meal on the table when he came home, whatever the hour, and scrubbing his filthy pit clothes. Except for the availability of modern labour-saving household devices, the lives of miners' wives did not significantly change from that of their forebears over almost a century before, although the installation of pit head baths had all but rendered obsolete the custom of scrubbing the man's back as he bathed in a zinc tub in front of the coal fire. There remained one abiding issue facing every miner's wife, mother and sister, however. Like the sword of Damocles, the ever-present possibility of injury and death hung over their heads. This was the conventional stereotype of the miner's wife. Events of 1984–1985 showed that, during the century and a half that had elapsed since they worked alongside men, even though their physical strength may have atrophied, their non-physical toughness remained.

Margaret Thatcher, believing that self-interest defeats class solidarity, predicted that the 1984–1985 miners' strike would end swiftly as a result of pressure exerted on the miners by their wives. The women, she was sure, were the ones who would get the men back to work. Evidently Margaret Thatcher had failed to heed the lessons of history. Working class women's activism has been well recorded. Many parallels have been drawn between the Miners' Strike of 1984–1985 and its 1926 predecessor. In the earlier dispute, women's enthusiastic participation was motivated by a congenital communal spirit and sense of shared values that was part of their DNA. The behaviour of the preceding generation of women in support of their men came from an inbred allegiance, not only towards their men, but towards the whole community. This ethos survived into 1984 and 1985.

Most women from both generations of miners' wives had no political affiliation prior to the strike. They were motivated by a spontaneous reaction to a common concern: husbands who worked together were now on strike together, fighting for their livelihoods and their communities. During 1984–1985 women's groups proliferated in every mining community in the country. They wanted the people to know the reasons behind the men's actions and why they supported them.

During 1984–1985, few miners' wives remained apolitical regardless of their attitude to the strike. At the beginning, many of them were plunged into what they considered the time of their lives. They mobilised in droves to save their communities and their way of life. Militant pro-strike groups sprung up spontaneously in almost every affected community. In May 1984, over 5,000 women from pit villages across the country attended a rally in Barnsley. Speaking at this rally, one of the miners' wives, Lorraine Bowler declared,

"This fight does not just belong to the men, it belongs to us all.... [being] active takes away the uncertainty that is involved in this strike .... We cannot allow this government to decimate our industry and our communities .... If this government thinks its fight is only with the miners, they are sadly mistaken. They are now fighting men, women and families."

> We don't need government approval for anything we do
> We don't need their permission to have a point of view
> We don't need anyone to tell us what to think or say
> We've strength enough and wisdom of our own, to go our own way.

This became the anthem of Women Against Pit Closures (WAPC), initiated by a group of miners' wives in Barnsley, part of the Yorkshire coal field. It was the beginning of a movement which generated WAPC groups in mining communities all over Britain.

Miners' wives demonstrating at Hemmingfield Colliery, Yorkshire, 1984.

For women the 1984–1985 Strike gave many women a voice in the protest and, for many, the year of conflict changed their lives irrevocably.

https://www.pinterest.com.au/pin/478929741599366738/?lp=true

Women against Pit Closures (WAPC) was formed in April 1984. At a national rally held in London in August 1984, over 15,000 women marched. "We caused a lot of havoc", said one member. Possibly the first working class women's movement in Britain, WAPC provided mutual support and solidarity for the wives of striking miners, affirming that they were all, men and women, part of the same cause. Anne Scargill, then wife of Arthur Scargill, president of the National Union of Mineworkers, became a leading figure in the movement. The 'call to arms' which had been delivered to the women at the Barnsley rally was a challenge to the traditional male bastion of trade unionism –and not all men were comfortable with this feminist assertion.

The original Barnsley group engendered numerous movements in mining communities across the country providing support, defending jobs, showing loyalty to their husbands and publicising their need to feed their families. Campaigning against pit closures, they adopted many of the tactics employed by the women of the Peace Camps at Greenham Common who protested against nuclear weapons. The wives spoke at meetings and rallies, raised funds and provided advice on welfare matters. They took part in picketing and they challenged the power of the state, especially the police.

These women's groups presented an opportunity for formerly unrelated communities to come together. Disparate groups such a Gay and Lesbian Communities, university students and members of CND all offered support, reminiscent of suffragists who, in 1926, had provided help and support for the Women's Committee for the Relief of Miners' Wives and Children. An essentially working man's struggle opened new territory for many women. In an evocation of the old Chinese adage 'Crisis brings change', Women against Pit Closures challenged the assumptions of the miners and trade unionists about gender roles *and* the feminist movement which had hitherto been a bastion of middle-class women.

One member remarked, "As women we have not been encouraged to be involved in…. trade unions and organising. Organisation has always been seen as belonging to the men…. we are seen to be the domestic element of the family."

Striking miners' wives demonstrated passionate determination, not only by their presence on the picket line. While tackling basic, practical issues first, they simultaneously provided solidarity and support for the cause, standing side by side with the miners. With plastic buckets emblazoned with *Save our Pits* and *When they close a pit, they kill a Community* as well as the most famous, *Coal not Dole*, they collected funds from the public to provide food for families who had no income. To supplement NUM funds paid to pickets they held jumble sales and market stalls and they organised raffles. They developed skills which cannot be underestimated: organizing large numbers of food parcels and preparing as many as three hundred meals a day. Each family which registered with the centres received one food parcel a week. Although not containing huge amounts, the idea of the parcels was to help prevent miners, whose families who were experiencing poverty, from having to return to work. Thus, the women's work was vital in prolonging the strike.

NUM branches relinquished the responsibility for providing food and welfare to the women's groups although the groups, initially, relied on the union for the necessary finance. Ironically, the sheer hard work of these women in backing up of the strike wasn't regarded as essential by the NUM who channeled their *masculine* efforts into aggressive strike action. Initially, women formed groups and cooked meals in their own homes to feed strike-affected families who had no food. They later set up soup kitchens, also reminiscent of sixty years earlier. Although the Miners' Union provided a hundred and twenty pounds to establish each centre, they still needed crockery, cutlery and cooking utensils. These were obtained with money the women raised from tirelessly knocking on doors, begging for spare food as well as money, from holding raffles and organising socials.

One group of women raised sixteen hundred pounds which the NUM then demanded they hand over. The women refused. They organised premises and arranged any necessary permission needed for their heroic ventures. Some of the kitchens were at pit tops while others were in town centres. In one instance, when denied the use of a local community hall, women negotiated the use of appropriate cooking facilities at a nearby school. To families who lived outside the mining communities, and were unable to attend the centres, they distributed food parcels as an alternative.

They set up crèches to allow women the freedom to become involved in supportive activities. Through involvement with the communal feeding of families, and providing help and advice on matters of benefit claims, women discovered that working as a group was more effective than as individuals. They demonstrated outside electricity showrooms to deter providers from disconnecting supplies to those who were unable to pay power bills — and they threatened to picket if their pleas fell on deaf ears. They became strong through working together. Gradually, the women became more politically active.

Men who, who had previously regarded the women as 'just housewives' gained a new respect for these women as they saw the work being done by them. Gradually, the women noticed that they were being treated differently and even being referred to, reported one woman, as 'women rather than 'ladies'! Customary gender roles began to blend as men helped in the home, freeing their wives to attend political commitments.

"As women we have not been encouraged to be involved in....trade unions and organizing. Organization has always been seen as belonging to the men....we are seen to be the domestic element of the family"
(Lorraine Bowler, WAPC 1984)

Miners' Strike: Birmingham Live News Gallery. Many wives, mothers, daughters, sisters and even granddaughters were as involved in strike action as were the miners themselves

https://www.birminghammail.co.uk/news/local-news/gallery/miners-strike-2572589

Women spoke at public meetings in support of the miners, shared community household chores and childminding, and even spent time on the picket lines. Front line activism such as picketing was a new experience for the women. Traditionally undertaken by striking men, the women were initially disparaged for undertaking this role. Unlike the men who protested in familiar territory, the women were bussed to often to unfamiliar areas with women whom they didn't know. They were usually able to pass though police road blocks, frequently impenetrable by the men. Although they gained the admiration of fellow pickets, police dealt with both men and women with equal severity.

Women picketers were spared none of the abuse and brutal treatment meted out by the police to the men.

https://www.walesonline.co.uk/lifestyle/nostalgia/gallery/miners-strike-8748011

There is often a tendency to sentimentalise the lives of miners' wives during the strike, although for many it proved a positive vehicle for change. Despite some transference of gender roles — some husbands helped with communal activities and/or looked after children while the women were occupied — traditionally it was the wives who bore the brunt of the hardship. For the men on strike, apart from the fact that they weren't going to work, there was no drastic upheaval in their routine. They were with their mates on the picket line, they still had a social life at the clubs and miners' lodge, although not the money for beer. In contrast the women's workloads had increased, organising food distribution and communal cooking while still carrying out their household chores and looking after the children — like the women of 1926. With little money coming in, they had the additional hardship of trying to cope on a strictly managed budget. Their whole world was turned upside down. Many women, never having been out to work since their marriages, had been torn from the familiar environment of their homes. Their lives were portrayed in nightly news bulletins, picketing where they were most needed, often in strange places among strange people. It was the women who worried about loss of income and how to make ends meet and yet the popular media portrayed them, as Margaret Thatcher had falsely predicted, as being unsupportive of the strike, urging the men to go back to work. Nothing could have been further from the truth. Yet again like their predecessors, they often got by on a slice of toast and a cup of tea after they'd used up rations feeding the rest of the family.

Although some of the men began to take up work usually done by their wives, the majority left it up to the women. If asked, the men would help but seldom, women reported, volunteered. When working in the communal kitchens, the women often had to take along their children as, without their husband's help, there was nowhere else for them to go until they improvised crèches. While picketing they developed a roster system, taking turns for some to remain behind to look after each other's children. Wives found mutual support and understanding in the groups where previously they had been strangers. As a result, many women became good friends and confidantes.

As families faced increasing hardship during the 1984–1985 miners' strike, women's groups set up communal feeding centres in any available accommodation which was large enough. Although they were given initial funding by the NUM, it was not enough to provide the necessary equipment and the ongoing cost of food. Funds were obtained through activities, money collecting and donations from sympathetic supporters.
Miners' Strike: WalesOnline https://www.walesonline.co.uk/lifestyle/nostalgia/gallery/miners-strike-8748011

The work got more difficult week by week as the hardship and privation of no work and no money began to tell on them. They were forced to decide who were the ones most in need, and who were those hardest affected by the strike. They had to negotiate who needed help the most. This, they felt to be their paramount responsibility, although traditionally it was the men who earned the money, it was the wives who had been primarily restricted to their own homes who had learned to make ends meet.

The women got little help or support from the NUM, an overwhelmingly male institution. Initially there had even been criticism from the NUM about the soup kitchens. They should be, insisted the union, primarily for the benefit of striking miners. The women stuck to their guns, even the NUM juggernaut failed to deter them. Some NUM members, at the invitation of the women, attended WAPC meetings, which they then attempted to dominate. Reciprocal invitations to the women to attend NUM meetings were never extended. In December 1984, WAPC sought affiliated membership with the NUM, but it was never granted. After the strike had ended there was a demand for the women to transfer any accrued funds, plus financial accounts to the NUM. The women declined and instead donated surplus money towards a national fund for sacked miners. This demand by the union caused acrimony on the part of the women which outlasted the strike.

Many of the men, born and bred into communities which had never known anything but a paternalistic way of life, felt insecure and confused in the face of this newly found female autonomy. Being wage earners endowed them with a sense of power — they were the breadwinners, the family heads. Except that, during the strike, they weren't earning wages. They were not even used to regarding their wives as equals, let alone independent beings functioning at quite high levels. By and large, any apprehension on the men's part was met with amusement by the women, although many men were genuinely worried that the women might be getting ideas 'above their station' and would never be able to return to a 'normal life' after the strike.

Some of the women were apprehensive for the same reason. Having relied on their mining husbands while they ran the household, would they ever be able to return to their usual domestic arrangements when, and if, life returned to normal? Many feared not.

However, mostly the women were focused on fighting for jobs and their communities without giving too much thought to the future.

Women gained a new respect for each other and from others as they shared good and bad times — humour, frustration, fear and sadness — as they battled the harsh winter of 1984–1985 with lack of money and lack of heating. Truckloads of toys arrived from Germany and Belgium in time for Christmas and were parcelled up and distributed by men *and* women.

The presence of women on the picket lines presented the police with a dilemma. Initially they were confused as to how to deal with them. The role of the police forces during the strike has been variously reported in the media from that of law enforcement — in what was essentially a violent upheaval — to reports of provocation and use of excessive violence on the part of some forces. Eight thousand police, from as many as fourteen different forces, equipped with riot shields and helmets were deployed each day throughout the strike. They were controlled like military. In fact, rumours abounded of the military being used, dressed in police uniforms. On picket lines and at the centre of rallies and demonstrations, miners could be sacked for trespassing if they stepped over the yellow picket line. Not being employed, women were free to do so.

There was little or no discretion in the amount of violence meted out to both men and women pickets by members of the police force. There were numerous reported instances of sexual harassment towards women by the police. Women related how they were propositioned by officers of a certain force to 'earn five pounds in the back of the van' and such instances were not isolated. Women described running the gauntlet of police insults: 'whores', 'lesbians' and 'Scargill's slags'. Police deliberately insulted and taunted the women in the hope of provoking the men to violence, Of the 11,291 arrested, 878 were charged with assaulting police. Police often singled out women from demonstrations and strip searched them, even in the presence of children. Perhaps because of the hard lives they had led, these women were able to call on reserves of strength they hadn't previously known to endure this intimidation.

At Christmas 1984, truckloads of toys arrived for the children of striking miners. They were donated by mining families of France, Belgium and Germany. These families also invited many of the children to spend the Christmas holidays in their homes.

Santa's Underground Grotto; National Mining Museum for England
https://www.ncm.org.uk/news/the-national-coal-mining-museum-for-england-invites-visitors-to-their-underground-christmas-pit-experience-this-december

For 363 days, 130,000 miners and their families endured unimaginable hardships to save jobs and communities. Surviving on fifteen pounds a week, two thirds below the national poverty line, families were not able even to provide the basic necessities of life –food, clothing, fuel and housing. Privation, a tactic used in 1926, was intended by the government to force the miners back to work. Although fund raising meant that the miners could hold out for almost a year, many 'hunger scabs' — desperate men who could no longer tolerate the harsh conditions — gradually returned to work.

On 3 March 1985, an NUM delegate conference voted to end the strike. Realising that life as they had known it was over, the men, accompanied by their wives and families, proudly, but with breaking hearts, marched back to work, carrying union banners, often preceded by brass bands made up of miners. Thatcher was graceless in victory declaring, "there is no such thing as society".

Margaret Thatcher was nowhere more thoroughly despised than in northern England's coal belt, where her crackdown against striking miners is blamed for wiping out an entire industry that had sustained a community for generations.

10 things we learn about Margaret Thatcher from her 1984 papers
The Telegraph
https://www.telegraph.co.uk/news/politics/margaret-thatcher/11137193/10-things-we-learn-about-Margaret-Thatcher-from-her-1984-papers.html

It was obvious, in the lead up to the strike, that the coal industry could not survive. Government strategy in provoking the strike demonstrated a total abrogation of social responsibility. Coal mining communities were heartlessly destroyed. It cost the government six billion pounds to destroy the NUM and a further 26 billion pounds to dismantle the coal industry.

Pit head infrastructure, including the winding wheels which hauled the 'cages' of miners to the pit bottom and back again at the end of their shift have gone. The mines have been flattened as though they had never existed. Even the pit 'buzzer' heard throughout the village sounding the demarcation of shift times is silent. Pit shafts have been filled with cement leaving spectres of once thriving coal communities and a legacy of unemployment, drug addiction and other anti-social behavior.

The lives of many miners' wives were irrevocably changed by the strike. After a year of upheaval, many realised that neither they nor their lives, could ever return to previous 'normality'. Many had been transformed from political passivity to political activism. Being as committed and involved as the men, when the strike ended in March 1985, they were understandably devastated. However, with the men back at work, many decided to continue their campaign. They gave support to other industrial disputes such as the Wapping printers and the Liverpool dockers, by joining picket lines to repay solidarity shown to them.

Most women had not entered the industrial fray with political intent, let alone the intention of advancing the cause of feminism. Their purpose was to save jobs and preserve their way of life and their communities. After the strike many women expected to return to their previous existence, although the yearlong turbulence had *ipso facto* altered their perspectives on that life. Nothing could now be taken for granted and even men were regarded in a different light. They were vulnerable and no longer the guaranteed breadwinner.

When no wages were coming into the home, the women had coped, not only with their own hardship, but helped others cope with theirs. They understood what they had accomplished individually and communally as women. They had gained a new set of skills, and realising what they were capable of in the face of adversity, gave many of them a new found confidence. Their horizons had been broadened and some had gained a new freedom from the drudgery and sameness of home. For many this was a novel experience.

Like the men, women emerged from the strike tired and bruised. Inevitably there was a post-strike anticlimax which would require a period of readjustment. The miners and their wives were defeated, but not humiliated. Despite good intentions, few of the women managed to maintain their supportive network and communal support collapsed as they returned to their homes. There was pressure to deal with debts accrued during the year long strike. For the majority there was a feeling of despondency, of being let down, and a fear of what lay in the future. It is the personal stories of the change which occurred in some of the women's lives which merit mention. Many returned to roles as housewives, although with the pits closed and the livelihoods gone, they would never be the same. No one in these communities was unaffected by the events of 1984 and 1985.

Many marriages did not survive the iconoclasm of altered traditional role models. Despite what had taken place, most women agreed the change had been positive. Some women found it impossible to turn away from the turmoil the strike had produced in their lives, and the skills and tenacity it had unexpectedly uncovered for them, harnessing these into opportunities.

Women involved in the strike believe their children and grandchildren are more politically active as a result of their actions during the strike. It was a turning point in their personal lives. Many left their husbands, started studying and commenced careers — in many cases, political careers. Turning fear into anger and anger into action was an intrinsic part of the strike and for many working-class women; this was a welcome catalyst for changing their lives.

20 We are women, we are strong.

We are women, we are strong,
We are fighting for our lives
Side by side with our men
Who work the nation's mines,
United by the past,
And it's — Here we go! Here we go!
For the women of the working class.

Arthur Scargill said at the end of the 1984–1985 miners' Strike, "[It] was truly a historic fight that gave birth to the magnificent Women Against Pit Closures and the miners' support groups …. I have always said that the greatest victory in the strike was the struggle itself …."

21

Extinguishing the Spark

Who put this pit-head wheel,
Smashed but carefully folded
In some sooty fields, into his stocking?
And this lifetime nightshift—a snarl
Of sprung celluloid? here's his tin flattened,
His helmet. And the actual sun closed
Into what looks like a bible of coal
That falls to bits as he lifts it. Very strange.
Ted Hughes, late Poet Laureate, 2003.

From 1850, the annual production of coal in Britain soared from 8.4 million tons to 40 million tons in 1870. By 1913 the annual production was 270 million tons. In 1900, coal accounted for 90% of the world's energy.

In 1865, Victorian economist and logician William Stanley Jevons proclaimed:

> 'Coal in truth stands not besides but entirely above all other commodities. It is the material energy of the country — the universal aid — the factor in everything we do. With coal almost any feat is possible or easy; without it we are thrown back into the laborious poverty of early times.'
> *Economics William Stanley Jevons' The Coal Question* (**1865**), *beyond the rebound effect Volume 82, October 2012, Pages 97-103 (*https://www.sciencedirect.com/science/article/pii/S0921800912002741

With the burgeoning coal industry in the 19th century there evolved a distinctive culture in mining communities which made them relatively isolated from the outside world. This is exemplified in the South Wales coalfield where, with its undulating geological features, communities developed in remote valleys, each relatively self-contained and separated from neighbouring valleys. Within these communities, specific patterns of behaviour emerged. When women were prohibited by an 1842 act from working underground in mines, a gender division evolved when men, by virtue of their earning capacity, ranked above women. Relegated to the home, round-the-clock working hours in dirty conditions made life hard for colliers' wives. It became largely impractical for them to work outside the home. The life of the community depended on the local pit which was usually the only means of employment. Even social life revolved around the pit. However, there was an ambivalent view of the industry which generated life into these communities. Loathing and fear for its harshness and cruelty were juxtaposed with a dread of its non-existence. Its absence presaged misery and despair.

Even before World War I, coal production in the US exceeded that of Britain and, post war, the production of cheaper coal on the European continent was further competition for the British coal industry. Although in 1913, the height of the British coal industry, coal production peaked at 287 million tons, its dominance lasted a mere six years, coming to an end in 1918. From then, for the next sixty five years, despite a temporary reversal in the trend during the inter-war period of 1918 to 1939, the coal industry entered a decline that ended with its extinction less than a century later.

By virtue of their sheer numbers, miners were, historically, able to organise into extremely disciplined, resilient trade unions which gradually came to be regarded as the 'elite' unions of the working class. In 1920, Prime Minister Stanley Baldwin declared, "There

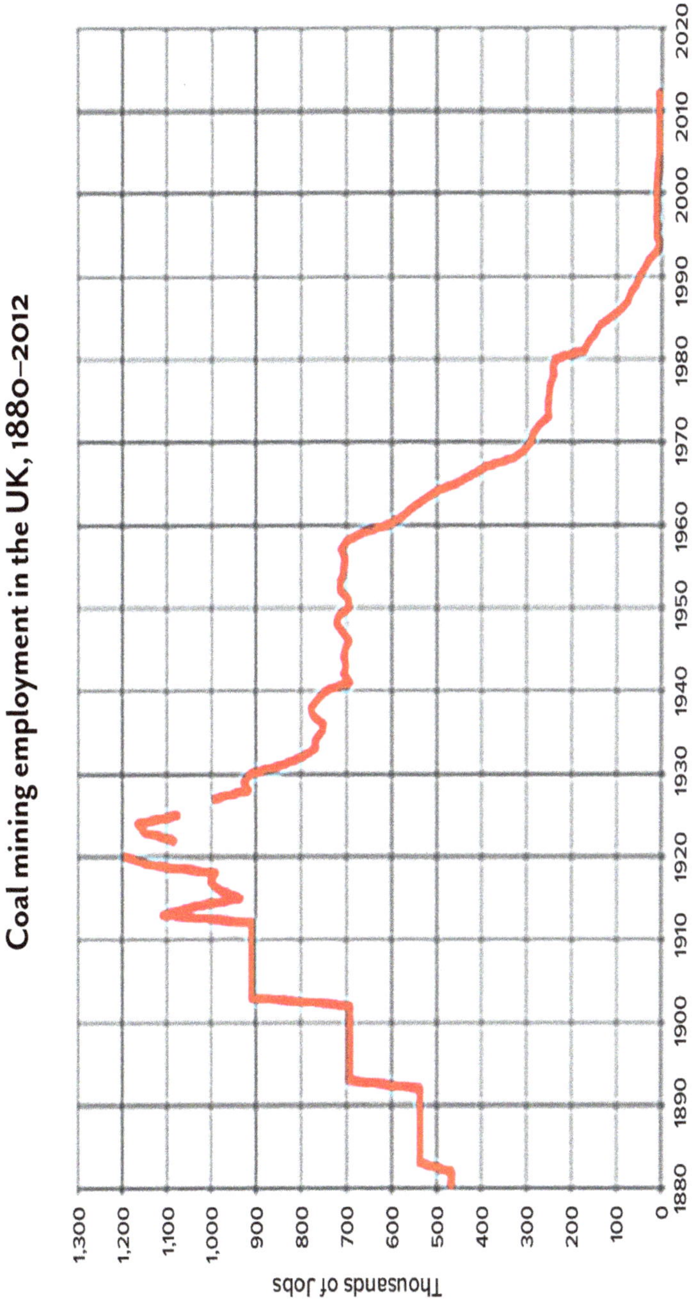

21 *Extinguishing the Spark*

Coal mining employment in the UK, 1880–2012

Numbers employed (millions) in coal industry, UK, 1880–2012. Employment peaked at 1.2 million in 1920, before a decline to 0.7 million through most of the 1940s and 1950s. A rvapid decline over the next three decades brought it to almost zero.
https://en.wikipedia.org/wiki/Coal_mining_in_the_United_Kingdom

are three institutions you couldn't possibly fight: the Vatican, the Treasury and the Miners' Union."

The first half of the 20th century saw hardship and large-scale disputes in the coal industry, most notably the General Strike and lockout of 1926 and 1927. Miners had always believed in the ideology of nationalisation of their industry. Despite coming close to achieving this goal in the second decade of the 20th century, it proved elusive until 1947. By that time, it came too late as most pits had been neglected and starved of badly needed infrastructure because of short-term profit maximisation by previous private ownership.

Although coal remained the major source of energy in Britain until the 1960s, during that decade and the previous ones there had been regular pit closures. Towards the end of the 1960s there was growing militancy within the National Union of Miners and an expansion of industrial action for higher wages. In the 1970s there was increased spending on infrastructure in some (but not all) mines, resulting in fewer closures.

However, by this time, the development of cheaper and cleaner sources of energy produced a further decline in the British coal industry. Steam power vanished from the rail transport system in favour of diesel and electricity. The introduction of the Clean Air Acts of the 1950s caused people to switch from coal to other forms of heating. Decreased dependence on coal, demands for higher wages and an inability to compete with foreign suppliers signalled a terminal decline for the British coal industry which was, by now, surviving mainly on government subsidies.

The militant strike of 1984–1985 was an attempt by miners to save a moribund industry. Beginning in March 1984, it lasted 51 weeks. When it ended in March 1985 the coal industry was in ruins. In December 2015, Kellingley Colliery in Yorkshire, the last working coal mine in Britain was closed, ending centuries of deep coal mining. Ten former miners, working in a team, took three hours to pour concrete down the pit shaft, encasing the mine forever. Mine buildings were demolished to be replaced two years later by housing developments of hundreds of homes. A memorial to 17 miners who lost their lives at the colliery was transferred to the National Coal Mining Museum in nearby Wakefield.

Miners leave work at Kellingley Colliery, Yorkshire, for the last time on 18 December 2015 ending centuries of coal mining in Britain. Known locally as 'The Big K', the largest deep pit in Europe could produce 900 tons of coal in an hour. Ten miners took three hours to pour concrete down the pit shaft, sealing it forever. A pipe from the centre of the pit was left to release methane gas, used by the on-site power station. Buildings were demolished.

BBC News: https://www.bbc.com/news/uk-england-york-north-yorkshire-35803048

Throughout Britain, all traces of the coal mines, which once supported thriving communities, have been similarly obliterated.

Like the buildings, slag heaps have been levelled, replaced, not just by housing developments but shopping centres, office complexes and motor vehicle repair workshops.

In the twenty years following the 1984–1985 strike, 162,500 men were forced out of coal mining work, equating to one in nine of the male population of Britain between the ages of 16 and 64. Job losses remain part of the everyday economic reality of most former mining communities. Although, after demolition, there is no longer any physical evidence of the industrial dynamo at the heart of these communities, psychological scars remain as evidence of its destruction.

Manipulated by the government, who told the miners in 1984 that their pits were safe from closure, the cynical actions of Thatcher's Conservative government to subsequently close pits such as Creswell — which had continued to work throughout the strike — along with the militant pits involved in the industrial action, was seen as an act of betrayal.

> "Our heritage, indeed, our very way of life, is summed up in the tragedy of the miner who achieves the near impossible every day, producing top-quality work in desperate conditions, and then describes himself as unskilled at the dole office."
> (Andrew Taylor; *The NUM and British Politics: Volume 2: 1969–1995; Studies in Labour History*)

Ten years after the end of the 1984–1985 miners' strike, 15 mining sites remained active, compared to 170 when the strike began. The culture of the demoralised miners was destroyed. Many never worked again and for those who did, employment was not long-term. In 2004, a BBC report estimated there were 5.5 million people living in former coal mining towns and villages, 9 per cent of the entire population of Great Britain.

Ian MacGregor, Margaret Thatcher's appointed Chairman of the National Coal Board at the time of the 1984 and erstwhile *agent provocateur*, served one term as President of the National Coal Board. In 1986 he was replaced, his ambition of transforming British Coal into a highly productive, capital intensive industry unfulfilled.

The effects of closures on communities totally reliant on the pit for employment were devastating and far-reaching. *The State of the Coalfields*, a report produced in 2014 by the Centre for Regional Economic and Social Research at Sheffield Hallam University, examines the economic and social conditions in the former mining communities of England, Scotland and Wales. The report states that across former coalfield communities there were fifty jobs available for every one hundred people and most people who were employed were likely to be in 'low grade' manual work since they usually lacked higher qualifications. Poor health was almost double that of South East England, and 7.9% of the population were receiving welfare payments.

The 1984–1985 strike, the longest ever, is considered to be the most acrimonious industrial dispute Britain has ever witnessed. Arguably, it was a dispute provoked by a government intent on revenge for events which occurred during the Heath government's tenure ten years previously. The Thatcher government understood there was no future for the industry. Not only was the miners' union fighting to save an industry whose demise was inevitable, a way of life which had evolved entirely around that industry was also as stake. The dispute, in hindsight, appears anachronistic and yet it became a symbol of class struggle. The archetypal working-class miner was opposed by an emergent *nouveau riche* class whose wealth was predicated on how much money could be made in a free market economy.

When the team of miners poured concrete into the shaft of Kellingley colliery, they sealed off seams of coal which could have produced energy into future centuries had its usefulness not been usurped by alternate, less polluting fuel. Long before the Romans occupied Britain, coal was being mined there. It was the spark which ignited and fuelled the Industrial Revolution. Lasting little more than a century and a half, in historical terms, it was a very short time. Even after the spark was extinguished, its influence remains.

Lewis Dartnell points out in his book *Origins*, until the most recent election in 2020, the geological distribution of coal affected and reflected the political landscape of Britain. Although the Conservative party won government in 2015 and 2117, the Labour party, with its origins in the coal mining unions, traditionally retained strong support in the old coal mining areas of the north of England, Midlands, South Wales and Kent. (Darnell, L: *Origins: How the Earth Made Us*; Bodley Head; London 2018)

(The election of December 2020 with its *Get Brexit Done* slogan produced a *volte face* in the former coal mining constituency of Bolsover which returned a Conservative candidate for the first time since it was created in 1950.)

In May 2019, amid the all-consuming Brexit debate, Britain went for seven days without using any coal-generated energy. Power was produced by natural gas and nuclear energy with the addition of renewable energy such as solar and wind power. Declaring a 'climate emergency', the government of then Prime Minister, Theresa May, laid out new rules to close all coal-fired power stations by 2025.

At the same time, Germany, which followed Britain into the Industrial Revolution, committed to stop using coal by mid-2030. The last coal mine in Germany was decommissioned in 2018. Not a single miner was sacked during the process. In 1968, all German coal mines were placed into one company which worked closely with state and federal governments to manage the closure of the industry. Mines were closed progressively so that miners who wanted to continue to work could be relocated to other pits. Men under 50 were offered re-training while those over 50 were offered generous voluntary pay outs. To enable former mining communities to continue to exist, new transport infrastructure was built, and many mining sites converted into parks and museums, much of the associated work being undertaken by former miners.

This initiative was in contrast to the British example where men whose families had worked the mines for generations were cast aside like the dross which made up the local slagheaps.

> *Was it worth it all those years ago?*
> *My answer, friends, is definitely "No".*
> *Seeing your man going down that dark hole*
> *Clawing at the earth for black coal.*
> *Their bodies marked and heavily scarred,*
> *Tired and grumpy from working so hard.*
> *But ask those old men, the miners of old*
> *Their answer "Yes" they enjoyed digging for black gold.*
> *"We knew no different", they would say,*
> *"It was a job, working hard for little pay".*
> *The valley is now a void of mines,*
> *Gone are the winding wheels and dram lines.*
> *The land is now picturesque and green,*
> *No sign of coal or colliers are to be seen.*
> **Yvonne Smith, South Australia.**

22

Last Look

On a warm, overcast day in August 2017, Davey with his wife Nicky by his side, drove along the old A161 road in his hire car. He had always associated warm, overcast days like this with summer in the mining village where the ever-present soot particles obscured the full force of the sun and created a sepia-like medium. It was so unlike the brilliantly clear, sunny days and cloudless cobalt skies he now associated with summer. The summers in which he basked now were the summers promised in the framed posters of the train compartments which carried him towards his annual fortnight in Scarborough or, on one occasion, as far as Newquay on the Cornish coast. It was the promise of golden sun, white sand and a clear blue ocean.

During his youth Davey had travelled along this road many times to and from school. Later it became the last leg of fewer journeys home from London. He knew it like the back of his hand, so he thought. It was now, however, over thirty years since his last foray and, exiting the motorway a few miles south of here, he had become somewhat disoriented by the intervening changes that had taken place.

It was comforting to see that some of the old houses along the route were still standing, although some of the larger ones had obviously been bought by people with enough money — if not taste — to renovate them. He wondered what sort of people now inhabited these houses and where they worked. At one point, he was compelled to pull over to the side of the road, quite distracted by the experience which heightened the feeling that he really didn't belong here anymore. Revisiting the past wasn't always a good idea; perhaps some memories are best left undisturbed. However, after travelling all this way, there was no point in turning back now, and besides he'd promised Nicky that during this trip he would try to share some of the history of his early life in the colliery village, the village where his life had begun only three years after the war.

He had never known his father who had been killed in the pit disaster of 1950 when he was only two. Freda, his mother had joined the increasing number of post war widows, but her loss was not as a result of the carnage of war. Like all the women widowed by the disaster, she received, in addition to a State widow's pension, a generous lump sum from the National Disaster Fund established in the wake of the mining tragedy. Hardly had the first bodies been recovered and the fire extinguished than the nation proved once again that it was at its best in times of adversity; people from all parts of the country donated generously.

The money was a godsend. No longer having a miner in the family, Freda had no choice but to vacate the house in the Model Village which, belonging to the pit, was intended to house its employees. Not only had she spent all her life in the Model, the house she was about to vacate was the same house in which Meg and Gwyn, Davey's grandparents, had settled almost thirty years earlier after migrating to escape the unemployment and overcrowded squalor of their native Welsh valley. With its bathroom with running hot and cold water and the little garden at the front, their new home had exceeded all their expectations of a better life. It was the house where Meg had given birth to her only child and later nursed Gwyn, who had died there. Although Gwyn's death had been hard on Meg, then largely without support, having eschewed the well-intentioned offers of friendship from the other wives, she accepted that his body had been defeated by years of working underground, breathing in the noxious, dust-laden air.

They had shared 20 years of married life, more than they could have hoped for if they'd stayed in Pontymawr like his brother, Gareth. Becoming a miner's wife all those years ago had come with a caveat which she, like all the wives, was prepared to accept: the mine would always have a claim on her husband's life. Somehow she never expected the same would apply to her only son. Owen was young, strong and healthy. Who knows what he could have achieved? Once Owen had gone, his son Davey, her only grandchild, was her only surviving flesh and blood.

Freda had lived her whole life within a stone's throw of the house she had shared with Owen and Meg, with its communal back yard and its front windows overlooking the once genteel but now sadly neglected park. By this time, all that remained of the once green oasis separating the newly built Top from Bottom Models was the decaying bandstand and a few rusty swings. Later, broken bottles and rusty cans would litter sparse tufts of grass and weeds. Meg's house, like the one in which Freda had been reared, was within walking distance of the pit which had taken *her* husband's life along with seventy-nine others one September night while the village slept. After the cataclysm, the house no longer offered warmth and security. It was filled with too many memories.

Freda was unsure how Meg would react to a proposed move, or how would she cope with the upheaval. Would she even survive the move? Both women had always regarded this house primarily as Meg's home and Freda never really lost the feeling of being an interloper. Not only would Meg be uprooted from her old home, the new house would be Freda's, and Meg would no longer be in charge. Leaving the old house would be an ambivalent experience for both women.

Meg appeared to have shrunk, physically, in the wake of the worst tragedy she could imagine, the death of her child. She now thought of the house as merely a shell, as though she had entered a holding pattern, moving, breathing and carrying out the most basic of personal chores mechanically until it was her turn to die. Uncharacteristically meek, she put up neither defence nor opposition to Freda's decision to move; she merely complied as she had nowhere else to go.

Freda found a detached bungalow at the edge of the village in a street consisting mostly of semi-detached and a few detached houses. In recognition of middle class aspirations, each house had a good size garden at the back and a manicured grass verge at the front which separated it from the road. In the past Freda would have felt though she were trespassing in such an environment but, like Meg, she too was now barely aware of her surroundings. With no stairs and enough bedrooms for the three of them, the bungalow would be eminently suitable. It was also within easy walking distance of her parents' house and, in a few years, Davey's school. Most importantly, it was close to the cemetery where Owen now lay.

When the last of Meg's furniture had been packed and loaded into the removal van both women walked silently through the empty, echoing house each with unique memories. What was it, after all, but a shell of coal blackened bricks and mortar? Memories had been made here but they weren't being left behind. There was no need to pack and unload them; they were embedded in their psyches, portable and able to be taken out and relived at will for the rest of their lives. Now with furniture and memories safely stowed, they were both ready to move on.

Although Meg's attitude to life was still influenced by memories of Sunday morning homilies delivered from the pulpit of the Non-Conformist Welsh Chapel, she was not a religious person *per se*.

She had taken the preaching and adjusted it to suit her moral code which provided a framework around which she built her life. After Gwyn's death, she had adopted a self-imposed mourning ritual and insisted on dressing in black. Any display of grief — in fact any emotion — was anathema to her. In the past, of course, she had Owen to support her and, although she never intended for him to go down the mine, once he did she found some solace in focusing on the familiar routine which now revolved around her son's shifts down the mine. It restored meaning to her life. After Owen's death, life ceased to have any meaning for her. She could not tolerate music in the house, even the new house, although she eventually relented, but only if it was 'serious' music.

Despite Meg's idiosyncrasies, the little family adapted well to the new house. As previously, the *ménage* was run on matriarchal lines but Freda was now the matriarch. She didn't, however, feel much at all, apart from the persistent pain in her heart which she had no wish to alleviate. This was the thread by which she remained attached to Owen.

After a life in the Model Village, the detached bungalow was light and airy with a lovely view at the back of the house — although the familiar pervasive smell of the pit was still present. Although, with the passing of time, the pain diminished for Freda, the emptiness never left her. Even though she had worried that Meg might not survive Owen's loss, she did, and gradually she began to resume an interest in life. Davey became the apple of *both* their eyes — indulged and, according to Freda's dad Joe, completely spoilt.

When it was time for Davey to begin school, Freda began to consider returning to work and was fortunate enough to be offered her old job at the co-op. By this time, some of the other disaster widows had remarried, but there were still a number of single women which meant that working mothers were no longer an anomaly.

The income was an added benefit and returning to work would be yet another milestone in Freda's life. She knew *she* would never remarry and, like the younger Meg, she resented the interruption of gossiping neighbours even into her uninspiring round of housework. In this respect the two women were similar.

When he was five, Davey, along with the neighbouring children, began his education at the local Church of England infants' school. Freda returned to work and Meg seemed to unexpectedly come to life as, once again she took up duster, polish and mop and, eventually, vacuum cleaner.

The little household functioned well and Freda was quite content to share the rearing of her son with his grandmother. Like his father, Davey was popular with his friends. Unlike his father, however, he was a good student to whom learning came naturally. He advanced from the infants' to the junior school from where, after passing the eleven-plus examination, entered grammar school several miles from the village, leaving many of his friends to continue their village education.

Many of the boys were destined to follow their fathers into a life of mining, and the girls to work at the local hosiery factory until they married. Freda hoped it wasn't premature for her to believe mining was not the future that awaited *her* son. Meg, whose life had been inextricably bound up with mining, considered it to be, despite its daily grind and hazards, courageous, *manly* work. Inexplicably she felt a faint pang of disappointment at the direction Davey's life was taking, even though it was what she had anticipated for her own son.

Davey's boyhood popularity endured, although he was, like his dad, a little 'different'. Yet he was bright, exceptionally bright. While many of his friends left school at sixteen Davey, with a smaller group, progressed to lower sixth form. In his upper sixth form year, he was made head boy and, after five years of grammar school, there was another parting of ways. His A-level marks were high — mathematics, physics, chemistry and biology — high enough to gain admission to London University to study medicine.

Most of his sixth form peers, boys *and* girls went on to university, but Davey was the only one to gain admission to medical school. Freda's heart swelled with pride, while at the same time fighting hard to quell the sense of impending loss. She had dreamed, worked and encouraged Davey towards this end but, deep down, knew that once he had left he would never return to live in the drab village whose only claims to fame were its pit and its band — although even that star attraction was beginning to dim with the advent of the 'Swinging Sixties'.

In mid-September 1966, the driver helped Davey to load his heavy trunk into the taxi and he and Freda set out for Chesterfield station to catch the London train. As they drew away from the house, Davey turned and saw Meg waving from the front gate. Not until that time did he notice how she had aged. With her upright Welsh demeanour, she had always been there, sometimes disapproving but always willing, in her brittle way, to indulge him. During the time he was growing up he had been fascinated by stories of her life in the Welsh valley, so long ago. She had spoken about the strike and the lockout, although it hadn't directly affected her or Gwyn, who had by then escaped the austerity and deprivation. Davey knew of the hard times — poverty, exploitation and industrial turmoil — endured by the family Meg and Gwyn had left behind in the village with the unpronounceable name. He had listened to tales of how women had shamed the men who had continued to work during the lockout — 'the blacklegs' — and those who had refused to join the unions. They had covered the men with pig slop, painted their faces black and chased them with poles strewn with women's clothes. He was the only one in whom she, his *Mamgu*, had confided her life story. How white now was her wispy hair as it was lifted by the breeze; how thin the hand that waved goodbye. Despite the constriction in his throat and the pang of guilt in the pit of his stomach, he was comforted by the thought that, while he was being carried south to a new future, Meg and Freda would at least have each other.

The next five years in London passed quickly. With his good nature and the lack of self-consciousness he had inherited from Owen, Davey failed to notice that some of his fellow medical students were bemused by his northern accent, his limited wardrobe — and the fact that, with a name like David Thomas, he had never played rugby. Although with his share of Welsh genes he soon demonstrated a natural talent for the game. He shared rooms above a dental surgery in Southwark with a fellow medical student, coincidentally, from Wales. Alun was a little older than the rest of the students, having already completed a science degree and worked as a teacher. He was already married with a young son who remained with his mother in Wales. Like Davey, Alun adhered to a strict budget. Unlike Davey, Alun was not free to pursue the pleasures of a single man in a big city.

Although he worked hard, especially during his pre-clinical years, once he entered his third year and began to work on the wards, Davey began to relax a little and allow himself to enjoy the work. As a clerk or 'dresser' it was his responsibility to take the histories of new patients, draw bloods and order simple investigations. He attended lectures and took part in ward rounds as he moved through various 'firms' — medical and surgical specialties headed by eminent consultants. However, by this time, it wasn't all work. He formed an eclectic social network, capable of letting down their hair during their spare time. Visits home became few and far between, although he remained a conscientious letter-writer.

He took holidays with friends — on one occasion hitch-hiking with a fellow student as far as Vienna. However, he found it a constant struggle to live within the confines of his student grant — even without indulging in the delights of 'Swinging London' in the 1960s. During his infrequent visits home to the grimy village, he felt it was becoming less and less his home. Although it was comforting to sleep in his old bed, settling into the familiar contours, this was not where his future lay. His mother, who was still working, had also begun to make quite a large circle of new friends. He knew she missed his company but never told him so and, with her dreamy, absent-minded nature she never made any demands on him. Oddly this made it more difficult for him to think about a future away from her. Nevertheless, when the time and the opportunity presented, he knew he would go wherever he had to to pursue his career. He knew that Freda would always prefer this for him to a life down the pit.

Around this time the future of the coal industry was threatened by the switch from coal to oil, which was cheaper and less polluting than coal. Several pits all over the county had closed and Davey was unsure about what the future held for his community and many of his friends now working in the mine.

At Christmas 1970, Davey was unable to return home because of his ward roster. This, however, gave him the opportunity to enjoy the hospital festive season — *work hard, play harder* seemed to be the axiom by which the students lived. Christmas Day was a whirlwind of ward visits which were definitely *not* work related. When he was a boy his grandfather Joe had taught him how to play the musical saw, drawing a bow over the bending instrument to create a dreamlike sound. Davey had mastered the art and, together with a fellow northern student performing percussion on a pair of spoons, they formed a popular duet much in demand as they went from ward to ward.

There was also another reason why Davey was happy to remain at the hospital that Christmas. He had become very fond of Nicky Baxter, a formidable house physician a couple of years ahead of him. Like Alun, she had experienced life outside the confines of a hospital medical school. She had taken a year after she qualified to work in a mining community in Western Australia before returning to complete her graduate year. Hospital Christmases are reputed to be memorable experiences and not, Davey discovered, without good reason.

On Christmas night when, exhausted but happy, he finally returned to his rooms there was a note pinned to his door. Freda had called from a neighbour's telephone as Meg was being carried into a waiting ambulance; she had suffered a stroke. Davey dashed into the hall and, although it was late, telephoned the neighbour who confirmed that Meg had been taken to nearby Worksop Hospital and that Freda was with her.

The euphoria of Christmas Day quickly evaporated. Davey's Boxing Day was spent travelling home where he was met by his uncle, Freda's brother-in-law, with the news that Meg had died a few hours after arriving at the hospital. She had never regained consciousness.

Meg was buried with Gwyn in the churchyard, away from their only son. Owen lay with his dead comrades in the new cemetery closer to Freda's house where a monument to honour their memory had since been erected. Although Freda still had her ageing parents, from now on she would be effectively on her own. The familiar pain returned to her heart at the thought of Davey leaving her again. Nevertheless, she adamantly refused to make any claim on him. At least he was going back to London and a life far removed from the mine; a life that could, like his grandfather and father, and like many of his peers, have been pre-ordained for him and then cut short. Sadly he returned to London on the dismal January day following the funeral, even more determined to transform his mother's dream for him into reality.

In 1973, Davey graduated with MBBS. Freda made a rare visit to London to see him take his place among the famous alumni which included such past luminaries as Alexander Fleming, Richard Bright and Astley Cooper. Although these names meant nothing to Freda, she was filled with pride and awe, barely conscious of her surroundings as she self-consciously greeted his friends.

"Now the world really is your oyster", she whispered in his ear as he saw her on to the train that evening, having refused his offer of accommodation.

Her son's world was now one in which she would never belong, nor did she wish to. Home for her was the blackened village where she had been born — a village built around the pit with its sulphur smell and its wailing siren. When she was away from the village she felt restless and insecure. Davey knew this and was reassured that she was happy in her own environment. Freda considered her mission now accomplished. She dozed as the train drew closer to home. What, she wondered, would Owen have thought of his son, the doctor?

In order to obtain full registration with the General Medical Council, Davey spent the following year at the hospital working as a house officer, the most underpaid and overworked member of the medical hierarchy. No longer a lowly student, his relationship with Nicky had endured and, at the end of his pre-registration year, they became engaged. Nicky was also an only child. Although from different backgrounds, her upbringing was not that different from Davey's. Her father had been a general practitioner in Kent where, coincidentally, he had worked as a medical officer in the mines of the Kent coal field. Coal was a common denominator in their lives, and Nicky was the first and only one of Davey's hospital friends to be invited to his home, ostensibly to meet Freda and to inform her of their coming marriage. To Freda's delight, Nicky showed an interest in the village and, through Grandad Joe's remaining connections, Davey was able to arrange a visit underground. Thus it was, with his fiancée, that Davey made his one and only excursion underground into a coal mine.

Conditions had not changed much since that day, almost a quarter of a century previously, when his father's body had been brought to the surface and, although harrowing, Davey could at last appreciate the conditions under which his forebears had made their living. He felt close to his roots as he trudged along the miles of subterranean passages, through caverns, sometimes ankle deep in dust. He closed his eyes and tried to imagine what it must have been like for his father, sitting with his workmates as the fire raged, waiting for help to arrive. Although he had no memory of his father, he felt close to him then. The fact that Nicky had been there with Davey made her even more special in Freda's estimation.

The year 1973 was not a good one to be living in Britain. Civil war was raging in Northern Ireland and bombs were being detonated in London and Manchester; strikes were common and it was a year of industrial unrest in the mining industry. Inflation was high, as were mortgage rates and, in spite of two reasonably good incomes, Davey and Nicky could see little hope of being able to afford a house of their own. Towards the end of the year, the simmering dispute between the government and miners caused fears of power shortages and there was talk of introducing a three day working week. Although half a world away, the prospect of beginning a new life in Australia gathered momentum for both Nicky *and* Davey.

The move meant that each would have to leave behind a lone, ageing parent. Davey knew Freda would never leave her roots. She would visit them but never stay. The situation was similar for Nicky's dad. Nevertheless, the decision was made to make the move.

Neither of them ever doubted they had made the right decision to migrate to the great antipodean continent. They worked hard and made many friends in the town where they lived in a rambling single storey house surrounded on three sides by corrugated iron covered verandas. With its endless horizon, clear blue skies — and Christmases in summer — it was a far cry from the grim mining village and, as Davey seemed to recall, overcast days more often than not.

It was here that they followed with interest and sadness the events of 1984 and 1985 — images of angry miners fighting for work and the survival of communities such as Davey's — and the police, equally as angry, fighting to restrain them.

On a dazzling antipodean summer morning in February 1991, while his home village was in the middle of winter, Davey received a telephone call to say that Freda was in hospital. She had slipped on the icy path outside the kitchen door and broken her femur. Unable to attract any attention, she had lain in the freezing cold for several hours until a passer-by heard her calls for help. Although only 70, the combination of lying on the cold ground and years of heavy smoking resulted in her contracting pneumonia. Davey made the long, lonely journey home.

He arrived at the hospital to be told that, because of the weakened state of Freda's lungs, any surgery to fix the fracture would not be immediately possible. During the almost twenty four hours it had taken Davey to arrive at her bedside, her condition had deteriorated. He agreed with the registrar that in the interim she should, with the aid of morphine injections, be made as comfortable as possible.

Freda was still conscious when Davey entered her room. "Hello, my love", she greeted him as though she had only recently seen him. She wanted to tell him all her news. He held her hand as she began to tell him all she had done during the previous few days. Suddenly she stopped, realising where she was. They sat in silence, still holding hands uttering a few intermittent words. After a while Freda's eyes closed and her breathing became irregular, the gaps between each breath became longer. Davey was familiar with the process of dying.

He stayed alone in the cold, empty bungalow until after the funeral, arranging for Freda to be buried next to Owen. A solicitor was engaged to organise the sale of the house and other effects and, with no reason to linger any longer, Davey returned to his wife and family.

Although Davey and Nicky returned to England for several visits after his mother's death, they never went north. There was no longer a reason to do so. He couldn't possibly imagine that the village would be the same anyway. Regardless of having worked throughout the 1984–1985 strike, the pit had closed in 1991, the demoralised miners abandoned by government policy. In Kent, Nicky's former home, circumstances were no different. Although it was hard not to think of all the harm that had been done, this state of affairs vindicated, even more strongly, Davey and Nicky's decision to leave twenty years previously,

At Christmas 2016, Davey and Nicky sold their joint practice, but not the house, and finally retired. Davey felt, it was now time to revisit his roots. Late in the afternoon of that overcast August day, he stood in front of his former home. Things had changed, a little. There was no manicured grass, the verge replaced by bitumen — surprisingly, for this had been a quiet street, there was a bus stop opposite the house. Did this mean that buses no longer had to make the journey to the top of the village before turning around to pick up passengers on the descent to the arterial A616? Had they discovered a way of tricking the people who, having seen the bus ascend the main street could calculate how long it would take before it was time to catch it on the way down?

The driveway to the house was no longer a steep incline from the front gate to the kitchen door but had been levelled and a garage built at the end of it. He looked at his old bedroom window; the small fanlight window was open, although the stained glass panes had been replaced by a single piece of plain glass. He smiled to himself as he remembered clambering head first through the little aperture one afternoon when the three of them had been to a matinee performance at the local picture house and forgotten to take a key. Freda had helped him up and he had landed with a belly flop on the bed before unlocking the kitchen door to admit Freda and Meg. It was one of the few times he'd seen Meg laugh as she watched his black boots slowly disappear. Did anyone else remember this? Did the house remember?

"Hello, House", he whispered as it stood there, inscrutable, as though it resented being abandoned by him all those years ago.

Its loyalty was now to its new occupants — and there had probably been quite a number in the intervening years. He looked at the familiar front door, now closed against him for ever.

He had parked the car near the house, having decided to walk around the once familiar streets. His first visit was to his father's grave which, so close to his old home, now also contained the remains of his mother. Once again he proudly showed Nicky the memorial to the dead miners on which his father's name appeared. The grave had been surprisingly well maintained and Nicky helped him to arrange the spray of pink roses — his mother's favourite. The other flowers he took with him as they walked through the village to the parish church where Meg and Gwyn also shared a grave. This was the church from which the bodies of many of the eighty men who perished beneath it all those years ago were farewelled in relays during a two day test of endurance in pouring rain. Davey had retrieved from Freda's possessions the now yellow battered order of service from the night of the fire

"... and God Himself will be among them ....He will wipe every tear from their eyes."

Davey was somewhat taken aback by the appearance of the church, surely it had been a dignified edifice built from stone; yet all he saw was an ugly red brick building. Perhaps it was the redness of the brick which surprised him; it would, after all, in his youth have been stained black from coal dust. The second surprise came when he turned the round handle of the heavy porch door and discovered it was locked, making it impossible to show Nicky the small choir stall where he had sat in his white surplice, longing for the final hymn to end so he could run home with the other boys to his traditional Sunday dinner. Somehow his mother, who had always been too busy, insisted that he attend Matins each Sunday. Meg, of course, had remained loyal to her Non-Conformist upbringing.

Here was the infants' school and next to it the secondary school where many of his friends had gone after they were segregated by the results of the eleven-plus. Both fine examples of Edwardian architecture, they were now no longer in use, their windows boarded. Did the school still contain the hall where he had played a series of percussion instruments in the school band, in front of large musical manuscripts covered with different coloured crotchets and quavers — blue for triangles, brown for tambourines and black for the drums? He couldn't recall the colour for the castanets, was it red?

A few metres away was the *art deco* cinema, scene of rowdy Saturday morning matinees when the film was frequently halted and the manager appeared on stage threatening to stop the film if the rowdiness continued. It did continue and so did the film. It was no longer a place of respite from the grimy outside world where his mother and her friends had been temporarily transported to the magnificent South Pacific or the mansions of Newport, Rhode

Island. Now it was the Bingo and Social Club where 'early and big link took place 7 nights a week.' As a boy Davey remembered being confused during the showing of *The Jolson Story*, not realising that the main character was in fact a white man with a blackened face. The film had a special screening for the Sunday School Christmas outing followed by a party in the Drill Hall, just up the street. When he came out he was embarrassed to see his grandmother waiting for him, even though it was dark. She had brought his cup, plate and bowl for the jelly which, in his haste, he had left behind. The silver spoon for the jelly had coloured cotton wound around the handle in the optimistic hope that it would not be lost. The Drill Hall, he noticed a few minutes later, had also been reborn as a social centre.

What struck Davey most was the almost deserted main street with its many boarded up shop fronts. Surely, during his childhood it was much busier than this. Of the many boarded up shops he recognised one that used to belong to the pork butcher where Meg had waited to be served one day. Like the rest of the customers she had been entertained by a rotund collier's wife whose house overlooked the weighbridge. Being constantly woken early each morning by shouting truck drivers waiting in line for their loads of coal to be weighed she threw own open the window one day and threatened, if their clamour continued, to appear naked in front of the window to shock them into silence. Obviously it was the wrong threat as one of the men shouted back "When ya gunna do it, missus?" He remembered the sheepish way Meg had related the story, describing how the customers (including Meg) had laughed. The weighbridge, he noted wryly, was still standing although now, like the men themselves, redundant.

He arrived at the Model Village; it looked different. Although the concentric octagonal circles containing the 281 houses remained, each house had been modernised and was now privately owned, the ubiquitous lines of washing still flapping in the yards. He was surprised again by the redness of the brickwork, no longer begrimed by the polluting smoke. How green and tidy the park looked. As he reached the end of the road bisecting top from bottom, he noticed Joe's villa. In different surroundings and with a garden, it would probably be described as 'desirable property'. Even more imposing was the Miners' Institute at the end of the road. He noted, for the first time what another fine, but squandered example of Edwardian architecture it was.

The biggest shock waited him as he neared the end of the roadway leading to the pit where large wire gates marked **Keep Out** had been erected. Beyond them he could see the green cricket oval to which the whole school had marched, two abreast, to compete in school sports days. Surrounding this oasis was a mess of broken concrete, detritus of the once prosperous mine. The winding wheel and the monolithic chimney had gone. He turned to Nicky who stood patiently by his side.

"Let's go," he said turning his back on the dilapidation. "I've seen enough".

They retraced their steps through the village to where they had left the car. He knew this would be his final visit. The few people they passed nodded to them. They were probably the same age as he was, but they looked, he thought, older; most walked with a stoop and without smiles. He recognised no one. To some he gave side-long glances, wondering if perhaps they had shared his classroom, played in the infant school band with him or run amok as Batman and Robin after the Saturday matinees. Could that overweight man with the dishevelled receding hair be Billy Rushton or Bernard Riley? Where were Janet Rowe, Mavis Bennet and Angela Jones, the popular girls who had organised communal skipping games in the junior school yard with lengths of washing line they'd 'borrowed' from their mums' washhouses? Had these boys followed their fathers and grandfathers into the mine to be made redundant with so many potential working years left? Had the girls shouted on picket lines as the wives of miners relegated to the scrap heap? They would have been too old to retrain once their livelihood had gone.

The village seemed like a faded, threadbare semblance of his past. Even though it was the middle of the long summer holiday there were very few children, no one playing in the streets or going for day-long bicycle excursions like Davey and his friends had once done, Freda's only condition being that he be back in time for tea. It wasn't until they reached the car that Davey realised that the place even smelled differently. The acrid, sulphurous fumes he had been forced to inhale during his childhood and adolescence were no longer present.

Sadly, without talking, they returned to the little Dukeries hotel, its 21st century makeover unable to disguise the fact that it was once, no doubt patronised by local miners, sitting outside on summer evenings, pint of bitter in hand while the *wife* sipped her port and lemon. It was comforting to hear the accent of his childhood, but Davey's visit had put him in an indifferent mood to start a conversation.

As he lay on the bed that night he realised how lucky he had been. His could have been one of the few anonymous, preoccupied, prematurely ageing faces of people he had seen that afternoon walking aimlessly along the main street. He would never return to the declining village that had once seemed the centre of his being — the weekly dances, the brass band playing on Armistice Day, the flower shows, the pit siren and the tramping of boots were all gone. He thought of his family; above all the two strong women who had shaped his life. His grandmother, Meg, living in a small colliery house overshadowed by a waste heap and a belching chimney, it may

Oblivion
https://www.oblivionstate.com/community/threads/creswell-pit.3945/

not have been luxury but it was a far cry from the starving families and overcrowded squalor of the Welsh Valley she had left behind. Her strict Welsh non-conformism may have seemed rigid but it had provided a set of boundaries inside which the family operated. She had mourned the fact that the pit had claimed the life of her husband, but miners' wives had been conditioned to accept that probability. She never forgave the pit for the loss of her son, yet she survived. Owen had inherited his mother's moral compass which had become part of Davey's genetic inheritance. Above all he was grateful to his mother, also the product of a mining culture, who had worked all her life, determined to ensure that culture ended with her son. All he had done, all he had achieved — his work, his family, his sense of right and wrong — Davey knew were the products of the combined strength of these two mining women.

Post Scriptum

https://www.pinterest.com.au/pin/716635359429043478/?lp=true

"Mrs Thatcher's hatchet man was brought in to close as many
pits as possible."
Arthur Scargill of Ian McGregor

"People are now discovering the price of insubordination and
insurrection. And boy, are we going to make it stick."
Ian MacGregor, NCB Chairman

For Annette and Steve, 1984 had been a time of upheaval and, much of the time, confusion. The events of that year were neither caused nor provoked by people like them. They were caught between the power of a government intent on revenge, and to a great extent, confrontational NUM action. Yet they were not victims. The events of that year forced them to confront everything that made them who they were — work, community, tradition. They were forced to re-evaluate their present, past and future lives. Although they didn't appreciate it at the time, the crisis offered opportunities which, albeit subconsciously, they grasped.

Unlike reported instances, neither Annette nor Steve experienced epiphanies which urged them to pursue careers in local government, become creative artists or undergo further studies leading to degrees in social science. Their experience resembled that of Plato's prisoners in the cave. After 1984, Anette and Steve's life seemed to them like the blank wall on which shadows appeared to be reality. Events surrounding the strike had shown them that there was a life beyond these confines. Their strike work emboldened them to embrace the consequences of the change which had been thrust upon them. Both had been hurt by the light of the discovery, yet they were brave enough to embrace change and the opportunities it presented.

Appendix

Igniting the Spark:
How this mineral changed so many lives.

How modest it seems, how bashful,
This lump dug up from the bowels of the earth,
Still giving off its vegetable gases.
Is it waiting to become a diamond?
From Ode to Coal by Steve Orlen (1998)

https://www.shutterstock.com/search/coal

A diamond or a coal?
A diamond, if you please:
Who cares about a clumsy coal
Beneath the summer trees?
A diamond or a coal?
A coal, sir, if you please:
One comes to care about the coal
What time the waters freeze.
— **Christina Georgina Rossetti**

Often referred to as 'the black diamond', coal unlike its namesake, coal is not a thing of beauty. Yet, like the true diamond, coal represents power and wealth. How then, did this black mineral transform the nature of a nation from a once agrarian society into the premier industrialised state of the world?

The Concise Oxford Dictionary describes coal as a "hard opaque black or blackish mineral mainly carbonized plant matter, found in seams or strata below the earth's surface and used as fuel ….for burning in a fire…" Coal is the end product of trees and vast swamps which covered the earth 300-400 million years ago. When the trees died, this vegetation returned to the soil and, over the course of millennia was, during the carboniferous period (*carbo* -coal, *fero*- I carry) converted to coal. Coal is based on the element carbon, which is locked into atoms of hydrogen and oxygen by chemical bonds. When coal is burned these bonds break, and energy is released in the form of heat.

When water is heated by burning coal, an "invisible gas into which water is changed by boiling, used as a motive for power…." (*ibid*). Steam power became, literally, the driving force of Britain at the end of the 17th century.

Used to pump water out of flooded mines, such innovations as the aptly named 'Miner's Friend', invented by Thomas Savery in 1698, were driven by steam. Built into such mechanical devices were a water tank and a space to burn the coal to heat the water to make steam. The steam was then captured in a cylinder and used to drive a piston which, by moving backwards and forwards, powered the engine. Steam power paved the way for technological progress, and in many instances, manpower could now be replaced by machinery.

Appendix   *Igniting the Spark: How this mineral changed so many lives.*

James Watt and Steam Power: Spartacus Educational
https://spartacus-educational.com/U3Ahistory16.htm

In 1763 James Watt was sent a Newcomen steam engine to repair. While putting it back into working order, he discovered how he could make the engine more efficient. Watt worked on the idea for several months and eventually produced a steam engine that cooled the used steam in a condenser separate from the main cylinder.

Watt took his ideas to a successful businessman from Birmingham who, for the next ten years produced and sold Watt's steam-engines. The machines were sold chiefly to colliery owners who used them to pump water from their mines (Miners' Friends).

One of Watt's steam-engines was purchased by John Wilkinson, who used it in his blast furnace. Wilkinson now helped Watt improve his steam-engine by developing a boring machine that was able to drill cylinders to a high standard of accuracy.

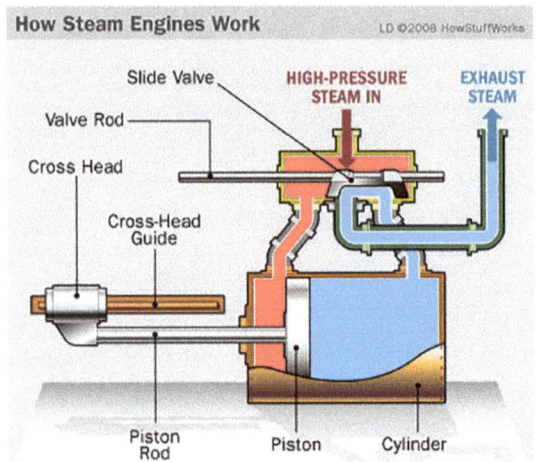

How steam engines work: How Stuff Works
https://science.howstuffworks.com/transport/engines-equipment/steam1.htm

Before the advent of steam power, coal had been used primarily as a source of domestic heating and cooking. Harnessing the power of that energy to drive the new heavy machinery, coal became synonymous with — and has been described as — the midwife of the Industrial Revolution. From James Watt's steam engine to Arkwright's Spinning Jenny, from Cartwright's loom to lighting houses and streets, to powering ships to increase trade and discovery, coal was behind the creation of abundant employment which propelled Britain towards 19th century greatness. It is therefore, an easy, but fallacious assumption that coal mining began with the Industrial Revolution.

HOW COAL WAS FORMED

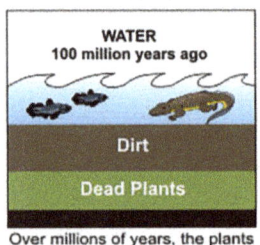
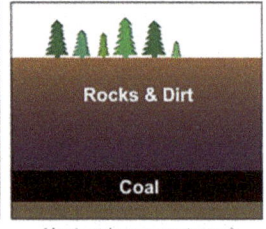

https://www.tes.com/lessons/yYUrNsuTi7IA8w/coal-formation

Appendix *Igniting the Spark: How this mineral changed so many lives.*

Throughout millennia coal lay dormant in its subterranean habitat. The Chinese first began to mine surface deposits as early at 1000 BCE and used it primarily as a source of fuel. In about 300 BCE the Greek scientist Theophrastus, a pupil of Aristotle, in his geological treatise on stone, described coal as a means of heating used by metal workers.

Although the Romans were aware of coal, it was rarely used by them as wood was in plentiful supply. However, as they invaded further north, they discovered coal mining. During the Roman occupation of Britain in the 2nd century BCE, coal was mined over a wide area of the Britain and used mainly for heating the villas of the wealthy and their public baths. This system of heating was known as Hypocaust (*Hypo:* under; *caust:* burnt).

Ruins of an old hypocaust (a system of central heating using coal) in Roman Villa

https://www.flickr.com/photos/anuwintschalek/5747315451

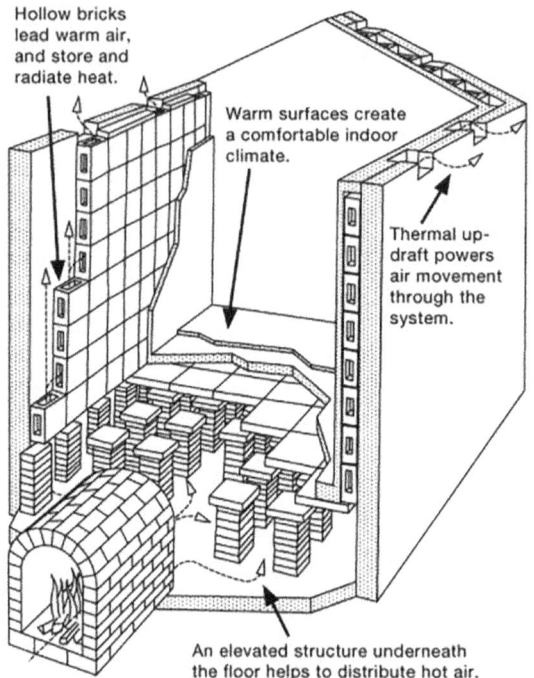

Hypocaust was probably the earliest form of central heating and was used by wealthy Romans to heat their homes and pubic baths using hot air which circulated under the floor and surrounding walls.

Floors were raised on pillars which supported a layer of tiles. A layer of concrete was placed over the tiles which were, in turn, covered by a further layer of tiles.

Built into the base of an outside wall, below floor level was a furnace, the heat from which was directed under the floor by a draft. It was carried up through the walls to chimneys in the corners of rooms which heated upstairs rooms. The sole source of heat was the coal furnace.

The Romans in Britain; Britain before, during and after the Roman occupation — 10 BCE to 450 CE.

https://www.romanobritain.org/12_innovations/inv_central_heating.php

The South American Aztecs in the 14th century discovered the dark mineral and used it for making jewellery and ornaments– not surprisingly it later became known, albeit for varying reasons, as the 'Black Diamond'

In the Middle Ages, coal was found to be excellent for heating forges and was used for metal working by village smiths. However, its use was limited as, when burned, it produced noxious fumes. Rather presciently, although coal was used by London artisans in the 14th century, a Royal Proclamation was issued forbidding its use in favour of wood and charcoal which were considered less pollutant.

However, a hundred years later when wood supplies were being severely depleted, coal again returned to favour for heating and industrial use. Further discoveries of coal deposits over widespread areas of Britain drove a gradual flourishing of the mining industry until, with the discovery of Watt's steam engine in the late 18th century, coal achieved its supreme importance as the means of enabling mechanical power.

Coal-fuelled industrialisation brought drastic changes to the social fabric of Britain. As the country took on the status of a premier industrialised nation, rapid urbanisation took place. People migrated from the countryside to work in towns and cities, eager to share in the economic boom times.

In pre-industrial Britain, although men had been the primary wage earners — usually working as tenant farmers or craftsmen — women also worked and produced goods primarily in home cooking, sewing and spinning. Even children performed basic tasks — looking after animals and crops and helping with household chores. This bucolic way of life, which involved all members of the family, was preserved longer in the Southern Counties of Britain while in the North, where most of the coal was mined, the Industrial Revolution was well underway.

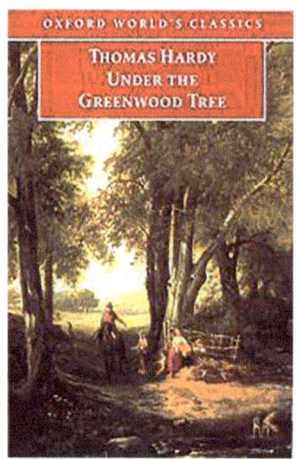

Under the Greenwood Tree is a portrayal of life in 19th century rural England. The writer, Thomas Hardy, paints four different portraits of country life appropriate to each season of the year, from singing carols and making cider in the winter to gathering nuts and collecting honey from beehives in the autumn. The book is a nostalgic study into the disappearance of old traditions and a move towards a more modern way of life.

This social dichotomy is appropriately captured and idealised in the novels of Thomas Hardy, and the rustic, unsophisticated lives of the characters inhabiting his fictitious county of Wessex. Whereas the mines, furnaces and coming of the railways in the smokestack north are aptly portrayed in the novels of Elizabeth Gaskell, particularly *North and South* and *Mary Barton*; southern rusticity is juxtaposed with northern pragmatism.

The simultaneous side effects of this new mechanical age on the lives of women provoke contentious debate. Some historians believe it had a negative outcome for women by relegating them to a role which was dependent on men. In the pre-industrial agricultural British economy where the home had been the locus of production and the whole family worked together there was equality between men and women. The arrival of industrialisation meant that, as varied well paid work became available to women, they left their homes to take up paid employment. Family productivity ceased. Women who remained in the home became reliant on the man's wage. Women's traditional independence and equality with men was replaced by dependency and lack of self-sufficiency.

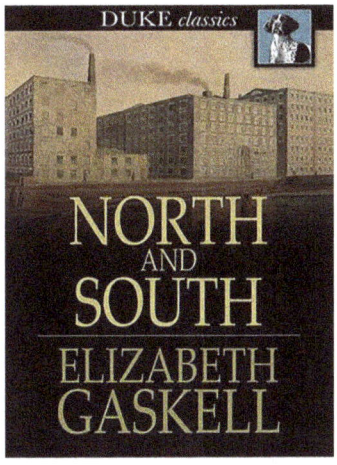

Elizabeth Gaskell's novel contrasts the values of bucolic southern England with the industrialised north. The book is also a reflection on the need for reconciliation among the English classes.

The lives of middle-class women who were relegated to the home became a relatively tedious domestic existence — supervising servants and generally living a life of leisure. While Victorian feminist activist, historian and later suffragette Helen Priestman Bright, (1840–1927) regarded industrialisation as having an unfavourable effect on better-off women, a less pessimistic view was taken by Ivy Pinchbeck (1898–1982) economist and social historian. She believed that, with men providing the family wage, these women's ability to withdraw from the workforce to devote their time to running the home was an advantage to them.

Rural life in Britain had not changed for centuries prior to industrialisation. Although idealised in art and literature, life based around agriculture was hard and could be a constant struggle. Whole families worked together on the land and farmers were still very much at the mercy of their landlords.

Life before the Industrial revolution: http://rishi-kumanan.tripod.com/id8.html

Although women had little part in creating the Industrial Revolution *per se*, they were greatly affected by it. For poor women it did not bring emancipation, it brought more hardship and rigid working lives. Poor women and children had always worked hard. What changed at this time was the type of work they did. In pre-industrial rural communities, the men ploughed and sowed, while the women carried manure to feed the crops. It was the women and the children who backbreakingly dug up the potatoes. In urban communities women managed shops, handled money *and* bore and raised children. Hard as this life was for many of these women, they were at least able to pace their working day.

Industrialisation turned women's working lives into rigid

regimes. They worked longer hours in unhealthy environments, were answerable to mine and factory overseers, became grist for the competitive business mill, a*nd* were paid less than men for equally hard work. The early days of the Industrial Revolution certainly changed working women's lives, but did not necessarily improve them.

The transformation of the landscape with the advent of the Industrialised Britain 1750–1850.

Spartacus Educational: https://spartacus-educational.com/U3Ahistory21.htm

With the large-scale urban migration which accompanied the development of industry, urban workers came to outnumber their rural peers by four to one, and the term 'working class' entered the lexicon. As factories developed and new machinery was installed to replace work previously done mainly by men, less physical work — weaving and piece work — was done by women and children. Children were particularly suited to working in factories. They were easy to train and with hands small enough to recover items dropped into machinery causing frequent obstructions. Also, they could be paid less than men *and* were usually compliant.

The labour of women and children was, therefore, the first

thing sought for by capitalists who used machinery. That mighty substitute for labour and labourers was forthwith changed into a means for increasing the number of wage-labourers by enrolling, under the direct sway of capital, every member of the workman's family, without distinction of age or sex. Compulsory work for the capitalist usurped the place, not only of the children's play, but also of free labour at home within moderate limits for the support of the family. (K. Marx, *Capital*, vol. 1. pp. 394-5.)

For most women, the advent of industrialism was a turning point in their working lives.

Bibliography

Bailey, C. (2007). Black Diamonds: The Rise and Fall of an English Dynasty. Penguin. London.

Barren, H. (2010). The 1926 Miners' Lockout: Meanings of Community in the Durham Coalfield. Oxford. Historical Monographs Series. New York: Oxford University Press.

Bourke, J. (1994). Working Class Cultures in Britain 1860–1960: Gender, Class, Ethnicity. Routledge. New York.

Britain, V. (1978) Testament of Youth. Fontana. London

Bright, G. (2014). "There's a kind of haunting going on": 30 years on from the 1984-85 miners' strike. ESRI Blog. Available at http://www.esriblog.info/theres-a-kind-of-haunting-going-on-30-years-on-from-the-1984-85-miners-strike/

Bruley, S. (2010). The Women and Men of 1926: A Gender and Social History of the General Strike and Miners' Lockout in South Wales. University of Wales Press. Cardiff.

Cambridge Family Law Practice. (2012). A Brief History of Divorce. 18 April. Available at http://www.cflp.co.uk/a-brief-history-of-divorce/

Cronin, A. J. (1948). The Citadel. Victor Gollancz .London

Cronin, A. J. (1935). The Stars Look Down. Victor Gollancz. London.

Darling, P. (ed). (2002) SME Mining Engineering Handbook. (3rd ed). The Society for Mining, Metallurgy and Exploration. Electronic Edition.

Dartnell, L. (2018) Origins: How the Earth Made Us. the Bodley Head. London

Evans, E. J. (1983). The Forging of the Modern State: Early industrial Britain 1783–1870. Longman Inc. New York.

Frost, N. (2017). The Women Miners in Pants who shocked Victorian Britain. Atlas Obscura. Available at https://www.atlasobscura.com/articles/pit-brow-lasses-women-miners-victorian-britain-pants

Funnell, E. (1963) Aids to Hygiene for Nurses. Bailliere, Tindall and Cox. London

Galsworthy, J. (1967). Swan Song. Penguin. Harmondsworth.

Gildart, D., Howell, D., Kirk, N., (eds). (2003). Dictionary of Labour Biography Vol Xl.

Palgrave MacMillan. Basingstoke.

Hopkins, E. (1979) A Social History of the English Working Classes 1815–1945. Edward Arnold. London.

Lawrence, D. H. (2011). Sons and Lovers. Vintage Books. London.

Lawrence, D. H. (1981). The Rainbow. Penguin. Harmondsworth.

Macmillan, H. (1966). The Winds of Change 1814–1939. Macmillan. London.

Mining.com. (2014). Let's talk about: women in the coal mining industry. Worldwide Recruitment Solution. 15 April. Available at https://www.mining.com/lets-talk-about-women-in-the-mining-industry-31775/

Ministry of Fuel and Power. (1950). Accident at Creswell Colliery Derbyshire Report. Available at http://www.dmm.org.uk/ukreport8574-03htm

Moore, C. (2015). Margaret Thatcher: The authorised biography: From Grantham to the Falklands. Vintage Books. New York.

Orwell, G. (1985). The Road to Wigan Pier. Penguin. Harmondsworth.

Piketty, T. (2014). Capital in the Twenty First Century. The Belknap Press of Harvard University. Cambridge Ma.

Rowland, P. (1976). David Lloyd George: A biography. Macmillan Publishing Co. Inc. New York.

Smart, C. (1999). A Moral Tale Divorce in England 1950–2000. CAVA Workshop Paper 2 Prepared for Workshop One: Frameworks for Understanding Policy Change and Culture. Available at https://www.leeds.ac.uk/cava/papers/wsp2.pdf

Spence, J., Stephenson, C. (2007). Female Involvement in the Miners' Strike 1984–1985: Trajectories of Activism. January 31. Sociological Research Online. Volume 12. Issue 1. doi:10.5153/sro.1461 Available at http://www.socresonline.org.uk/12/1/spence.html

Stopes, M. (2013). Married Love: A book for married couples. Scribe Publications. Carlton North.

Stopes, M. (1932). Wise Parenthood: The treatise on birth control and contraception. (52nd ed.). G.P Puttnams. London.

Thompson, G., Hawkins, O., Dar, A., Taylor, M. (2012). Olympic Britain: Social and economic change since the 1908 and 1948 London Games. House of Commons Library. London.

Walker, A. (1997). Pleasurable homes? Victorian model miners' wives and the family wages of a South Yorkshire colliery district. Women's History Review. Vol. 6.3. pp: 317-336. Available at https://www.tandfonline.com/doi/abs/10.1080/09612029700200147

Wilson, A. N. (2003). The Victorians. Arrow Books. London.

Wilson, A. N. (2005). After the Victorians: The world our parents knew. Hutchinson. London

Wilson, A. N. (2008). Our Times: The Age of Elizabeth II. Arrow Books. London.

Wilson, H. (1977). A Prime Minister on Prime Ministers. Summit Books. New York.

Woolfe, V. (1992) Mrs. Dalloway. Penguin. Harmondsworth

Index

NB: Photographs are in **Bold**.

Numbers

2nd Battalion Sherwood Foresters, 363
1887 Coal Mines Act, 289
1902 Midwives Act, 158
1911 Census, 121
1911 Coal Mines Act, 40, 127, 289–290, 301, 329
1912 Coal Mines Act, 183
   provision of ambulances, 289
1914 Defence of the Realm Act, 55
1916 Defence of the Realm Act, 186
1920 Emergency Powers Act, 193
1951 Festival of Britain Gala Day, 320
1987 General Election, 397
2020 General Election, 456

A

Abertillery Constructive Birth Control Committee, 174
Abertillery Hospital, 154, 172, 173
abortions, induced, 162
Accrington Stanley (football team), matches, 362
Act of 1842, 17
Agricola, Georgius, his accounts about miners working with heavy metals, 292
Albert, Prince Consort, 318
Albert Hall, 273
Allen, Megan, *Miner's Wives* (poem), 327
Anderson, Elizabeth Garrett, 158, **160**
   first woman in England to qualify as a medical practitioner, 160
   opened St Mary's Dispensary for Women and Children, 160
Andrews, Elizabeth (née Smith), 218, 230
   account, 224–228
   became a member of Women's Political and Social Union, 225
   death, 228
   joined the Women's Suffrage Movement, 225
   A Woman's Work is Never Done, **226**, 228

Andrews, Thomas
   established a local branch of the Women's Cooperative, 225
   a founder member of the Rhondda Independent Labour Party, 225
animals, treatment of, 315
Annette, her account of the miner's strike, 405–429
Arab-Israeli (Yom Kippur) War, ending, 378
Arkwright's Spinning Engine, 484
Army Nursing Corps, 57
Ashley-Cooper, Anthony, 29
   7th Earl of Shaftesbury, 24
   a devout Christian, 24
Ashton Moss Colliery, 65
Ashton-Under-Lyne District Infirmary, 64–65, 240
Atlee, Clement Richard (Prime Minister), xi, 257, 328, 374
   Dale Enquiry, 300

B

Baily, Catherine, *Black Diamonds*, 211
Bainbridge, Emerson Mushchamp, **94**, 178
   founded Bolsover Colliery Company, 94
   as a member of Parliament, 94, 95
   as a philanthropist, 95
Baker-Carr, Major, **115**
Baldwin, Stanley (Prime Minister), 193, 197, 199, 201, 450
Barnsley Coal Bed, 86
Barnsley Girls High, 62
Barnsley or Top Hard Coal Field, 92
   sinking of, 95
Battle of Passchendaele, Belguim, **51**
BBC, restrictions, 379
Bell, Gertrude, 13
Bennett family, 245
Bentink, Victoria, **115**
Bethesda Baptist Chapel, 129
Bevan, Aneurin
   architect of Britain's National Health Service, 228, 262, 300
   a Minister for Health, 228, 262

Bevin, Ernest
   General Secretary of the Transport Workers' Union, 267
   Minister for Mines and National Service, 267
Bevin Boys, named after Ernest Bevin, 267
Bevin Hostels, 267, 281
Birch Hill Infirmary Rochdale, 65, 264
birching, 315
Birkenhead, Lord, 197
birth control, 162
   clinics, 175
Black Friday, 192, 194
Bolsover Colliery Company, 95, 96, 100, 109, 178, 270, 273, 328
Bolsover Cooperative Society, 103–104
Booth, Rebecca, 3
   marriage, 11
Booth, Samuel, 11
Bowler, Lorraine, 432, 437
Branson, Rev, 346
Bridge Inn, 39, **40**
Bright, Helen Priestman, 489
Bright, Richard, 469
Britain, Vera, *Testament of Youth*, 57
British Airways, privatisation under Thatcher, 385
British coal industry, 61
   deaths, 288
British coal mines, ceased operation in 2015, 398
British Expeditionary Force, 50
British Medical Association, 158
British Miners' Strike of 1984-1985, 377, 388–389, 390, 432, 452
   statistics, 454–455
   women picketers, 437
   women's groups, 432
British Steel Corporation, 383
British Telecom, privatisation under Thatcher, 385
British Worker, The, **207**
Brown, John and Jennie, 253
Bryan, Andrew, 348
burns, treatment, 297–298

C

Callahan, James, 383
Carburton (hamlet), 69, 70
Carlton-in-Lindrick, 247, 258, 260
   St John's Church, 249
Cartwright's loom, 484

Catholic Women's League, 171
Cavendish-Bentink, William, 95, **113**
Cavendish-Bentink, Winifred, **113**
Central Rescue Brigades, 338
Charles II, King, 288
Charlton Brook, a country village, 39
Chesterfield (market town), 90
Chesterfield hospital, 311, 313
Child Welfare, 170
childbirth, and limited amounts of analgesia, 274
Churchill, Winston, 182, 392
Clarke, Fred, xv
Clarke, May, xv, 284
Clarke, Robert Coldwell, 21–22, 23
Clean Air Acts of the 1950s, 452
Clumber Park, 72
coal
   definition, 482
   as an essential commodity, 266
coal industry, health and safety issues, 287
Coal Industry Nationalisation Act, 262
   received Royal Assent, 373
coal miners
   clothing, 267
   diseases, 181
   labour shortages in World War II, 266
   living in Nissen Huts, 267
Coal Miners (poem), 177
Coal Miners' Strike of 1984-1985 *See also* British Miner's Strike of 1984-1985
coal miner's wives
   account, 111
   family story, 352–372
Coal Mines Act, passing of bill, 42
coal mining
   accidents, 12, 30, 313, 327, 334–349
   banning of children, 9
   cancer, 291
   dangers, 286
   electronic detectors, 291
   hazards, 308
   use of canaries, 291
Coal Nationalisation Act, 301
Colliery Worker's Magazine, The (journal), 228
Colmans, mustard maker company, 296
Colman's Sick Society, 296
Communist, Party, 217–218
Contagious Diseases Act, 160
Cook, Arthur J, 195, 200
Cooper, Ashley, 469

Index

Cooper, Gertie, 276
Corrie, Joe (poet), 117
Creswell (mining village), xi, xxiv, 69, 72, 86, **101–102**, 246, 265, 266, 360
    acception of evacuated children, 269
    Drill Hall, xvii, 79, 104, 106, **106**, 272, 321, 362, 475
    inducted into the war effort, 269
    location of, **87m**
    Model Village, xv, 74, 82, 100, **101**, 105, **108**, 112, 271, 285, 322, 358, 360, 460, 462, 475
    as a provider of coal, 268
    scene of the miner's strike, 402
    statistics, 98
Creswell Colliery, 94, **96**, 328, 342
    account, 329
    conveyor belt, 331–332
    disaster, 368
    Disaster Plan, 339
    No 2 District, 337
    sinking of, 95
    South West District, 334–335, 340
Creswell Colliery and District Band, 107, **108**, 272
Creswell Colliery football team, matches, 362
Creswell conveyor system, account, 332–333
Creswell Crags, 88, **89**, 109
Cronin, A J (physician and author), 281
    appointed to Ministry of Mines, 162
    The Citadel, 299
    The Stars Look Down, 162
Cullen, Edie, 368

D

Daggar, David "Dai," 172, 229
Dale, Jim, xii
Dale, Mrs, xiii
Dartnell, Lewis, *Origins*, 456
Davey and Nicky's account, 459–480
Davies, Idris, *The Angry Summer*, 206
Davies, Joyce, *The Miner's Tale (poem)*, 287
Declaration of The Rights of Man, 188
Derbyshire Coal Field, also known as Barnsley Bed coal seam, 41
Derbyshire County Council, 264, 271
Derbyshire Miners' Holiday Camp, opening, 318
Dig for Britain (campaign), 270
Domesday Book, 89
Donnelly, Robert, poem, 352
Drill Hall *See also* Creswell (mining village)

Duchess of Hohenberg, **115**
Duke and Duchess of Portland, 273
Duke and Duchess Street, 72
Durham, coal mining areas, 105
Durham coalfield, 236
Durham Women's Advisory Council, 236

E

Edwardian Miners' Institute, xx
Edwinstowe, home of Robin Hood, 73
Elizabeth Garrett Anderson Hospital
    lectured at the London School of Medicine for Women, 160
    various names, 160
Ellis, Havelock, 168
Elm Tree Hotel, Elmton, **110**
Emily and Harry (Nan's parents), 39
English Channel, 46
epidemics, 99, 125

F

Factory Act of 1833, 295
Falklands War, 391
female tram driver, 52
Ferdinand, Franz, (Archduke of Austria), 78, 114, **115**
Fitzwilliam, Peter, 211
Fitzwilliam Wentworth dynasty, 211
Fleming, Alexander, 469
Fletcher, Mrs, 82
Floral Art Society, 321
Flowerday, Phillippa, 296
Forest of Dean (coalfield), 408
Forrest of Dean (coalfield), 42
Forsyte Saga, The, Swan Song, 208–209
Funnell, Edith, *Aids to Hygiene for Nurses*, 273

G

Galsworthy, John, 208
Galtieri, General, 391
Galton, Francis, 167
Gaskell, Elizabeth
    Mary Barton, 488
    North and South, 488
Geddes, Will, poem, 352
General Election, 257
General Medical Council, 469
General Nursing Council, 64

General Strike of 1926, 175, 195, 199, 209, 210, 212, 213, 218, 230, 236, 240, 360
    lockout, 223
George V, King, 112, 202, 272
George VI, King, xi
Gilbert, Mr, 277
Gittins, Jean, 403, 429
Gloucester Echo, 274
Gold Standard, 196
Great Depression, 221
Great Exhibition of 1851, 318
Green, Beatrice (née Dykes)
    account, 228–233
    as an advocate of birth control, 230
    became President Monmouthshire Labour Women's Council, 230
    burial at Blaenau Chapel Monmouthshire, 232
    had a role at Ebenezer Baptist Church Sunday School, 229
    secretary of the Abertillery Hospital League, 229
Green, Jenny, 69, 77
    her relationship and friendship with Tommy, 75
    lived at Model Village, 80
    marriage, 80
    went into service at the Abbey, 76
Green, Ronald Emlyn, 229
Green, Tommy, 69
    account, 74
Greenham Common, 416
Guy Fawkes, 75

H

Haldane, John Scott, 290
Halle Orchestra, performance, 362
Haque, Md Ziaul, 177
Hardy, Thomas, *Under the Greenwood Tree*, 488
Harry (Nan's father), 254
    drafted into the Durham Light Infantry, 50
    employed as a miner, 39–41
    left for the front, 48
Hatfield Colliery, closure of, 398
Heath, Edward, 387
    ordered a wage freeze, 379
Heath, Edward (Prime Minister), defeat of his government, 381
Hemmingfield Colliery, 433
hewing, 4

High Green, 39
High Peak District, Glossop, 244
HM Inspectors of Mines, 339
Holger-Nielsen, 317
Holmes, Enoch, 3
    death, 12
    worked at hewing, 3
Holmes, Thirza (née Booth), 3
    account, 5
    coal miner's clothes, 5
    death, 11
    her views on coal mining, 6
    worked as a hurrier, 4
Home Office, 32
Hopkins, Sid, 354
Horner, Arthur, 346
Houfton, Percy Bond, 100, 104
Houfton, John Plowright, 95
House of Commons, 25
House of Lords, 30
Housewives Choice (BBC Radio Program), xii, xiii
housework, 125
housing, overcrowding, 122
Houston, Minnie, 253
Houston family, 252
Hughes, Ted, Poet Laureate, 449
hurriers, 4, 17
Huskar Colliery, 20
    accident, 30
Hyde Park (London), 210
Hypocast, 485, 486

I

Industrial Revolution, 86, 95, 99, 107, 178, 290, 430, 484, 487, 490–491
ITV, restrictions, 379

J

Jackson, Harry, 247, 253, 284
Jackson, Nan, 253, 274, 284
    friend of Nan Stewart, 247
Jehovah's Witness, xxiv
Jenkins, Mrs, 83
Jevons, William Stanley, 449
Jones, Aneurin, 130, 148, 151

Index

K

Karrakatta Cemetary, Perth, xxiii
Kellingley Colliery, 456
   closure of, 398, 452
King, Joe, 358
King's Lynn, Norfolk, 56
Kinnock, Neil, 391
Kitchener, Herbert, as a Field Marshall, 44
Korean Peninsula, xi

L

Lanarkshire, Scotland, 47
   coal mining areas, 105
Lawrence, D H, 169
   The Rainbow, 93
Lawson, Nigel, as Chancellor of the Exchequer, 381
Llewellyn, Dr, 150, 152
Lloyd-George, David, 187, 188, 192, 197
   produced a "People's Budget," 182
London General Omnibus Company, 52
Lord Melbourne, 24
Lowestoft, a Suffolk port, 269

M

McCulloch, Dr, 252, 264
MacDonald, Ramsey, 188, 236
McGahey, Mick, president of NUM, 398
MacGregor, Ian
   account, 382–383
   appointed chairman of the National Coal Board, 382
   as Chairman of the National Coal Board, 455
   death, 397
   effigy, 420
   employed at Ministry of Aircraft production, 383
   employed at Ministry of Supply, 383
   known as Mac the Knife, 383
MacMillan, Harold (Prime Minister), 391
Maerdy Pit, 224
Major, John (Prime Minister), 397
Malcolm, Jeanne, **210**
Malcolm, John, 210
male nurses, rates of pay, 307
Malthus, Thomas, *An Essay on the Principle of Population*, 167
Malthusianism, 167
Manchester Royal Infirmary, 63
Mansfeld hospital, 411
Mansfield (market town), 90
Manson, Dr, 84
Markham Colliery, mandatory training, 311
Markland Grips, 109
Markland Grips Nature Reserve, **110**
Martineau, Harriet, 35
Marx, Karl, 15
Mary, Queen, 272
Mary Harriet, (Nan's Aunt), 63, 65
   trained as a nurse, 63
Mason, Roy, MP for Barnsley South, 398
maternal death, principal causes, 158–159
May, Theresa (Prime Minister), 456
Mead, Mr (solicitor), 260
Meco-Moore cutter loader, 329, 329–330
Meteorological Office, 328
Metham, Nurse, 83–84
Michael Mont (book character), 208
Midland Railway, 94
midwives, 279–281
Midwives Act of 1902, 49
   account, 46
Military Service Act, 44–45
Mine Owners Association, 200
Miners' Federation of Great Britain (MEGB), 183
Miners' Federation of Great Britain (MFGB), 41, 184, 217, 235, 387–388
   women's section, 220–221
Miner's Institute, **109**, 111, 354, 476
Miners's Welfare Committee, 226
mines, closure of, 378
Mines and Colliery Act of 1842, 295
   passing of bill, 30
Mines and Safety Station at Buxton, 348
Mines Regulations Act, 32
Mining Qualifications Board, establishment, 290
mining safety, 111
Minister for Fuel and Power, 348
Ministry of Food, 234
Ministry of Fuel and Energy, 342
Ministry of Health, 161, 170, 306
Ministry of Munitions, 300
Model Village *See also* Creswell (mining village)
Monk Bretton, Yorkshire, 3
Mother's Clinic, 168
Mountbatten, Edwina, **210**
Mountbatten, Lord, 210
Munby, Arthur J (photographer), 35

N

National Association of Colliery Overmen, Deputies and Shot Firers (NACODS), 390
National Coal Board (NCB), xiv, xv, 262, 270, 283, 300, 301, 323, 341, 373, 374, 379, 384, 390, 395, 396
    ambulance, 313
    appointment of Medical Officers, 305
    East Midlands division, 328
    privatisation under Thatcher, 385
    responsible for nationalisation of coal mines, 375
    staffed by State Registered Nurses, 305
National Coal Mining Museum, Wakefield, 453
National Health Insurance Act, 172
National Health Service, Britain (NHS), 66, 245, 262, 264, 319–320, 380
    establishment, 300
National Health Services Act, 301
National Service, 270
National Union of Mineworkers (NUM), 183, 323, 341, 377, 379, 381, 390–391, 392, 395–396, 414, 427, 435–436, 440–441, 444, 452, 480
    fine, 378
    National Delegates Conference, 388
    participation in strikes, 387–388
National Union of Railwayman, 184
Nightingale, Florence, 13
Noblethorpe (hamlet), 21
Noblethorpe Hall, 22
Non-Conformist Welsh Chapel, 462
North Sea gas, 377
Nottinghamshire pits, 395
Nurses' Registration Act, 64
Nursing Employment, duty statement, 302–304

O

Oaks Pit (coal mine), 3
oil, as a replacement for coal, 377
Oldham, Samuel, 65
Ollerton, Nottinghamshire, 411
Organisation of Petroleum Exporting Countries (OPEC), 378
Orgreave coking works, 393
Orwell, George, *The Road to Wigan Pier*, 123, 222
Otlen, Steve, Ode to Coal (poem), 481
Owen, Wilfred (poet), 85–86
Oxford University, 118
Oxley, Walter, 348

P

Parish of Elmton-with- Creswell, also known as Helmtune, 89
Parry, Hubert
    All of an April Evening, 364
    Jerusalem, 364
Payton, George, 328
Pear Tree Cottage, 249
    location of, 247
Pennines, Yorkshire, xiv
Phillips, Marion, 235
    awarded Coben Medal, 234
    became an MP, 236
    buried at Golders Green Cemetery, 237
    educated at PLC, **233**
    joined the Independent Labour Party, 234
    joined the non-militant National Union of Women's Suffrage, 234
    a member of the Fabian Society, 234
Pinchbeck, Ivy, 489
Pit Brow Women, **33**, 35
pit brow women, 6
pit head baths, 124
Pontymawr pit, 359, 461
Portland, Winifred, **115**
Portland Estate, 70
Post Traumatic Stress Disorder, xviii, 59
Pott, Percival (surgeon), 290–291
Pottersgate Farm, Cumberworth, 62
Presbyterian Ladies' College, Melbourne (PLC), 233
Price, Lil, 217
Primitive Methodist Chapel, 114
Pritchard, Meg, 129
    account, 135–155
    employment as a maid/housekeeper, 130
    marriage to Gwyn Thomas, 132
    move to Pontymawr, 132
Probert, Tom, dispatched to the Western Front, 131

Q

Queen Alexandra's Royal Imperial Army Nursing Service, 306

Index

R

Red Cross, 58
Red Friday, 195
Red Lion Inn, inquest, 21
Redding Colliery, Falkirk Scotland, **31**
Regors Cinema, xii
Relief Office, 213
Representation of the People Act, The, 225
Resusci Anne, 317
    rescussitation mannequin, 317
Rhayendd, (mining village), South Wales, 129
Rhondda Labour Party Executive, 225
Rhondda Valley, 224
Ridley, Nicholas, *The Ridley Report*, 381–382
Robin Hood, 73
Rose Bridge Pit (coal mine), **11**
Rossetti, Christina Georgina, 481
Royal Commission of 1907, 288
Royal Commission into the coal industry, 187
Royal Society for the Protection of Birds, 112
Rushton, Frank, 355
Russell, John, 16

S

Samuel Commission, 198, 201
Sanderson, Elizabeth (midwife), 47
Sanger, Margaret, 169
Sankey, John, 187–189
Sankey Commission, 190–191, 226
Savery, Thomas (inventor), 482
Scargill, Anne, 434
Scargill, Arthur, 386, 389, 391, 396, 398, 406, 409, 434, 447
    became Yorkshire Head of NUM, 387
    General Secretary of NUM, 377
Schonburg, Countess, **115**
Scriven, Samuel, 25
Seaton Carew, 249
Senghenydd pit, Aber Valley South Wales, explosion, 127
Sheffield hospital, 311
Sherwood Forest, 73
Sherwood Lodge, 283
Shinwell, Manny, as Minister for Fuel and Power, 373
Shire Hill Hospital, Glossop, 244
Silkstone, Yorkshire, 20
    monument, 21, **23**
    Parish Council, 21
Silkstone Colliery, Yorkshire, 39
Six Bells Lodge, 172

Skelton, Helen, 306, 322
Smith, Herbert, as member of the Miner's Federation, 217
Smith, John, Shadow Energy Minister, 382
Smith, Samuel, 114
Smith, Yvonne, 457
Soames Forsyte, 208, 209
Society for Constructive Birth Control and Racial Progress (CBC), 167
Soldier Settlement Scheme, 60
South American Aztecs, 487
South Wales, coal mining areas, 105
Soviet Union, 231
Spanish Flu Pandemic of 1918, 60
Special Committee of the General Council of the Trades Union Congress, 199
Spry, Constance, 321
St Giles, Carburton, 71
St John's Ambulance Brigade, 272, 296, 298, 300, 305, 317
Standing Joint Committee of Industrial Worker's Organisation, 235
State Certificate of Training Miners, 32
State of the Coalfields, The (report), 455
steam power, 482
Stewart, Alistair (son), xiii
    birth, 252
    death, 402
    education, 276
Stewart, Annie Elizabeth (Nan), 39, 118, 239
    account of her working hours as a nurse, 308–311
    appointment as a District Midwife, 274
    became a midwife, 65
    became a State Certified Midwife, 66
    became a State Registered Nurse, 66
    child mining of her children, 283
    education, 62
    employment as a Registered Nurse, 306
    her move to Australia, 402
    house sale, 265
    marriage to Jack Stewart, 248
    nursing training at Ashton-Under-Lyne, 240
    pregnancies, 251
    purchase of a black Ford Anglia, 277
    purchase of a house, 401
    responsible to the County Supervisor of Midwives, 278
    retirement, 324
    social life and friendships, 281
    training at Birch Hill, 278

wearing of gown and facemask, 274
worked as a nurse in Worksop, 249
Stewart, Elizabeth (daughter), 276
   birth, 252
   her move to Australia, 402
Stewart, Jack (Nan's husband), 248
Stockton, Lord, 391
Stopes, Marie Carmichael, 168, 171, 175, 244
   her opposition to abortion, 164
   Married Love, 165, 169
   Wise Parenthood, 165–166
Strand Palace Hotel, 251
Sullivan, Arthur, *Box and Cox*, 123

T

Territorial Force Nursing Service, 58
Thatcher, Margaret Hilda (Prime Minister), 389, 391, 406, 409, 426, 431, 455
   account, 384–385
   death, 397
   despised by coal miners, 444
   determined to destroy trade unions, 381
   effegy, 420
   first female British Prime Minister, 384–385
   her economic policies, 383
   known as The Iron Lady, 384
   leadership issues, 397
Theophrastus, 485
Thomas, Carys (Gareth's wife), 134–135, 360
   account, 135–155
Thomas, Elwyn, 135
Thomas, Gareth, 132
   account, 135–155
Thomas, Gwyn, 129
   account, 135–155
   death, 360, 460
Thomas, Hugh, 133
Thomas, Lucy, 22
Thomas, Mared, 135
Thomas, Mauriel, 135
Thorseby Colliery, closure of, 398
Tommy-shop, 26
Top and Bottom Model Village, 74, 75, 273
Trade Union Act, 203
Trade Union Council, 183, 198
Trades Union Congress (TUC), 195, 197, 208
Transport Workers Federation, 184
Treaty of Versailles, 196
Tredegar Medical Society, 300
Triple Alliance, 183, 192

Truman, Harry S, xi
typhus, 3

V

Vesting Day, 373
Victoria, Queen, 24, 88, 318
Victorian era, 13–14
Voluntary Aid Detachment, 57, 119
Volunteer Defence Force, 192
von Hohenheim, Philippus Theophrastus Aureolus Bombastus
   also known as Paracelsus, 292–295
   a pioneer of Medical Revolution, 292

W

Warner Pathe News, 355
water, heating of, 482
Watt, James, 484
   sent a Newcomen steam engine, 483
Webb, Beatrice
   1662 petition, 288
   founder of the LSE, 234
Webb, Sydney
   1662 petition, 288
   founder of the LSE, 234
Welbeck, 72
Welbeck Abbey, 70, **115**
Welbeck Estate, 100
   country seat of the Dukes of Portland, 69–70
Wellington Bomber, crash of, 269
Wentworth Estate, 212
Wentworth House, 212
Wentworth Woodhouse, **181**
Wentworth-FitzWilliam, Maud, 213
Wentworth-FitzWilliam, William "Billy"
   Charles de Meuron, 180
Wertheimer, Ella, 235
White Shirting, definition, 216
Whitelaw, William, 391
Whitwell pit, 76
Whitwell (village), 76
Wilkinson, John, purchase of Watt's steam engine, 483
William the Conqueror, 89
Williams, Spike, 355
Wilson, A N, 15
Wilson, Harold (Prime Minister), 178, 378
   A Prime Minister on Prime Minister, 178
Wollsonecraft, Mary, 35
women
   childbirth, 126

in coal mining communities, 431
in colliery villages, xii
domestic duties, xii
family planning, 126
marital relationships, 446
professions, 118
routines, 431
working conditions, 120
Women Against Pit Closures (WAPC), 413, 441, 447
formation, 433–434
women coal miners
fighting and conflicts, 19
work duties, 17
working conditions, 18
Women's Auxiliary Corp, 57
Women's Committee for the Relief of Miners' Wives and Children, 216, 230, 232, 235, 236, 434
Women's Guild of Empire (WGE), 217, 218
Women's Land Army, 58
Women's Social and Political Union (WSPU), 58
Woolley Colliery, 386
Woolton, Lord, 365
Worksop and Mansfield (factories), 73
Worksop Victoria Hospital, 246, 311
World Health Organisation, 157
World War I, 41, 78, 131, 184, 234, 359
Armistice, 58, 131, 430
Battles, 50, 55
conscription, 44
mining labour shorters, 266
shell shock or Combat Stress Reaction, 59
Western Front, 59
World War II, xi, 300
outbreak, 223, 269
ration books, 271
rations, 270
wounds, treatment, 297
Wright, Tylden, 95

Y

York House, 104, **105**, 273
Yorkshire/Nottinghamshire/Derbyshire Coal Field, 92

Z

Zeppelin airships, 56

www.ingramcontent.com/pod-product-compliance
Lightning Source LLC
Chambersburg PA
CBHW042117300426
44117CB00021B/2973